OECD Factbook 2015-2016

ECONOMIC, ENVIRONMENTAL AND SOCIAL STATISTICS

This work is published on the responsibility of the Secretary-General of the OECD. The opinions expressed and arguments employed herein do not necessarily reflect the official views of the Organisation or of the governments of its member countries.

This document and any map included herein are without prejudice to the status of or sovereignty over any territory, to the delimitation of international frontiers and boundaries and to the name of any territory, city or area.

Please cite this publication as:
OECD (2016), *OECD Factbook 2015-2016: Economic, Environmental and Social Statistics*, OECD Publishing, Paris.
http://dx.doi.org/10.1787/factbook-2015-en

ISBN 978-92-64-23256-3 (print)
ISBN 978-92-64-25111-3 (PDF)
ISBN 978-92-64-25524-1 (HTML)

Annual:
ISSN 1995-3879 (print)
ISSN 1814-7364 (online)

The statistical data for Israel are supplied by and under the responsibility of the relevant Israeli authorities. The use of such data by the OECD is without prejudice to the status of the Golan Heights, East Jerusalem and Israeli settlements in the West Bank under the terms of international law.

Photo credits:
Chapter 2: © Image Source/Getty Images | Chapter 3: © Istockphoto/Dan Barnes | Chapter 4: © Stockbyte/Getty Images | Chapter 5: © Lawrence Lawry/Photodisc/Getty Images | Chapter 6: © Larry Lee Photography/Corbis | Chapter 7: © Cocoon/Digital Vision/Getty Images | Chapter 8: © Comstock Images/Comstock Images/Getty Images | Chapter 9: © Digital Vision/Getty Images | Chapter 10: © Jacobs Stock Photography/Getty Images | Chapter 11: © OCDE.

Corrigenda to OECD publications may be found on line at: *www.oecd.org/publishing/corrigenda*.

OECD Factbook 2015-2016

FOREWORD

For over 10 years now, the *OECD Factbook* has been one of the most comprehensive OECD publications on statistics. The 2015-2016 edition continues this tradition. The *OECD Factbook* now contains close to 100 internationally comparable indicators, allowing users to assess and compare the performance of countries over time in a wide range of topics that match the interests of policy-makers and citizens alike.

To give just a few examples, the 2015-2016 *OECD Factbook* shows that: CO_2 emissions from fuel combustion in the OECD as whole during 2014 were below the levels seen between 2003 and 2008; that the contribution of renewables to the energy supply remains just under 10% on average in the OECD; that expenditure on health has risen steadily, accounting for more than 9% of GDP on average; and, that the elderly population as a percentage of the total population continues to increase in most OECD countries, with an average ratio of 16% across the OECD in 2014. This latest edition of the *Factbook* also includes new indicators in the fields of education on the connection between students, computers and learning, as well as early childhood education and care, and for regional statistics on GDP by metropolitan area.

Written in a non-technical language, the *OECD Factbook* provides data and indicators for all 34 OECD member countries and, when available and considered internationally comparable, for Brazil, India, Indonesia, the People's Republic of China, Russia and South Africa.

As part of an on-going effort to make OECD data more readily available, virtually all the indicators presented in the *OECD Factbook 2015-2016* are also available online through *OECD.Stat*, the OECD platform for data dissemination, and through the new *OECD Data* portal.

I trust that the *OECD Factbook*, in its various formats, will continue to be a first-stop, easy tool for all those who are looking for reliable, trustworthy and internationally comparable statistics, providing the evidence which ultimately helps to deliver better policies for better lives.

Martine Durand
OECD Chief Statistician and Director of Statistics

ACKNOWLEDGEMENTS

The *OECD Factbook*, comprising the paper and e-publications, as well as the online rolling dataset is the result of ongoing statistical co-operation among virtually all OECD directorates, more specifically: the *Centre for Tax Policy and Administration*; the *Directorate for Financial and Enterprise Affairs*; the *Development Co-operation Directorate*; the *Directorate for Education and Skills*; the *Directorate for Employment, Labour and Social Affairs*; the *Environment Directorate*; *Public Governance and Territorial Development*; the *Statistics Directorate*; and the *Directorate for Science, Technology and Innovation*. A number of OECD agencies are also included, namely: the *International Energy Agency* (IEA), the *Nuclear Energy Agency* (NEA) and the *International Transport Forum* (ITF). It also reflects the continuous and effective collaboration with OECD and partner countries' statistical authorities.

The OECD *Statistics Directorate* is responsible for the overall co-ordination of the *OECD Factbook*, led by David Brackfield (Editor) and Ingrid Herrbach (technical production). The OECD *Public Affairs and Communications Directorate* provides editorial guidance, led by Eileen Capponi with Damian Garnys and Margaret Simmons. The *Knowledge and Information Services* section of the *Digital, Knowledge and Information Service* in the OECD *Executive Directorate* provides the IT support.

TABLE OF CONTENTS

☼ Environment and science

☉ Education

→ Government

❀ Health

READER'S GUIDE

Main features

- Tables and charts are preceded by short texts that explain how the statistics are defined (Definition) and that identify any problems there may be in comparing the performance of one country with another (Comparability). To avoid misunderstandings, the tables and charts must be viewed in conjunction with the texts that accompany them.

- Tables and charts can be downloaded as Excel files.

- While media comment on statistics usually focuses on the short term – what has happened to employment, prices, GDP and so on in the last few months – the *OECD Factbook* takes a longer view; the text and charts mostly describe developments during at least the last ten years. This long-term perspective provides a good basis for comparing the successes and failures of policies in raising living standards and improving social conditions in countries.

- To facilitate cross-country comparisons, many indicators in the *OECD Factbook* have been standardised by relating them to each country's gross domestic product (GDP). In cases where GDP needs to be converted to a common currency, purchasing power parities (PPPs) have been used rather than exchange rates. When PPPs are used, differences in GDP levels across countries reflect only differences in the volume of goods and services, that is, differences in price levels are eliminated.

Conventions

Unless otherwise specified:

- OECD refers to all 34 OECD countries; the indicator is presented either as the weighted average of country values or an unweighted arithmetic average.

- For each country, the average value in different periods takes into account only the years for which data are available. The *average annual growth rate* of an indicator over a period of time is the geometric average of the growth rates of that indicator across the period (that is, the annual compound growth rate).

- Each table and chart specifies the period covered. The mention, *XXXX or latest available year* (where XXXX is a year or a period) means that data for later years are not taken into account..

Signs, abbreviations and acronyms

..	Missing value, not applicable or not available
0	Less than half of the unit precision level of the observation
-	Absolute zero
USD	US dollars
DAC	OECD Development Assistance Committee
ILO	International Labour Organization
IMF	International Monetary Fund
ITF	International Transport Forum
UN	United Nations
UNECE	United Nations Economic Commission for Europe
WTO	World Trade Organization

The OECD Factbook uses ISO codes for countries

AUS	Australia	JPN	Japan	DAC	DAC total
AUT	Austria	KOR	Korea	EA19	Euro area
BEL	Belgium	LUX	Luxembourg	EU28	European Union
CAN	Canada	MEX	Mexico	OECD	OECD area
CHL	Chile	NLD	Netherlands	WLD	World
CZE	Czech Republic	NZL	New Zealand		
DNK	Denmark	NOR	Norway	BRA	Brazil
EST	Estonia	POL	Poland	CHN	China
FIN	Finland	PRT	Portugal	IND	India
FRA	France	SVK	Slovak Republic	IDN	Indonesia
GRC	Greece	SVN	Slovenia	RUS	Russian Federation
DEU	Germany	ESP	Spain	ZAF	South Africa
HUN	Hungary	SWE	Sweden		
ISL	Iceland	CHE	Switzerland		
IRL	Ireland	TUR	Turkey		
ISR	Israel	GBR	United Kingdom		
ITA	Italy	USA	United States		

StatLinks

This publication includes the OECD **StatLink** service, which enables users to download Excel versions of tables and figures. **StatLinks** are provided at the bottom of each table and figure. **StatLinks** behave like Internet addresses: simply type the **StatLink** into your Internet browser to obtain the corresponding data in Excel format.

For more information about OECD **StatLinks**, please visit: *www.oecd.org/statistics/statlink*.

Accessing OECD publications

- OECD publications cited in the *OECD Factbook* are available through OECD iLibrary (*www.oecd-ilibrary.org*).
- All the OECD working papers can be downloaded from OECD iLibrary.
- All OECD databases mentioned can be accessed through OECD iLibrary.
- Print editions of all OECD books can be purchased via the OECD online bookshop (*www.oecd.org/bookshop*).

POPULATION AND MIGRATION

TOTAL POPULATION

The size and growth of a country's population provides important contextual information to help understand other social and economic outcomes.

Definition

Data refer to the resident population, which for most countries is defined as all nationals present in, or temporarily absent from the country, and aliens permanently settled in the country. It includes the following categories: national armed forces stationed abroad; merchant seamen at sea; diplomatic personnel located abroad; civilian aliens resident in the country; and displaced persons resident in the country. Excluded are the following categories: foreign armed forces stationed in the country; foreign diplomatic personnel located in the country; and civilian aliens temporarily in the country.

For countries with overseas colonies, protectorates or other territorial possessions, their populations are generally excluded. Growth rates are the annual changes resulting from births, deaths and net migration during the year.

Data for total population may be compiled following two basic concepts: "Present-in-area population" or *de facto*, i.e. persons actually present in the country on the date of the census; or, "Resident population" or *de jure*, i.e. persons regularly domiciled in the country on the date of the census.

Comparability

For most OECD countries, population data are based on regular, ten-yearly censuses, with estimates for intercensal years derived from administrative data. In several European countries, population estimates are based entirely on administrative records. Population data are fairly comparable. Some nations are capable of generating population statistics from administrative records or through a combination of data sources. The vast majority of countries, however, produce these data on population and housing by conducting a traditional census, which in principle entails canvassing the entire country, reaching every single household and collecting information on all individuals within a brief stipulated period.

For some countries, the population figures shown here differ from those used for calculating GDP and other economic statistics on a per capita basis, although differences are normally small.

Overview

Within the OECD, in 2013, the United States accounted for 25% of the OECD total, followed by Japan (10%), Mexico (9%), Germany and Turkey (6%), France, Italy and the United Kingdom (5%), Korea and Spain (4%), Canada and Poland (3%). In the same year, the population of China was 10% higher than that of the whole OECD while the population of India was equal to that of the whole OECD.

In the three years to 2014 (or latest available period), population annual growth rates above 1% were recorded in Chile, Israel, Mexico and Turkey (high birth rate countries) and in Luxembourg, Australia, Canada, Norway, and Switzerland (high net immigration).

Over the same period, the highest population annual declines were observed in Portugal (due to a low birth rate and a negative net migration rate) and Hungary (for which birth and net migration rates are low). Growth rates were also negative in Estonia, Greece, Japan and Spain, while the population was stable in Poland.

Among emerging economies, in the three years to 2013, population annual growth rates were above 1% in South Africa, Brazil, India and Indonesia. By contrast, Russian population rose more slowly.

Sources

- For OECD member countries: national sources, United Nations and Eurostat.
- For Brazil, China, India, Indonesia, the Russian Federation and South Africa: United Nations, *World Population Prospects: The 2012 Revision.*

Further information

Analytical publications

- OECD (2011), *Doing Better for Families*, OECD Publishing.
- OECD (2011), *The Future of Families to 2030*, OECD Publishing.

Statistical publications

- OECD (2014), *Society at a Glance: OECD Social Indicators*, OECD Publishing.

Methodological publications

- OECD (2014), *OECD Labour Force Statistics*, OECD Publishing.

Online databases

- *OECD Employment and Labour Market Statistics.*
- *OECD Social and Welfare Statistics, Family indicators.*
- *United Nations World Population Prospects.*

Websites

- OECD Family Database, *www.oecd.org/social/family/database.*

Population levels
Thousands

	2002	2003	2004	2005	2006	2007	2008	2009	2010	2011	2012	2013	2014
Australia	19 495	19 721	19 933	20 177	20 451	20 828	21 249	21 692	22 032	22 340	22 728	23 126	23 491
Austria	8 082	8 118	8 169	8 225	8 268	8 295	8 322	8 341	8 361	8 389	8 426	8 469	..
Belgium	10 333	10 376	10 421	10 479	10 548	10 626	10 710	10 796	10 920	11 048	11 128	11 178	11 227
Canada	31 354	31 640	31 941	32 245	32 576	32 928	33 318	33 727	34 127	34 484	34 880	35 154	35 540
Chile	15 668	15 838	16 002	16 165	16 332	16 505	16 687	16 877	17 066	17 256	17 445	17 632	17 819
Czech Republic	10 201	10 202	10 207	10 234	10 267	10 323	10 430	10 491	10 517	10 497	10 509	10 511	10 525
Denmark	5 376	5 391	5 405	5 419	5 437	5 461	5 494	5 523	5 548	5 571	5 592	5 615	..
Estonia	1 379	1 371	1 363	1 355	1 347	1 341	1 337	1 335	1 331	1 327	1 323	1 318	1 316
Finland	5 201	5 213	5 228	5 246	5 267	5 289	5 313	5 339	5 363	5 388	5 414	5 439	5 472
France	59 894	60 304	60 734	61 182	61 597	61 965	62 300	62 615	62 918	63 223	63 514	63 786	64 062
Germany	82 456	82 502	82 491	82 465	82 369	82 257	82 135	81 904	81 715	80 249	80 413	80 611	80 896
Greece	10 983	11 016	11 057	11 093	11 131	11 163	11 186	11 185	11 153	11 124	11 090	..	..
Hungary	10 159	10 130	10 107	10 087	10 071	10 056	10 038	10 023	10 000	9 972	9 920	9 893	9 863
Iceland	288	289	293	296	304	311	319	319	318	319	321	324	327
Ireland	3 917	3 980	4 045	4 134	4 233	4 376	4 485	4 533	4 555	4 575	4 585	4 593	4 610
Israel	6 570	6 690	6 809	6 930	7 054	7 180	7 309	7 486	7 624	7 766	7 911	8 059	..
Italy	57 474	57 478	57 297	57 716	57 984	58 272	58 740	59 140	59 420	59 660	59 898	60 225	60 448
Japan	127 435	127 619	127 687	127 768	127 770	127 771	127 692	127 510	128 057	127 799	127 515	127 298	..
Korea	47 622	47 859	48 039	48 138	48 372	48 598	48 949	49 182	49 410	49 779	50 004	50 220	50 424
Luxembourg	446	450	455	461	469	476	484	494	502	512	525	537	550
Mexico	100 909	102 000	103 002	107 151	108 409	109 787	111 299	112 853	114 256	115 683	117 054	118 395	119 713
Netherlands	16 149	16 225	16 282	16 320	16 346	16 382	16 446	16 530	16 615	16 693	16 755	16 804	..
New Zealand	3 949	4 027	4 088	4 134	4 185	4 224	4 260	4 303	4 351	4 384	4 408	4 442	4 510
Norway	4 538	4 564	4 592	4 623	4 661	4 709	4 768	4 829	4 889	4 953	5 019	5 080	5 137
Poland	38 232	38 195	38 180	38 161	38 132	38 116	38 116	38 153	38 517	38 526	38 534	38 502	38 484
Portugal	10 420	10 459	10 484	10 503	10 522	10 543	10 558	10 568	10 573	10 558	10 515	10 457	..
Slovak Republic	5 377	5 373	5 372	5 373	5 373	5 375	5 379	5 386	5 391	5 398	5 408	5 416	..
Slovenia	1 996	1 997	1 997	2 001	2 009	2 019	2 023	2 042	2 049	2 052	2 056	2 059	2 062
Spain	41 424	42 196	42 859	43 663	44 361	45 236	45 983	46 368	46 562	46 736	46 766	46 593	46 464
Sweden	8 925	8 958	8 994	9 030	9 081	9 148	9 220	9 299	9 378	9 449	9 519	9 609	..
Switzerland	7 285	7 339	7 390	7 437	7 484	7 551	7 648	7 744	7 828	7 912	7 997	8 140	..
Turkey	66 003	66 795	67 599	68 435	69 295	70 158	71 052	72 039	73 142	74 224	75 176	76 055	76 903
United Kingdom	58 570	58 839	59 149	59 591	60 003	60 482	60 982	61 424	61 915	62 435	62 859	63 238	63 650
United States	287 625	290 108	292 805	295 517	298 380	301 231	304 094	306 772	309 347	311 722	314 112	316 498	318 857
EU 28	489 827	491 624	493 577	495 518	497 369	499 299	501 194	502 630	503 833	505 035	506 100	506 736	..
OECD	1 168 022	1 176 212	1 184 415	1 192 754	1 201 155	1 210 194	1 219 475	1 227 932	1 236 914	1 243 751	1 250 277	1 257 114	
Brazil	175 077	177 360	183 439	185 651	187 852	189 954	192 000	193 995	193 253	197 825	199 689	201 467	..
China	1 295 322	1 302 810	1 310 414	1 318 177	1 326 146	1 334 344	1 342 733	1 351 248	1 359 822	1 368 440	1 377 065	1 385 567	
India	1 076 706	1 093 787	1 110 626	1 127 144	1 143 289	1 159 095	1 174 662	1 190 138	1 205 625	1 221 156	1 236 687	1 252 140	..
Indonesia	215 038	218 146	221 294	224 481	227 710	230 973	234 244	237 487	240 677	243 802	246 864	249 866	..
Russian Federation	145 306	144 649	144 067	143 519	143 050	142 805	142 742	142 785	142 849	142 961	143 207	143 507	..
South Africa	45 545	46 127	46 727	47 350	47 991	48 658	49 345	50 055	50 792	51 554	52 341	53 158	54 002

StatLink http://dx.doi.org/10.1787/888933336107

Population growth rates
Annual growth in percentage

3 year average at end of period 2012-14 or latest available period   3 year average at beginning of period 2002-04

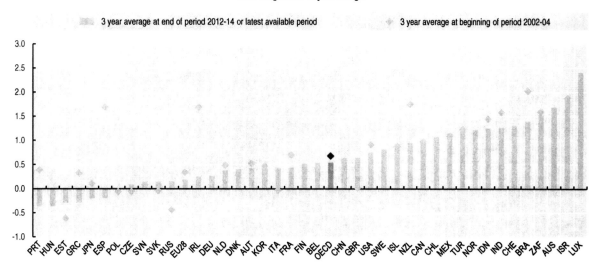

StatLink http://dx.doi.org/10.1787/888933334925

FERTILITY

Together with mortality and migration, fertility is a core driver of population growth, which reflects both the causes and effects of economic and social developments.

Total fertility rates in OECD countries have declined dramatically over the past few decades, falling from an average of 2.8 children per woman of childbearing age in 1970 to 1.7 in the early 2000s. The decline has been especially pronounced – by around or greater than three children per woman on average – in Korea, Mexico and Turkey, but a number of other OECD countries have also seen the total fertility rate fall by at least one child per woman on average since 1970. There are many reasons behind the decline in fertility, but the postponement of family formation and a decrease in desired family size –

themselves driven by rising female education and employment, insufficient support for families juggling work and children, the need to generate a secure job and income, and growing housing problems – have played a central role.

Definition

The total fertility rate in a specific year is the total number of children that would be born to each woman if she were to live to the end of her child-bearing years and give birth to children in agreement with the prevailing age-specific fertility rates.

Comparability

The total fertility rate is generally computed by summing up the age-specific fertility rates defined over a five-year interval. Assuming there are no migration flows and that mortality rates remain unchanged, a total fertility rate of 2.1 children per woman generates broad stability of population: it is also referred to as the "replacement fertility rate", as it ensures replacement of the woman and her partner with another 0.1 children per woman to counteract infant mortality.

Data are collected every year from national statistical institutes.

Overview

Prior to the start of the economic crisis in 2008, fertility rates in many – although not all – OECD countries were recovering slightly from the record lows observed in the early 2000s. Fertility rates continued to decline or remained stable in Austria, Japan, Korea and Switzerland – all low fertility countries. Fertility rebounded in countries with higher initial fertility rates, and even exceeded the replacement level in New Zealand and Iceland.

This fertility rebound stalled in many OECD countries in 2008, possibly as a consequence of the economic crisis. Since 2008, fertility rates have fallen in more than two-thirds of OECD countries, with the decline greater than two decimal points in three European OECD countries (Denmark, Estonia and Iceland) and the United States (a relatively high fertility country). Israel and Japan have seen the largest increases since the start of the economic crisis, but no OECD country has seen the total fertility rate increase by more than 1 decimal point since 2008.

In 2013, the highest fertility rate was recorded in Israel, where women had almost one child more than in the second country, Mexico. Israel and Mexico were in fact the only two OECD countries with a total fertility rate above the replacement fertility rate (2.1 children per woman). Anglophone and Nordic countries were typically at the higher end, while continental Europe (France being the one major exception) generally reported low fertility, along with even lower fertility rates in the East Asian and Southern Europe OECD countries. Fertility rates were particularly low in Portugal and Korea, with two parents replacing themselves in the next generation by little more than one child, on average.

Fertility rates were generally higher but have declined sharply in the emerging economies; with current rates only above replacement levels in India, Indonesia and South Africa.

Sources
- For OECD member countries and Brazil, Russia and South Africa: National statistical offices.
- For China, India and Indonesia: World Bank *World Development indicators*.
- Fertility rates: OECD (2015), "Family Indicators", *OECD Social and Welfare Statistics* (database).

Further information
Analytical publications
- OECD (2011), *Doing Better for Families*, OECD Publishing.

Statistical publications
- OECD (2014), *Society at a Glance: OECD Social Indicators*, OECD Publishing.

Methodological publications
- Adema, W., N. Ali and O. Thévenon (2014), "Changes in Family Policies and Outcomes: Is there Convergence?", *OECD Social Employment and Migration Working Papers*, No. 157, OECD Publishing.

Online databases
- *United Nations World Population Prospects.*

Websites
- OECD Family Database, *www.oecd.org/social/family/database.*
- World Bank – World Development Indicators, *http://data.worldbank.org/indicator.*

Total fertility rates

Number of children born to women aged 15 to 49

	1970	1980	1990	2000	2005	2006	2007	2008	2009	2010	2011	2012	2013
Australia	2.86	1.89	1.90	1.76	1.85	1.88	1.99	2.02	1.97	1.95	1.92	1.93	1.88
Austria	2.29	1.65	1.46	1.36	1.41	1.41	1.39	1.42	1.40	1.44	1.43	1.44	1.44
Belgium	2.25	1.68	1.62	1.64	1.74	1.78	1.80	1.86	1.83	1.84	1.81	1.79	1.76
Canada	2.33	1.68	1.71	1.49	1.54	1.59	1.66	1.68	1.67	1.63	1.61	..	..
Chile	3.95	2.72	2.59	2.05	1.84	1.83	1.88	1.92	1.92	1.89	1.85	1.80	..
Czech Republic	1.91	2.10	1.89	1.14	1.28	1.33	1.44	1.50	1.49	1.49	1.43	1.45	1.46
Denmark	1.95	1.55	1.67	1.77	1.80	1.85	1.84	1.89	1.84	1.87	1.75	1.73	1.67
Estonia	..	2.02	2.05	1.36	1.52	1.58	1.69	1.72	1.70	1.72	1.61	1.56	1.52
Finland	1.83	1.63	1.79	1.73	1.80	1.84	1.83	1.85	1.86	1.87	1.83	1.80	1.75
France	2.48	1.95	1.78	1.87	1.92	1.98	1.95	1.99	1.99	2.02	2.00	1.99	1.98
Germany	2.03	1.56	1.45	1.38	1.34	1.33	1.37	1.38	1.36	1.39	1.39	1.40	1.41
Greece	2.40	2.23	1.40	1.27	1.32	1.38	1.38	1.47	1.49	1.47	1.40	1.35	1.30
Hungary	1.97	1.92	1.84	1.33	1.32	1.35	1.32	1.35	1.33	1.26	1.24	1.34	1.34
Iceland	2.81	2.48	2.31	2.08	2.05	2.07	2.09	2.14	2.22	2.20	2.02	2.04	1.93
Ireland	3.87	3.23	2.12	1.90	1.88	1.94	2.03	2.07	2.07	2.06	2.04	2.01	1.96
Israel	..	3.14	3.02	2.95	2.84	2.88	2.90	2.96	2.96	3.03	3.00	3.05	3.03
Italy	2.42	1.68	1.36	1.26	1.32	1.35	1.37	1.42	1.41	1.41	1.39	1.42	1.39
Japan	2.13	1.75	1.54	1.36	1.26	1.32	1.34	1.37	1.37	1.39	1.39	1.41	1.43
Korea	4.53	2.82	1.57	1.47	1.08	1.12	1.25	1.19	1.15	1.23	1.24	1.30	1.19
Luxembourg	1.98	1.50	1.62	1.78	1.62	1.64	1.61	1.60	1.59	1.63	1.51	1.57	1.55
Mexico	6.72	4.71	3.36	2.65	2.45	2.42	2.38	2.35	2.32	2.28	2.26	2.24	2.22
Netherlands	2.57	1.60	1.62	1.72	1.71	1.72	1.72	1.77	1.79	1.80	1.76	1.72	1.68
New Zealand	3.17	2.03	2.18	1.98	1.97	2.01	2.18	2.19	2.13	2.17	2.09	2.10	2.01
Norway	2.50	1.72	1.93	1.85	1.84	1.90	1.90	1.96	1.98	1.95	1.88	1.85	1.78
Poland	2.20	2.28	1.99	1.37	1.24	1.27	1.31	1.39	1.40	1.38	1.30	1.30	1.26
Portugal	2.83	2.18	1.56	1.56	1.42	1.38	1.35	1.40	1.35	1.39	1.35	1.28	1.21
Slovak Republic	2.40	2.31	2.09	1.29	1.25	1.24	1.25	1.32	1.41	1.40	1.45	1.34	1.34
Slovenia	2.21	2.11	1.46	1.26	1.26	1.31	1.38	1.53	1.53	1.57	1.56	1.58	1.55
Spain	2.90	2.22	1.36	1.23	1.33	1.36	1.38	1.45	1.38	1.37	1.34	1.32	1.27
Sweden	1.94	1.68	2.14	1.55	1.77	1.85	1.88	1.91	1.94	1.98	1.90	1.91	1.89
Switzerland	2.10	1.55	1.59	1.50	1.42	1.44	1.46	1.48	1.50	1.54	1.52	1.53	1.52
Turkey	5.00	4.63	3.07	2.27	2.12	2.12	2.16	2.15	2.08	2.06	2.03	2.09	2.07
United Kingdom	2.43	1.90	1.83	1.64	1.76	1.82	1.86	1.91	1.89	1.92	1.91	1.92	1.83
United States	2.48	1.84	2.08	2.06	2.06	2.11	2.12	2.07	2.00	1.93	1.89	1.88	1.86
EU 28	2.43	2.01	1.78	1.48	1.49	1.52	1.54	1.60	1.60	1.59	1.55	1.56	1.52
OECD	2.76	2.17	1.91	1.67	1.66	1.69	1.72	1.76	1.74	1.75	1.71	1.71	1.67
Brazil	5.02	4.07	2.81	2.36	2.07	2.00	1.94	1.90	1.86	1.84	1.82	1.81	1.80
China	5.47	2.71	2.51	1.51	1.59	1.60	1.62	1.63	1.64	1.65	1.66	1.66	1.67
India	5.49	4.68	3.88	3.15	2.82	2.75	2.69	2.64	2.60	2.56	2.53	2.51	2.48
Indonesia	5.47	4.43	3.12	2.48	2.49	2.50	2.49	2.48	2.46	2.43	2.40	2.37	2.34
Russian Federation	2.01	1.90	1.89	1.20	1.29	1.31	1.42	1.50	1.54	1.57	1.58	1.69	1.71
South Africa	5.59	4.79	3.66	2.87	2.56	2.53	2.53	2.52	2.51	2.50	2.44	2.39	2.34

StatLink http://dx.doi.org/10.1787/888933336165

Total fertility rates

Number of children born to women aged 15 to 49

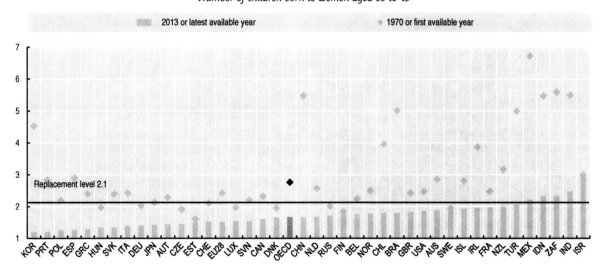

StatLink http://dx.doi.org/10.1787/888933334982

POPULATION BY REGION

Population is unevenly distributed among regions within countries. Differences in climatic and environmental conditions discourage human settlement in some areas and favour concentration of the population around a few urban centres. This pattern is reinforced by higher economic opportunities and wider availability of services stemming from urbanisation itself.

Definition

The number of inhabitants of a given region, i.e. its total population, can be measured as either its average annual population or as the population at a specific date during the year considered. The average population during a calendar year is generally calculated as the arithmetic mean of the population on 1 January of two consecutive years, although some countries estimate it on a date close to 1 July.

Comparability

The main problem with economic analysis at the sub-national level is the unit of analysis, i.e. the region. The word "region" can mean very different things both within and among countries, with significant differences in area and population.

The population across OECD regions ranges from about 600 inhabitants in Stikine, British Columbia (Canada) to 39 million in California (the United States).

To address this issue, the OECD has classified regions within each member country to facilitate comparability at the same territorial level. The classification is based on two territorial levels: the higher level (TL2) consists of 362 large regions and the lower level (TL3) consists of 1 802 small regions. These two levels are used as a framework for implementing regional policies in most countries. In Brazil, China, India, Russia and South Africa only TL2 large regions have been identified. This classification (which, for European Union countries, is largely consistent with the Eurostat NUTS classification) facilitates comparability of regions at the same territorial level.

All the regional data refer to small regions with the exception of Brazil, China, India, Russia and South Africa.

In addition, the OECD has established a regional typology to take into account geographical differences and enable meaningful comparisons between regions belonging to the same type. Regions have been classified as predominantly rural, intermediate and predominantly urban on the basis of the percentage of population living in local rural units.

The metropolitan database identifies about 1 200 urban areas (with a population of 50 000 or more) in 30 OECD countries. Urban areas are defined on the basis of population density and commuting patterns to better reflect the economic function of cities in addition to their administrative boundaries. Functional urban areas can extend across administrative boundaries, reflecting the economic geography of where people actually live and work.

Urban areas in Turkey refer to the 144 cities classified according the national definition and refer to the year 2012. Comparability with other countries is, therefore, limited.

Overview

In 2014, 10% of regions accounted for approximately 40% of the total population in OECD countries. The concentration of population was highest in Canada and Australia where differences in climatic and environmental conditions discourage human settlement in some areas.

In 2014, two-thirds of the OECD urban population live in cities (above 50 000 inhabitants). However the urban experience is very different from country to country. In Korea, 90% of the national population is concentrated in cities (more than 45 million people), while only 40% in the Slovak Republic live in cities (more than 2 million people).

In 2014, almost half of the total OECD population (48%) lived in predominantly urban regions, which accounted for around 6% of the total area.

Predominantly, rural regions accounted for one-fourth of the total population and 83% of land area. In Ireland, Finland and Slovenia the share of national population in rural regions was twice as high as the OECD average.

Sources
• OECD (2013), OECD Regions at a Glance, OECD Publishing.

Further information

Analytical publications
• OECD (2014), OECD Regional Outlook, OECD Publishing.
• OECD (2014), OECD Territorial Reviews, OECD Publishing.

Statistical publications
• OECD (2014), OECD Labour Force Statistics, OECD Publishing.

Online databases
• OECD Regional Statistics.

Websites
• Regions at a Glance interactive, rag.oecd.org.
• Regional statistics and indicators, www.oecd.org/gov/regional/statisticsindicators.

Share of national population in the ten per cent of regions with the largest population

Percentage, 2000 and 2014

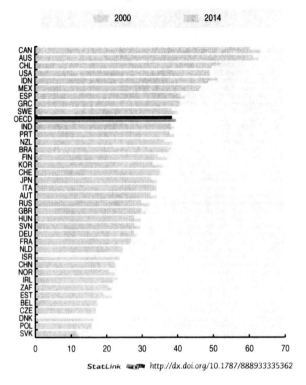

StatLink http://dx.doi.org/10.1787/888933335362

Distribution of the national population into urban, intermediate and rural regions

Percentage, 2014

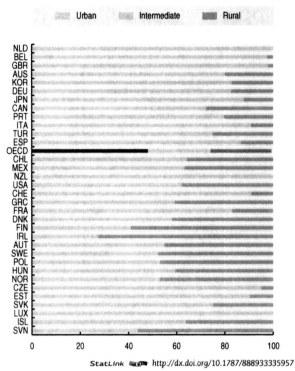

StatLink http://dx.doi.org/10.1787/888933335957

Urban population by city size

2014

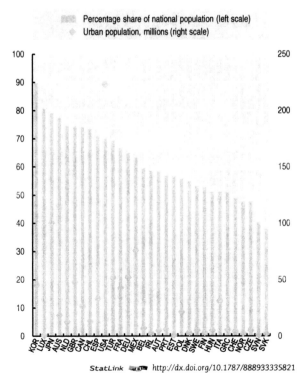

StatLink http://dx.doi.org/10.1787/888933335821

Distribution of the national area into urban, intermediate and rural regions

Percentage, 2014

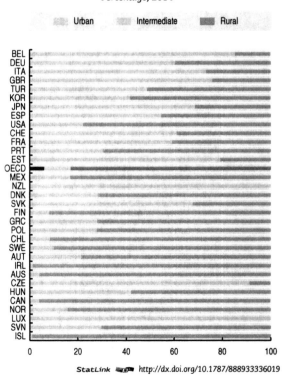

StatLink http://dx.doi.org/10.1787/888933336019

ELDERLY POPULATION BY REGION

In all OECD countries, populations aged 65 years and over have dramatically increased over the last decades, both in size and as a percentage of total population. Elderly people, it turns out, tend to be concentrated in few areas within each country, which means that a small number of regions will have to face a number of specific social and economic challenges raised by ageing population.

Definition

The elderly population is the number of inhabitants of a given region aged 65 or older. The population can be either the average annual population or the population at a specific date during the year considered.

The elderly dependency rate is defined as the ratio between the elderly population and the working age (15-64 years) population.

Comparability

As for the other regional statistics, the comparability of elderly population data is affected by differences in the definition of the regions and the different geography of rural and urban communities, both within and among countries. In order to better show the rural/urban divide, elderly dependency rates are presented for rural and urban regions, but not for intermediary regions, which explains that for some countries, the country average can be outside the rural/urban range.

All the regional data shown here refer to small regions with the exception of Brazil, China, India, Russia and South Africa.

Overview

In most OECD countries the population is ageing. Due to higher life expectancy and low fertility rates, the elderly population (those aged 65 years and over) accounts for almost 16% of the OECD population in 2014, up from just over 13% 14 years earlier. The proportion of elderly population is remarkably lower in the emerging economies (South Africa, Brazil and China) and Mexico, Turkey, Chile and Israel.

The elderly population in OECD countries has increased more than three times faster than the total population between 2000 and 2014. The rate of ageing between different parts of a country can be quite different, as an increase in the geographic concentration of the elderly may arise from inward migration of the elderly or by ageing "in place" because the younger generations have moved out of the regions.

The ratio of the elderly to the working age population, the elderly dependency rate, is steadily growing in OECD countries. The elderly dependency rate gives an indication of the balance between the retired and the economically active population. In 2014 this ratio was 24% in OECD countries, with substantial differences between countries (42% in Japan versus 11% in Turkey). Differences among regions within the same countries are also large. The higher the regional elderly dependency rate, the higher the challenges faced by regions in generating wealth and sufficient resources to provide for the needs of the population. Concerns may arise about the financial self-sufficiency of these regions to generate taxes to pay for the services for the elderly.

Sources
- OECD (2013), *OECD Regions at a Glance*, OECD Publishing.

Further information

Analytical publications
- OECD (2015), *Ageing and Employment Policies*, OECD Publishing.
- OECD (2014), *OECD Regional Outlook*, OECD Publishing.
- OECD (2011), *The Future of Families to 2030*, OECD Publishing.
- Oliveira Martins J., et al. (2005), "The Impact of Ageing on Demand, Factor Markets and Growth", *OECD Economics Department Working Papers*, No. 420.

Statistical publication
- OECD (2014), *Society at a Glance: OECD Social Indicators*, OECD Publishing.

Online databases
- OECD Regional Database.

Websites
- Regions at a Glance Interactive, *rag.oecd.org*.
- Regional statistics and indicators, *www.oecd.org/gov/regional/statisticsindicators*.

Elderly population

As a percentage of total population, 2000 and 2014

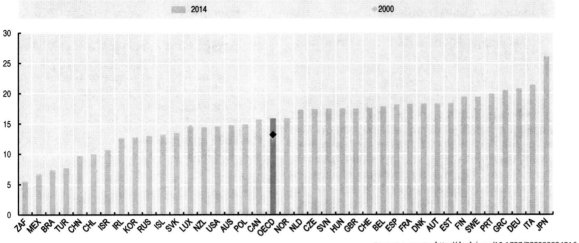

StatLink http://dx.doi.org/10.1787/888933334816

Regional elderly population

Average annual growth in percentage, 2000-14

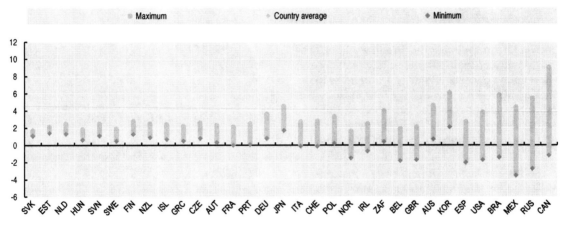

StatLink http://dx.doi.org/10.1787/888933335744

Elderly dependency rate in urban and rural regions

Percentage, 2014

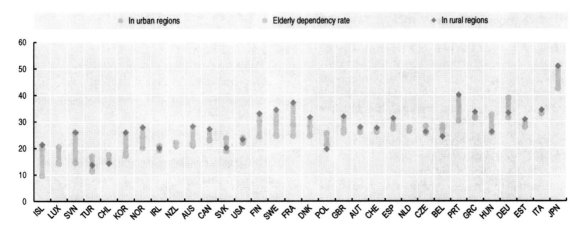

StatLink http://dx.doi.org/10.1787/888933335890

IMMIGRANT AND FOREIGN POPULATION

As a result of successive waves of migration flows from varying destinations, countries differ in the share and composition of immigrants and foreign population. The definition of these populations is key for international comparisons.

Definition

Nationality and place of birth are the two criteria most commonly used to define the "immigrant" population. The foreign-born population covers all persons who have ever migrated from their country of birth to their current country of residence. The foreign population consists of persons who still have the nationality of their home country. It may include persons born in the host country.

Comparability

The difference across countries between the size of the foreign-born population and that of the foreign population depends on the rules governing the acquisition of citizenship in each country. In some countries, children born in the country automatically acquire the citizenship of their country of birth while in other countries, they retain the nationality of their parents. In some others, they retain the nationality of their parents at birth but receive that of the host country at their majority. Differences in the ease with which immigrants may acquire the citizenship of the host country explain part of the gap between the two. For example, residency requirements vary from as little as four years in Canada to as much as ten years in some other countries.

In general, the foreign-born criterion gives substantially higher percentages for the immigrant population than the definition based on nationality because of naturalisations. The place of birth changes only if country borders change.

Overview

The share of the foreign-born population in the total population is especially high in Luxembourg, Switzerland, New Zealand, Australia, Israel and Canada where it ranges from 20% to 44%. In a number of other countries e.g. Austria, Ireland, Slovenia, Sweden, Belgium, Norway, Spain and the United States the share is above 13%. It has increased in the past decade in all countries for which data are available with the exception of Israel and Estonia.

The proportion of foreign-born in the population as a whole roughly doubled over the past 13 years in Ireland, Norway and Spain. By contrast, the foreign population tends to increase more slowly, because inflows of foreign nationals tend to be counterbalanced by persons acquiring the nationality of the host country.

Most data are taken from the contributions of national correspondents who are part of the *OECD Expert Group on International Migration*.

The foreign-born population data shown here include persons born abroad as nationals of their current country of residence. The prevalence of such persons among the foreign-born can be significant in some countries, in particular France and Portugal who received large inflows of repatriates from former colonies.

The EU28 aggregate is a weighted average and does not include Croatia or Malta.

Sources
- OECD (2015), *International Migration Outlook*, OECD Publishing.

Further information

Analytical publications
- Arslan C. et al. (2014), "A New Profile of Migrants in the Aftermath of the Recent Economic Crisis", *OECD Social, Employment and Migration Working Papers*, No. 160, OECD Publishing.
- OECD (2011), "Tackling the Policy Challenges of Migration, Regulation, Integration, Development", *Development Centre Studies*, OECD Publishing.

Statistical publications
- OECD (2015), *Connecting with Emigrants, A Global Profile of Diasporas 2015*, OECD Publishing.
- OECD (2015), *OECD Indicators of Immigrant Integration 2015*, OECD Publishing.

Methodological publications
- Lemaître, G. and C. Thoreau, (2006), *Estimating the foreign-born population on a current basis*, OECD, Paris.

Online databases
- OECD International Migration Statistics.

Websites
- International migration policies and data, *www.oecd.org/migration/mig*.

Foreign-born and foreign populations

	As a percentage of total population								As a percentage of all foreign-born
	Foreign-born population				Foreign population				Foreign-born nationals
	2000	2005	2010	2013	2000	2005	2010	2013	2011 or latest available year
Australia	23.0	24.1	26.6	27.6	..	..	..	..	..
Austria	10.4	14.5	15.7	16.7	8.8	9.7	10.9	12.6	36.5
Belgium	10.3	12.1	14.9	15.5	8.4	8.6	10.2	10.9	44.2
Canada	17.4	18.7	19.9	20.0	..	..	..	..	..
Chile	..	1.5	2.2	..	..	..	..	..	..
Czech Republic	4.2	5.1	6.3	7.1	1.9	2.7	4.0	4.2	59.1
Denmark	5.8	6.5	7.7	8.5	4.8	5.0	6.2	7.1	40.8
Estonia	18.4	16.9	16.0	10.1	..	19.0	16.3	16.1	37.4
Finland	2.6	3.4	4.6	5.6	1.8	2.2	3.1	3.8	46.3
France	10.1	11.3	11.7	..	..	5.8	6.1	..	53.2
Germany	12.5	12.6	13.0	12.8	8.9	8.2	8.3	9.3	52.6
Greece	..	..	7.4	..	2.9	5.0	7.3	6.2	20.0
Hungary	2.9	3.3	4.5	4.5	1.1	1.5	2.1	1.4	71.9
Iceland	6.0	8.3	10.9	11.5	..	4.7	6.6	7.0	47.5
Ireland	8.7	12.6	17.0	16.4	..	..	12.3	..	29.0
Israel	32.2	28.1	24.5	22.6	..	..	..	..	..
Italy	..	..	8.9	..	2.4	4.6	7.6	8.1	25.0
Japan	1.0	..	..	..	1.3	1.6	1.7	1.6	..
Korea	0.3	..	..	..	0.4	1.1	2.0	2.0	..
Luxembourg	33.2	36.2	40.5	43.7	37.3	41.1	43.5	45.8	13.9
Mexico	0.5	0.5	0.8	0.8	..	..	0.2	..	..
Netherlands	10.1	10.6	11.2	11.6	4.2	4.2	4.6	4.9	67.3
New Zealand	17.2	20.3	27.3	28.2	..	..	..	..	..
Norway	6.8	8.2	11.6	13.9	4.0	4.8	7.6	9.5	46.2
Poland	..	..	-	..	..	..	..	..	84.8
Portugal	5.1	7.1	8.1	..	2.1	4.0	4.2	3.7	67.3
Slovak Republic	..	4.6	..	3.2	0.5	0.5	1.3	1.1	79.9
Slovenia	..	..	11.2	16.1	..	..	4.7	5.4	74.5
Spain	4.9	11.1	14.3	13.4	..	9.5	12.4	10.7	22.1
Sweden	11.3	12.5	14.8	16.0	5.4	5.3	6.8	7.2	66.6
Switzerland	21.9	23.8	26.5	28.3	19.3	20.3	22.0	23.3	31.9
Turkey	1.9	..	-	..	..	..	..	..	..
United Kingdom	7.9	9.2	11.2	12.3	4.0	5.0	7.2	7.7	41.6
United States	11.0	12.1	12.9	13.1	..	7.2	7.3	7.0	49.1
EU 28	..	..	..	..	..	..	..	..	..
OECD	..	..	..	..	..	..	..	..	..
Brazil	..	..	..	..	..	..	..	..	..
China	..	..	..	..	..	..	..	..	..
India	..	..	..	..	..	..	..	..	..
Indonesia	..	..	..	..	..	..	..	..	..
Russian Federation	..	..	..	..	..	..	..	..	..
South Africa	..	..	..	..	..	..	..	..	..

StatLink ⟶ http://dx.doi.org/10.1787/888933336396

Foreign-born population
As a percentage of total population

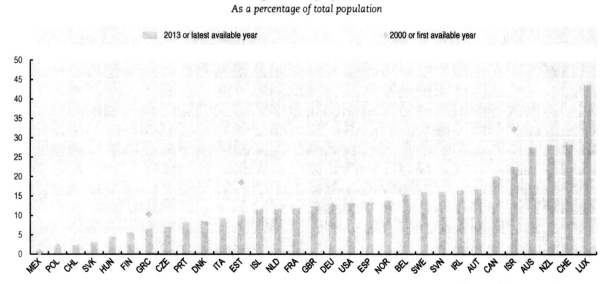

StatLink ⟶ http://dx.doi.org/10.1787/888933335230

TRENDS IN MIGRATION

Permanent immigrant inflows are presented by category of entry which is a key determinant of immigrant results on the labour market. They cover regulated movements of foreigners as well as free movement migration.

Definition

Permanent immigrant inflows cover regulated movements of foreigners considered to be settling in the country from the perspective of the destination country. In countries such as Australia, Canada, New Zealand and the United States, this consists of immigrants who receive the right of "permanent" residence. In other countries, it generally refers to immigrants who are granted a residence permit which is indefinitely renewable, although the renewability is sometimes subject to conditions, such as the holding of a job. Excluded are international students, trainees, persons on exchange programmes, seasonal or contract workers, service providers, installers, artists entering the country to perform or persons engaging in sporting events, etc. Permits for persons in this latter group may be renewable as well, but not indefinitely.

Migrants are defined as "free movement" when they have some kind of basic rights, usually accorded through international agreements, to enter and leave a country that result in few restrictions being placed on their movements or durations of stay, such as citizens of EU countries within the EU. Their movements are not always formally recorded and sometimes have to be estimated.

Comparability

This standardisation according to the concept of "permanent immigrant inflows" represents a considerable improvement compared with compilations of national statistics, whose coverage can vary by a factor of one to three. However, the extent to which changes in status are identified and the coverage of "permanent" free movement may vary somewhat across countries. Overall, the standardisation is applied to 23 OECD countries.

The year of reference for these statistics is often the year when the permit was granted rather than the year of entry. Some persons admitted on a temporary basis are sometimes allowed to change to a permanent status. They are counted in the year the change of status occurred. For example, asylum seekers are not considered migrants but are candidates for humanitarian migrant status. Only those who are recognised as refugees – or who obtain another permanent-type residence title – will be included in the permanent immigrant inflows statistics, in the year they are granted refugee or another permanent-type status. As a consequence, the unprecedented inflows of asylum seekers observed in the EU in 2015 (1.3 million requests filed) will appear in the permanent immigrant inflows in the subsequent years only, and only a part of these will figure there.

Sources

- OECD (2015), *International Migration Outlook*, OECD Publishing.

Further information

Analytical publications

- Arslan C. et al. (2014), "A New Profile of Migrants in the Aftermath of the Recent Economic Crisis", *OECD Social, Employment and Migration Working Papers*, No. 160, OECD Publishing.
- OECD (2015), "Is this humanitarian migration crisis different?", *Migration Policy Debates*, No. 7, Paris.

Statistical publications

- OECD (2015), *Connecting with Emigrants, A Global Profile of Diasporas*, OECD Publishing.
- OECD (2015), *OECD Indicators of Immigrant Integration 2015*, OECD Publishing.

Methodological publications

- Dumont, J.C. and Lemaître G. (2005), "Counting Immigrants and Expatriates in OECD Countries: A New Perspective", *OECD Social, Employment and Migration Working Papers*, No. 25.
- Lemaître G. (2005), "The Comparability of International Migration Statistics: Problems and Prospects", *OECD Statistic Brief*, No. 9.

Online databases

- OECD International Migration Statistics.

Websites

- International migration policies and data, *www.oecd.org/migration/mig*.

Overview

Total permanent immigration increased by about 1.6% overall in OECD countries in 2013 relative to 2012, with the migration picture being a mixed one at the country level. More than half of OECD countries showed increases, with Germany, Korea and Denmark being among the countries which progressed the most. Permanent migration flows diminished markedly in 2013 in Spain, Italy and the United States.

Migration to European countries continues to be characterised by free circulation within the European Economic Area (EEA). In Austria, Switzerland, Germany and Norway, it represents 78%, 78%, 76% and 63%, respectively, of permanent international migration.

Family reunification accounted for over one third of all permanent migration to OECD countries in 2013 (minus 1% compared to 2012) and free movement for 30% (up 4% compared to 2012).

Permanent inflows by category of entry

Thousands, 2013

	Work	Free movements	Accompanying family of workers	Family	Humanitarian	Other	Total
Australia	61.3	40.3	67.7	60.2	20.0	4.0	253.5
Austria	1.3	50.5	0.3	10.2	2.5	0.3	65.0
Belgium	7.8	27.3	-	22.3	3.0	..	60.3
Canada	64.7	..	83.3	79.6	31.0	0.0	258.6
Chile	..	..	..	..	..	..	..
Czech Republic	..	..	..	..	..	..	..
Denmark	7.9	27.7	3.5	5.2	3.9	4.2	52.4
Estonia	..	..	..	..	..	..	..
Finland	1.2	10.2	-	8.9	3.1	0.5	23.9
France	26.8	95.9	-	104.6	11.7	20.9	259.8
Germany	24.3	354.8	-	56.0	30.7	2.4	468.8
Greece	..	..	..	..	..	..	..
Hungary	..	..	..	..	..	..	..
Iceland	..	..	..	..	..	..	..
Ireland	2.7	23.1	0.3	13.9	0.2	..	40.2
Israel	..	..	..	..	..	..	..
Italy	73.1	77.9	2.5	78.6	8.8	4.9	245.8
Japan	25.1	..	-	20.6	0.2	11.5	57.3
Korea	1.6	..	5.1	31.4	0.0	28.6	66.7
Luxembourg	..	..	..	..	..	..	..
Mexico	16.6	..	-	19.2	0.2	18.4	54.4
Netherlands	9.2	65.2	-	21.1	10.0	..	105.5
New Zealand	10.1	3.7	10.3	16.9	3.4	..	44.4
Norway	3.8	37.8	-	11.9	6.7	..	60.3
Poland	..	..	..	..	..	..	..
Portugal	6.4	10.6	3.2	9.6	0.1	3.2	27.0
Slovak Republic	..	..	..	..	..	..	..
Slovenia	..	..	..	..	..	..	..
Spain	39.8	105.1	-	41.2	0.5	8.8	195.3
Sweden	3.9	22.0	2.4	29.5	28.9	..	86.7
Switzerland	2.2	105.8	-	21.3	5.1	2.0	136.2
Turkey	..	..	..	..	..	..	..
United Kingdom	86.4	98.3	37.6	27.1	20.7	20.7	291.0
United States	75.9	..	85.2	649.8	119.6	59.4	989.9
EU 28	..	..	..	..	..	..	..
OECD	..	..	..	..	..	..	..
Brazil	..	..	..	..	..	..	..
China	..	..	..	..	..	..	..
India	..	..	..	..	..	..	..
Indonesia	..	..	..	..	..	..	..
Russian Federation	..	..	..	..	..	..	..
South Africa	..	..	..	..	..	..	..

StatLink http://dx.doi.org/10.1787/888933336420

Permanent inflows by category of entry

Percentage of total permanent inflows, 2013

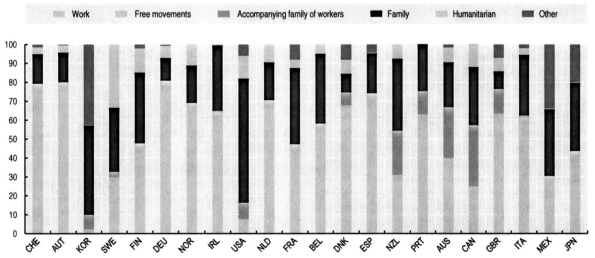

StatLink http://dx.doi.org/10.1787/888933335265

MIGRATION AND EMPLOYMENT

Changes in the size of the working-age population affect more strongly the foreign-born than the native-born for whom such changes are hardly noticeable from one year to another. This is notably due to the impact of net migration. In most OECD countries, employment rates for immigrants are lower than those for native-born persons. However, the situation is more diverse if one disaggregates employment rates by educational attainment.

Definition

The employment rate is calculated as the share of employed persons in the 25-64 population (active and inactive persons). In accordance with ILO definitions, employed persons are those who worked at least one hour or who had a job but were absent from work during the reference week. The classification of educational attainment shown is based on the *International Standard Classification of Education* (ISCED) categories. Generally speaking, "low" corresponds to less than upper secondary education; "intermediate" to upper secondary education; and "high" to tertiary education. Tertiary education includes programmes of high-level vocational education whose graduates feed into technical or semi-professional occupations.

Comparability

Data for the European countries are from the *European Union Labour Force Survey*. Data for other countries are mostly taken from national labour force surveys. Even if employment levels can at times be affected by changes in survey design and by survey implementation problems (e.g. non-response), data on employment rates are generally consistent over time.

However, comparability of education levels between immigrants and the native-born population and across countries is only approximate. The educational qualifications of some origin countries may not fit exactly into national educational categories because the duration of study or the programme content for what appear to be equivalent qualifications may not be the same. Likewise, the reduction of the ISCED classification into three categories may result in some loss of information regarding the duration of study, the programme orientation, etc. For example, high educational qualifications can include programmes of durations varying from two years (in the case of short, university-level technical programmes) to seven years or more (in the case of PhDs).

The EU28 aggregate is a weighted average.

Overview

Labour market outcomes of immigrants and native-born vary significantly across OECD countries, and differences by educational attainment are even larger. In all OECD countries, the employment rate increases with education level. While people with tertiary education find work more easily and are less exposed to unemployment, access to tertiary education does not necessarily guarantee equal employment rates for immigrants and native-born persons. In all OECD countries but Chile, employment rates are higher for native-born persons with high educational qualifications than for their foreign-born counterparts.

The situation is more diverse for persons with low educational attainment. In the United States, Luxembourg and to a lesser extent in some southern European countries such as Italy and Greece, foreign-born immigrants with low educational qualifications have higher employment rates than their native-born counterparts. The opposite is true in most other countries, in particular in Sweden, the Netherlands, Denmark and the United Kingdom. The higher employment rate of foreign-born persons with low educational attainment in some countries may reflect the persistent demand for workers in low-skilled jobs which are hardly taken up by the in-coming cohorts of native-born workers.

Sources
- OECD (2015), *International Migration Outlook*, OECD Publishing.

Further information

Analytical publications
- OECD (2014), *Jobs for Immigrants (Vol. 4), Labour Market Integration in Italy*, OECD Publishing.
- OECD (2014), *Matching Economic Migration with Labour Market Needs*, OECD Publishing.

Statistical publications
- OECD (2015), *Connecting with Emigrants, A Global Profile of Diasporas 2015*, OECD Publishing.
- OECD (2015), *OECD Indicators of Immigrant Integration 2015*, OECD Publishing.

Methodological publications
- Dumont, J.C. and Lemaître G. (2005), "Counting Immigrants and Expatriates in OECD Countries: A New Perspective", *OECD Social, Employment and Migration Working Papers*, No. 25.

Online databases
- OECD International Migration Statistics.

Websites
- International migration policies and data, *www.oecd.org/migration/mig*.

Employment rates of native- and foreign-born population by educational attainment

As a percentage of population aged 25-64

	2007						2014					
	Native-born			Foreign-born			Native-born			Foreign-born		
	Low	High	Total	Low	High	Total	Low	High	Total	Low	High	Total
Australia	..	..	77.2	..	..	71.1	..	..	76.5	..	..	72.7
Austria	57.1	89.5	76.5	57.5	75.5	67.3	54.2	87.5	77.1	50.9	76.6	67.4
Belgium	51.8	86.3	71.9	39.5	73.8	55.3	49.4	87.0	73.4	42.1	72.8	57.7
Canada	..	..	..	..	..	..	56.6	83.2	77.2	52.7	77.5	73.3
Chile	..	..	..	..	..	..	..	..	..	..	..	..
Czech Republic	45.7	85.3	74.6	45.7	81.9	69.6	42.7	84.6	76.8	46.9	81.9	74.9
Denmark	67.4	88.8	81.3	54.1	76.4	63.9	63.1	87.6	79.3	51.9	76.0	66.6
Estonia	56.5	88.3	80.1	45.7	83.1	75.2	60.3	85.6	78.1	69.3	73.4	68.8
Finland	58.0	85.6	76.2	54.1	76.5	70.7	53.4	84.3	75.6	54.4	68.4	63.9
France	59.0	85.0	73.7	54.3	70.8	62.1	55.3	85.6	74.2	50.5	71.6	60.6
Germany	56.1	87.7	76.2	52.3	70.5	62.8	57.9	89.8	81.0	58.1	78.0	70.8
Greece	56.7	83.8	68.3	74.8	70.9	72.7	45.5	69.4	56.2	55.9	54.4	54.3
Hungary	38.4	80.5	65.4	50.1	77.5	70.7	45.1	81.8	69.5	59.5	81.6	75.0
Iceland	82.3	92.5	87.8	86.9	88.4	86.8	76.0	90.5	84.8	83.3	83.7	83.9
Ireland	58.6	88.3	74.0	60.3	80.9	75.9	47.0	83.6	69.3	43.7	73.7	66.9
Israel	42.8	85.4	71.2	43.0	80.4	69.0	..	..	..	..	..	..
Italy	51.5	80.6	64.4	66.9	75.2	71.0	48.0	78.8	62.8	58.9	69.0	63.5
Japan	..	..	..	..	..	..	..	..	..	..	..	..
Korea	..	..	..	..	..	..	..	..	..	..	..	..
Luxembourg	52.3	83.8	69.8	70.5	85.1	76.3	55.6	86.6	74.8	64.9	83.5	76.4
Mexico	63.0	82.8	67.8	66.6	69.3	65.5	63.4	79.2	67.7	64.5	76.8	67.2
Netherlands	63.7	88.4	79.2	50.9	77.7	64.3	61.5	89.1	79.0	48.6	79.6	64.2
New Zealand	69.7	85.3	81.5	60.7	80.0	75.3	68.7	89.8	81.7	61.9	83.1	77.6
Norway	66.5	90.3	82.3	58.1	86.6	75.3	62.5	91.2	82.7	58.1	81.7	73.8
Poland	41.2	84.6	65.7	15.3	65.7	36.3	39.3	86.3	69.0	..	80.7	71.8
Portugal	71.3	85.8	74.3	75.4	87.0	79.2	62.8	83.2	70.2	66.0	79.1	72.7
Slovak Republic	29.0	84.2	70.0	40.4	87.2	70.1	32.6	80.0	69.4	42.2	75.5	67.0
Slovenia	56.1	88.0	75.0	56.7	81.8	69.2	49.4	84.0	71.6	45.5	68.2	60.8
Spain	57.8	85.5	69.7	71.4	78.8	74.9	49.3	78.7	63.5	49.8	66.8	57.9
Sweden	71.1	90.5	84.8	51.5	78.3	67.7	71.3	91.9	86.5	51.8	78.3	68.9
Switzerland	65.0	93.0	84.5	67.3	82.7	75.5	68.5	92.1	86.3	70.1	83.0	78.3
Turkey	..	..	..	..	..	..	47.6	76.5	54.5	38.8	68.3	55.8
United Kingdom	54.7	88.9	76.8	47.1	83.2	70.6	60.8	86.4	78.2	53.1	81.1	74.0
United States	51.5	84.0	76.5	68.8	80.3	75.2	45.0	81.8	73.2	65.8	77.1	72.4
EU 28	57.0	86.2	72.1	59.5	77.8	68.6	52.3	84.8	72.1	53.8	75.7	66.1
OECD	..	..	..	..	..	..	..	..	..	..	..	..
Brazil	..	..	..	..	..	..	..	..	..	..	..	..
China	..	..	..	..	..	..	..	..	..	..	..	..
India	..	..	..	..	..	..	..	..	..	..	..	..
Indonesia	..	..	..	..	..	..	..	..	..	..	..	..
Russian Federation	..	..	..	..	..	..	..	..	..	..	..	..
South Africa	27.8	79.9	36.3	60.8	75.3	63.7	..	..	..	..	..	..

StatLink http://dx.doi.org/10.1787/888933336388

Gap in employment rates between foreign- and native-born population by educational attainment

Percentage points, 2014

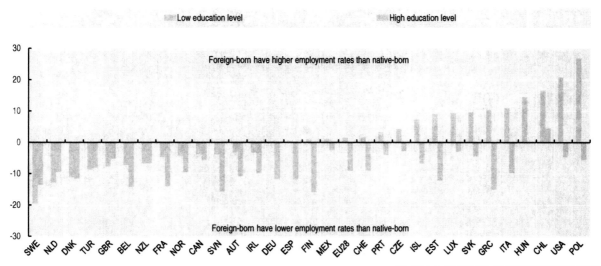

StatLink http://dx.doi.org/10.1787/888933335228

MIGRATION AND UNEMPLOYMENT

Immigrant workers are more affected by unemployment than native-born workers in traditional European immigration countries. Conversely, in some settlement countries (Australia, New Zealand and the United States) as well as in Hungary, the unemployment rate depends less on the place of birth. Some groups, such as young immigrants, women or older immigrants have greater difficulties in finding jobs.

Definition

The unemployment rate is the share of the unemployed aged 15-64 in the total labour force (the sum of employed and unemployed persons aged 15-64). In accordance with the ILO standards, unemployed persons consist of those persons who report that they are without work during the reference week, that they are available for work and that they have taken active steps to find work during the four weeks preceding the interview.

Comparability

Data for the European countries are from the *European Union Labour Force Survey*. Data for the United States come from the *Current Population Survey*; those for other countries are taken from their national labour force surveys. Even if unemployment levels can at times be affected by changes in the survey design and by survey implementation problems (e.g. non-response), data on unemployment rates are generally consistent over time.

The EU28 aggregate is a weighted average.

Overview

Immigrants were hard hit, and almost immediately, by the economic downturn in most OECD countries. This is mainly explained by their greater presence in sectors that have been strongly affected by the crisis (e.g. construction, manufacturing, hotels and restaurants) as well as by their greater likelihood of being in precarious or informal jobs. However, differences exist across OECD countries and between migrant groups.

The ongoing economic downturn has seen unemployment rates increase, both for foreign- and native-born persons, in most OECD countries. However, immigrants in most European OECD countries were more affected by unemployment than the native-born population. In Spain, Greece and Ireland, immigrant unemployment increased by 25, 25 and 11 percentage points respectively between 2007 and 2014 whereas that of the native-born increased by 15, 15 and 10 percentage points respectively. In 2014, the unemployment rate of immigrants living in Greece or Spain was still above 30%. The unemployment rate was more than twice the level observed for the native-born population in Sweden, Belgium, Switzerland, Austria and Finland.

Sources
- OECD (2015), *International Migration Outlook*, OECD Publishing.

Further information

Analytical publications
- OECD (2014), *Jobs for Immigrants (Vol. 4), Labour Market Integration in Italy*, OECD Publishing.
- OECD (2014), *Matching Economic Migration with Labour Market Needs*, OECD Publishing.

Statistical publications
- OECD (2015), *Connecting with Emigrants, A Global Profile of Diasporas 2015*, OECD Publishing.
- OECD (2015), *OECD Indicators of Immigrant Integration 2015*, OECD Publishing.

Methodological publications
- Dumont, J.C. and Lemaître G. (2005), "Counting Immigrants and Expatriates in OECD Countries: A New Perspective", *OECD Social, Employment and Migration Working Papers*, No. 25.
- Lemaître G. (2005), "The Comparability of International Migration Statistics: Problems and Prospects", *OECD Statistic Brief*, No. 9.

Online databases
- OECD International Migration Statistics.

Websites
- International migration policies and data, *www.oecd.org/ migration/mig*.

Unemployment rates of native- and foreign-born population

As a percentage of total labour force

	Women				Men				Total			
	Native-born		Foreign-born		Native-born		Foreign-born		Native-born		Foreign-born	
	2007	2014	2007	2014	2007	2014	2007	2014	2007	2014	2007	2014
Australia	4.6	6.1	5.5	6.6	4.1	6.3	4.3	5.6	4.3	6.2	4.9	6.1
Austria	4.1	4.5	9.7	9.5	3.1	4.8	8.4	10.8	3.5	4.7	9.0	10.1
Belgium	7.5	6.5	17.2	16.3	5.6	7.2	15.8	18.7	6.4	6.9	16.4	17.6
Canada	..	5.9	..	8.4	..	7.5	..	7.4	..	6.7	..	7.9
Chile	..	..	..	..	..	..	..	..	..	..	..	..
Czech Republic	6.7	7.4	10.8	8.8	4.2	5.2	7.7	5.7	5.3	6.2	9.1	7.0
Denmark	3.8	6.0	7.8	13.9	3.0	6.0	8.6	10.8	3.4	6.0	8.2	12.3
Estonia	3.9	6.7	4.6	9.7	5.3	7.9	7.1	8.8	4.6	7.3	5.7	9.3
Finland	6.9	7.5	17.4	17.1	6.5	9.1	12.0	16.5	6.7	8.3	14.5	16.8
France	8.1	8.8	14.5	15.7	6.9	9.3	11.9	16.4	7.4	9.1	13.1	16.0
Germany	8.0	4.2	13.8	7.4	7.6	4.8	15.2	8.3	7.8	4.5	14.6	7.9
Greece	12.8	29.8	14.3	35.4	5.3	22.6	4.9	33.8	8.4	25.8	8.7	34.5
Hungary	7.7	7.9	6.1	8.3	7.2	7.7	2.6	4.0	7.5	7.8	4.3	6.0
Iceland	2.2	4.5	3.9	7.9	2.3	5.0	2.1	7.3	2.2	4.7	3.0	7.6
Ireland	4.0	8.6	5.8	12.7	4.6	13.0	6.0	14.2	4.3	11.0	5.9	13.5
Israel	8.6	..	6.8	..	7.1	..	6.3	..	7.8	..	6.5	..
Italy	7.6	13.3	11.4	17.4	4.9	11.6	5.3	15.6	6.0	12.3	7.9	16.4
Japan	..	..	..	..	..	..	..	..	..	..	..	..
Korea	..	..	..	..	..	..	..	..	..	..	..	..
Luxembourg	4.4	4.0	5.1	7.3	3.0	4.7	4.3	7.1	3.6	4.4	4.6	7.2
Mexico	4.2	5.0	10.7	6.1	3.6	5.0	4.1	7.2	3.8	5.0	6.2	6.8
Netherlands	3.6	5.9	7.7	11.8	2.7	6.3	7.5	12.2	3.1	6.1	7.6	12.0
New Zealand	3.8	6.5	5.0	7.5	3.5	5.3	3.5	5.2	3.6	5.9	4.2	6.3
Norway	2.3	2.5	4.0	8.3	2.3	3.2	6.1	7.6	2.3	2.9	5.1	7.9
Poland	10.4	9.7	9.2	14.8	9.1	8.6	9.5	9.8	9.7	9.1	9.4	12.1
Portugal	9.9	14.6	12.1	16.7	7.0	13.9	7.3	17.2	8.4	14.2	9.6	16.9
Slovak Republic	12.7	13.7	5.9	9.1	9.9	12.9	7.7	6.0	11.2	13.3	6.8	7.4
Slovenia	5.8	10.3	7.8	15.7	4.1	8.9	4.0	11.1	4.9	9.6	5.7	13.0
Spain	10.5	24.1	12.6	32.6	6.0	21.8	8.3	34.0	7.9	22.8	10.3	33.3
Sweden	5.5	5.9	12.6	16.2	5.1	6.6	11.7	16.6	5.3	6.2	12.1	16.4
Switzerland	3.2	3.3	8.8	8.3	2.0	3.4	5.8	7.1	2.6	3.3	7.1	7.7
Turkey	..	12.0	..	14.7	..	9.2	..	10.5	..	10.0	..	12.0
United Kingdom	4.5	5.5	8.6	8.2	5.4	6.6	6.9	6.1	5.0	6.1	7.6	7.1
United States	4.6	6.1	4.7	6.6	5.1	6.8	4.1	5.1	4.9	6.5	4.4	5.8
EU 28	7.4	9.8	11.4	15.2	6.2	9.7	8.6	14.6	6.8	9.8	9.9	14.9
OECD	..	..	..	..	..	..	..	..	..	..	..	..
Brazil	..	..	..	..	..	..	..	..	..	..	..	..
China	..	..	..	..	..	..	..	..	..	..	..	..
India	..	..	..	..	..	..	..	..	..	..	..	..
Indonesia	..	..	..	..	..	..	..	..	..	..	..	..
Russian Federation	..	..	..	..	..	..	..	..	..	..	..	..
South Africa	..	..	..	..	..	..	..	..	..	..	..	..

StatLink ⏴📊 http://dx.doi.org/10.1787/888933336406

Gap in unemployment rates between foreign- and native-born populations

Percentage points, 2014

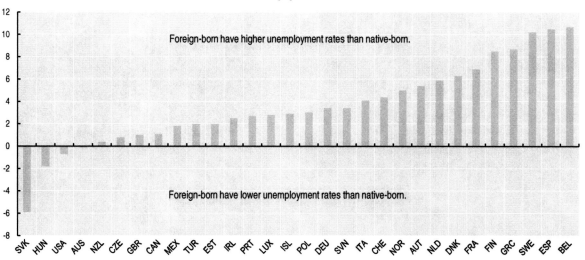

StatLink ⏴📊 http://dx.doi.org/10.1787/888933335247

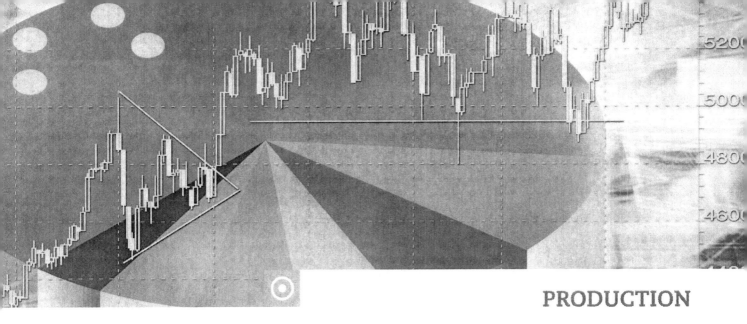

PRODUCTION

SIZE OF GDP

Gross Domestic Product (GDP) is the standard measure of the value of final goods and services produced by a country during a period minus the value of imports. While GDP is the single most important indicator to capture economic activity, it should not be looked upon as an all-encompassing measure for societies' well-being, as it does not include several aspects of people's material living standards let alone other aspects of people's quality of life.

GDP per capita is a core indicator of economic performance and commonly used as a broad measure of average living standard despite some recognised shortcomings.

Definition

What does gross domestic product mean? "Gross" signifies that no deduction has been made for the depreciation of machinery, buildings and other capital products used in production. "Domestic" means that it relates to the output produced on the economic territory of the country. The products refer to final goods and services, that is, those that are purchased, imputed or otherwise, as: the final consumption of households, non-profit institutions serving households and government; gross capital formation; and exports (minus imports).

Comparability

All countries compile data according to the 2008 SNA "System of National Accounts, 2008" with the exception of Chile, Japan, and Turkey, where data are compiled according to the 1993 SNA. When changes in international standards are implemented, countries often take the opportunity to implement improved compilation methods; therefore also implementing various improvements in sources and estimation methodologies. In some countries the impact of the 'statistical benchmark revision' could be higher than the impact of the changeover in standards. As a consequence the GDP level for the OECD total increased by 3.8% in 2010 based on the available countries.

For some countries, the latest year has been estimated by the Secretariat. Historical data have also been estimated for those countries that revise their methodologies but only supply revised data for some years.

For GDP per capita some care is needed in interpretation, for example Luxembourg and, to a lesser extent, Switzerland, have a relatively large number of frontier workers. Such workers contribute to GDP but are excluded from the population figures.

Overview

Per capita GDP for the OECD as a whole was USD 38 865 in 2014. Five OECD countries exceed this amount by more than 25 percent – Luxembourg, Norway, Switzerland, the United States and Ireland. Nine OECD countries had a per capita GDP that was between 10 to 25 percent higher than the per capita GDP for the OECD average in 2014: the Netherlands, Austria, Sweden, Germany, Australia, Denmark, Canada, Iceland and Belgium while nine countries had a more than 25 percent lower GDP per capita than the OECD average: Mexico, Turkey, Chile, Poland, Hungary, Greece, Estonia, the Slovak Republic, and Portugal.

In the ten year time period between 2004 and 2014, the countries whose GDP per capita relative to the OECD average has increased the most (by more than 10 percentage points) were Luxembourg, the Slovak Republic, Estonia, Poland, Switzerland, Norway, Chile, and Turkey.

On the other hand, the relative position of GDP per capita to the OECD average has deteriorated in 14 countries. The largest decreases were observed in Greece, the United Kingdom, and Italy.

Sources
• OECD (2015), National Accounts of OECD Countries, OECD Publishing.

Further information
Analytical publications
• OECD (2015), OECD Economic Outlook, OECD Publishing.
• OECD (2015), OECD Economic Surveys, OECD Publishing.
• OECD (2015), Towards Green Growth, OECD Green Growth Studies, OECD Publishing.

Statistical publications
• OECD (2015), National Accounts at a Glance, OECD Publishing.

Methodological publications
• OECD, et al. (eds.) (2010), System of National Accounts 2008, United Nations, Geneva.

Online databases
• OECD National Accounts Statistics.
• OECD Economic Outlook: Statistics and Projections.

Websites
Sources & Methods of the OECD Economic Outlook, www.oecd.org/eco/sources-and-methods.htm.

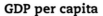
GDP per capita

US dollars, current prices and PPPs

	2002	2003	2004	2005	2006	2007	2008	2009	2010	2011	2012	2013	2014
Australia	30 603	32 088	33 699	35 440	37 583	39 343	39 704	41 138	42 253	43 802	43 676	44 706	44 971
Austria	31 261	32 212	33 820	34 702	37 653	39 240	41 151	40 642	41 876	44 039	44 870	45 133	46 171
Belgium	30 776	31 059	31 997	33 057	35 110	36 596	37 857	37 664	39 276	41 118	41 595	41 595	42 839
Canada	30 634	32 054	33 654	36 051	37 822	39 226	40 108	38 709	40 055	41 567	42 283	43 038	44 057
Chile	10 279	10 760	11 704	12 690	15 496	16 709	16 327	16 136	18 173	20 189	21 108	21 888	22 254
Czech Republic	18 311	19 593	20 970	22 237	24 350	26 622	26 994	26 895	26 941	28 603	28 636	28 963	30 366
Denmark	31 597	31 269	33 162	34 083	37 192	38 685	40 843	39 625	41 812	43 319	43 565	43 797	44 889
Estonia	11 770	13 193	14 628	16 510	19 255	21 803	22 487	20 195	21 070	23 914	25 206	26 160	26 902
Finland	28 421	28 813	31 092	32 065	34 523	37 509	39 730	37 546	38 296	40 251	40 209	40 017	39 987
France	28 523	28 110	29 056	30 398	32 311	34 064	35 170	34 837	35 896	37 353	37 281	37 617	38 870
Germany	28 438	29 365	30 709	32 186	34 716	36 783	38 434	37 137	39 622	42 152	42 807	43 282	44 985
Greece	22 719	23 804	25 432	25 396	28 290	29 309	31 161	30 662	28 961	26 626	25 177	25 523	25 950
Hungary	14 918	15 640	16 466	17 314	18 664	19 339	20 811	20 867	21 562	22 603	22 556	23 507	24 709
Iceland	31 972	31 751	34 897	35 987	36 685	38 729	41 115	39 831	38 592	39 558	40 498	41 987	43 330
Ireland	34 441	36 016	38 183	40 446	44 030	46 727	43 839	41 845	43 223	45 670	45 757	46 858	48 733
Israel	25 138	23 696	25 124	24 774	25 634	27 499	27 358	27 589	28 948	30 585	31 938	32 713	33 243
Italy	27 890	28 422	28 712	29 554	31 832	33 531	34 941	33 893	34 396	35 494	35 044	34 781	35 015
Japan	27 251	27 960	29 384	30 446	31 795	33 319	33 500	31 861	33 748	34 312	35 601	36 225	36 456
Korea	20 785	21 389	22 968	24 220	25 863	27 872	28 718	28 393	30 465	31 327	32 022	33 089	34 356
Luxembourg	59 353	60 831	65 407	67 003	77 306	82 733	84 920	80 265	84 440	90 889	91 256	93 234	97 273
Mexico	10 319	10 808	11 438	12 342	13 505	14 132	14 743	14 394	15 139	16 366	16 808	16 891	17 831
Netherlands	33 954	33 741	35 424	37 313	40 854	43 673	46 156	44 413	44 752	46 389	46 387	46 749	47 635
New Zealand	23 209	23 886	25 005	25 666	27 589	29 104	29 482	30 390	30 942	32 221	32 861	34 989	36 810
Norway	37 726	38 991	43 202	48 370	54 720	56 901	62 421	56 205	58 775	62 738	66 358	65 635	64 837
Poland	11 592	12 047	13 054	13 808	15 157	16 894	18 051	19 145	20 612	22 250	23 054	23 616	24 430
Portugal	19 332	19 822	20 303	22 073	23 887	25 224	26 096	26 217	26 924	26 932	27 001	27 651	28 382
Slovak Republic	13 133	13 889	14 965	16 482	18 760	21 354	23 728	23 046	24 325	25 169	25 809	26 586	27 711
Slovenia	20 123	20 938	22 693	23 884	25 873	27 670	29 589	27 488	27 586	28 513	28 441	28 675	29 969
Spain	24 664	25 329	26 484	27 863	30 906	32 800	33 708	32 804	32 361	32 535	32 393	32 546	33 169
Sweden	30 790	32 062	34 269	34 332	37 594	40 565	41 881	39 670	41 727	43 709	43 869	44 586	45 153
Switzerland	36 134	36 174	37 523	38 916	43 140	47 175	50 226	49 722	51 121	54 551	55 857	56 897	57 246
Turkey	8 667	8 806	10 168	11 394	12 905	13 896	15 021	14 495	16 001	17 692	18 002	18 599	19 027
United Kingdom	30 088	31 184	33 112	34 616	36 921	37 509	37 765	36 383	35 859	36 575	37 605	38 743	39 709
United States	38 122	39 606	41 857	44 237	46 369	47 987	48 330	46 930	48 302	49 710	51 368	52 592	54 353
EU 28	24 663	25 302	26 519	27 727	30 063	31 817	33 125	32 339	33 180	34 493	34 804	35 271	36 237
OECD	26 678	27 484	28 972	30 479	32 492	34 035	34 809	33 860	35 053	36 347	37 135	37 815	38 865
Brazil	9 326	9 523	10 183	10 737	11 434	12 365	13 160	13 114	14 179	15 065	..	..	..
China	3 454	3 853	4 333	4 948	5 717	6 665	7 412	8 118	9 031	10 017	10 917	11 874	..
India	..	..	2 722	3 022	3 355	3 729	3 863	4 247	..	..	..	..	..
Indonesia	5 372	5 663	6 026	6 483	6 959	7 499	8 003	8 167	8 489	8 907	9 433	10 023	..
Russian Federation	8 029	9 254	10 231	11 822	14 916	16 649	20 164	19 387	20 498	22 570	24 069	25 151	..
South Africa	8 408	8 737	9 277	9 946	10 652	11 441	11 957	11 598	11 772	12 292	12 715	13 002	13 146

StatLink 🔗 http://dx.doi.org/10.1787/888933336587

GDP per capita

US dollars, current prices and PPPs, 2014 or latest available year

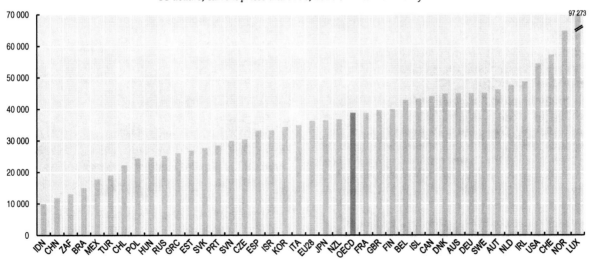

StatLink 🔗 http://dx.doi.org/10.1787/888933335492

EVOLUTION OF GDP

Changes in the size of economies are usually measured by changes in the volume (often referred to as real) levels of GDP. Real reflects the fact that changes in GDP due to inflation are removed. This provides a measure of changes in the volume of production of an economy.

Definition

Converting nominal values of GDP to real values requires a set of detailed price indices, implicitly or directly collected. When applied to the nominal value of transactions, the corresponding volume changes can be captured. The *System of National Accounts* recommends that weights should be representative of the periods for which growth rates are calculated. This means that new weights should be introduced every year, giving rise to chain-linked (volume) indices.

Comparability

All countries compile data according to the 2008 SNA "System of National Accounts, 2008" with the exception of Chile, Japan, and Turkey, where data are compiled according to the 1993 SNA. It's important to note that differences between the 2008 SNA and the 1993 SNA did not have a significant impact on the growth rates of real GDP and therefore, the comparability of the indicators presented here are highly comparable across countries. However, there is generally some variability in how countries calculate their volume estimates of GDP, particularly in respect of services produced by government such as health and education.

With the exception of Mexico, all OECD countries derive their annual estimates of real GDP using annual chain-linked volume indices (that is the weights are updated every year). Mexico, like many non-OECD countries, revise their weights less frequently.

Overview

In 2014, the annual rate of economic growth for the OECD as a whole was 1.8%, an acceleration from the 1.2% growth rate seen in 2013.

Several countries after 2 or more years of contraction rebounded in 2014: Slovenia, Greece, Spain, the Czech Republic, Portugal, Denmark, and the Netherlands. Seven countries experienced a growth rate of 3% or higher. The largest economic growth rates were recorded in Ireland (5.2%), Luxembourg (4.1%), Hungary (3.7%), Poland (3.3%), Korea (3.3%), Slovenia (3.0%) and New Zealand (3.0 %).

However, in some countries growth rates slowed or turned negative between 2013 and 2014. Chile slowed from 4.2% in 2013 to 1.9% in 2014, Iceland from 3.9% to 1.8%, Japan 1.6% to minus 0.1% and Turkey from 4.2% to 2.9%.

Moreover, two other countries experienced negative growth in 2014: Finland (minus 0.4%), Italy (minus 0.4%).

Sources
• OECD (2015), *National Accounts of OECD Countries*, OECD Publishing.
• For non-member countries: National sources.

Further information

Analytical publications
• OECD (2015), *Economic Policy Reforms*, OECD Publishing.
• OECD (2015), *OECD Economic Outlook*, OECD Publishing.
• OECD (2015), *OECD Journal: Economic Studies*, OECD Publishing.

Statistical publications
• OECD (2015), *National Accounts at a Glance*, OECD Publishing.

Online databases
• *OECD National Accounts Statistics*.
• *OECD Economic Outlook: Statistics and Projections*.

Websites
Sources & Methods of the OECD Economic Outlook, *www.oecd.org/eco/sources-and-methods.htm*.

Real GDP growth
Annual growth in percentage

	2002	2003	2004	2005	2006	2007	2008	2009	2010	2011	2012	2013	2014
Australia	3.1	4.2	3.2	3.0	3.8	3.7	1.7	2.0	2.3	3.7	2.5	2.5	2.7
Austria	1.7	0.8	2.7	2.1	3.4	3.6	1.5	-3.8	1.9	2.8	0.8	0.3	0.4
Belgium	1.8	0.8	3.6	2.1	2.5	3.4	0.7	-2.3	2.7	1.8	0.2	0.0	1.3
Canada	2.8	1.9	3.1	3.2	2.6	2.0	1.2	-2.7	3.4	3.0	1.9	2.0	2.4
Chile	2.7	3.8	7.0	6.2	5.7	5.2	3.3	-1.0	5.8	5.8	5.5	4.2	1.9
Czech Republic	1.6	3.6	4.9	6.4	6.9	5.5	2.7	-4.8	2.3	2.0	-0.9	-0.5	2.0
Denmark	0.5	0.4	2.6	2.4	3.8	0.8	-0.7	-5.1	1.6	1.2	-0.7	-0.5	1.1
Estonia	6.1	7.4	6.3	9.4	10.3	7.7	-5.4	-14.7	2.5	7.6	5.2	1.6	2.9
Finland	1.7	2.0	3.9	2.8	4.1	5.2	0.7	-8.3	3.0	2.6	-1.4	-1.1	-0.4
France	1.1	0.8	2.8	1.6	2.4	2.4	0.2	-2.9	2.0	2.1	0.2	0.7	0.2
Germany	0.0	-0.7	1.2	0.7	3.7	3.3	1.1	-5.6	4.1	3.7	0.4	0.3	1.6
Greece	3.9	5.8	5.1	0.6	5.7	3.3	-0.3	-4.3	-5.5	-9.1	-7.3	-3.2	0.7
Hungary	4.5	3.8	4.9	4.4	3.8	0.4	0.8	-6.6	0.7	1.8	-1.7	1.9	3.7
Iceland	0.5	2.7	8.2	6.0	4.2	9.5	1.5	-4.7	-3.6	2.0	1.2	3.9	1.8
Ireland	5.9	3.8	4.4	6.3	6.3	5.5	-2.2	-5.6	0.4	2.6	0.2	1.4	5.2
Israel	-0.1	1.2	5.1	4.4	5.8	6.1	3.1	1.3	5.5	5.0	2.9	3.3	2.6
Italy	0.3	0.2	1.6	0.9	2.0	1.5	-1.0	-5.5	1.7	0.6	-2.8	-1.7	-0.4
Japan	0.3	1.7	2.4	1.3	1.7	2.2	-1.0	-5.5	4.7	-0.5	1.8	1.6	-0.1
Korea	7.4	2.9	4.9	3.9	5.2	5.5	2.8	0.7	6.5	3.7	2.3	2.9	3.3
Luxembourg	3.6	1.4	4.4	3.2	5.1	8.4	-0.8	-5.4	5.7	2.6	-0.8	4.3	4.1
Mexico	0.8	1.4	4.2	3.1	5.0	3.2	1.4	-4.7	5.2	3.9	4.0	1.4	2.1
Netherlands	0.1	0.3	2.0	2.2	3.5	3.7	1.7	-3.8	1.4	1.7	-1.1	-0.5	1.0
New Zealand	4.9	4.6	3.8	3.4	2.8	3.0	-1.6	-0.3	1.4	2.2	2.2	2.5	3.0
Norway	1.4	0.9	4.0	2.6	2.4	2.9	0.4	-1.6	0.6	1.0	2.7	0.7	2.2
Poland	2.0	3.6	5.1	3.5	6.2	7.2	3.9	2.6	3.7	5.0	1.6	1.3	3.3
Portugal	0.8	-0.9	1.8	0.8	1.6	2.5	0.2	-3.0	1.9	-1.8	-4.0	-1.1	0.9
Slovak Republic	4.5	5.4	5.3	6.4	8.5	10.8	5.7	-5.5	5.1	2.8	1.5	1.4	2.5
Slovenia	3.8	2.8	4.4	4.0	5.7	6.9	3.3	-7.8	1.2	0.6	-2.7	-1.1	3.0
Spain	2.9	3.2	3.2	3.7	4.2	3.8	1.1	-3.6	0.0	-1.0	-2.6	-1.7	1.4
Sweden	2.1	2.4	4.3	2.8	4.7	3.4	-0.6	-5.2	6.0	2.7	-0.3	1.2	2.3
Switzerland	0.1	0.0	2.8	3.0	4.0	4.1	2.3	-2.1	3.0	1.8	1.1	1.8	1.9
Turkey	6.2	5.3	9.4	8.4	6.9	4.7	0.7	-4.8	9.2	8.8	2.1	4.2	2.9
United Kingdom	2.5	3.3	2.5	3.0	2.7	2.6	-0.5	-4.2	1.5	2.0	1.2	2.2	2.9
United States	1.8	2.8	3.8	3.3	2.7	1.8	-0.3	-2.8	2.5	1.6	2.2	1.5	2.4
Euro area	0.9	0.7	2.3	1.7	3.2	3.0	0.5	-4.6	2.0	1.6	-0.8	-0.3	0.9
EU 28	1.3	1.5	2.5	2.0	3.4	3.1	0.5	-4.4	2.1	1.7	-0.5	0.2	1.4
OECD	1.7	2.1	3.3	2.8	3.1	2.7	0.3	-3.5	3.0	1.9	1.3	1.2	1.8
Brazil	3.1	1.2	5.7	3.1	4.0	6.0	5.0	-0.2	7.6	3.9	..	..	..
China	9.1	10.0	10.1	11.3	12.7	14.2	9.6	9.2	10.4	9.4	7.8	7.7	7.4
India	..	..	..	9.3	9.3	9.8	4.9	9.1	..	..	..	..	..
Indonesia	4.5	4.8	5.0	5.7	5.5	6.3	6.0	4.7	6.4	6.2	6.0	5.6	5.0
Russian Federation	4.7	7.3	7.2	6.4	8.2	8.5	5.2	-7.8	4.5	4.3	3.4	1.3	0.6
South Africa	3.7	2.9	4.6	5.3	5.6	5.4	3.2	-1.5	3.0	3.2	2.2	2.2	1.5

StatLink http://dx.doi.org/10.1787/888933336096

Real GDP growth
Average annual growth in percentage

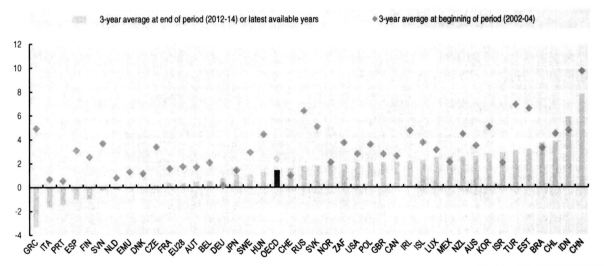

■ 3-year average at end of period (2012-14) or latest available years   ◆ 3-year average at beginning of period (2002-04)

StatLink http://dx.doi.org/10.1787/888933334916

GDP BY METROPOLITAN AREA

Metropolitan areas are the prime engine of growth. A better understanding how cities function offers a unique opportunity to identify solutions for the problems faced by individual cities.

Definition

281 metropolitan areas have been identified across 30 OECD countries. They are defined as the functional urban areas (FUA) with population above 500 000. The functional urban areas are defined as densely populated municipalities (city cores) and adjacent municipalities with high levels of commuting towards the densely populated urban cores (commuting zone). Functional urban areas can extend across administrative boundaries, reflecting the economic geography of where people actually live and work.

GDP is the standard measure of the value of the production activity (goods and services) or resident producer units. Values of the GDP in the metropolitan areas are estimated by adjusting the GDP values of small (TL3) regions.

GDP per capita is the ratio between GDP and population in a metropolitan area.

Comparability

Functional urban areas have not been identified in Iceland, Israel, New Zealand and Turkey. The FUA of Luxembourg does not appear in the figures since it has a population below 500 000 inhabitants.

GDP values in metropolitan areas are estimates based on GDP data at TL3 level except for Australia, Canada, Chile and Mexico were it is TL2. The figures for the United States were provided by the U.S. Bureau of Economic Analysis.

Overview

The aggregate GDP growth of metropolitan areas in the period 2000-13, appeared for a large part due to a small number of large metropolitan areas. Indeed, fourteen metropolitan areas (around 5% of the total) contributed to 40% of the GDP metropolitan growth in the OECD area. Seoul Incheon, Houston and New York recorded the highest contribution to the GDP growth in the OECD area.

The role of metropolitan areas for the national GDP growth can be quite different across OECD countries. Metropolitan areas in Norway, Japan and Denmark accounted for more than 75% of the national growth in the period 2000-13. In contrast, in Switzerland and the Netherlands, metropolitan areas accounted for less than 30% of the national growth.

Metropolitan areas tend to be wealthier than the rest of the economy. The GDP per capita gap between the metropolitan areas and the rest of the economy in the OECD area was around 37% in 2013. Such a gap is higher in the Americas and in Europe than in Asia. Overall, GDP per capita is on average higher in large metropolitan areas (with population above 1.5 million).

Sources
- OECD (2013), *OECD Regions at a Glance*, OECD Publishing.

Further information

Analytical publications
- OECD (2012), *Promoting Growth in All Regions*, OECD Publishing.
- OECD (2012), *Redefining "Urban": A New Way to Measure Metropolitan Areas*, OECD Publishing.
- Piacentini, M. et K. Rosina (2012), "*Measuring the Environmental Performance of Metropolitan Areas with Geographic Information Sources*", OECD Regional Development Working Papers, No. 2012/05, OECD Publishing.

Online databases
- *Metropolitan areas.*

Websites
- Regional Statistics and Indicators, *www.oecd.org/gov/regional-policy/regionalstatisticsandindicators.htm.*
- Regions at a Glance Interactive, *http://rag.oecd.org.*

Contribution of metropolitan areas to OECD aggregate growth
Percentage, 2000-13; contribution (y-axis), aggregate growth (x-axis)

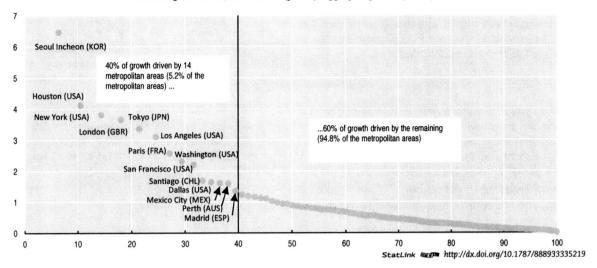

StatLink http://dx.doi.org/10.1787/888933335219

Per cent of national GDP growth contributed by the metropolitan areas
Percentage, 2000-13

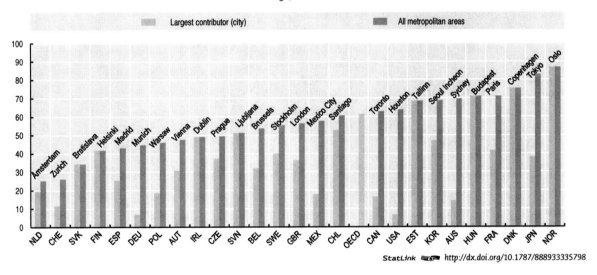

StatLink http://dx.doi.org/10.1787/888933335798

GDP per capita gap between metropolitan areas and the rest of the economy
Percentage, 2013

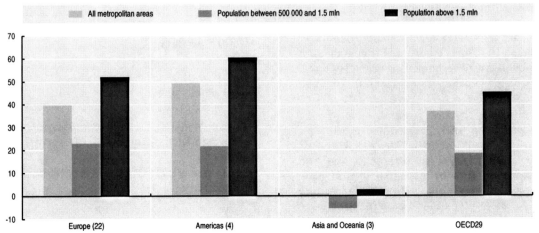

StatLink http://dx.doi.org/10.1787/888933335930

INVESTMENT RATES

Investment, or to be more precise, gross fixed capital formation, is an important determinant of future economic growth and an essential variable in economic analyses, such as analyses of demand and productivity.

Definition

Gross fixed capital formation (GFCF) is defined in the national accounts as acquisition less disposals of produced fixed assets. The relevant assets relate to products that are intended for use in the production of other goods and services for a period of more than a year.

Acquisition includes both purchases of assets (new or second-hand) and the construction of assets by producers for their own use.

The term produced assets signifies that only those assets that come into existence as a result of a production process recognised in the national accounts are included. The national accounts also record transactions in non-produced assets such as land, oil and mineral reserves for example; which are recorded as (acquisitions less disposals of) non-produced assets in the capital account and the balance sheet.

Acquisition prices of capital goods include transport and installation charges, as well as all specific taxes associated with purchase.

Comparability

All countries compile data according to the 2008 SNA "System of National Accounts, 2008" with the exception of Chile, Japan, and Turkey, where data are compiled according to the 1993 SNA. The most important changes between the 1993 SNA and the 2008 SNA was the extension of the scope of assets to be recorded as GFCF.

According to the 2008 SNA, expenditures on research and development and military weapons (warships, submarines, military aircraft, tanks, etc.) are now included in GFCF.

Overview

Investment grew on average by 1.8% over the period 2012-14 for the OECD as a whole, reflecting an overall improvement since the financial crisis. While the majority of the OECD countries experienced positive growth rates, ten countries recorded negative growth in 2014: Australia, Austria, Chile, Estonia, Finland, France, Greece, Israel, Italy, and Turkey. Although Greece recorded a negative average growth rate of 12.3% for the period 2012-14, the decrease was by less than 3% in 2014 improving by 6.6 percentage points compared to 2013. The growth rate of investment, on the other hand, fell by 8.2 percentage points from 2.1% in 2013 in Chile to minus 6.1% in 2014.

Belgium, Hungary, Iceland, Ireland, Luxembourg New Zealand, Poland, Sweden, and the United Kingdom all recorded growth rates of investment larger than 5%. In Hungary, Iceland, and Ireland investment grew by more than 10% in 2014, which is particularly notable for the latter two countries because investment growth rates were negative in 2013.

Sources
- OECD (2015), *National Accounts of OECD Countries*, OECD Publishing.
- For Brazil: National sources.

Further information

Analytical publications
- OECD (2015), *OECD Economic Outlook*, OECD Publishing.
- OECD (2015), *OECD Investment Policy Reviews*, OECD Publishing.

Statistical publications
- OECD (2015), *National Accounts at a Glance*, OECD Publishing.

Methodological publications
- Ahmad, N. (2004), "Towards More Harmonised Estimates of Investment in Software", *OECD Economic Studies*, No. 37, 2003/2.
- OECD, et al. (eds.) (2010), *System of National Accounts 2008*, United Nations, Geneva.

Websites
Sources & Methods of the OECD Economic Outlook, *www.oecd.org/eco/sources-and-methods.htm*.

Gross fixed capital formation

Annual growth in percentage

	2002	2003	2004	2005	2006	2007	2008	2009	2010	2011	2012	2013	2014
Australia	12.6	8.5	6.3	9.3	5.1	9.5	2.1	2.1	3.8	11.5	2.0	-1.5	-2.0
Austria	-2.9	3.8	0.9	0.2	1.1	4.6	1.4	-7.3	-2.1	6.7	1.3	-0.3	-0.2
Belgium	-4.3	-0.4	8.9	6.1	2.0	6.8	1.9	-6.6	-0.8	4.2	0.2	-1.7	7.0
Canada	1.0	5.2	8.4	9.2	6.3	3.2	1.6	-11.5	11.5	4.8	4.8	0.4	0.2
Chile	2.2	6.5	11.3	23.5	4.3	10.8	17.9	-12.1	11.6	15.0	11.6	2.1	-6.1
Czech Republic	2.2	1.8	3.9	6.4	5.9	13.5	2.5	-10.1	1.3	1.1	-3.2	-2.7	2.0
Denmark	-0.7	0.0	4.2	4.8	15.1	0.7	-3.3	-14.3	-4.0	0.3	0.6	0.9	4.0
Estonia	23.9	17.8	5.5	15.3	22.9	10.3	-13.1	-36.7	-2.6	34.4	6.7	3.2	-3.1
Finland	-3.0	2.8	4.7	3.2	1.3	10.0	0.3	-12.5	1.1	4.1	-2.2	-5.2	-3.3
France	-0.9	1.9	3.5	2.9	3.6	5.5	0.9	-9.1	2.1	2.1	0.2	-0.6	-1.2
Germany	-5.8	-1.3	0.0	0.7	7.5	4.1	1.5	-10.1	5.4	7.2	-0.4	-1.3	3.5
Greece	-0.3	15.1	3.0	-11.9	19.4	15.9	-7.2	-13.9	-19.3	-20.5	-23.5	-9.4	-2.8
Hungary	7.8	1.3	7.6	3.6	0.7	4.2	1.0	-8.3	-9.5	-1.3	-4.4	7.3	11.2
Iceland	-12.8	9.8	26.7	32.0	23.4	-11.2	-19.0	-47.8	-8.6	11.6	5.3	-1.0	15.4
Ireland	5.6	7.9	9.8	16.7	7.5	-0.2	-11.5	-16.9	-15.5	3.2	8.6	-6.6	14.3
Israel	-5.4	-5.3	2.0	3.2	6.5	10.1	5.1	-2.9	10.0	14.6	3.6	3.6	-2.0
Italy	4.2	-0.3	2.1	1.7	3.2	1.6	-3.1	-9.9	-0.5	-1.9	-9.3	-6.6	-3.5
Japan	-4.9	0.2	0.4	0.8	1.5	0.3	-4.1	-10.6	-0.2	1.4	3.4	3.2	2.6
Korea	6.9	4.8	2.9	2.0	3.6	5.0	-0.9	0.3	5.5	0.8	-0.5	3.3	3.1
Luxembourg	0.2	4.4	6.4	-3.3	4.7	14.9	7.3	-13.2	0.0	17.2	-0.3	-7.2	9.9
Mexico	-0.6	0.4	7.5	5.9	8.7	6.0	5.0	-9.3	1.3	7.8	4.8	-1.6	2.3
Netherlands	-4.5	-1.6	0.2	3.1	7.2	6.5	4.1	-9.2	-6.5	5.6	-6.3	-4.4	3.5
New Zealand	7.9	14.2	8.1	5.7	-2.0	7.8	-7.4	-9.3	3.3	5.5	7.2	10.4	8.8
Norway	-0.3	0.4	10.0	12.0	9.1	11.7	0.9	-6.8	-6.6	7.4	7.6	6.8	0.6
Poland	-6.1	1.2	6.7	8.7	13.3	19.2	8.4	-1.9	-0.4	8.8	-1.8	-1.1	9.8
Portugal	-3.4	-7.3	0.1	0.1	-0.8	3.1	0.4	-7.6	-0.9	-12.5	-16.6	-5.1	2.8
Slovak Republic	0.0	-3.2	4.7	16.5	9.1	8.9	1.6	-18.7	7.2	12.7	-9.2	-1.1	3.5
Slovenia	0.5	5.8	5.4	3.5	10.2	12.0	7.0	-22.0	-13.3	-4.9	-8.8	1.7	3.2
Spain	4.6	7.0	5.1	7.5	7.4	4.4	-3.9	-16.9	-4.9	-6.9	-7.1	-2.5	3.5
Sweden	-2.3	2.5	5.8	5.1	9.3	8.1	0.6	-13.4	6.0	5.7	-0.2	0.6	7.6
Switzerland	0.2	-1.0	5.1	3.2	4.7	4.9	0.7	-7.5	4.4	4.3	2.9	1.2	2.1
Turkey	14.7	14.2	28.4	17.4	13.3	3.1	-6.2	-19.0	30.5	18.0	-2.7	4.4	-1.3
United Kingdom	2.8	2.3	2.8	3.4	3.0	5.7	-5.9	-14.4	5.0	2.0	1.5	2.6	7.5
United States	-1.8	3.9	5.8	5.6	2.2	-1.2	-4.8	-13.1	1.1	3.7	6.3	2.4	4.1
Euro area	-1.2	1.3	2.7	2.8	5.5	4.9	-0.6	-11.3	-0.4	1.6	-3.6	-2.6	1.2
EU 28	-0.6	1.7	3.1	3.0	5.8	5.8	-0.5	-12.0	0.2	2.0	-2.8	-1.6	2.5
OECD	-0.6	2.8	4.5	4.6	4.1	2.6	-2.2	-10.9	2.0	3.6	1.8	0.8	2.8
Brazil	-1.5	-3.9	8.4	2.3	6.1	12.0	12.7	-1.9	17.8	6.6	..	..	..
China	..	..	..	..	..	..	..	..	..	..	..	..	..
India	..	..	..	16.2	13.8	16.2	1.5	7.3	..	..	..	..	..
Indonesia	4.7	0.6	14.7	10.9	2.6	9.3	11.9	3.9	6.7	8.9	9.1	5.3	4.1
Russian Federation	3.1	13.9	12.0	10.2	17.9	21.1	9.7	-14.7	6.4	9.2	7.0	0.6	-2.1
South Africa	3.5	10.2	12.9	11.0	12.1	13.8	12.8	-6.7	-3.9	5.7	3.6	7.6	-0.4

StatLink http://dx.doi.org/10.1787/888933336335

Gross fixed capital formation

Average annual growth in percentage

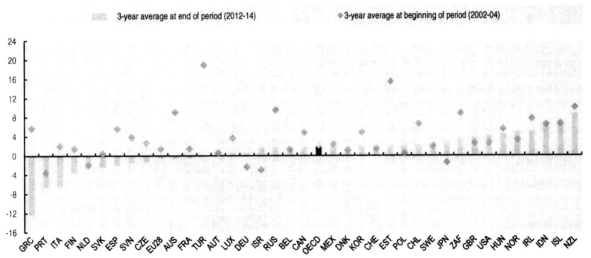

StatLink http://dx.doi.org/10.1787/888933335155

LABOUR PRODUCTIVITY LEVELS

Productivity is a measure of the efficiency with which available resources are used in production. Labour productivity, together with use of labour resources, is one of the main determinants of living standards.

Definition

Labour productivity is measured as GDP per hour worked. GDP data at current prices are from the *OECD Annual National Accounts*. For international comparisons and to obtain a volume or "real" measure of GDP, data are converted to a common currency using the OECD Purchasing Power Parities (PPPs) for the year 2014. Hours worked data are derived from two sources, the *OECD Annual National Accounts* and the *OECD Employment Outlook*.

Labour productivity and income levels in each country are calculated with respect to the labour productivity and income levels of the United States. Differences in GDP per

Overview

In 2014, the top three countries with the highest levels of GDP per hour worked, were Luxembourg, Norway and the United States. In Luxembourg, the level of labour productivity was roughly five times that observed in Mexico. Despite low labour productivity levels, Mexico and Chile recorded the highest average working time (well above 2 000 hours annually for the former) among other OECD countries.

In the same year, differences in per capita GDP with respect to the United States varied widely across countries. Much of the differences observed in GDP per capita reflect differences in labour productivity, with gaps relative to the United States ranging from minus 68 percentage points in Mexico, to plus 19 and 80 percentage points in Norway and Luxembourg, respectively. In 2014, Norway and Luxembourg were, once again, the only OECD countries to maintain substantial positive gaps in GDP per capita and in GDP per hour worked vis-à-vis the United States.

Cross-country differences in labour utilisation reflect high unemployment and low participation rates of the working age population, on the one hand, and lower working hours among employed people, on the other hand. Relative to the United States, gaps in labour utilisation were significantly smaller than gaps in GDP per capita and per hour worked. In 2014, the gap in labour utilisation vis-à-vis the United States worsened in several countries and remained substantially negative in Belgium, France, South Africa, Spain and Turkey. In the same year, Iceland, Korea, Luxembourg, Switzerland and Russia showed a relatively positive gap in labour utilisation, therefore contributing to narrow their gap with the United States in GDP per capita.

capita levels with respect to the United States can be decomposed into differences in labour productivity levels and differences in the extent of labour utilisation, measured as the number of hours worked per capita.

Comparability

Cross-country comparisons of productivity and income levels require comparable data on output. Currently, OECD countries use the 2008 *System of National Accounts*, except Chile, Japan and Turkey for which data are based on the 1993 SNA. Comparable labour input estimates are also required. In many cases, employment data are derived from labour force surveys and may not be fully consistent with national account concepts. This reduces the comparability of labour utilisation across countries. Hours worked data are derived either from national labour force surveys or from business surveys. Several OECD countries estimate hours worked by combining these sources, or integrate these sources in a system of labour accounts which is comparable to the national accounts. Cross-country comparability of hours worked remains limited, generating a margin of uncertainty in productivity levels estimates.

Sources
- OECD (2015), *OECD National Accounts Statistics* (Database).
- OECD (2015), *OECD Productivity Statistics* (Database).

Further information
Analytical publications
- OECD (2011), *OECD Reviews of Labour Market and Social Policies*, OECD Publishing.

Statistical publications
- OECD (2015), *OECD Compendium of Productivity Indicators*, OECD Publishing.

Methodological publications.
- OECD (2001), *Measuring Productivity – OECD Manual: Measurement of Aggregate and Industry-level Productivity Growth*, OECD Publishing.

Websites
- Productivity statistics, *www.oecd.org/statistics/productivity*.

GDP per hour worked

US dollars, current prices and PPPs, 2014

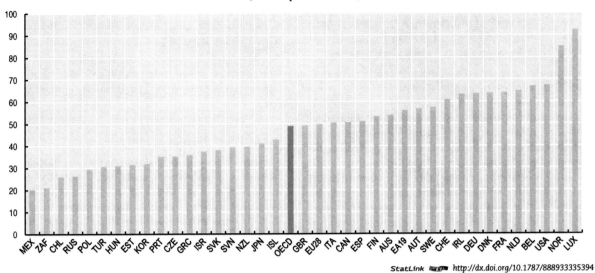

StatLink ⬛ http://dx.doi.org/10.1787/888933335394

Levels of GDP per capita and labour productivity

Percentage point differences with respect to the United States, 2014

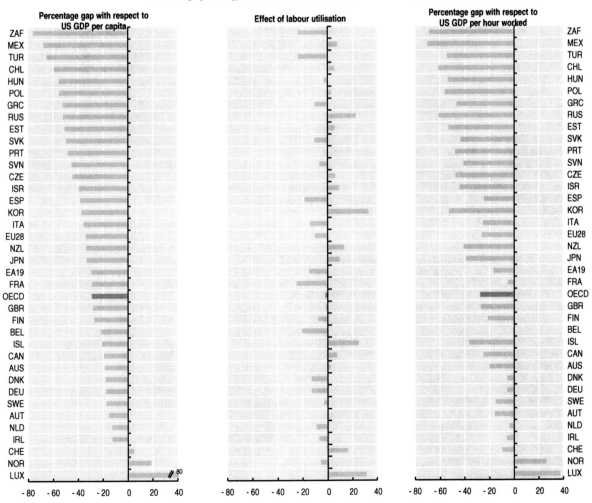

StatLink ⬛ http://dx.doi.org/10.1787/888933335835

VALUE ADDED BY ACTIVITY

Value added reflects the contribution of labour and capital to production. The sum of value added in the economy equals GDP, so value added is also a measure of output and frequently used in productivity and structural analysis.

One of the major advantages of value added is that it avoids problems inherent in the measurement of gross output – gross in the sense that it counts the output of all production units including those that produce intermediate inputs for other units. Countries with fragmented production networks therefore will have, all other things equal, higher output than those with more consolidated networks, complicating international comparisons. This is also a temporal problem as production networks can become more or less consolidated (through outsourcing for example) within a country from one year to another.

Definition

Value added at basic prices can be simply defined as the difference between gross output (at basic prices) and intermediate consumption (at purchasers' prices) and can be decomposed into the following components:

Overview

The importance of each activity varies across OECD countries with the most important sector groupings being industry; distributive trade, repairs, transport, accommodation and food services; and public administration, defence, education, and human health and social work activities. The share of industry in total value added has trended downward in recent decades. However, looking at changes in the share between 2002 and the most recent year, eight countries show an increase; most notably in Korea, the Czech Republic, and Hungary.

The share of industry also fell in non-member countries but remains at considerably higher levels than in most OECD countries, with the share for China and Indonesia remaining at over 30%. Norway, where mining and quarrying are large contributors to activity, Korea with consumer electronics, automotive, steel industries and shipbuilding, the Czech Republic with a strong automotive and energy sector come closest to these rates within the OECD.

As regards the share of financial and insurance activities, many OECD countries have regained or exceeded their 2002 levels, among them Luxembourg at 26.3%, representing the largest share of value added.

The share of agriculture in total value added within the OECD is generally small. In only five countries (Turkey, Iceland, New Zealand, Hungary and the Slovak Republic) does agriculture account for more than 4% of total value added.

compensation of employees; gross operating surplus; mixed income; and other taxes on production less subsidies on production.

The *System of National Accounts* recommends the basic price valuation for value added but it can also be measured on different price bases such as producers' prices and at factor cost.

Comparability

All countries compile data according to the 2008 SNA "System of National Accounts, 2008" with the exception of Chile, Japan, and Turkey, where data are compiled according to the 1993 SNA. It's important to note however that differences between the 2008 SNA and the 1993 SNA do not have a significant impact on comparability implying that data are highly comparable across countries.

However, not all countries produce value added on the basis of basic prices. Japan uses approximately market prices. New Zealand uses producer prices, and Iceland and the United States use factor costs.

Activity is based on the *International Standard Industrial Classification of All Economic Activities (ISIC Rev.4)* system except for Indonesia which is based on ISIC Rev.3. Countries generally collect information using their own industrial classification systems. The conversion from a national classification system to ISIC may create some comparability issues. That said, for most countries the activities presented here are generally comparable.

Sources
- OECD (2015), *National Accounts of OECD Countries*, OECD Publishing.

Further information

Analytical publications
- OECD (2002), *Measuring the Non-Observed Economy: A Handbook*, OECD Publishing.

Statistical publications
- OECD (2015), *National Accounts at a Glance*, OECD Publishing.

Online databases
- STAN: *OECD Structural Analysis Statistics*.

Websites
- OECD National Accounts, *www.oecd.org/std/na*.

Value added by activity

As a percentage of total value added, 2014 or latest available year

	Agriculture, hunting, forestry, fishing	Industry including energy	Construction	Distributive trade, repairs, transport, accommodation and food services	Information and communication	Finance and insurance	Real estate	Professional, scientific, technical, administration and support services	Public administration, defence, education human health and social work	Other services
Australia	2.5	18.6	8.4	16.5	3.0	9.0	12.1	9.8	17.4	2.7
Austria	1.4	21.7	6.4	22.9	3.3	4.6	9.9	9.5	17.4	2.9
Belgium	0.7	16.5	5.7	19.8	4.1	6.2	8.6	13.6	22.6	2.2
Canada	..	..	..	..	..	..	..	..	..	..
Chile	3.3	27.2	7.9	15.3	2.0	5.6	..	15.3	14.8	8.6
Czech Republic	2.7	32.4	5.6	18.0	4.9	4.5	8.3	6.7	14.8	2.2
Denmark	1.4	18.0	4.4	19.5	4.3	6.2	10.2	9.0	23.3	3.6
Estonia	3.4	21.6	6.5	22.7	5.3	3.8	10.1	9.2	14.8	2.6
Finland	2.8	20.3	6.2	16.2	5.5	3.0	12.3	8.4	22.1	3.1
France	1.7	13.8	5.7	17.7	4.9	4.5	12.9	12.8	23.2	3.0
Germany	0.7	25.7	4.6	15.5	4.9	4.1	11.1	11.1	18.2	4.1
Greece	3.8	12.8	2.9	24.9	3.2	4.6	17.8	5.2	20.6	4.2
Hungary	4.5	26.8	4.4	18.2	5.2	5.2	3.7	9.0	17.4	3.0
Iceland	6.9	18.8	4.9	17.9	4.9	7.4	9.4	7.4	19.5	3.0
Ireland	1.6	22.7	2.9	15.8	11.7	8.9	7.6	10.2	16.3	2.3
Israel	1.3	16.8	5.6	13.1	8.5	5.8	14.9	12.3	18.5	3.1
Italy	2.2	18.6	4.9	20.2	3.7	5.9	14.1	9.2	17.3	4.0
Japan	1.2	20.4	5.9	19.4	5.6	4.5	11.8	..	11.4	19.9
Korea	2.3	33.3	4.9	14.9	3.8	5.6	8.0	7.4	17.0	2.8
Luxembourg	0.3	6.1	5.8	17.3	6.3	26.3	8.0	11.9	15.9	2.0
Mexico	3.3	27.1	7.4	25.1	2.4	3.7	11.4	6.4	11.0	2.1
Netherlands	1.8	16.7	4.5	20.2	4.7	7.8	5.7	13.6	22.2	2.7
New Zealand	6.9	17.6	5.8	17.1	3.2	5.9	13.5	9.9	16.3	3.7
Norway	1.7	32.4	5.8	14.1	3.8	5.1	6.7	7.4	21.1	1.9
Poland	2.9	25.0	7.4	26.0	3.9	4.4	5.2	7.7	14.9	2.4
Portugal	2.3	17.1	4.5	24.7	3.4	5.2	12.8	6.9	20.2	2.9
Slovak Republic	4.4	25.3	8.4	22.1	4.4	4.2	6.7	7.4	13.6	3.6
Slovenia	2.2	27.4	5.7	20.2	4.1	4.0	6.9	9.8	17.0	2.7
Spain	2.5	17.0	5.4	24.1	4.3	4.1	12.0	7.4	18.8	4.3
Sweden	1.4	20.0	6.0	17.0	5.6	4.6	8.5	9.5	24.4	3.0
Switzerland	0.8	20.9	5.3	20.2	4.1	9.8	1.0	9.9	19.0	8.9
Turkey	8.0	22.0	5.1	29.8	2.1	3.4	11.0	6.2	10.7	1.7
United Kingdom	0.7	14.7	6.2	18.2	6.2	8.2	11.2	12.2	18.1	4.3
United States	1.4	16.6	3.9	15.7	6.1	7.4	11.4	11.7	22.6	3.2
Euro area	1.6	19.4	5.0	18.9	4.6	5.0	11.6	10.6	19.6	5.0
EU 28	1.6	18.9	5.4	19.0	4.9	5.5	11.2	10.7	19.3	5.5
OECD	..	..	..	..	..	..	..	..	..	..
Brazil	5.1	20.9	6.3	19.5	3.7	6.3	8.4	7.6	16.1	6.0
China	10.0	37.0	6.9	16.6	..	5.9	5.9	..	..	17.7
India	..	..	..	..	..	..	..	..	..	..
Indonesia	13.7	32.8	10.1	21.3	3.6	4.0	2.9	1.6	8.4	1.6
Russian Federation	..	..	..	..	..	..	..	..	..	..
South Africa	..	..	..	..	..	..	..	..	..	..

StatLink http://dx.doi.org/10.1787/888933336760

Value added in industry, including energy

As a percentage of total value added

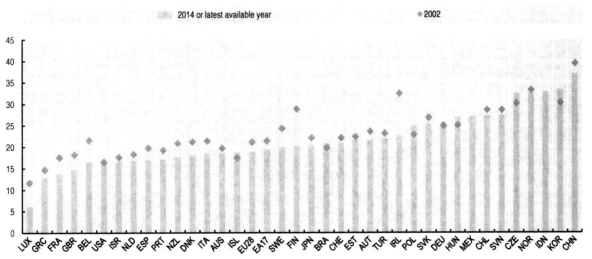

StatLink http://dx.doi.org/10.1787/888933335692

REAL VALUE ADDED BY ACTIVITY

Like its nominal counterpart, real value added can be derived as the difference between real output and real intermediate consumption, an approach known as double-deflation.

One of the major advantages of value added is that it avoids problems inherent in the measurement of gross output – gross in the sense that it counts the output of all production units including those that produce intermediate inputs for other units. Countries with fragmented production networks therefore will have, all other things equal, higher output than those with more consolidated networks, complicating international comparisons. Production networks have become increasingly globalised in recent years, further affecting temporal and cross-country comparability. Value added avoids these problems by measuring the value that a resident unit adds to that of the units that supply its inputs.

Definition

Growth rates refer to volume estimates of gross value added. Value added at basic prices can be simply defined as the difference between gross output (at basic prices) and intermediate consumption (at purchasers' prices) and can be decomposed into the following components:

Overview

OECD countries have returned to positive growth rates of real value added for agriculture. Strategies such as "Food Harvest 2020" in Ireland have begun to show their results with 21.3% annual growth in real value added. The growth rate in real value added for agriculture in Spain on the other hand fell by minus 3.7%.

In the industry sector, declines in the growth rate greater than 10% were recorded only in Greece (minus 10.2%), while in Ireland growth was strong, 6.8% in 2014 rebounding from minus 0.4% in 2004.

Ten OECD countries registered negative growth rates in the construction sector: Austria, Estonia, Finland, France, Greece, Israel, Italy, Mexico, Portugal, and Spain; whereas the construction sector in Hungary and Sweden increased by more than 12%.

In Slovenia real value added by the real estate sector fell by 25.6% in contrast to a 9.5% increase in Ireland. The growth rate of real value added for the information and communication sector was positive in most OECD countries except Austria, Greece, Italy, Luxembourg and Portugal.

Finland, Mexico, Poland and the Slovak Republic showed strong increases in their real value added for financial and insurance activities with 11.6%, 9.1%, 9.4% and 10.7% annual growth rates, respectively.

compensation of employees; gross operating surplus; mixed income; and other taxes on production less subsidies on production.

The *System of National Accounts* recommends the basic price valuation for value added but it can also be measured on different price bases such as producers' prices and at factor cost.

Comparability

All countries compile data according to the 2008 SNA "System of National Accounts, 2008" with the exception of Chile, Japan, and Turkey, where data are compiled according to the 1993 SNA. It's important to note however that differences between 2008 SNA and the 1993 SNA do not have a significant impact on comparability implying that data are highly comparable across countries.

However, not all countries produce value added on the basis of basic prices. Japan uses approximately market prices. New Zealand uses producer prices, and Iceland and the United States use factor costs.

Activity is based on the *International Standard Industrial Classification of All Economic Activities* (ISIC Rev.4) system except for Indonesia which is based on ISIC Rev.3. Countries generally collect information using their own industrial classification systems. The conversion from a national classification system to ISIC may create some comparability issues. That said, for most countries the activities presented here are generally comparable.

Sources
- OECD (2015), *National Accounts of OECD Countries*, OECD Publishing.

Further information

Analytical publications
- OECD (2015), *OECD Economic Outlook*, OECD Publishing.

Statistical publications
- OECD (2015), *National Accounts at a Glance*, OECD Publishing.

Methodological publications
- OECD, *et al.* (eds.) (2010), *System of National Accounts 2008*, United Nations, Geneva.

Online databases
- STAN: OECD Structural Analysis Statistics.

Real value added by activity

Annual growth in percentage, 2014 or latest available year

	Agriculture, hunting, forestry, fishing	Industry, including energy	Construction	Distributive trade, repairs, transport, accommodation and food services	Information and communication	Finance and insurance	Real estate	Professional, scientific, technical, administration and support services	Public administration, defence, education human health and social work	Other services
Australia	2.1	3.2	3.9	-0.2	2.4	5.3	3.6	-0.2	4.1	2.2
Austria	4.1	1.3	-2.0	-0.4	-2.7	-1.5	2.8	1.2	-0.2	0.4
Belgium	1.8	1.7	3.3	0.0	1.3	3.8	1.2	1.9	0.9	0.2
Canada	0.7	0.9	5.2	2.0	1.6	2.4	2.6	1.8	1.1	0.5
Chile	2.3	1.0	1.5	1.1	6.6	3.0	..	1.9	4.3	1.7
Czech Republic	5.9	4.7	3.4	1.5	5.9	-0.5	-0.3	4.9	0.3	0.9
Denmark	11.8	-0.1	3.4	0.8	8.5	1.1	-2.2	4.6	0.0	1.7
Estonia	5.1	4.4	-4.2	2.1	3.8	4.7	-2.3	6.1	0.3	0.8
Finland	-0.2	-0.3	-3.7	-1.2	5.1	11.6	0.6	-1.7	-1.5	-1.2
France	8.5	-0.9	-3.6	0.2	1.2	-0.8	1.0	0.7	1.0	0.4
Germany	7.5	1.6	2.6	1.3	2.4	0.6	1.0	2.4	1.0	0.1
Greece	10.9	-10.2	-4.9	7.2	-4.5	-4.4	1.6	-2.3	-0.4	1.1
Hungary	13.9	6.7	12.3	3.6	1.4	-2.9	-0.4	5.8	-2.1	4.3
Iceland	3.3	3.7	8.2	5.5	6.9	-1.0	1.6	5.8	0.7	2.8
Ireland	21.3	6.8	7.6	3.0	8.9	5.2	9.5	5.4	0.1	7.7
Israel	-3.5	1.9	-2.9	1.0	9.0	-5.0	4.1	7.3	0.7	4.4
Italy	-1.7	-1.2	-3.3	0.4	-1.7	-0.1	1.5	-2.3	0.1	0.3
Japan	2.7	0.3	3.7	0.6	4.3	4.5	0.2	..	-0.4	2.0
Korea	2.6	3.8	0.6	2.5	3.1	5.7	1.8	4.1	3.1	2.8
Luxembourg	13.5	-0.1	7.9	5.3	-5.3	2.1	7.6	8.6	2.5	2.6
Mexico	2.6	0.7	-4.9	2.3	4.8	9.1	0.9	2.9	0.8	2.0
Netherlands	3.4	-2.1	3.2	2.5	4.4	-3.0	3.9	3.3	0.1	0.6
New Zealand	-3.0	1.2	10.9	2.5	0.9	4.4	1.2	3.4	2.7	2.2
Norway	6.1	2.3	4.4	2.1	4.3	3.7	1.0	0.6	1.7	3.4
Poland	1.1	4.9	5.0	0.5	4.3	9.4	5.4	5.4	1.3	5.4
Portugal	1.2	0.8	-1.4	2.3	-1.4	-6.4	0.3	3.5	0.1	3.0
Slovak Republic	18.1	8.1	7.9	7.1	0.2	10.7	-25.6	-2.7	-5.7	3.2
Slovenia	10.0	4.8	9.5	3.5	1.4	-1.2	1.4	7.7	1.0	1.6
Spain	-3.7	1.2	-2.1	3.2	4.7	-1.0	1.2	3.4	-0.4	4.4
Sweden	2.9	-0.5	12.1	3.3	4.2	1.8	0.8	3.6	1.4	2.3
Switzerland	7.6	1.9	2.1	1.5	1.4	1.8	1.9	2.4	2.8	0.8
Turkey	-1.9	3.8	2.2	2.1	3.4	7.0	2.6	8.5	4.6	2.9
United Kingdom	13.1	1.0	7.7	4.6	0.6	-0.9	2.4	7.1	0.0	5.4
United States	12.1	1.8	1.9	1.3	4.0	4.6	1.4	2.0	0.6	1.5
Euro area	3.4	0.5	-0.9	1.3	2.0	-0.4	1.3	1.5	0.6	0.6
EU 28	3.8	0.9	1.6	1.9	2.0	-0.5	1.3	2.7	0.6	1.5
OECD	0.8	1.9	0.4	2.5	2.9	1.0	..	..	0.9	0.8
Brazil	5.6	2.9	8.3	-9.1	6.5	5.3	1.8	5.7	1.2	2.2
China	4.5	7.7	9.3	9.0	..	10.0	4.1	..	..	7.9
India	..	..	..	..	..	..	..	..	..	..
Indonesia	4.2	3.5	7.0	5.6	10.0	4.9	5.0	9.8	4.8	8.9
Russian Federation	..	..	..	..	..	..	..	..	..	..
South Africa	..	..	..	..	..	..	..	..	..	..

StatLink  http://dx.doi.org/10.1787/888933336116

Real value added in industry, including energy

Annual growth in percentage

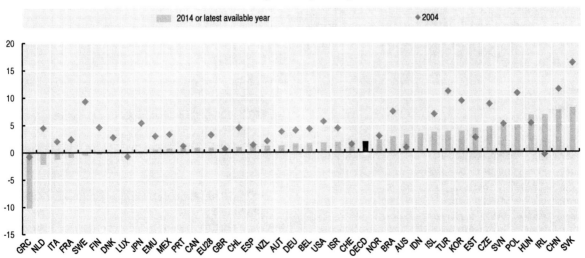

StatLink http://dx.doi.org/10.1787/888933334934

SMALL AND MEDIUM-SIZED ENTERPRISES

Small firms, and especially start-ups in specialised sectors, can be very dynamic and innovative. A few very high-performance firms can make an important contribution to employment creation and economic growth. Although the majority of small firms have modest economic impacts individually, taken together they make an important economic and social contribution.

Definition

An enterprise is an entity possessing the right to conduct business on its own; for example to enter into contracts, own property, incur liabilities and establish bank accounts. It may consist of one or more establishments situated in a geographically separate area.

Employees include all persons covered by a contractual arrangement, working in the enterprise and receiving compensation for their work. Included are persons on sick leave, paid leave or vacation, while excluded are working proprietors, active business partners, unpaid family workers and home-workers.

Number of persons employed is defined as the total number of persons who worked in or for the concerned unit. Excluded are directors of incorporated enterprises and members of shareholders' committees, labour force made available to the concerned unit by other units and charged for, persons carrying out repair and maintenance work in the unit on the behalf of other units, and home-workers. It also excludes persons on indefinite leave, military leave or those whose only remuneration from the enterprise is by way of a pension.

Comparability

An area where differences do arise concerns the coverage of data on enterprises/establishments. Data are typically compiled based on information coming from business registers, economic censuses or business surveys that may have a size or turnover cut-off. Also, countries may apply thresholds depending on tax legislation and legal provisions, for instance to reduce administrative burdens (including respondent burdens) on very small enterprises.

The size-class breakdown 1-9, 10-19, 20-49, 50-249, 250+ provides for the best comparability given the varying data collection practices across countries. Some countries use different conventions: the size class "1-9" refers to "1-19" for Australia and Turkey; the size class "20-49" refers to "20-199" for Australia; the size class "50-249" refers to "50-299" for Japan; and finally, the size class "250+" refers to "200+" for Australia and "300+" for Japan.

For Israel, Mexico, Turkey and the United States data refer to employees. Data refer to 2009 for Mexico, 2010 for Australia and 2013 for Israel.

Overview

Enterprises with less than ten persons employed (i.e. micro-enterprises) in the manufacturing sector represent, on average, 80% of the total business population, ranging between 70% and 90% in most OECD countries. The share of these micro-enterprises in employment of the manufacturing sector is, however, considerably less. Across countries, the contribution of manufacturing micro-enterprises to employment is around 10 to 15%; there are a few exceptions, notably Greece where micro-enterprises account for 42.2% of employment in manufacturing.

Sources
• OECD (2015), *Structural and Demographic Business Statistics* (Database).

Further information

Analytical publications
• OECD (2015), *Financing SMEs and Entrepreneurs*, OECD Publishing.
• OECD (2015), *OECD Studies on SMEs and Entrepreneurship*, OECD Publishing.

Statistical publications
• OECD (2015), *Entrepreneurship at a Glance*, OECD Publishing.
• OECD (2010), *Structural and Demographic Business Statistics 2009*, OECD Publishing.

Methodological publications
• OECD and Eurostat (2008), *Eurostat-OECD Manual on Business Demography Statistics*, OECD Publishing.

Number of employees and number of enterprises in manufacturing

Breakdown by size-class of enterprise, as a percentage of total, 2012 or latest available year

	Number of persons employed					Number of enterprises in manufacturing				
	Less than 10	10-19	20-49	50-249	250 or more	Less than 10	10-19	20-49	50-249	250 or more
Australia	30.2	..	31.7	..	38.2	94.0	..	5.5	..	0.5
Austria	8.9	6.5	10.8	26.0	47.8	71.8	11.8	8.6	5.9	1.9
Belgium	11.6	6.3	12.9	25.1	44.1	81.9	7.4	6.2	3.6	0.9
Canada	..	..	..	..	..	63.5	15.5	13.1	7.2	0.8
Chile	..	..	..	..	..	..	..	..	..	..
Czech Republic	15.8	5.3	10.0	26.6	42.4	92.8	2.7	2.3	1.8	0.4
Denmark	8.3	7.2	11.9	25.7	46.8	71.4	12.3	9.0	6.0	1.3
Estonia	12.2	8.1	15.7	39.5	24.5	73.2	9.8	9.1	7.0	1.0
Finland	10.2	6.6	11.1	24.0	48.2	81.5	7.8	5.9	3.9	0.9
France	13.7	6.9	11.9	23.0	44.6	85.8	6.1	4.7	2.7	0.7
Germany	6.9	8.0	7.6	24.5	53.1	62.1	20.0	7.8	8.1	2.0
Greece	42.2	7.1	11.6	19.8	19.3	94.5	2.6	1.8	0.9	0.2
Hungary	13.0	6.5	10.4	26.0	44.1	85.0	6.4	4.5	3.3	0.8
Iceland	..	..	..	..	..	..	..	..	..	..
Ireland	4.6	5.6	11.3	31.8	46.7	54.1	16.4	14.5	11.8	3.3
Israel	8.9	7.3	12.2	29.8	41.7	81.0	7.9	5.9	4.3	0.8
Italy	24.6	14.5	15.9	21.7	23.3	82.7	10.0	4.9	2.1	0.3
Japan	7.6	6.0	10.7	23.7	52.0	75.9	10.1	8.1	5.1	0.8
Korea	..	..	..	..	..	..	..	..	..	..
Luxembourg	6.8	..	..	..	93.2	61.7	13.0	12.3	10.0	3.0
Mexico	29.4	4.6	6.0	14.8	45.2	93.9	2.8	1.6	1.2	0.5
Netherlands	14.9	8.4	13.9	31.7	31.0	83.8	6.7	5.2	3.7	0.6
New Zealand	12.9	10.7	15.8	24.3	36.3	68.6	15.3	10.2	4.9	0.9
Norway	11.0	8.0	14.2	27.2	39.5	81.9	7.8	6.1	3.6	0.7
Poland	15.8	4.9	9.4	28.6	41.3	86.9	4.5	4.2	3.5	0.9
Portugal	20.0	11.9	18.3	29.9	19.9	82.9	8.2	5.7	2.9	0.4
Slovak Republic	18.4	4.6	8.3	22.7	46.0	94.1	2.2	1.9	1.4	0.4
Slovenia	15.4	6.6	9.1	28.2	40.7	87.8	5.4	3.3	2.9	0.6
Spain	20.4	10.7	16.3	23.7	28.9	83.4	8.2	5.6	2.4	0.4
Sweden	12.0	6.7	10.9	22.6	47.8	87.7	5.3	3.9	2.5	0.6
Switzerland	7.5	8.7	13.8	28.9	41.0	56.6	18.9	13.4	9.1	2.0
Turkey	22.6	..	17.2	26.4	33.9	92.0	..	5.2	2.4	0.5
United Kingdom	9.7	7.6	13.7	27.9	41.2	75.6	10.6	7.7	5.0	1.1
United States	5.5	4.9	8.7	17.7	63.2	67.5	13.6	10.7	6.7	1.6
EU 28	13.7	8.3	11.7	25.3	41.0	82.1	8.5	5.2	3.4	0.8
OECD	..	..	..	..	..	..	..	..	..	..
Brazil	9.3	8.3	12.4	20.5	49.4	64.9	16.8	11.3	5.8	1.3
China	..	..	..	..	..	..	..	..	..	..
India	..	..	..	..	..	..	..	..	..	..
Indonesia	..	..	..	..	..	..	..	..	..	..
Russian Federation	..	..	..	..	..	..	..	..	..	..
South Africa	..	..	..	..	..	..	..	..	..	..

StatLink http://dx.doi.org/10.1787/888933336596

Manufacturing enterprises with less than ten persons employed: number of persons employed and number of enterprises

As a percentage of total number of persons employed or total number of enterprises in manufacturing, 2012 or latest available year

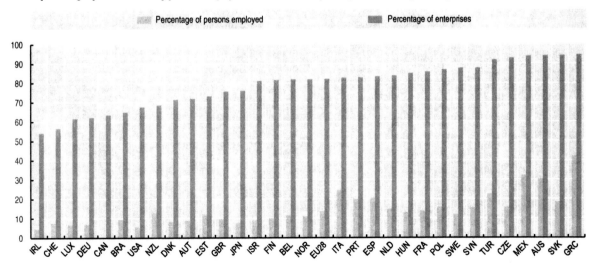

StatLink http://dx.doi.org/10.1787/888933335509

HOUSEHOLD INCOME AND WEALTH

NATIONAL INCOME PER CAPITA

While per capita gross domestic product is the indicator most commonly used to compare national income levels, two other measures are preferred by many analysts. These are per capita Gross National Income (GNI) and Net National Income (NNI). Whereas GDP refers to the income generated by production activities on the economic territory of the country, GNI measures the income generated by the residents of a country, whether earned in the domestic territory or abroad. NNI is the aggregate value of the balances of net primary incomes summed over all sectors.

Definition

GNI is defined as GDP plus receipts from abroad less payments to abroad of wages and salaries and of property income plus net taxes and subsidies receivable from abroad. NNI is equal to GNI net of depreciation.

Wages and salaries from abroad are those that are earned by residents who essentially live and consume inside the economic territory but work abroad (this happens in border areas on a regular basis) or for persons that live and work abroad for only short periods (seasonal workers) and whose centre of economic interest remains in their home country. Guest-workers and other migrant workers who live abroad for twelve months or more are considered to be resident in the country where they are working. Such persons may send part of their earnings to relatives at home, but these remittances are treated as transfers between resident and non-resident households and are recorded in national disposable income but not national income.

Property income from/to abroad includes interest and dividends. It also includes all or part of the retained earnings of foreign enterprises owned fully or in part by residents (and *vice versa*). In this respect, it is important to note that retained earnings of foreign enterprises owned by residents do not actually return to the residents concerned. Nevertheless, the retained earnings are recorded as a receipt.

Comparability

All countries compile data according to the 2008 SNA "System of National Accounts, 2008" with the exception of Chile, Japan, and Turkey, where data are compiled according to the 1993 SNA. When changes in international standards are implemented countries often take the opportunity to implement improved compilation methods; therefore also implementing various improvements in sources and estimation methodologies. In some countries the impact of the 'statistical benchmark revision' could be higher than the impact of the changeover in standards. As a consequence the GDP level for the OECD total increased by 3.8% in 2010 based on the available countries. The level changes in NNI are generally more moderate than the changes in the levels of GDP. For the OECD, the impact of the changes on NNI is about 0.5 percentage points on average in 2010.

However, there are practical difficulties in the measurement both of international flows of wages and salaries and property income and of depreciation. It is for that reason that GDP per capita is the most widely used indicator of income or welfare, even though, GNI is theoretically superior.

Overview

On average for the OECD, GNI per capita is around 15-25% higher than NNI per capita. The country rankings are not greatly affected by the choice of income measure. Only three countries would be more than one place higher in the ranking if GNI per capita were used instead of NNI: the Slovak Republic, the Czech Republic, and Finland. Only four countries would be more than two places lower in the ranking if GNI per capita were used: Russia, Israel, Ireland and the United Kingdom.

GNI per capita does not differ significantly from GDP per capita. Usually, the differences are smaller than USD 3 000. There are, however, two exceptions. For Luxembourg, GNI per capita in 2014, although still highest in the OECD, is nearly USD 33 000 lower than GDP per capita. In Ireland, GNI is USD 8 000 lower than GDP per capita in 2013.

Sources
- OECD (2015), *National Accounts of OECD Countries*, OECD Publishing.

Further information

Analytical publications
- OECD (2015), *OECD Economic Outlook*, OECD Publishing.
- OECD (2014), *Perspectives on Global Development*, OECD Publishing.
- OECD (2003), *The Sources of Economic Growth in OECD Countries*, OECD Publishing.

Statistical publications
- OECD (2015), *National Accounts at a Glance*, OECD Publishing.

Methodological publications
- OECD, et al. (eds.) (2010), *System of National Accounts 2008*, United Nations, Geneva.

Online databases
- OECD National Accounts Statistics.
- OECD Economic Outlook: Statistics and Projections.

Websites
- Sources & Methods of the OECD Economic Outlook, *www.oecd.org/eco/sources-and-methods*.

Gross national income per capita

US dollars, current prices and PPPs

	2002	2003	2004	2005	2006	2007	2008	2009	2010	2011	2012	2013	2014
Australia	29 740	31 173	32 446	34 061	35 906	37 736	38 317	39 539	40 554	42 467	42 575	43 672	44 098
Austria	31 109	32 150	33 770	34 593	37 755	39 162	41 451	40 632	42 227	44 188	44 916	45 263	45 878
Belgium	31 287	31 631	32 421	33 445	35 586	37 076	38 745	37 711	40 438	41 475	42 549	42 190	43 484
Canada	29 851	31 259	32 923	35 310	37 218	38 647	39 498	38 026	39 278	40 808	41 548	42 414	43 361
Chile	9 879	10 137	10 780	11 629	13 657	14 888	15 153	15 091	16 950	19 069	20 211	21 037	21 494
Czech Republic	17 675	18 942	20 004	21 231	22 872	24 918	25 243	25 001	24 914	26 434	26 840	27 214	27 984
Denmark	31 226	31 076	33 307	34 342	37 642	38 882	41 299	40 023	42 501	44 239	44 566	45 365	46 182
Estonia	11 218	12 478	13 907	15 864	18 255	20 302	21 270	19 578	19 974	22 721	24 220	25 630	26 283
Finland	28 506	28 643	31 311	32 199	34 848	37 627	39 804	38 028	38 815	40 434	40 419	40 157	39 943
France	28 812	28 462	29 479	30 929	32 961	34 773	35 921	35 459	36 629	38 213	37 810	38 205	39 636
Germany	28 097	29 099	30 925	32 472	35 314	37 324	38 805	37 971	40 402	43 216	43 826	44 222	46 016
Greece	22 678	23 699	25 095	25 397	27 722	28 539	30 188	29 932	28 390	25 998	25 734	25 805	..
Hungary	14 168	14 940	15 597	16 380	17 708	18 063	19 536	19 919	20 559	21 505	21 588	22 836	23 616
Iceland	31 940	31 276	33 434	34 646	34 524	37 065	32 826	32 465	32 398	34 541	36 547	41 087	..
Ireland	28 679	30 824	32 781	34 920	38 523	40 531	38 004	34 850	36 357	36 857	37 324	38 832	..
Israel	24 222	22 839	24 390	24 558	25 535	27 460	26 828	26 917	28 310	30 184	31 084	32 065	32 844
Italy	27 761	28 277	28 655	29 586	31 942	33 546	34 614	33 857	34 307	35 377	34 971	34 691	35 006
Japan	27 690	28 423	29 931	31 156	32 702	34 445	34 622	32 745	34 655	35 380	36 729	37 556	37 929
Korea	20 701	21 307	22 921	24 031	25 767	27 787	28 716	28 326	30 496	31 512	32 351	33 335	34 622
Luxembourg	47 715	47 224	53 696	56 087	53 473	62 392	63 476	54 142	62 819	63 276	63 475	61 126	64 780
Mexico	10 132	10 611	11 275	12 124	13 226	13 822	14 490	14 166	14 975	16 083	16 461	16 405	17 318
Netherlands	34 010	34 217	36 051	37 461	41 696	44 336	45 298	44 452	45 115	47 237	47 342	47 672	48 235
New Zealand	22 041	22 752	23 599	24 013	25 735	27 022	27 323	29 135	29 390	30 739	31 528	33 620	35 369
Norway	37 840	39 230	43 284	48 900	54 759	56 725	62 138	56 517	59 403	63 328	66 904	66 353	66 306
Poland	11 553	11 930	12 635	13 566	14 836	16 327	17 733	18 566	19 735	21 251	22 063	22 840	..
Portugal	18 994	19 573	19 999	21 733	23 128	24 420	25 080	25 257	26 019	26 413	26 346	27 279	28 002
Slovak Republic	13 081	13 196	14 367	16 023	18 196	20 719	23 286	22 889	23 757	24 263	25 270	26 114	26 815
Slovenia	20 024	20 790	22 458	23 743	25 640	27 127	28 906	27 120	27 329	28 287	28 240	28 515	29 922
Spain	24 390	25 125	26 240	27 460	30 367	32 007	32 804	32 202	31 907	31 970	32 165	32 395	33 034
Sweden	30 857	32 601	34 458	34 796	38 485	42 006	43 581	40 688	42 950	45 016	45 298	45 926	46 719
Switzerland	37 142	38 604	39 908	42 241	46 430	47 526	46 998	50 744	54 214	55 079	57 094	57 964	..
Turkey	..	..	..	..	..	..	..	..	..	..	..	..	..
United Kingdom	30 595	31 725	33 732	35 466	37 355	37 924	37 898	36 515	36 325	37 038	37 630	38 367	38 986
United States	38 544	39 884	42 190	44 669	47 322	48 346	48 568	47 176	48 808	50 622	52 770	53 943	55 842
Euro area	22 766	23 152	24 143	25 238	27 337	28 899	29 498	28 698	29 675	30 881	30 812	30 931	38 631
EU 28	24 488	25 198	26 508	27 753	25 337	26 787	27 574	26 825	27 638	28 765	28 917	29 222	29 948
OECD	26 725	27 521	29 057	30 625	32 772	34 135	34 818	33 912	35 222	36 626	37 548	38 213	..
Brazil	..	..	..	..	..	..	..	..	..	..	..	..	..
China	3 419	3 829	4 321	4 913	5 706	6 680	7 459	8 104	8 992	9 920	10 891	11 818	..
India	..	..	2 703	3 001	3 329	3 714	3 840	4 223	..	..	..	..	..
Indonesia	..	..	..	..	..	..	..	..	..	..	..	..	..
Russian Federation	7 876	8 972	10 010	11 527	14 475	16 256	19 572	18 757	19 844	21 857	23 254	24 183	..
South Africa	8 205	8 507	9 102	9 755	10 450	11 068	11 584	11 338	11 521	11 977	12 370	12 661	12 795

StatLink http://dx.doi.org/10.1787/888933336415

Gross and net national income per capita

US dollars, current prices and PPPs, 2014 or latest available year

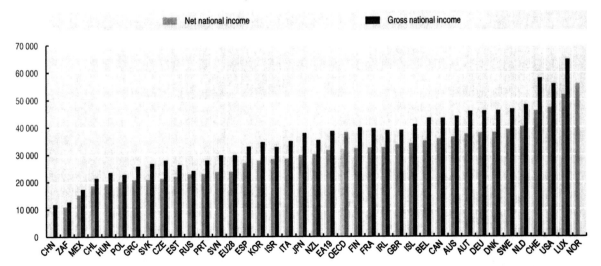

Net national income   ■ Gross national income

StatLink http://dx.doi.org/10.1787/888933335255

HOUSEHOLD DISPOSABLE INCOME

Disposable income, as a concept, is closer to the concept of income generally understood in economics, than either national income or GDP. At the total economy level it differs from national income in that additional income items are included, mainly other current transfers such as remittances. For countries where these additional items form significant sources of income the importance of focusing on disposable income in formulating policy is clear. Another important difference between national income and disposable income reflects the fact that the latter concerns the share of national income that is allocated to households only. Disposable income can be seen as the maximum amount that a household can afford to spend on the consumption of goods or services without having to reduce its financial or non-financial assets or by increasing its liabilities.

Definition

Household disposable income is the sum of wages and salaries, gross operating surplus (income earned from renting a dwelling or the imputed rental income of owner-occupiers), mixed income, net property income, net current transfers and social benefits other than social transfers in kind, less taxes on income and wealth and social security contributions paid by employees, the self-employed and the unemployed.

The indicator for the household sector includes the disposable income of non-profit institutions serving households (NPISH).

Comparability

All countries compile data according to the 2008 SNA "System of National Accounts, 2008" with the exception of Chile, Japan, and Turkey, where data are compiled according to the 1993 SNA. It's important to note however that differences between the 2008 SNA and the 1993 SNA do not have a significant impact of the comparability and implies that data are highly comparable across countries.

Overview

On average over the period 2012-14, household disposable income in real terms increased in 20 out of 30 OECD countries for which data is available. Chile (7.5%), Norway (3.5%) and Mexico (3.1%) showed the highest growth rates. In contrast, Greece's household disposable income fell by 8.6% and the household disposable income for Italy, Spain, Portugal, and Slovenia fell around 2% in the three year period.

In most OECD countries, the growth rate of real household disposable income over the three years to 2014 was lower than in the three years to 2004. In fact, in the three years to 2004 only two countries recorded small declines in disposable income (the Netherlands and Belgium) whereas 10 countries recorded declines in the three years to 2014. In Chile and Russia, however, disposable income showed very strong growth. Over that period, inequalities in household disposable income continued to increase in the majority of OECD countries.

Sources
- OECD (2015), *National Accounts at a Glance*, OECD Publishing.
- OECD (2015), *National Accounts of OECD Countries*, OECD Publishing.

Further information

Statistical publications
- OECD (2015), *Taxing Wages*, OECD Publishing.
- OECD (2015), *OECD Pensions at a Glance*, OECD Publishing.
- OECD (2014), *Society at a Glance: OECD Social Indicators*, OECD Publishing.

Methodological publications
- Lequiller, F. and D. Blades (2014), *Understanding National Accounts: Second Edition*, OECD Publishing.
- OECD, et al. (eds.) (2010), *System of National Accounts 2008*, United Nations, Geneva.

Online databases
- OECD Social Expenditure Statistics.

Real household disposable income
Annual growth in percentage

	2002	2003	2004	2005	2006	2007	2008	2009	2010	2011	2012	2013	2014
Australia	0.7	5.6	5.6	2.7	5.5	7.1	6.8	1.3	4.9	3.7	0.9	1.5	..
Austria	0.9	2.0	2.2	4.0	2.7	2.1	0.7	-0.3	-1.1	-0.3	2.0	-2.0	0.5
Belgium	-0.6	-0.1	-0.4	0.8	2.2	2.0	2.2	2.1	-1.2	-1.1	0.4	-0.7	0.3
Canada	2.4	2.3	3.6	2.9	6.1	3.7	4.0	1.6	2.4	2.3	2.7	2.4	1.5
Chile	..	..	..	..	..	..	..	6.4	6.3	9.2	7.4	5.8	..
Czech Republic	2.9	4.0	2.4	4.6	5.6	3.1	2.3	2.1	0.1	-1.6	-1.1	-0.9	1.7
Denmark	3.1	2.4	2.5	2.6	2.4	-0.8	-0.9	2.7	3.6	1.0	-0.5	-1.4	-0.4
Estonia	1.7	8.2	5.5	9.1	11.9	11.0	5.3	-9.2	-4.3	3.8	0.3	6.3	2.0
Finland	3.0	3.9	4.5	1.2	2.6	3.5	2.3	1.1	2.9	1.0	-0.2	0.3	-1.0
France	3.2	0.6	2.1	0.8	2.2	2.9	0.1	1.7	1.3	0.1	-0.9	0.0	1.1
Germany	-0.7	0.7	0.8	0.2	1.0	0.0	0.6	-0.6	0.4	0.9	0.5	0.5	1.3
Greece	..	..	..	..	..	3.2	0.9	0.0	-11.0	-9.8	-7.6	-8.4	..
Hungary	4.6	6.6	4.7	4.0	1.4	-3.2	-2.4	-4.4	-2.5	3.9	-3.2	1.6	2.9
Iceland	..	..	..	..	..	..	..	..	..	..	..	..	..
Ireland	2.1	2.5	5.1	7.6	3.8	6.3	6.7	0.3	-2.7	-3.5	-1.0	-2.3	0.6
Israel	..	..	..	..	..	..	..	..	..	..	..	..	..
Italy	0.9	0.5	1.3	0.5	1.1	1.3	-1.4	-2.3	-1.8	-0.5	-5.7	-0.6	-0.3
Japan	1.0	0.0	1.1	0.9	0.8	0.8	-1.2	1.3	2.6	0.7	1.0	0.7	..
Korea	4.0	3.3	4.0	2.8	3.1	2.9	1.4	1.1	3.5	2.0	1.5	4.0	2.6
Luxembourg	..	..	..	..	..	..	..	..	..	..	..	..	..
Mexico	..	..	3.7	3.6	6.6	2.5	2.0	-7.5	6.3	3.3	2.6	3.2	..
Netherlands	-0.4	-1.4	-0.3	-0.6	0.2	1.9	-0.9	0.7	-0.7	0.6	-1.2	-0.9	1.3
New Zealand	0.8	9.5	5.0	3.0	4.6	5.0	-1.9	2.8	3.5	1.4	3.9	..	..
Norway	8.4	4.6	3.4	8.3	-6.6	6.0	3.4	3.2	2.3	4.1	4.4	3.0	2.9
Poland	-0.3	0.8	-0.1	0.9	4.3	5.2	4.3	6.0	1.8	0.0	1.1	2.8	..
Portugal	1.1	-1.6	2.7	0.7	0.0	1.4	1.0	1.5	1.0	-5.6	-5.1	-0.9	0.2
Slovak Republic	5.3	0.5	4.3	5.6	3.5	9.6	5.0	1.4	2.9	-2.3	-1.8	1.7	3.1
Slovenia	2.5	0.5	3.5	4.8	3.1	4.6	2.8	-1.3	-0.5	0.1	-4.2	-2.1	1.5
Spain	3.1	3.9	2.2	2.3	1.8	0.4	1.8	3.0	-3.5	-1.3	-5.3	-1.5	0.7
Sweden	3.2	0.7	1.7	2.2	4.1	5.6	2.0	2.6	1.7	4.1	3.8	1.7	2.2
Switzerland	-0.2	-0.5	1.3	1.7	3.4	3.9	1.1	2.1	1.2	1.7	4.0	3.2	..
Turkey	..	..	..	..	..	..	..	..	..	..	..	..	..
United Kingdom	2.1	1.5	0.8	2.0	1.3	2.6	0.9	3.3	0.7	-2.1	2.6	-1.1	-0.7
United States	3.3	2.9	3.5	1.4	3.8	1.9	1.8	-0.3	1.3	2.7	3.3	-1.5	2.7
Euro area	1.2	1.2	1.6	0.9	1.6	1.5	0.3	0.3	-0.8	-0.1	-1.9	-0.5	0.9
EU 28	1.1	1.7	1.5	1.3	1.7	1.8	0.9	1.2	-0.7	-0.2	-1.2	-0.1	0.8
OECD	..	..	..	..	..	..	..	..	..	..	..	..	..
Brazil	..	..	..	..	..	..	..	..	..	5.0	..	..	..
China	..	..	..	..	..	..	..	..	..	..	..	..	..
India	..	..	..	..	..	..	..	..	..	..	..	..	..
Indonesia	..	..	..	..	..	..	..	..	..	..	..	..	..
Russian Federation	..	7.7	9.4	11.9	13.6	14.1	8.0	-2.0	8.6	4.7	6.1	3.1	..
South Africa	..	..	..	..	..	..	..	0.8	5.1	5.3	2.7	3.3	2.2

StatLink http://dx.doi.org/10.1787/888933336269

Real household disposable income
Average annual growth in percentage

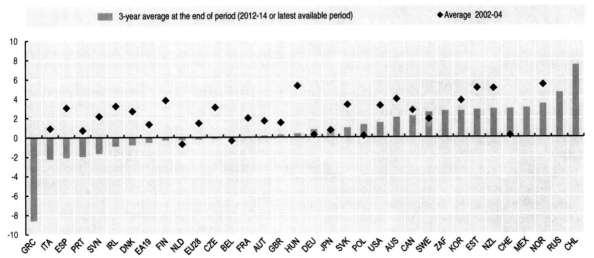

■ 3-year average at the end of period (2012-14 or latest available period)   ◆ Average 2002-04

StatLink http://dx.doi.org/10.1787/888933335075

HOUSEHOLD SAVINGS

Household savings is the main domestic source of funds to finance capital investment, which is a major driver of long-term economic growth. Household savings rates vary considerably between countries because of institutional, demographic and socio-economic differences. For example, government provisions for old-age pensions and the demographic age structure of the population will influence the rate at which populations save (older persons tend to run down their financial assets during their retirement to the detriment of savings). Equally the availability and price of credit, as well as attitudes towards debt, may influence choices made by individuals regarding whether to spend or save.

Definition

Household savings is estimated by subtracting household consumption expenditure from household disposable income plus the adjustment for the change in pension entitlements.

Household disposable income consists essentially of income from employment and from the operation of unincorporated enterprises, plus receipts of interest, dividends and social benefits minus payments of current taxes, interest and social contributions. Note that enterprise income includes the imputed rental income earned by owner-occupiers of dwellings.

Household consumption expenditure consists mainly of cash outlays for consumer goods and services but it also includes the imputed expenditures that owner occupiers pay, as occupiers, to themselves as owners of their dwellings and the production of goods for own-final use such as agricultural products; the values of which are also included in income.

The household savings rate is calculated as the ratio of household savings to household disposable income (plus the adjustment for the change in pension entitlements).

Comparability

All countries compile data according to the 2008 SNA "System of National Accounts, 2008" with the exception of Chile, Japan, and Turkey, where data are compiled according to the 1993 SNA. One of the changes in the standards of the 2008 SNA that directly impacts the savings rates, concerns the treatment of pension schemes. These changes may have a significant impact on households' savings rates in countries with (partially) funded defined benefit pension schemes, as is the case, for example, in the United Kingdom. For pensions provided by government to their employees, countries have some flexibility in the recording of the unfunded liabilities, which may hamper comparability across countries.

Savings rates may be measured on either a net or a gross basis. Net savings rates are measured after deducting consumption of fixed capital (in respect of assets used in unincorporated enterprises and in respect of owner-occupied dwellings), from savings and from the disposable income of households, so that both savings and disposable income are shown on a net basis.

Overview

Household savings rates differ significantly across countries. From 2002-14 three countries had savings rates consistently above 9%: France, Germany and Switzerland. From 2007 Sweden also registered a savings rate above 9%.

In contrast, six countries showed several years of negative savings rates over the period 2002-14; most notably in Greece (2006-13); New Zealand (2002-08); and Estonia (2002-07).

Sources

- OECD (2015), *National Accounts of OECD Countries*, OECD Publishing.

Further information

Analytical publications

- Fournier, J. and I. Koske (2010), "A Simple Model of the Relationship between Productivity, Saving and the Current Account", *OECD Economics Department Working Papers*, No. 816.
- Laiglesia, J. de and C. Morrison (2008), "Household Structures and Savings: Evidence from Household Surveys", *OECD Development Centre Working Papers*, No. 267.
- OECD (2015), *OECD Economic Outlook*, OECD Publishing.

Statistical publications

- OECD (2015), *National Accounts at a Glance*, OECD Publishing.

Websites

- Sources & Methods of the OECD Economic Outlook, *www.oecd.org/eco/sources-and-methods*.

Household net saving rates
As a percentage of household disposable income

	2002	2003	2004	2005	2006	2007	2008	2009	2010	2011	2012	2013	2014
Australia	0.0	0.5	1.5	1.1	1.8	4.0	10.0	9.1	10.2	11.2	10.3	9.7	..
Austria	8.9	9.2	9.2	10.7	11.3	12.1	11.9	11.3	9.3	7.9	9.2	7.3	7.8
Belgium	11.0	10.6	8.9	8.5	9.2	9.4	10.0	11.4	8.2	6.6	6.4	5.0	5.1
Canada	2.3	1.7	2.3	1.5	3.5	2.9	3.9	5.1	4.3	4.3	5.0	4.9	3.8
Chile	..	..	..	..	..	..	7.0	12.3	8.8	8.6	9.9	9.7	..
Czech Republic	6.3	5.7	4.9	6.1	7.8	7.0	6.3	8.5	7.6	5.9	6.2	5.5	5.7
Denmark	1.2	1.8	-2.2	-4.6	-1.7	-3.1	-4.2	0.8	2.1	0.9	0.0	-0.4	-6.4
Estonia	-9.5	-9.3	-11.0	-10.7	-11.2	-7.3	1.6	6.9	3.3	4.1	1.4	3.9	3.1
Finland	..	..	..	..	..	..	..	..	..	..	..	..	..
France	11.6	10.9	11.0	9.4	9.4	9.8	9.5	10.8	10.4	10.0	9.5	9.1	9.6
Germany	9.6	10.1	10.1	10.1	10.1	10.2	10.5	10.0	10.0	9.6	9.3	9.1	9.5
Greece	..	..	..	..	-3.4	-3.5	-5.6	-4.5	-9.0	-8.2	-8.3	-16.4	..
Hungary	3.1	1.7	4.5	5.7	6.3	2.2	1.5	3.6	3.6	4.1	2.6	3.9	4.9
Iceland	..	..	..	..	..	..	..	..	..	..	..	..	..
Ireland	0.0	0.4	1.2	1.9	-0.6	-0.7	6.3	12.2	9.6	7.3	8.5	8.1	..
Israel	..	..	..	..	..	..	..	..	..	..	..	..	..
Italy	9.6	9.1	9.5	9.0	8.4	8.0	7.7	7.0	4.1	3.6	1.8	3.9	3.4
Japan	3.3	2.7	2.3	1.6	1.3	1.1	0.6	2.3	2.1	2.6	1.4	0.0	..
Korea	..	..	..	..	..	..	..	..	4.7	3.9	3.9	5.6	..
Luxembourg	..	..	..	..	..	..	..	..	..	..	..	..	..
Mexico	..	10.1	8.6	8.2	9.1	8.4	8.1	8.4	8.8	6.9	6.1	5.4	..
Netherlands	7.9	7.4	6.8	5.7	3.8	3.9	3.7	7.1	4.9	5.8	6.8	7.3	8.2
New Zealand	-6.6	-4.1	-3.8	-5.9	-3.3	-1.0	-1.1	1.1	3.0	1.7	2.2	..	..
Norway	..	..	..	..	..	..	..	..	..	..	..	..	..
Poland	9.0	7.9	4.0	3.0	2.7	2.2	0.8	3.2	3.0	-0.5	-0.5	0.7	..
Portugal	3.9	2.7	2.7	1.8	0.4	-0.8	-1.1	2.7	1.3	-0.9	-0.5	-0.2	-2.3
Slovak Republic	..	..	..	..	..	..	..	..	..	..	..	..	..
Slovenia	8.5	6.1	7.1	9.4	11.1	9.4	9.7	7.7	6.1	5.5	3.2	5.7	6.5
Spain	5.2	6.7	5.0	3.2	1.4	-1.0	1.6	7.3	3.7	4.6	2.6	4.2	3.9
Sweden	7.8	6.6	5.8	5.4	6.9	9.4	12.7	12.2	11.0	12.7	15.3	15.1	15.3
Switzerland	15.3	14.8	13.7	14.0	15.8	17.4	16.7	17.1	17.0	17.8	18.5	19.0	..
Turkey	..	..	..	..	..	..	..	..	..	..	..	..	..
United Kingdom	3.8	2.4	0.5	-0.3	-1.2	-0.7	-0.8	4.0	6.1	3.4	2.9	0.0	-1.9
United States	5.2	5.0	4.7	2.7	3.4	3.1	5.1	6.3	5.8	6.2	7.9	4.9	5.0
Euro area	8.9	9.0	8.7	7.8	7.1	6.9	7.1	8.5	6.9	6.5	6.0	6.1	6.1
EU 28	7.3	7.2	6.4	5.7	4.9	4.6	5.0	7.4	6.1	5.4	4.9	4.7	4.3
OECD	..	..	..	..	..	..	..	..	..	..	..	..	..
Brazil	..	..	..	..	..	..	..	..	..	..	..	..	..
China	31.5	33.9	33.8	35.4	37.2	39.2	39.9	40.4	42.1	40.9	40.7	..	..
India	..	..	..	..	..	..	..	..	..	..	..	..	..
Indonesia	..	..	..	..	..	..	..	..	..	..	..	..	..
Russian Federation	..	..	..	11.0	12.4	12.1	10.1	13.1	15.5	13.8	12.5	10.9	..
South Africa	..	..	..	..	..	..	-1.1	-0.5	-0.8	-1.1	-2.1	-2.5	-2.4

StatLink http://dx.doi.org/10.1787/888933336288

Household net saving rates
As a percentage of household disposable income

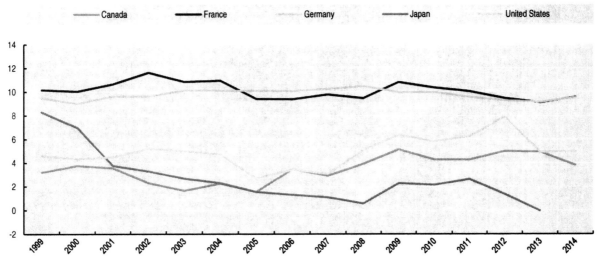

StatLink http://dx.doi.org/10.1787/888933335091

INCOME INEQUALITY

Income inequalities are one of the most visible manifestations of differences in living standards within each country. In many OECD countries, income inequalities reflect developments in the labour market, as well as in tax and transfer systems.

Definition

Income is defined as household disposable income in a particular year. It consists of earnings, self-employment and capital income and public cash transfers; income taxes and social security contributions paid by households are deducted. The income of the household is attributed to each of its members, with an adjustment to reflect differences in needs for households of different sizes.

The Gini coefficient is based on the comparison of cumulative proportions of the population against cumulative proportions of income they receive, and it ranges between 0 in the case of perfect equality and 1 in the case of perfect inequality. The Palma index is the ratio between the income share of the top 10% and the bottom 40%; S90/S10 is the ratio of the average income of the 10% richest to the 10% poorest; S80/S20 of the average income of the 20% richest to the 20% poorest. P90/P10 is the ratio of the upper bound value of the ninth decile (i.e. the 10% of people with highest income) to that of the first decile; P90/P50 of the upper bound value of the ninth decile to the median income; and P50/P10 of median income to the upper bound value of the first decile.

Comparability

Data have been provided by national experts applying common methodologies and standardised definitions. In many cases, experts made several adjustments to source data to conform to standardised definitions. While this approach improves comparability, full standardisation cannot be achieved. Small differences between periods and across countries are usually not significant.

Results refer to different years. "2012 or latest year available" data refer to the income in 2012 in all countries except Japan (2009); Indonesia and Russia (2010); Brazil, Canada and Chile (2011); India (2013); and China (2014). "Mid-1990s" data refer to the income earned between 1993 and 1996. "Mid-1980s" data refer to the income earned between 1983 and 1987 in all countries for which data are available except Czech Republic (1992) and Hungary (1991).

For the emerging economies except Russia, Gini coefficients are not strictly comparable with OECD countries as they are based on per capita incomes except India and Indonesia for which per capita consumption was used.

Overview

There is considerable variation in income inequality across OECD countries. Inequality as measured by the Gini coefficient ranges from 0.25 in Denmark to approximately twice that value in Chile and Mexico. The Nordic and Central European countries have the lowest inequality in disposable income while inequality is high in Chile, Israel, Mexico, Turkey and the United States. Alternative indicators of income inequality suggest similar rankings. The gap between the average income of the richest and the poorest 10% of the population was almost 10 to 1 on average across OECD countries in 2012, ranging from 5 to 1 in Denmark to five times larger in Chile and Mexico.

From the mid-1980s to around 2012, inequality rose in 16 out of 18 countries for which longer-run data are available. The increase was strongest in Finland, Luxembourg and Sweden. Declines occurred in Turkey, and Greece to a lesser extent. Income inequality generally rose faster from the mid-1980s to the mid-1990s than in the following periods.

With measurement-related differences in mind, the emerging economies have higher levels of income inequality than most OECD countries, particularly Brazil and South Africa. Comparable data from the early 1990s suggest that inequality increased in Asia, decreased in Latin America and remained very high in South Africa.

Sources
• OECD (2015), OECD Social and Welfare Statistics (Database).

Further information

Analytical publications
• OECD (2015), How's Life? Measuring Well-being, OECD Publishing.
• OECD (2015), In It Together: Why Less Inequality Benefits All, OECD Publishing.
• OECD (2011), Divided We Stand, Why Inequality Keeps Rising, OECD Publishing.
• OECD (2008), Growing Unequal? Income Distribution and Poverty in OECD Countries, OECD Publishing.

Statistical publications
• OECD (2014), Society at a Glance: OECD Social Indicators, OECD Publishing.

Websites
• OECD Centre for Opportunity and Equality, http://oe.cd/cope.
• OECD Income Distribution Database (supplementary material), www.oecd.org/social/incomedistribution-database.htm.

Income inequality

Different summary inequality measures, 2012 or latest year available

	Gini coefficient (disposable income, post taxes and transfers)	Palma ratio (S90/S40 disposable income decile share)	S90/S10 disposable income decile share	S80/S20 disposable income quintile share	P90/P10 disposable income decile ratio	P90/P50 disposable income decile ratio	P50/P10 disposable income decile ratio
Australia	0.33	1.2	8.8	5.5	4.4	2.0	2.2
Austria	0.28	1.0	7.0	4.3	3.5	1.8	2.0
Belgium	0.27	0.9	5.9	4.0	3.4	1.7	2.0
Canada	0.32	1.2	8.6	5.2	4.2	1.9	2.1
Chile	0.50	3.3	26.5	13.0	8.5	3.3	2.6
Czech Republic	0.26	0.9	5.4	3.6	3.0	1.8	1.7
Denmark	0.25	0.9	5.2	3.5	2.8	1.6	1.7
Estonia	0.34	1.3	9.6	5.8	4.7	2.2	2.1
Finland	0.26	0.9	5.4	3.7	3.1	1.7	1.8
France	0.31	1.2	7.4	4.6	3.6	1.9	1.9
Germany	0.29	1.1	6.6	4.3	3.5	1.9	1.9
Greece	0.34	1.3	12.3	6.3	4.9	1.9	2.5
Hungary	0.29	1.0	7.3	4.5	3.8	1.8	2.0
Iceland	0.26	0.9	5.6	3.7	3.0	1.7	1.7
Ireland	0.30	1.1	7.4	4.7	3.8	2.0	1.9
Israel	0.37	1.6	13.7	7.5	6.1	2.2	2.7
Italy	0.33	1.3	11.4	5.8	4.4	2.0	2.2
Japan	0.34	1.3	10.7	6.2	5.2	2.0	2.6
Korea	0.31	1.1	10.2	5.5	4.8	1.9	2.5
Luxembourg	0.30	1.1	7.1	4.6	3.6	1.9	1.9
Mexico	0.46	2.5	25.1	11.5	8.1	2.8	2.9
Netherlands	0.28	1.0	6.8	4.2	3.3	1.8	1.9
New Zealand	0.33	1.3	8.2	5.3	4.2	2.1	2.0
Norway	0.25	0.9	6.2	3.8	3.0	1.6	1.9
Poland	0.30	1.1	7.3	4.7	3.9	1.9	2.0
Portugal	0.34	1.3	10.1	5.9	4.7	2.1	2.2
Slovak Republic	0.25	0.8	5.7	3.7	3.2	1.7	1.9
Slovenia	0.25	0.8	5.5	3.7	3.3	1.7	2.0
Spain	0.34	1.3	11.7	6.1	4.9	2.0	2.4
Sweden	0.27	1.0	6.3	4.1	3.3	1.7	1.9
Switzerland	0.29	1.0	6.7	4.3	3.5	1.8	1.9
Turkey	0.40	1.9	14.0	7.8	6.0	2.5	2.4
United Kingdom	0.35	1.5	10.5	5.9	4.2	2.1	2.0
United States	0.39	1.8	17.9	8.5	6.2	2.3	2.8
EU 28	0.29	1.1	7.7	4.7	3.8	1.9	2.0
OECD	0.32	1.3	9.5	5.5	4.3	2.0	2.1
Brazil	0.55	..	..	..	..	..	..
China	0.47	..	..	..	..	..	..
India	0.34	..	..	..	..	..	..
Indonesia	0.41	..	..	..	..	..	..
Russian Federation	0.40	..	..	..	..	..	..
South Africa	0.67	..	..	..	..	..	..

StatLink http://dx.doi.org/10.1787/888933336302

Trends in income inequality

Percentage point changes in the Gini coefficient

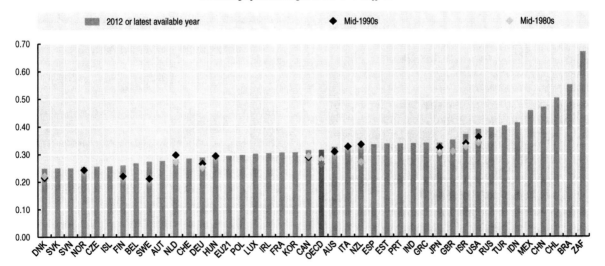

■ 2012 or latest available year   ◆ Mid-1990s   ◇ Mid-1980s

StatLink http://dx.doi.org/10.1787/888933335119

POVERTY RATES AND GAPS

Avoiding economic hardship is a primary objective of social policy. As perceptions of "a decent standard of living" vary across countries and over time, no commonly agreed measure of "absolute" poverty across OECD countries exists. A starting point for measuring poverty is therefore to look at "relative" poverty, whose measure is based on the income that is most typical in each country in each year.

Definition

The poverty rate is the ratio of the number of people (in a given age group) whose income falls below the poverty line, taken as half the median household income of the total population. However, two countries with the same poverty rates may differ in terms of the relative income level of the poor. To measure this dimension, the poverty gap, i.e. the percentage by which the mean income of the poor falls below the poverty line.

Income is defined as household disposable income in a particular year. It consists of earnings, self-employment and capital income and public cash transfers; income taxes and social security contributions paid by households are deducted. The income of the household is attributed to each of its members, with an adjustment to reflect differences in needs for households of different sizes (i.e. the needs of a household composed of four people are assumed to be twice as large as those of a person living alone).

Overview

Across OECD countries, the average poverty rate was about 11% around 2012. There is considerable diversity across countries: poverty rates are almost 20% in Israel and Mexico, but below 6% in the Czech Republic and Denmark. Poverty rates vary across age groups: in Japan and Korea, older people are more likely to be poor, while in Turkey child poverty is a greater issue. The United States, Chile, Israel and Mexico share higher overall poverty rates, while the Nordic countries combine lower poverty rates.

On average, in OECD countries, the mean income of poor people is 31% below the poverty line (poverty gap), with larger gaps in countries hard hit by the recent crisis like Italy, Greece, Spain and the United States and lower ones in Belgium, Finland, Germany, New Zealand and Slovenia. In general, countries with higher poverty rates also have higher poverty gaps.

From the mid-1980s to around 2012, poverty rates rose in 15 out of 18 countries for which data are available, resulting in an overall increase of 2.7 percentage points for the OECD as a whole. The largest rises were experienced by Israel and Sweden, and the only decline was registered in Denmark.

Comparability

Data have been provided by national experts applying common methodologies and standardised definitions. In many cases, experts made several adjustments to source data to conform to standardised definitions. While this approach improves comparability, full standardisation cannot be achieved.

Measurement problems are especially severe at the top but also at the bottom end of the income scale. As large proportions of the population are clustered around the poverty line, small changes in their income can lead to large swings in poverty measures. Small differences between periods and across countries are usually not significant.

Results refer to different years. "2012 or latest year available" data refer to the income in 2012 in all countries except Japan (2009), Russia (2010), Canada and Chile (2011). "Mid-1990s" data refer to the income earned between 1993 and 1996. "Mid-1980s" data refer to the income earned between 1983 and 1987 in all countries for which data are available except the Czech Republic (1992) and Hungary (1991).

Sources
- OECD (2015), "Income Distribution", OECD Social and Welfare Statistics (database).

Further information

Analytical publications
- Förster, M. (1994), "Measurement of Low Incomes and Poverty in a Perspective of International Comparisons", OECD Labour Market and Social Policy Occasional Papers, No. 14.
- OECD (2015), How's Life? Measuring Well-being, OECD Publishing.
- OECD (2015), In It Together: Why Less Inequality Benefits All, OECD Publishing.
- OECD (2011), Divided We Stand, Why Inequality Keeps Rising, OECD Publishing.
- OECD (2008), Growing Unequal?: Income Distribution and Poverty in OECD Countries, OECD Publishing.

Statistical publications
- OECD (2014), Society at a Glance: OECD Social Indicators, OECD Publishing.

Websites
- OECD Income Distribution Database (supplementary material), www.oecd.org/social/income-distribution-database.htm

Poverty rates and poverty gaps

2012 or latest available year

	Relative poverty rates (50% median income)				Poverty gap (mean)
	Entire population	Children (age 0-17)	Working-age population (age 18-65)	Retirement-age population (over 65)	Entire population
Australia	0.14	0.13	0.11	0.34	0.27
Austria	0.10	0.10	0.09	0.11	0.34
Belgium	0.10	0.11	0.10	0.11	0.23
Canada	0.12	0.14	0.12	0.07	0.30
Chile	0.18	0.24	0.15	0.21	0.33
Czech Republic	0.05	0.08	0.05	0.03	0.25
Denmark	0.05	0.03	0.07	0.05	0.31
Estonia	0.12	0.12	0.12	0.12	0.31
Finland	0.07	0.03	0.07	0.09	0.23
France	0.08	0.11	0.08	0.04	0.25
Germany	0.08	0.07	0.08	0.09	0.22
Greece	0.15	0.21	0.16	0.07	0.39
Hungary	0.10	0.17	0.10	0.06	0.31
Iceland	0.06	0.08	0.06	0.03	0.29
Ireland	0.08	0.09	0.09	0.07	0.30
Israel	0.18	0.25	0.15	0.21	0.35
Italy	0.13	0.18	0.12	0.09	0.41
Japan	0.16	0.16	0.14	0.33	0.33
Korea	0.15	0.09	0.10	0.49	0.39
Luxembourg	0.08	0.13	0.08	0.03	0.26
Mexico	0.19	0.23	0.16	0.27	0.38
Netherlands	0.08	0.10	0.08	0.02	0.31
New Zealand	0.10	0.13	0.09	0.08	0.23
Norway	0.08	0.06	0.10	0.04	0.37
Poland	0.10	0.13	0.10	0.08	0.27
Portugal	0.13	0.18	0.13	0.08	0.31
Slovak Republic	0.08	0.15	0.08	0.04	0.30
Slovenia	0.09	0.09	0.08	0.16	0.23
Spain	0.14	0.21	0.14	0.07	0.39
Sweden	0.09	0.08	0.09	0.09	0.26
Switzerland	0.09	0.08	0.06	0.23	0.24
Turkey	0.18	0.26	0.14	0.17	0.30
United Kingdom	0.11	0.10	0.10	0.13	0.33
United States	0.18	0.21	0.16	0.21	0.40
EU 28	0.10	0.12	0.10	0.08	0.29
OECD	0.11	0.13	0.10	0.13	0.31
Brazil	..	..	..	..	..
China	..	..	..	..	..
India	..	..	..	..	..
Indonesia	..	..	..	..	..
Russian Federation	0.14	0.19	..	..	0.27
South Africa	..	..	..	..	..

StatLink 🔗 http://dx.doi.org/10.1787/888933336319

Trends in poverty rates

Relative poverty rates in mid-1980s, mid-1990s and 2012 or latest available year

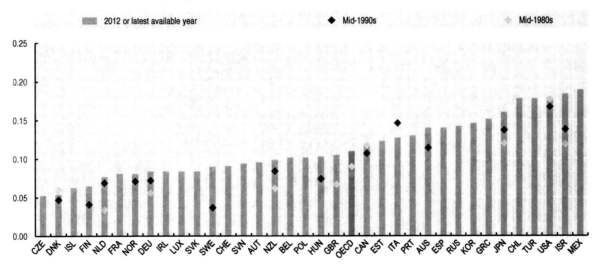

StatLink 🔗 http://dx.doi.org/10.1787/888933335124

HOUSEHOLD FINANCIAL ASSETS

Along with income, wealth is a key measure of households' economic resources. Households hold both non-financial and financial wealth. The structure of financial assets affects households financial risks as different types of securities carry different risk levels.

Definition

Household financial assets are classified according to the 2008 *System of National Accounts* (currency and deposits; debt securities; equity, investment funds shares; life insurance and annuity entitlements; and pension entitlements and entitlements to non-pension benefits). They relate to the households and the non-profit institutions serving households (NPISHs) sector. They exclude financial derivatives, loans and other accounts receivable.

The financial assets are classified according to their liquidity.

Comparability

International comparability may be hampered by differences in the way pension systems are organised and operated in the various countries. According to the 2008 SNA employment related pension entitlements that are expected or likely to be enforceable, are to be recognised as liabilities towards households regardless of whether the necessary assets exist in segregated schemes or not. However, for pensions provided by a government to their employees, countries have some flexibility in the recording of the unfunded liabilities, which may hamper comparability across countries.

Any changes in the stocks of financial assets over a period are the result of two components: net acquisitions of financial assets; and changes in valuations (holding gains and losses depending on the performance of financial markets), of which those for quoted shares are the most relevant.

Overview

The comparison of the structure of households' stocks of financial assets between 2008 and 2014 gives some insight into the impact of recent economic developments on the restructuring of their portfolio towards financial instruments better adapted to the new environment, i.e. more liquid and less risky. There is a slight decrease in the share of both currency and deposits, and debt securities for two-thirds of OECD countries over the period 2008-14. The largest decreases were recorded for Hungary and Italy (minus 8 percentage points) for currency and deposits and debt securities respectively. The share of life insurance remained relatively stable in a large number of OECD countries. On the other hand, the share of pension entitlements, equity, and investment fund shares became more popular in most OECD countries, the largest rise being observed in Greece (13 percentage points) for equity, and in the Netherlands (11 percentage points) for pension entitlements.

Considerable differences in national preferences for financial instruments can be observed across the OECD. Currency and deposits, the most liquid of the asset categories and also considered the one with the least risk, represented more than 50% in five OECD countries (the Czech Republic, Greece, Luxembourg, the Slovak Republic and Turkey) in 2014, and in Japan in 2013. The proportion of debt securities held by households was low in most OECD countries in 2014 with the exception of Italy (13%). Furthermore, despite the financial crisis, equity remained a predominant portfolio asset held by households in for example Estonia (53%), Finland (36%), and Sweden (35%). Household reserves in life insurance and pension funds represented more than half of the stock of total financial assets in the Netherlands (65%), Chile (62%), the United Kingdom (59%), Australia (56%) and Denmark (49%), whereas they remained at a very low level in Greece (3%).

Sources

- OECD (2015), "Financial Balance Sheets", *OECD National Accounts Statistics* (Database).

Further information

Analytical publications

- OECD (2015), *OECD Business and Finance Outlook*, OECD Publishing.
- OECD (2015), *OECD Economic Outlook*, OECD Publishing.
- Ynesta, I. (2009), "Households' Wealth Composition across OECD Countries and Financial Risks Borne by Households", *Financial Market Trends*, Vol. 2008/2.

Statistical publications

- OECD (2015), *National Accounts at a Glance*, OECD Publishing.
- OECD (2014), *National Accounts of OECD Countries, Financial Balance Sheets*, OECD Publishing.

Methodological publications

- Lequiller, F. and D. Blades (2014), *Understanding National Accounts: Second Edition*, OECD Publishing.
- OECD, et al. (eds.) (2010), *System of National Accounts 2008*, United Nations, Geneva.

Online databases

- OECD National Accounts Statistics.

Websites

- Financial statistics, *www.oecd.org/std/fin-stats*.

Financial assets of households by type of assets

As a percentage of total financial assets

	Currency and deposits		Debt securities		Equity		Investment funds shares		Life insurance and annuities		Pension funds	
	2008	2014	2008	2014	2008	2014	2008	2014	2008	2014	2008	2014
Australia	23.7	22.2	0.7	0.2	18.8	18.0	0.0	0.0	0.0	0.0	50.1	56.0
Austria	44.5	41.0	8.8	7.1	16.6	20.4	7.2	8.4	12.9	12.1	6.3	6.4
Belgium	30.3	30.5	10.0	6.5	23.0	25.8	12.4	12.4	14.7	15.0	6.3	6.7
Canada	26.6	23.3	3.2	1.8	16.2	19.2	15.0	18.0	..	..	..	..
Chile	14.4	13.7	0.0	0.0	26.0	17.9	4.2	5.4	13.0	12.7	41.9	49.8
Czech Republic	52.9	50.9	0.6	3.9	25.1	21.7	4.9	5.5	5.8	5.7	5.2	6.5
Denmark	21.3	16.4	4.9	1.6	20.9	23.6	5.3	7.3	24.5	27.8	20.2	21.3
Estonia	22.7	28.0	0.8	0.1	63.4	52.8	0.4	0.8	1.4	2.0	4.6	9.9
Finland	39.1	31.5	2.1	3.6	29.4	36.5	6.0	9.1	7.3	6.9	11.3	8.3
France	30.4	28.7	2.2	1.7	17.9	20.5	7.9	6.5	33.6	34.4	0.0	0.0
Germany	39.4	39.3	6.3	3.8	9.4	9.9	9.0	9.5	16.5	16.8	13.1	14.1
Greece	71.4	66.9	9.0	1.4	6.9	20.4	2.1	2.6	2.5	2.2	0.4	1.1
Hungary	37.5	29.1	5.6	8.4	26.9	29.0	6.9	10.7	5.2	4.6	10.0	3.6
Iceland	24.1	..	4.3	..	..	..	..	..	..	..	..	..
Ireland	42.7	36.9	0.1	0.1	16.2	13.7	0.0	0.0	15.0	16.2	22.0	28.5
Israel	27.4	..	17.6	..	10.2	..	0.0	..	9.2	..	29.4	..
Italy	29.2	31.5	21.3	13.4	24.4	22.0	6.0	9.7	9.1	13.2	5.7	6.3
Japan	53.7	..	4.3	..	6.4	..	3.2	..	14.5	..	13.8	..
Korea	..	42.0	..	5.8	..	15.6	..	3.7	..	21.1	..	3.8
Luxembourg	54.5	50.8	11.8	7.7	11.6	12.6	11.1	11.9	7.8	12.2	2.0	3.2
Mexico	..	..	..	..	..	..	..	..	..	..	..	..
Netherlands	22.7	19.6	1.8	0.5	12.0	8.1	3.1	2.9	10.4	8.4	45.8	56.9
New Zealand	..	..	..	..	..	..	..	..	..	..	..	..
Norway	29.4	28.6	0.8	0.4	21.2	21.5	3.2	4.1	4.2	3.2	24.1	27.1
Poland	46.4	46.7	1.0	0.3	19.6	18.6	5.6	6.0	7.0	4.8	15.1	10.2
Portugal	41.8	43.0	5.2	3.9	20.7	21.1	4.4	3.6	12.3	12.7	7.4	5.7
Slovak Republic	61.8	61.8	0.2	1.4	0.3	0.2	7.1	7.3	8.3	7.3	8.4	13.9
Slovenia	47.9	49.0	1.4	0.7	25.2	22.2	3.3	3.6	5.1	7.5	4.9	7.4
Spain	46.7	43.0	2.2	1.3	23.7	26.0	8.8	11.4	5.9	7.5	8.1	8.0
Sweden	16.4	14.3	2.5	1.4	29.5	35.0	7.2	8.3	14.2	9.5	27.5	29.6
Switzerland	28.8	..	9.4	..	9.3	..	8.9	..	5.6	..	34.6	..
Turkey	..	79.8	..	2.6	..	8.6	..	1.6	..	0.6	..	4.4
United Kingdom	28.1	24.0	1.4	1.7	7.3	7.0	2.5	4.2	12.6	10.4	43.3	48.5
United States	14.3	13.2	9.2	4.6	28.9	34.1	10.5	13.0	2.3	1.9	32.0	31.2
EU 28	..	..	..	..	..	..	..	..	..	..	..	..
OECD	..	..	..	..	..	..	..	..	..	..	..	..
Brazil	..	..	..	..	..	..	..	..	..	..	..	..
China	..	..	..	..	..	..	..	..	..	..	..	..
India	..	..	..	..	..	..	..	..	..	..	..	..
Indonesia	..	..	..	..	..	..	..	..	..	..	..	..
Russian Federation	..	..	..	..	..	..	..	..	..	..	..	..
South Africa	..	..	..	..	..	..	..	..	..	..	..	..

StatLink ᵇ http://dx.doi.org/10.1787/888933336294

Financial assets of households by type of assets

As a percentage of their total financial assets, 2014 or latest available year

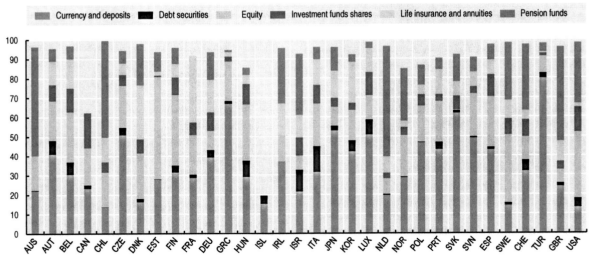

StatLink ᵇ http://dx.doi.org/10.1787/888933335102

HOUSEHOLD DEBT

The household debt ratio measures the indebtedness of households in relation to their income, that is their spending and saving capacity. High debt ratios are often interpreted as a sign of financial vulnerability though one should also take into account the availability of assets (e.g. dwellings) in such an assessment. High indebtedness levels generally increase the financing costs of the borrower, deteriorate balance sheet positions and may restrict access to new financing.

Definition

Debt is a commonly used concept, defined as a specific subset of liabilities identified according to the types of financial instruments included or excluded. Generally, debt is defined as all liabilities that require payment or payments of interest or principal by the debtor to the creditor at a date or dates in the future.

Consequently, all debt instruments are liabilities, but some liabilities such as equity and investment fund shares and financial derivatives are not considered as debt. Debt is thus obtained as the sum of the following liability categories, whenever available/applicable in the financial balance sheet of the households and non-profit institutions serving households (NPISHs) sector: monetary gold and Special Drawing Rights (SDRs), currency and deposits; debt securities; loans; insurance, pension, and standardised guarantees; and other accounts payable. For the households sector, liabilities predominantly consist of loans, and more particularly mortgage loans for the purchase of houses.

Comparability

As a number of OECD countries are not able to provide a breakdown between households and NPISHs, household debt refers to the aggregated sector "Households and NPISHs" to ensure the highest level of comparability between countries.

Overview

Households remain highly indebted in a large number of OECD economies. In 2013, the ratio of household debt to net disposable income (NDI) was far higher than the OECD average (134%), in Denmark, the Netherlands, Norway, Ireland, Australia and Switzerland. Hungary had the lowest debt ratio at 57% in 2013.

The level of household debt rose in most OECD countries over the period 2007-13. As a percentage of NDI, Greece recorded the largest increase during this period (around 31 percentage points). Belgium, Canada, the Netherlands and Poland showed increases of around 20 percentage points, followed by the Slovak Republic with 19 percentage points. A net fall of respectively 31 and 28 percentage points were observed in the United Kingdom and the United States, and to a lesser extent in Estonia, Spain and Ireland.

Long-term loans, mainly consisting of mortgage loans, remain the largest component of household debt, contributing more than 80% of the total household debt in twenty four OECD countries and even more than 90% in eighteen countries. In 2013, the highest levels were recorded in Estonia (98%) and Norway (97%) and the lowest ratios were observed in the United States (72%), and Korea (82%).

Sources
• OECD (2015), "Financial Balance Sheets", *OECD National Accounts Statistics* (Database).

Further information

Analytical publications
• OECD (2015), *Economic Policy Reforms*, OECD Publishing.
• OECD (2015), *OECD Economic Outlook*, OECD Publishing.
• OECD (2015), *OECD Economic Surveys*, OECD Publishing.
• Schich S. and J.-H. Ahn (2007), "Housing Markets and Household Debt: Short-term and Long-term Risks", *Financial Market Trends*, Vol. 2007/1.

Statistical publications
• OECD (2015), *National Accounts at a Glance*, OECD Publishing.
• OECD (2014), *National Accounts of OECD Countries, Financial Balance Sheets*, OECD Publishing.

Methodological publications
• Lequiller, F. and D. Blades (2014), *Understanding National Accounts: Second Edition*, OECD Publishing.
• OECD, et al. (eds.) (2010), *System of National Accounts 2008*, United Nations, Geneva.

Online databases
• OECD National Accounts Statistics.

Websites
• Financial statistics, *www.oecd.org/std/fin-stats*.

Household debt

Debt of households and non-profit institutions serving households, as a percentage of net disposable income

	2002	2003	2004	2005	2006	2007	2008	2009	2010	2011	2012	2013	2014
Australia	154.6	165.0	178.4	186.4	190.3	192.8	188.1	195.3	195.5	194.2	196.6	200.4	..
Austria	79.3	79.4	83.3	87.5	88.8	88.6	90.2	90.3	94.2	93.5	89.5	89.3	89.1
Belgium	68.3	70.7	74.6	79.5	83.3	87.4	89.8	90.8	96.0	102.4	104.2	107.3	111.9
Canada	114.4	119.4	124.8	132.1	135.2	143.4	148.4	157.4	160.2	161.5	163.1	163.8	166.1
Chile	..	..	..	..	..	..	58.9	57.2	57.5	57.2	56.8	57.9	..
Czech Republic	27.1	29.2	34.1	39.4	43.6	52.9	58.8	60.3	61.9	64.4	65.8	67.6	68.9
Denmark	242.9	248.7	261.9	282.1	299.4	324.7	339.4	338.7	325.1	319.5	314.6	313.0	313.3
Estonia	32.7	41.7	54.0	71.7	93.6	104.7	101.1	108.6	107.1	95.6	92.8	83.6	83.7
Finland	75.6	79.9	88.6	99.2	109.4	114.7	117.1	117.5	119.6	121.0	124.0	123.3	126.7
France	77.5	81.1	81.9	88.4	93.6	96.6	98.7	104.3	107.5	107.1	103.4	103.8	104.7
Germany	113.6	112.0	110.4	108.1	105.7	102.6	99.4	100.3	98.3	96.5	95.5	94.5	93.6
Greece	..	..	..	..	72.7	80.8	85.3	86.7	104.3	111.5	109.0	112.4	..
Hungary	27.0	35.8	41.2	47.1	53.8	62.2	76.1	76.6	81.1	74.5	63.1	57.1	54.4
Iceland	..	..	..	..	..	..	..	..	..	..	..	..	..
Ireland	125.3	146.1	168.7	199.0	223.2	233.3	227.1	235.6	231.3	230.3	221.9	214.1	..
Israel	..	..	..	..	..	..	..	..	..	..	..	..	..
Italy	59.4	62.5	66.2	71.3	76.1	80.2	81.6	86.5	90.4	89.9	92.0	90.6	90.1
Japan	139.5	138.1	137.4	137.9	137.3	133.6	132.2	132.4	131.9	128.3	127.1	129.2	..
Korea	..	..	..	..	..	..	..	..	..	157.8	159.4	160.3	164.2
Luxembourg	..	..	..	..	..	..	..	..	..	..	..	..	..
Mexico	..	..	..	..	..	..	..	..	..	..	..	..	..
Netherlands	204.4	222.9	233.0	251.5	256.9	261.4	274.3	286.6	293.9	287.8	288.4	280.9	273.6
New Zealand	..	..	..	..	..	..	..	..	..	..	..	..	..
Norway	147.8	151.4	161.6	167.4	199.2	207.9	207.6	207.0	212.1	216.8	220.2	221.9	223.9
Poland	..	19.7	21.6	25.0	31.2	39.2	51.5	52.8	57.2	60.7	58.6	59.5	..
Portugal	121.6	123.6	126.8	135.9	140.6	145.7	148.9	151.4	154.4	144.9	150.9	141.3	140.8
Slovak Republic	24.2	27.7	25.9	29.8	32.8	38.9	42.5	42.1	43.1	49.4	54.8	57.6	62.3
Slovenia	33.6	35.4	36.0	40.3	44.9	52.2	53.5	56.2	58.9	57.7	59.5	58.8	57.6
Spain	94.1	102.3	113.6	128.2	144.3	154.1	150.1	145.2	148.6	142.7	141.2	134.1	128.0
Sweden	121.6	128.2	137.0	146.7	153.8	157.4	159.5	163.5	170.7	168.5	167.1	169.7	173.4
Switzerland	173.3	182.5	184.2	188.2	187.6	182.1	180.4	184.0	189.3	194.0	196.0	197.4	..
Turkey	..	..	..	..	..	..	..	..	..	..	..	..	..
United Kingdom	138.8	151.6	164.9	167.2	178.9	183.3	178.2	167.5	158.7	159.1	153.7	152.0	155.7
United States	112.4	120.3	126.9	134.6	139.7	143.1	135.3	133.7	127.2	119.0	113.6	115.1	113.4
EU 28	..	..	..	..	..	..	..	..	..	..	..	..	..
OECD	..	..	..	..	..	..	..	..	..	..	..	..	..
Brazil	..	..	..	..	..	..	..	..	..	..	..	..	..
China	..	..	..	..	..	..	..	..	..	..	..	..	..
India	..	..	..	..	..	..	..	..	..	..	..	..	..
Indonesia	..	..	..	..	..	..	..	..	..	..	..	..	..
Russian Federation	..	..	..	..	..	..	..	..	..	..	..	..	..
South Africa	..	..	..	..	..	..	..	..	..	..	..	..	..

StatLink http://dx.doi.org/10.1787/888933336257

Households and NPISHs debt

As a percentage of net disposable income

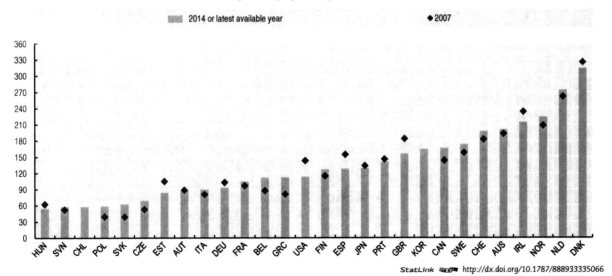

StatLink http://dx.doi.org/10.1787/888933335066

NON-FINANCIAL ASSETS OF HOUSEHOLDS

Non-financial assets held by households reflect the assets owned by unincorporated household enterprises and dwellings owned by households, with the latter representing by far the bulk of non-financial assets held by households. They form an important part of overall wealth and can provide an important additional source of revenue; either through their sale or refinancing, or as income via rentals of residential property for example. Estimates of non-financial assets held by households also play an important role in economic analyses, such as studies of asset bubbles, and analyses of living standards.

Definition

Non-financial assets held by households include, in theory, both produced and non-produced non-financial assets, i.e. dwellings, other buildings and structures and land improvements; machinery and equipment including livestock; and intellectual property products, such as software and literary originals, and non-produced assets such as land and taxi-licenses. In practice dwellings form by far the most significant component.

Except for dwellings, only those assets owned by household unincorporated enterprises, and used in production, are included as non-financial assets. For example a car used by a household purely for household transport is not a non-financial asset whereas a car used by a self-employed taxi driver is.

Non-financial assets are valued at the market prices at the time of the balance sheet, and are recorded net of depreciation.

Comparability

Information on non-financial assets held by households typically relies on household based surveys. As a consequence, the quality of this information, except for that pertaining to dwellings and land, is generally of lower quality than it is for similar information collected on incorporated businesses.

Moreover, in practice, countries use a variety of methods to differentiate between the value of dwellings and the land on which the dwellings sit, meaning that comparisons of these subcomponents across countries are challenging. Some countries include the value of land under dwellings within the figures for dwellings. This matters not only for international comparability but also because dwellings, as produced assets depreciate whereas land, as a non-produced asset, does not. A particular challenge arises from capturing quality change and quality differences in the housing stock and valuing it accordingly.

The caveats above, pertaining to the distinction between land and dwellings, mean that users should be particularly careful in using the figures in making international comparisons. The OECD is working with national statistics institutes so that future versions of these data reflect a greater degree of international comparability.

Data are assets net of depreciation for all countries except for the Slovak Republic and Poland (gross recording).

Overview

The non-financial assets of households in dwellings constitute a large share of household wealth. This indicator is of particular interest since the financial crisis because it may indicate risks of a speculative bubble.

In most OECD countries dwelling values per capita have grown steadily since 2010. In contrast, dwelling values per capita have fallen since 2010 in the Netherlands. The Netherland's land values have also exhibited sizable declines in recent years (minus 10% in 2012 and minus 9.7% in 2013).

Only nine OECD countries currently provide data on land. For those countries reporting data the value of the land exceeds that of dwellings in 5 of them in 2013.

Sources
- OECD (2015), *National Accounts of OECD Countries*, OECD Publishing.

Further information

Analytical publications
- Babeau, A. and T. Sbano (2003), "Household Wealth in the National Accounts of Europe, the United States and Japan", *OECD Statistics Working Papers*, No. 2003/02.
- OECD (2015), *Economic Policy Reforms*, OECD Publishing.

Statistical publications
- OECD (2015), *National Accounts at a Glance*, OECD Publishing.

Methodological publications
- OECD, et al. (eds.) (2010), *System of National Accounts 2008*, United Nations, Geneva.

Online databases
- OECD National Accounts Statistics.

Websites
- National accounts, *www.oecd.org/std/na*.

Non-financial assets of households
US dollars at current PPPs, per capita

	Dwellings				Land				Other			
	2010	2011	2012	2013	2010	2011	2012	2013	2010	2011	2012	2013
Australia	44 748	45 479	46 291	47 711	92 678	86 630	89 250	98 839	16 627	16 661	16 971	17 278
Austria	48 602	50 804	52 312	53 533	..	..	..	..	..	..	..	..
Belgium	49 853	51 629	53 280	53 408	..	..	..	..	..	..	..	..
Canada	38 617	39 560	41 261	42 163	35 659	37 687	39 448	43 026	1 869	1 903	1 827	1 843
Chile	12 976	13 930	13 998	14 504	..	..	..	..	..	..	..	..
Czech Republic	26 575	28 554	28 226	28 410	7 549	8 044	8 139	8 267	5 568	6 440	6 579	6 626
Denmark	37 431	41 738	42 083	42 153	..	..	..	..	..	..	..	..
Estonia	23 446	24 609	24 213		..	..	..	..	..	..	..	..
Finland	42 709	45 142	47 617	48 108	21 335	22 256	22 850	23 239	..	..	..	..
France	55 254	58 282	58 939	59 891	63 576	66 525	62 926	60 568	7 194	7 408	7 202	7 033
Germany	53 494	56 475	58 551	59 648	..	..	..	..	..	..	..	..
Greece	44 516	44 514	44 676		..	..	..	..	..	..	..	..
Hungary	24 321	24 993	24 991	..	..	..	..	..	..	..	..	..
Iceland	..	..	..	..	..	..	..	..	..	..	..	..
Ireland	..	..	..	..	..	..	..	..	..	..	..	..
Israel	26 791	28 532	30 052	31 037	..	..	..	..	..	..	..	..
Italy	49 145	52 164	53 517	54 618	..	..	..	..	..	..	..	..
Japan	21 083	21 645	21 985	22 850	52 882	53 479	54 129	53 928	4 550	4 601	4 649	4 684
Korea	23 117	23 927	24 402	25 329	72 576	76 634	78 033	78 994	9 086	9 511	9 414	9 370
Luxembourg	46 548	48 939	49 958	49 768	..	..	..	..	..	..	..	..
Mexico	..	..	..	..	..	..	..	..	..	..	..	..
Netherlands	53 266	53 003	51 881	50 849	53 982	54 145	48 740	43 999	..	..	..	..
New Zealand	..	..	..	..	..	..	..	..	..	..	..	..
Norway	..	..	..	..	..	..	..	..	..	..	..	..
Poland	5 626	5 775	5 895		..	..	..	..	..	..	..	..
Portugal	..	..	..	..	..	..	..	..	..	..	..	..
Slovak Republic	31 836	32 296	32 767	33 865	..	..	..	..	..	..	..	..
Slovenia	28 367	29 519	30 440	..	..	..	..	..	..	..	..	..
Spain	..	..	..	..	..	..	..	..	..	..	..	..
Sweden	29 677	30 534	31 134		..	..	..	..	..	..	..	..
Switzerland	..	..	..	..	..	..	..	..	..	..	..	..
Turkey	..	..	..	..	..	..	..	..	..	..	..	..
United Kingdom	..	..	..	..	..	..	..	..	..	..	..	..
United States	50 256	50 218	51 190	54 214	33 460	33 785	39 144	46 095	..	..	..	..
EU 28	..	..	..	..	..	..	..	..	..	..	..	..
OECD	..	..	..	..	..	..	..	..	..	..	..	..
Brazil	..	..	..	..	..	..	..	..	..	..	..	..
China	..	..	..	..	..	..	..	..	..	..	..	..
India	..	..	..	..	..	..	..	..	..	..	..	..
Indonesia	..	..	..	..	..	..	..	..	..	..	..	..
Russian Federation	..	..	..	..	..	..	..	..	..	..	..	..
South Africa	..	..	..	..	..	..	..	..	..	..	..	..

StatLink http://dx.doi.org/10.1787/888933336271

Non-financial assets of households per capita: dwellings
US dollars at current PPPs

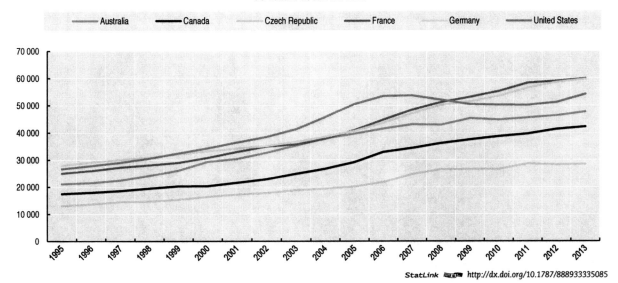

StatLink http://dx.doi.org/10.1787/888933335085

GLOBALISATION

SHARE OF INTERNATIONAL TRADE IN GDP

In today's increasingly globalised world, exports and imports are key aggregates in the analysis of a country's economic situation. Whenever an economy slows down or accelerates, all other economies are potentially affected through trade linkages.

Definition

Exports of goods and services consist of sales, barter or gifts or grants, of goods and services (included in the production boundary of GDP) from residents to non-residents. Equally, imports reflect the same transactions from non-residents to residents.

Not all goods need to physically enter a country's border to be recorded as an export or import. Transportation equipment, goods produced by residents in international waters sold directly to non-residents, and food consumed in ships or planes are but a few examples of transactions which may be recorded as exports or imports without physically crossing borders.

Equally not all goods that enter a country's borders are necessarily imports or exports. Transportation equipment, goods sent abroad for minor processing (or which enter and leave a country in their original state and ownership) are examples of goods that cross borders but are not recorded as imports or exports.

Comparability

Goods (merchandise trade) reflect the bulk of import and exports, and these are generally well covered and afford good comparability across countries; although discrepancies between total imports and exports of traded goods at the global level reveal that measurement in practice is not trivial. Growth in trade through the Internet has increased measurement difficulties.

The comparability of trade in services is more affected by practical measurement issues however; even if the conceptual approach, as it is for goods, is the same for all OECD countries.

Increases in outsourcing, merchanting, processing services and transactions in intellectual property, such as software and artistic originals, have increased the difficulties inherent in the measurement of trade in services.

Overview

International trade measured as the ratio of exports and imports to GDP increased for almost all OECD countries in 2010 and 2011, following sharp declines during the financial crisis. For 2010 and 2011, exports and imports as a share of GDP increased by more than 2 percentage points for the OECD total. The GDP ratio for imports fell in 15 countries in 2012 and fell even further in 2013 and 2014 for many OECD countries reflecting a weak demand for imported products as many economies slowed. However, the GDP ratio for exports also fell in 2012-14 but fewer countries saw declines as compared to the drops in the import share.

Looking at the balance of exports and imports in 2014, Luxembourg shows the largest surplus at 32.4% of GDP. Other countries showing a surplus greater than 10% are Ireland, the Netherlands and Switzerland, whereas Norway, Slovenia, Hungary, Germany, the Czech Republic, Iceland, Denmark and Korea have trade surpluses of more than 5% of GDP. On the other hand Turkey, Japan, the United States and Greece have deficits of more than 2% of GDP.

Sources
• OECD (2015), *National Accounts of OECD Countries*, OECD Publishing.

Further information

Analytical publications
• OECD (2012), *Policy Priorities for International Trade and Jobs*, OECD Publishing.
• OECD (2011), *Globalisation, Comparative Advantage and the Changing Dynamics of Trade*, OECD Publishing.

Statistical publications
• OECD (2015), *International Trade by Commodity Statistics*, OECD Publishing.
• OECD (2014), *OECD Statistics on International Trade in Services*, OECD Publishing.
• OECD (2014), *National Accounts at a Glance*, OECD Publishing.

Methodological publications
• OECD, et al. (2010), *Manual on Statistics of International Trade in Services*, United Nations.

Websites
• International Trade and Balance of Payments Statistics, *www.oecd.org/std/its*.

International trade in goods and services

As a percentage of GDP

	Imports						Exports					
	2009	2010	2011	2012	2013	2014	2009	2010	2011	2012	2013	2014
Australia	20.4	20.1	21.5	21.1	21.3	21.2	19.5	21.2	21.3	19.9	20.9	20.8
Austria	41.9	47.7	51.2	51.2	50.2	49.5	44.9	51.0	53.7	53.8	53.2	53.2
Belgium	67.0	74.7	81.1	81.7	80.9	83.1	69.3	76.4	81.6	82.3	82.2	84.0
Canada	29.9	31.0	31.8	32.1	31.8	32.5	28.4	29.1	30.6	30.2	30.2	31.6
Chile	29.6	31.7	34.9	34.5	33.1	32.3	37.2	38.1	38.1	34.3	32.4	33.8
Czech Republic	54.9	63.1	67.7	71.7	71.5	77.1	58.8	66.2	71.6	76.6	77.3	83.8
Denmark	42.4	43.6	47.4	48.6	48.5	48.3	46.7	49.7	52.9	54.0	54.3	53.7
Estonia	55.8	68.7	80.8	85.6	84.6	80.5	60.8	75.1	86.5	86.6	86.8	83.9
Finland	34.3	37.4	40.0	40.9	39.8	38.7	36.3	38.7	39.2	39.5	39.0	37.9
France	25.5	27.9	30.4	30.7	30.4	30.5	24.1	26.0	27.8	28.5	28.5	28.7
Germany	32.9	37.1	39.9	39.9	39.5	39.0	37.8	42.3	44.8	46.0	45.5	45.7
Greece	28.8	30.7	32.3	33.1	33.4	35.2	19.0	22.1	25.5	28.7	30.6	32.7
Hungary	70.8	77.0	81.1	80.1	80.7	82.0	74.8	82.3	87.2	86.8	88.0	89.3
Iceland	40.8	43.5	48.6	50.9	47.7	47.4	49.8	53.7	56.6	57.0	55.7	53.6
Ireland	80.1	87.1	83.3	90.0	87.4	95.4	93.6	103.1	101.2	107.2	106.7	113.7
Israel	30.4	32.8	35.4	35.6	31.4	30.6	33.3	35.0	36.1	36.9	33.2	32.3
Italy	23.1	27.1	28.6	27.6	26.5	26.5	22.5	25.2	27.0	28.6	28.9	29.6
Japan	12.3	14.0	16.0	16.7	19.0	20.8	12.7	15.2	15.1	14.7	16.2	17.7
Korea	42.9	46.2	54.3	53.5	48.9	45.3	47.5	49.4	55.7	56.3	53.9	50.6
Luxembourg	136.5	147.1	154.8	158.9	161.9	170.9	166.5	179.0	185.6	189.2	195.6	203.3
Mexico	28.8	31.1	32.6	33.8	32.7	33.5	27.3	29.9	31.3	32.7	31.8	32.6
Netherlands	55.8	63.6	68.8	72.3	71.6	71.5	63.2	72.0	77.4	81.9	82.6	82.9
New Zealand	26.6	28.2	29.2	28.5	27.6	27.4	29.0	30.5	30.8	29.2	29.3	29.2
Norway	27.9	28.6	28.5	27.7	28.6	29.6	39.2	39.8	41.3	40.6	38.8	38.3
Poland	38.3	42.1	44.5	44.9	44.4	46.2	37.6	40.0	42.5	44.4	46.3	47.4
Portugal	34.0	37.4	38.6	38.2	38.5	39.7	27.1	29.9	34.3	37.7	39.5	40.0
Slovak Republic	69.3	78.0	86.2	88.1	89.6	88.2	67.8	76.6	85.3	91.8	93.8	91.9
Slovenia	55.4	62.9	68.5	69.1	69.3	68.7	57.2	64.3	70.4	73.3	75.2	76.5
Spain	23.8	26.8	29.2	29.1	28.7	30.1	22.7	25.5	28.9	30.6	32.0	32.5
Sweden	38.7	40.7	42.0	41.4	39.3	40.8	44.5	46.2	46.7	46.3	43.8	44.5
Switzerland	49.9	53.5	57.3	56.9	60.2	53.0	57.4	64.2	65.8	67.3	72.3	64.3
Turkey	24.4	26.8	32.6	31.5	32.2	32.2	23.3	21.2	24.0	26.3	25.6	27.7
United Kingdom	29.2	31.3	32.3	32.2	32.0	30.3	26.8	28.6	30.7	30.1	30.0	28.4
United States	13.8	15.8	17.3	17.1	16.6	16.6	11.0	12.4	13.6	13.6	13.6	13.5
Euro area	33.4	37.5	40.4	40.9	40.5	40.7	34.8	38.9	41.8	43.6	43.9	44.5
EU 28	33.8	37.6	40.3	40.6	40.2	40.2	34.8	38.5	41.4	42.6	42.9	43.0
OECD	24.3	27.0	29.4	29.3	29.0	29.1	24.0	26.3	28.3	28.7	28.7	28.9
Brazil	11.3	11.8	12.2	..	..	..	10.9	10.7	11.5	..	..	..
China	22.3	25.6	25.9	24.5	23.8	..	26.7	29.4	28.5	27.3	26.2	..
India	25.0	..	..	..	..	..	19.8	..	..	..	..	..
Indonesia	21.1	22.4	23.9	25.0	24.8	24.5	23.6	24.3	26.3	24.6	24.0	23.7
Russian Federation	20.5	21.1	21.7	22.3	22.7	22.9	27.9	29.2	30.3	29.5	28.6	30.0
South Africa	27.5	27.4	29.6	31.0	33.2	33.1	27.9	28.6	30.4	29.7	31.0	31.3

StatLink http://dx.doi.org/10.1787/888933336720

International imports and exports in goods and services

As percentage of GDP, 2014 or latest available year

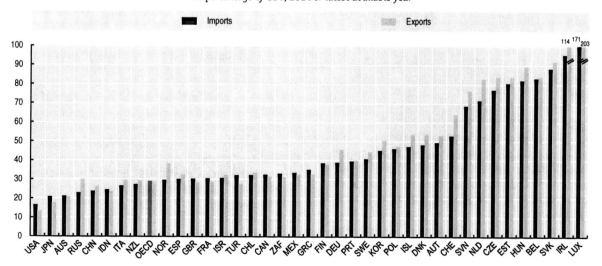

StatLink http://dx.doi.org/10.1787/888933335659

INTERNATIONAL MERCHANDISE TRADE

For the majority of countries, international merchandise trade flows have grown steadily over the long term. However, in the recent years since the economic crisis, trade growth has remained flat, raising questions about the role of international trade as a driver of growth, and whether the slowdown is structural or pro-cyclical.

Definition

According to United Nations guidelines, international merchandise trade statistics record all goods which add to, or subtract from, the stock of material resources of a country by entering (as imports) or leaving (as exports) its economic territory. Goods being transported through a country or temporarily admitted or withdrawn (except for goods for inward or outward processing) are not included in merchandise trade statistics.

All OECD countries use the United Nations guidelines to the extent that their data sources allow. There are some, generally minor, differences across countries in the coverage of certain types of transactions such as postal trade, imports and exports of military equipment under defence agreements, sea products traded by domestic vessels on the high seas and goods entering or leaving bonded customs areas.

Overview

For a substantial number of OECD countries, notably in Europe, total imports in 2014 (in current US dollars) were below those recorded in 2011, reflecting a combination of an appreciating US dollar, lower oil prices, and weak domestic demand. In the United States and the United Kingdom, merchandise imports grew, but only modestly compared to earlier periods.

Merchandise exports likewise remained stable in the recent years. Petroleum exporters such as Brazil and Russia, saw their trade values decline, especially in 2014, in light of the drop in oil prices. In contrast, the European countries most severely affected by the crisis (Greece, Spain, Portugal and Italy) noted modest merchandise trade growth rates since 2010.

Overall, the merchandise trade balance deteriorated in several OECD countries in recent years, for instance in the United States, the United Kingdom, France and Turkey. However, Germany, Korea, the Netherlands, China and Russia have continued to run a merchandise trade surplus.

The Japanese merchandise trade balance has deteriorated sharply since 2011, resulting in annual trade deficits for these years after 30 years of surpluses. This reversal is related to the rise in energy imports in the aftermath of the tsunami and earthquake in 2011.

Comparability

Exports are usually valued free on board (f.o.b.), with the exception of the United States which values exports free alongside ship (f.a.s.), which is lower than f.o.b. by the cost of loading the goods on board. Imports are valued by most countries at cost, insurance and freight (c.i.f.) i.e. the cost of the goods plus the costs of insurance and freight to bring the goods to the borders of the importing country. Canada, however, reports imports at f.o.b. values.

The introduction by the European Union of the single market in 1993 resulted in a loss of accuracy for intra-EU trade because custom documents were no longer available to record all imports and exports. Note that while the OECD data mostly follow the UN recommendations, trade statistics reported by Eurostat follow Community definitions, and are not strictly comparable.

The OECD aggregate includes all 34 members only from 1999. The EU28 aggregate excludes Croatia.

Sources
- OECD (2015), *International Trade by Commodity Statistics*, OECD Publishing.
- United Nations (2013), *United Nations Commodity Trade Statistics* (Database).

Further information

Analytical publications
- OECD (2011), *Globalisation, Comparative Advantage and the Changing Dynamics of Trade*, OECD Publishing.
- OECD (2006), *Aid for Trade: Making it Effective*, The Development Dimension, OECD Publishing.

Statistical publications
- OECD (2014), *Monthly Statistics of International Trade*, OECD Publishing.

Methodological publications
- OECD (2015), *International Trade by Commodity Statistics*, OECD Publishing.
- United Nations, *et al.* (2011), *International Merchandise Trade Statistics: Concepts and Definitions (IMTS 2010)*, United Nations.

Online databases
- *International Trade by Commodity Statistics.*
- *Monthly Statistics of International Trade.*

Websites
- International Trade and Balance of Payments Statistics, *www.oecd.org/std/its.*

International trade in goods
Billion US dollars

	Trade balance				Imports				Exports			
	2000	2005	2010	2014	2000	2005	2010	2014	2000	2005	2010	2014
Australia	-4.0	-12.8	18.6	12.9	67.8	118.9	193.3	227.5	63.8	106.0	211.8	240.4
Austria	-5.2	-2.2	-5.7	-2.7	67.4	120.0	150.6	172.4	62.3	117.7	144.9	169.7
Belgium	10.8	13.8	21.0	19.4	177.0	320.2	390.1	452.8	187.8	334.0	411.1	472.2
Canada	37.6	46.1	-5.5	10.9	240.0	314.4	392.1	462.0	277.6	360.6	386.6	472.9
Chile	1.6	9.0	11.5	4.3	16.6	32.9	59.4	72.3	18.2	42.0	70.9	76.6
Czech Republic	-3.2	1.7	6.5	21.1	32.2	76.5	125.7	153.2	29.1	78.2	132.1	174.3
Denmark	5.2	8.3	12.3	11.2	44.4	75.0	84.5	99.6	49.6	83.3	96.8	110.7
Estonia	-1.2	-2.8	-0.4	-2.5	5.1	11.0	13.2	20.1	3.8	8.2	12.8	17.6
Finland	11.6	6.8	1.4	-2.4	33.9	58.5	68.8	76.8	45.5	65.2	70.1	74.3
France	-8.5	-41.6	-87.5	-93.2	304.0	476.0	599.2	659.9	295.6	434.4	511.7	566.7
Germany	54.8	197.3	204.3	287.3	495.4	779.8	1 066.8	1 223.8	550.2	977.1	1 271.1	1 511.1
Greece	-18.8	-37.4	-41.8	-26.4	29.8	54.9	63.3	62.2	11.0	17.5	21.6	35.8
Hungary	-4.0	-3.6	7.3	9.2	32.1	65.9	87.4	103.2	28.1	62.3	94.7	112.4
Iceland	-0.7	-1.9	0.7	-0.3	2.6	5.0	3.9	5.4	1.9	3.1	4.6	5.1
Ireland	25.6	39.7	57.8	47.2	50.6	70.3	60.5	71.0	76.3	110.0	118.3	118.3
Israel	-4.3	-2.3	-0.8	-3.4	35.7	45.0	59.2	72.3	31.4	42.8	58.4	69.0
Italy	1.9	-11.9	-39.9	56.7	238.1	384.8	486.6	471.7	239.9	373.0	446.8	528.4
Japan	99.6	79.1	75.7	-138.4	379.7	515.9	694.1	822.3	479.2	594.9	769.8	683.8
Korea	11.8	23.2	41.2	47.5	160.5	261.2	425.2	525.6	172.3	284.4	466.4	573.1
Luxembourg	-2.8	-4.9	-6.5	-9.2	10.6	17.6	20.4	23.9	7.9	12.7	13.9	14.7
Mexico	-13.1	-7.6	-3.2	-2.9	179.4	221.8	301.5	400.0	166.3	214.2	298.3	397.1
Netherlands	5.4	36.9	52.7	63.3	174.7	283.2	440.0	508.0	180.1	320.1	492.6	571.3
New Zealand	-0.6	-4.5	0.8	-0.9	13.9	26.2	30.2	42.5	13.3	21.7	30.9	41.6
Norway	25.5	48.3	54.1	53.7	34.4	55.5	77.3	89.2	59.9	103.8	131.4	142.8
Poland	-17.2	-12.2	-17.1	-2.2	48.8	101.5	174.1	216.7	31.6	89.4	157.1	214.5
Portugal	-15.6	-23.1	-26.5	-14.2	39.9	61.2	75.2	78.1	24.4	38.1	48.8	64.0
Slovak Republic	-0.9	-2.4	-0.4	4.6	12.7	34.2	64.4	81.4	11.8	31.9	64.0	86.0
Slovenia	-1.4	-1.7	-2.2	0.5	10.1	19.6	26.4	30.0	8.7	17.9	24.2	30.5
Spain	-39.5	-96.8	-70.6	-32.3	152.9	289.6	318.2	351.0	113.3	192.8	247.6	318.6
Sweden	14.2	18.9	9.6	1.9	73.1	111.4	148.8	162.5	87.4	130.3	158.4	164.3
Switzerland	-2.0	4.4	19.3	36.1	82.5	126.6	176.3	275.1	80.5	130.9	195.6	311.1
Turkey	-26.7	-43.3	-71.6	-84.5	54.5	116.8	185.5	242.2	27.8	73.5	114.0	157.7
United Kingdom	-56.6	-131.4	-156.6	-183.2	339.4	515.8	562.4	694.3	282.9	384.4	405.8	511.1
United States	-477.7	-828.0	-689.4	-726.3	1 258.1	1 732.3	1 966.5	2 346.0	780.3	904.3	1 277.1	1 619.7
EU 28	..	-155.4	-231.2	..	..	1 465.5	2 026.9	..	..	1 310.1	1 795.8	..
OECD	-398.4	-738.8	-630.7	-637.3	4 898.0	7 499.6	9 590.9	11 295.0	4 499.5	6 760.7	8 960.2	10 657.7
Brazil	-0.7	44.9	16.9	-4.0	55.9	73.6	180.5	229.1	55.1	118.5	197.4	225.1
China	24.1	102.0	181.8	384.3	225.1	660.0	1 396.0	1 958.0	249.2	762.0	1 577.8	2 342.3
India	-10.6	-40.5	-129.6	-141.8	52.9	140.9	350.0	459.4	42.4	100.4	220.4	317.5
Indonesia	28.6	28.0	22.1	-2.1	33.5	57.7	135.7	178.2	62.1	85.7	157.8	176.0
Russian Federation	69.2	142.7	168.2	211.2	33.9	98.7	228.9	286.6	103.1	241.5	397.1	497.8
South Africa	-0.5	-8.0	-0.3	-9.3	26.8	55.0	82.9	99.9	26.3	47.0	82.6	90.6

StatLink http://dx.doi.org/10.1787/888933336374

Evolution of the merchandise trade balance
Annual growth rate in percentage

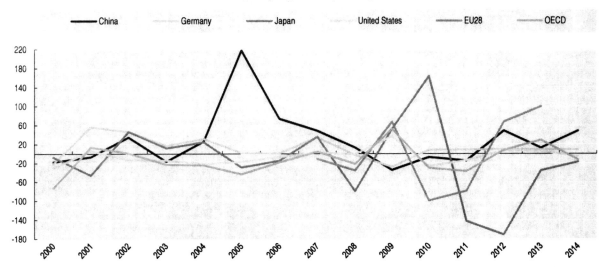

—— China —— Germany —— Japan —— United States —— EU28 —— OECD

StatLink http://dx.doi.org/10.1787/888933335205

INTERNATIONAL TRADE IN SERVICES

International trade in services is growing in importance both among OECD countries and in the rest of the world. Traditional services – transport, insurance on merchandise trade, and travel – account for about half of international trade in services, but trade in newer types of services, particularly those that can be conducted via the Internet, is growing rapidly.

Definition

International trade in services is defined according to the International Monetary Fund (IMF) *Balance of Payments and International Investment Manual* as well as by the *Manual on Statistics on International Trade in Services*. Services include: manufacturing services on physical inputs owned by others; maintenance and repair services n.i.e.; transport; travel (mainly expenditure on goods and services by tourists and business travellers); construction; insurance and pension services; financial services; charges for the use of intellectual property n.i.e.; telecommunications, computer and information services; other business services (research and development services, operational leasing, technical and professional services, etc.); personal cultural and recreational services (rents for films, fees for actors and other performers, but excluding purchases of films, recorded music, books, etc.); and government goods and services n.i.e.

Comparability

Almost all OECD countries now report international trade in services broadly according to the *Balance of Payments and International Investment Manual, Sixth Edition* (BPM6) framework.

Two recent changes introduced with BPM6 are worth highlighting here.

A stricter application of the change of ownership principle means that that goods sent abroad for processing are excluded from exports and imports in the goods accounts. Instead, the exchange of processing fees is recorded under services in the economies concerned: the outward processing economy recording payment of fees as imports of services, the inward processing economy recording the receipt of fees as exports of services.

To improve consistency on international merchandise and services trade statistics, purchase of goods under merchanting arrangements are registered as negative exports with subsequent sales registered as exports; the difference reflecting the merchanting margin, with all transactions recorded on the goods account. Previously the margin was recorded on the services account.

Both changes create differences between the balance of payments goods statistics and merchandise trade statistics.

Overview

Between 2010 and 2014 international trade in services in the OECD area grew significantly (imports by 22% and exports by 24%) despite the backdrop of slow global economic growth and low growth in merchandise trade. The United States, by some distance in 2014, was the largest exporter of international trade in services at 710.6 million USD, followed by the United Kingdom (361.7 million USD), Germany (277.7 million USD) and France (276.0 million USD). China, (232.0 million USD) emerged as the fifth largest exporter in the word, following a near doubling (up 97%) since 2010.

Measuring exports of international trade in services as a percentage of total exports in international trade in services and goods provides a picture of the relative importance of services in international trade. Amongst larger OECD countries, the percentage increased significantly, for example, in the United Kingdom (from around 30% in 1999 to just over 40% in 2014). Although growth in other major economies was less dramatic, this in part reflects the increasing services content of goods exports, and the growing knowledge content of goods, i.e. an increased blurring between goods and services.

Sources
- OECD (2015), *Main Economic Indicators*, OECD Publishing.
- OECD (2014), *OECD Statistics on International Trade in Services*, OECD Publishing.

Further information

Analytical publications
- OECD (2012), *Strategic Transport Infrastructure Needs to 2030*, OECD Publishing.

Statistical publications
- OECD (2015), *International Trade by Commodity Statistics*, OECD Publishing.

Methodological publications
- OECD, et al. (2010), *Manual on Statistics of International Trade in Services*, United Nations.

Websites
- International trade and balance of payments statistics, *www.oecd.org/std/trade-services*.
- Services Trade Restrictiveness Index (STRI), *www.oecd.org/trade/stri*.

International trade in services
Billion US dollars

	Trade balance				Imports				Exports			
	2000	2010	2013	2014	2000	2010	2013	2014	2000	2010	2013	2014
Australia	0.6	-4.9	-14.5	-9.4	19.3	51.5	68.0	63.5	19.9	46.6	53.4	54.2
Austria	..	13.7	13.5	13.9	..	38.8	51.0	53.3	..	52.5	64.5	67.3
Belgium	1.9	10.8	8.5	6.9	35.5	87.7	104.0	117.0	37.4	98.4	112.5	123.9
Canada	-2.8	-21.5	-22.6	-21.2	43.0	98.4	112.6	107.9	40.2	76.9	90.1	86.7
Chile	..	-1.9	-3.4	-3.8	..	13.0	15.9	14.7	..	11.1	12.5	11.0
Czech Republic	4.2	4.1	3.6	2.7	5.6	17.8	20.4	22.5	9.8	21.9	24.0	25.1
Denmark	..	6.8	8.8	10.6	..	54.7	62.4	62.3	..	61.5	71.2	72.8
Estonia	0.7	1.8	1.8	2.2	0.9	2.9	4.7	4.8	1.6	4.7	6.5	7.1
Finland	-1.8	0.2	-1.9	-2.4	10.1	28.8	31.5	30.5	8.3	29.0	29.6	28.1
France	12.1	20.4	29.7	23.7	84.8	181.7	226.6	252.3	96.9	202.1	256.4	276.0
Germany	-53.8	-36.4	-59.4	-53.0	137.0	263.3	326.0	330.8	83.2	226.9	266.6	277.7
Greece	..	16.1	20.9	24.2	..	21.7	16.3	17.0	..	37.8	37.2	41.2
Hungary	2.5	3.5	5.3	6.8	4.9	15.9	17.3	17.9	7.4	19.4	22.6	24.7
Iceland	0.0	0.8	1.2	1.2	1.1	2.2	2.8	3.1	1.1	3.0	4.0	4.3
Ireland	..	-19.5	-2.1	-11.7	..	109.6	123.6	145.1	..	90.2	121.5	133.4
Israel	3.9	6.6	13.6	12.9	12.3	18.8	20.8	22.5	16.3	25.4	34.5	35.4
Italy	0.6	-12.1	0.9	-1.7	58.7	113.1	110.8	115.8	59.3	101.0	111.7	114.1
Japan	-48.8	-30.3	-35.5	-29.3	118.2	164.7	170.9	192.3	69.4	134.4	135.2	163.2
Korea	-1.0	-14.2	-6.5	-8.2	33.6	97.5	110.2	115.0	32.7	83.3	103.7	106.9
Luxembourg	7.2	16.8	21.6	22.9	13.7	45.6	67.4	77.1	20.9	62.4	89.0	99.9
Mexico	-3.6	-10.6	-11.0	-12.5	17.1	25.8	31.2	33.5	13.5	15.2	20.2	21.1
Netherlands	..	-9.8	-7.3	-4.9	..	134.5	151.9	159.9	..	124.6	144.6	155.0
New Zealand	0.7	1.3	0.8	1.2	4.5	10.3	12.6	13.2	5.2	11.6	13.5	14.4
Norway	..	-1.1	-7.7	-6.7	..	42.8	56.4	56.1	..	41.7	48.7	49.4
Poland	..	4.4	10.1	11.4	..	31.1	34.5	36.8	..	35.5	44.6	48.1
Portugal	2.9	8.6	14.7	15.2	6.4	14.3	14.5	16.1	9.4	22.8	29.2	31.3
Slovak Republic	..	-0.9	0.5	0.1	..	7.3	8.6	9.0	..	6.4	9.1	9.1
Slovenia	0.6	1.6	2.3	2.3	1.7	4.6	4.7	5.1	2.4	6.2	7.1	7.4
Spain	19.9	44.9	63.3	64.3	33.0	68.2	63.2	68.4	53.0	113.1	126.4	132.7
Sweden	-3.9	6.9	12.3	9.2	24.6	47.4	60.7	65.9	20.7	54.3	73.0	75.1
Switzerland	15.2	25.5	22.0	20.0	30.7	69.3	92.4	98.6	45.9	94.8	114.4	118.5
Turkey	11.3	16.6	22.8	25.2	8.1	19.6	23.8	25.4	19.4	36.2	46.6	50.6
United Kingdom	20.1	83.9	126.6	146.1	103.6	185.1	209.2	215.6	123.7	269.0	335.8	361.7
United States	74.3	154.0	224.2	233.1	216.1	409.3	463.7	477.4	290.4	563.3	687.9	710.6
EU 28	..	..	..	..	..	..	..	..	..	..	..	..
OECD	..	286.1	457.2	491.3	..	2 497.2	2 890.8	3 046.5	..	2 783.4	3 347.8	3 537.9
Brazil	..	-30.0	-46.2	-48.1	..	60.8	84.4	88.1	..	30.8	38.2	40.0
China	..	-23.4	-123.5	-151.0	..	140.9	330.4	383.0	..	117.5	206.9	232.0
India	..	42.5	70.5	75.9	..	81.4	78.1	80.4	..	123.9	148.6	156.3
Indonesia	..	-9.8	-12.1	-10.0	..	26.5	35.0	33.5	..	16.7	22.9	23.5
Russian Federation	-5.0	-26.1	-58.3	-55.3	16.3	75.3	128.4	121.0	11.3	49.2	70.1	65.7
South Africa	-0.8	-4.5	..	..	5.8	18.5			5.0	14.0		

StatLink http://dx.doi.org/10.1787/888933336643

Exports of services as a percentage of total exports of goods and services
Percentage

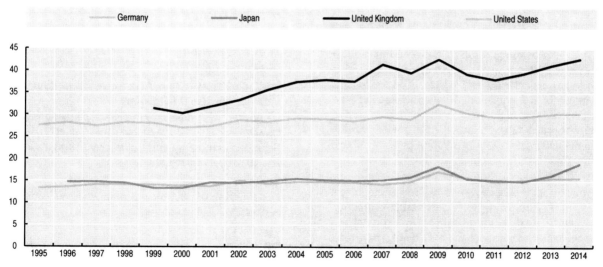

Germany — Japan — United Kingdom — United States

StatLink http://dx.doi.org/10.1787/888933335572

TRADE IN VALUE ADDED

Trade in value added data are statistical estimates of the source(s) of the value (by country and industry) that is added in producing goods and services for export (and import). It recognises that growing global value chains mean that a country's exports increasingly rely on significant intermediate imports (and, so, value added by industries in upstream countries). The consequence of the significant growth in global value chains is a multiple counting of trade in intermediates that may distort trade policy analysis.

The joint OECD-WTO Trade in Value Added (TiVA) initiative addresses this issue by considering the value added by each country in the production of goods and services that are consumed worldwide.

Definition

The OECD-WTO database includes a number of indicators that help to better understand the nature of global value chains and how value and where value is created. These indicators are derived from an inter-country input-output table that is constructed by combining national input-output tables and international trade in goods and services statistics, and benchmarked to countries' latest national accounts figures.

The share of foreign value added embedded in exports reflects how much of a country's gross exports contains value added that is produced outside the domestic economy (and imported).

Domestic value added embodied in foreign final demand shows how much domestic value added is included, via direct final exports and via indirect exports of intermediates through other countries, in the demand of foreign final consumers (households, charities, government, and as investment).

Foreign value added embodied in final domestic demand shows how much value added in final goods and services (purchased by households, government, non-profit institutions serving households and as investment) originates from abroad.

Comparability

The indicators in the TiVA database are estimates. The inter-country input-output tables from which the TiVA indicators are derived by necessity have to eliminate inconsistencies within and between official national statistics, and balance bilateral trade asymmetries to achieve a coherent picture of global production, trade and consumption of goods and services. This means that while for the countries for which data is presented, all data (including total exports and imports) are made consistent with official national accounts estimates, the bilateral trade positions presented in TiVA and those published by national statistics institutions may differ.

Overview

The foreign value added content of exports has generally increased over the past two decades, up to a weighted OECD average of 24.3%. Yet economies differ significantly in this respect. The share of foreign value added in exports clearly depends on economies' size and pattern of specialisation. Smaller economies tend to have higher shares of foreign value added embodied in their exports; larger economies have a wider variety of domestically sourced intermediate goods available and are therefore less reliant on foreign imports of intermediaries.

In particular, for Asian countries like India and Korea, but also for Poland, Hungary, Turkey and Luxembourg, the share of foreign value added in exports has increased substantially since the mid-1990s. The strong effects of the economic crisis has had on international trade is also evident in the decline of the share of foreign value added in gross exports from 2008 to 2009. This share recovered in 2011.

Sources
- OECD/WTO (2016), *OECD-WTO: Statistics on Trade in Value Added* (Database).

Further information
Analytical publications
- OECD (2013), *Interconnected economies: Benefiting from Global Value Chains*, OECD Publishing.
- De Backer, K. and N. Yamano (2012), "*International Comparative Evidence on Global Value Chains*", OECD Science, Technology and Industry Working Papers, No. 2012/03, OECD Publishing.

Statistical publications
- OECD (2014), *OECD Statistics on International Trade in Services*, OECD Publishing.

Methodological publications
- OECD (2012), "*Trade in Value-Added: Concepts, Methodologies, and Challenges (Joint OECD-WTO Note)*", Paris.

Websites
- Measuring Trade in Value Added: An OECD-WTO joint initiative, *www.oecd.org/trade/valueadded*.

Foreign value added as a share of gross exports
Percentage

	1995	2000	2005	2008	2009	2010	2011
Australia	12.1	15.9	12.2	13.8	13.1	13.0	14.1
Austria	21.4	24.8	26.5	28.1	24.7	26.4	27.8
Belgium	31.0	34.4	31.3	36.6	30.6	30.9	34.5
Canada	24.4	27.0	23.5	22.8	22.3	23.4	23.5
Chile	13.9	21.7	18.9	24.7	18.8	17.8	20.2
Czech Republic	30.6	38.7	42.6	42.3	40.2	44.1	45.3
Denmark	23.2	26.1	27.7	34.1	30.7	29.9	32.6
Estonia	36.0	44.6	42.7	33.0	28.4	33.0	35.2
Finland	24.2	30.6	31.8	33.6	30.6	31.8	34.7
France	17.3	22.8	23.4	24.8	21.6	23.7	25.1
Germany	14.9	20.2	21.3	24.8	21.9	23.3	25.5
Greece	16.4	23.9	21.3	25.3	20.7	21.8	25.0
Hungary	29.9	51.6	48.1	46.4	45.0	48.9	48.7
Iceland	17.4	24.2	29.0	29.6	30.4	31.2	33.2
Ireland	38.5	43.0	41.9	43.6	42.0	43.7	43.6
Israel	21.9	21.0	26.0	27.0	22.0	23.6	25.3
Italy	17.2	20.0	22.0	25.8	21.2	25.0	26.5
Japan	5.6	7.4	11.1	15.8	11.2	12.7	14.7
Korea	22.3	29.8	33.0	41.8	37.5	39.2	41.7
Luxembourg	41.0	52.9	54.7	58.9	55.2	57.5	59.0
Mexico	27.3	34.4	33.0	32.8	33.6	34.5	31.7
Netherlands	23.2	22.5	18.6	19.6	17.8	19.4	20.1
New Zealand	16.9	22.2	15.6	18.7	15.2	16.1	16.7
Norway	19.9	16.1	15.9	16.2	17.5	17.7	17.2
Poland	16.1	24.0	28.3	31.1	27.1	31.3	32.4
Portugal	27.4	30.2	31.8	33.8	28.6	31.6	32.8
Slovak Republic	31.9	44.2	47.2	46.5	43.6	45.9	46.8
Slovenia	32.3	36.5	37.9	36.2	31.1	34.9	36.2
Spain	19.2	25.8	26.3	27.6	22.2	24.8	26.9
Sweden	26.3	29.2	29.1	32.1	28.7	28.9	29.2
Switzerland	17.6	21.3	25.9	22.9	21.4	22.1	21.8
Turkey	8.9	13.1	21.0	25.0	21.6	22.6	25.7
United Kingdom	18.3	18.1	17.1	19.5	18.9	21.1	23.1
United States	11.5	12.6	13.1	15.6	11.6	13.4	15.0
EU 28	19.2	23.5	24.4	27.6	24.5	26.4	28.2
OECD	14.9	18.1	20.8	24.6	21.2	22.5	24.3
Brazil	7.8	11.5	11.7	12.5	10.0	10.3	10.8
China	33.4	37.3	37.4	31.8	30.8	32.0	32.2
India	9.4	11.3	17.5	22.7	21.0	22.3	24.1
Indonesia	12.6	17.4	16.6	14.6	11.1	11.1	12.0
Russian Federation	13.3	18.3	12.8	13.9	12.7	13.1	13.7
South Africa	13.2	17.8	19.5	23.8	18.8	17.9	19.5

StatLink 🔗 http://dx.doi.org/10.1787/888933336694

Value added in domestic and foreign final demand
Billion US dollars, 2011

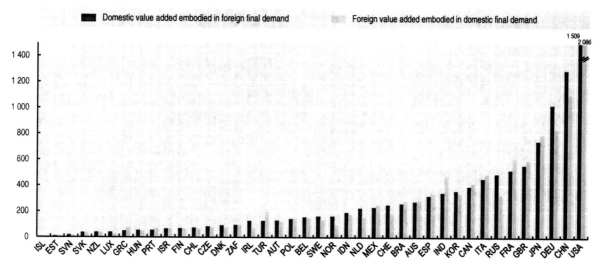

StatLink 🔗 http://dx.doi.org/10.1787/888933335612

TRADE IN VALUE ADDED: ROLE OF INTERMEDIATES AND SERVICES

The data on Trade in Value Added (TiVA) highlight the significance of intermediate imports used in producing goods and services for export in many economies. They emphasise that being competitive on international markets requires access to the most efficient inputs – either domestically produced or imported – and that tariffs on imports can harm the competitiveness of downstream exporters. The data also stress the important role played by upstream services in producing exports of goods, and, so, the importance of ensuring that producers have access to the most efficient services (again either domestically produced or imported).

Definition

Re-exported intermediates reflect the share of intermediate imports that are used (indirectly and directly) in producing goods and services for exports, as a percentage of total intermediate imports (by import category).

Overview

On average, 45% of intermediate imports are destined for the export market in 2011. Not surprisingly, the smaller the economy the higher the share, while the larger and more diversified economies see relative low share of imports in intermediates. The United States and Japan have the lowest such shares amongst OECD countries, at 20.6% and 20.4% respectively for the total economy, with noticeably higher percentages for some sectors. In Japan for example for basic metals and fabricated metal products, transport equipment and electrical and optical equipment sectors, around 35% of intermediate imports end up in exports.

In other countries, the share of intermediate imports embodied in exports is significantly higher. In Hungary for example, over 70% of all intermediate imports are destined for the export market after further processing, with the share reaching 88.6% for electronic intermediate imports in 2011. In China and Korea, around two thirds of all intermediate imports of electronics are embodied in exports. The TiVA database also reveals that close to 90% of China's intermediate imports of textile products end up in exports.

While services comprise about two-thirds of GDP in most developed economies, they typically account for just over one-quarter of total gross trade in goods and services in OECD countries. However, from a trade in value added perspective, the services sector contributes over 50% of total exports in the United States, the United Kingdom, France, Germany and Italy, and more than 40% in China, and services are provided by both foreign and domestic service providers.

Total services value added embodied in gross exports shows the total value added provided by the services sector in generating direct exports of services and also embodied in the exports of goods using intermediate services. The indicator contains a breakdown showing the contributions from domestic or foreign services.

Comparability

The indicators in the TiVA database are estimates. The global input-output tables from which the TiVA indicators are derived by necessity have to eliminate inconsistencies within and between official national statistics, and balance bilateral trade asymmetries to achieve a coherent picture of global production, trade and consumption of goods and services. This means that while for the countries for which data is presented, all data (including total exports and imports) are made consistent with official national accounts estimates, the bilateral trade positions presented in TiVA and those published by national statistics institutions may differ.

Sources

- OECD/WTO (2016), OECD-WTO: Statistics on Trade in Value Added (Database).

Further information

Analytical publications

- OECD (2013), Interconnected economies: Benefiting from Global Value Chains, OECD Publishing.
- Beltramello, A., K. De Backer and L. Moussiegt (2012), "The Export Performance of Countries within Global Value Chains (GVCs)", OECD Science, Technology and Industry Working Papers, No. 2012/02, OECD Publishing.
- De Backer, K. and N. Yamano (2012), "International Comparative Evidence on Global Value Chains", OECD Science, Technology and Industry Working Papers, No. 2012/03, OECD Publishing.

Methodological publications

- OECD (2012), "Trade in Value-Added: Concepts, Methodologies, and Challenges (Joint OECD-WTO Note)", Paris.

Websites

- Measuring Trade in Value Added: An OECD-WTO joint initiative, www.oecd.org/trade/valueadded.

Re-exported intermediates as percentage of total intermediate imports by selected industries

Percentage, 2011

	Agriculture, hunting, forestry and fishing	Food products, beverages and tobacco	Textiles, textile products, leather and footwear	Wood paper, paper products, printing and publishing	Chemicals and non-metallic mineral products	Basic metals and fabricated metal products	Machinery and equipment	Transport equipment	Transport and storage, post and telecommunication	Business services
Australia	25.2	18.7	19.5	14.4	20.7	26.7	35.2	25.6	25.6	23.9
Austria	40.7	37.7	53.4	45.7	45.7	64.4	65.1	64.2	64.2	44.8
Belgium	38.1	37.9	43.9	41.2	56.1	57.7	47.6	58.1	58.1	48.1
Canada	31.1	23.6	35.4	27.1	35.5	53.8	37.0	71.3	71.3	31.8
Chile	33.2	28.5	24.8	32.2	35.3	43.0	36.8	25.4	25.4	37.8
Czech Republic	38.1	35.7	64.5	57.5	65.3	75.2	63.4	74.6	74.6	53.5
Denmark	50.0	46.5	44.5	36.3	54.7	44.0	61.5	63.1	63.1	53.5
Estonia	52.8	47.2	65.5	51.9	51.0	58.5	60.3	61.3	61.3	57.0
Finland	38.3	28.8	45.7	40.3	46.1	62.7	55.8	53.8	53.8	43.8
France	27.4	24.6	48.4	28.3	40.2	44.9	41.7	52.2	52.2	34.2
Germany	27.1	25.1	50.8	38.4	50.7	64.8	60.4	60.7	60.7	44.4
Greece	20.3	23.0	37.5	26.9	35.6	37.0	29.7	30.3	30.3	36.9
Hungary	50.1	49.3	80.1	59.0	67.5	72.8	80.5	84.5	84.5	63.7
Iceland	72.6	63.6	63.0	24.7	44.3	70.3	50.9	82.0	82.0	67.4
Ireland	67.9	64.4	59.3	63.6	68.9	64.6	70.4	74.0	74.0	70.4
Israel	13.6	19.5	53.6	51.4	52.5	49.7	50.5	46.1	46.1	42.6
Italy	25.3	25.1	46.9	31.2	39.7	57.8	50.6	46.3	46.3	34.5
Japan	7.0	6.0	17.4	12.0	20.7	36.8	32.5	35.1	35.1	17.7
Korea	16.1	13.1	39.9	36.1	52.9	56.6	49.9	58.6	58.6	49.1
Luxembourg	89.3	74.8	80.8	86.1	84.6	83.5	85.0	86.7	86.7	92.4
Mexico	13.4	19.9	63.4	42.4	40.7	69.0	71.7	63.4	63.4	47.0
Netherlands	40.3	38.0	34.6	31.7	47.9	39.6	39.1	38.1	38.1	38.0
New Zealand	47.7	46.2	37.1	28.4	29.6	32.8	36.9	29.4	29.4	31.3
Norway	31.1	32.8	36.3	24.6	45.6	65.2	50.9	41.8	41.8	41.8
Poland	31.0	31.3	54.5	41.0	44.5	58.9	57.1	67.0	67.0	42.3
Portugal	33.6	27.4	57.5	42.5	44.3	56.6	52.0	69.2	69.2	41.1
Slovak Republic	51.3	42.9	75.6	54.7	68.4	75.4	65.9	88.1	88.1	59.4
Slovenia	37.7	36.4	67.3	57.5	58.5	71.7	58.1	73.5	73.5	53.2
Spain	30.2	27.1	48.0	31.5	41.3	50.5	42.5	64.8	64.8	35.7
Sweden	41.6	34.2	47.6	43.3	51.7	66.6	57.7	66.6	66.6	47.7
Switzerland	27.9	30.3	50.4	44.5	52.9	59.2	57.2	55.6	55.6	52.1
Turkey	14.1	17.5	28.0	21.4	25.4	36.4	26.8	35.6	35.6	25.8
United Kingdom	22.7	20.3	37.8	27.2	39.2	56.2	48.8	43.5	43.5	33.2
United States	15.5	10.6	21.0	15.3	20.3	30.6	23.4	24.9	24.9	16.0
EU 28	31.7	29.5	50.0	37.0	46.4	58.5	54.1	58.3	58.3	44.8
OECD	23.9	23.4	37.4	29.9	38.6	50.5	42.2	50.2	50.2	37.4
Brazil	21.9	14.2	11.2	16.7	17.3	20.1	22.3	15.0	15.0	16.2
China	34.8	36.3	88.3	49.3	48.3	54.3	48.1	26.5	26.5	48.7
India	14.9	18.2	27.3	23.0	26.3	16.5	24.2	29.9	29.9	28.1
Indonesia	16.7	11.9	30.9	20.8	16.9	10.9	21.4	16.2	16.2	18.7
Russian Federation	11.5	14.3	21.7	27.7	37.3	54.4	30.1	30.0	30.0	31.8
South Africa	17.1	19.6	22.4	24.6	29.3	31.4	43.3	31.2	31.2	32.6

StatLink http://dx.doi.org/10.1787/888933336685

Total domestic and foreign services value added embodied in gross exports

As a percentage of gross exports, 2011

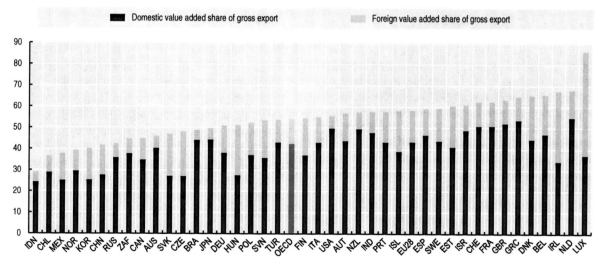

StatLink http://dx.doi.org/10.1787/888933335625

FOREIGN DIRECT INVESTMENT FLOWS

Foreign direct investment (FDI) is a key element in international economic integration. FDI creates direct, stable and long-lasting links between economies. It encourages the transfer of technology and know-how between countries, and allows the host economy to promote its products more widely in international markets. FDI is key to the creation of many global value chains by allowing firms to link and organise production across countries. FDI is also an additional source of funding for investment and, under the right policy environment, can be an important vehicle for development.

Definition

Foreign direct investment is a category of investment that reflects the objective of establishing a lasting interest by a resident enterprise in one economy in an enterprise that is resident in an economy other than that of the direct investor. The direct or indirect ownership of 10% or more of the voting power is evidence of such a relationship.

FDI flows are cross-border financial transactions within a given period (e.g. year) and between affiliated enterprises that are in a direct investment relationship. FDI flows include equity capital, reinvestment of earnings and inter-company debt.

Comparability

In 2014, the implementation of the latest international standards for compiling FDI statistics came into widespread use, which generally enhanced the comparability of FDI statistics across countries. However, some differences remain. For example, data for Brazil, India, Korea, Norway, South Africa and Switzerland are on an asset/liability basis while data for the other countries are on a directional basis. Implementation of the new standards also caused major changes to FDI statistics. Therefore, long historical series are not available for all countries.

Data for Austria, Chile, Denmark, Hungary, Iceland, Luxembourg, Mexico, the Netherlands, Poland, Portugal and Spain exclude resident Special Purpose Entities.

The EU28 aggregate has an evolving composition: EU15 until end 2003; EU25 in 2004-06; and EU27 for 2007-12.

Overview

Despite large quarterly fluctuations, global FDI flows remained stable overall in 2014 as compared to 2013, at around USD 1 385 billion. FDI activity gained momentum in the second half of 2014 after falling sharply in the first quarter due to a single large deal which reduced both inward FDI flows in the United States and outward FDI flows from the United Kingdom. Preliminary information for 2015 indicate that global FDI flows continued to rise in the first half of 2015. However, global FDI flows have stalled at levels substantially below the peak levels reached before the financial crisis (at USD 2 077 billion) and ensuing global recession that began in 2008.

OECD investors accounted for around 65% of global FDI outflows in 2014 at USD 895 billion and were up 2% as compared to 2013. The top three investing countries were the United States, Japan and Germany, representing 40% of global FDI outflows. OECD countries received 42% of global FDI inflows at USD 588 billion, representing an 18% decrease as compared to 2013. 40% of global FDI inflows were hosted by four countries: China (the top recipient of FDI worldwide since 2010), the United States, Brazil and Canada.

Sources
- OECD (2015), *OECD International Direct Investment Statistics* (Database).

Further information

Analytical publications
- OECD (2015), *OECD Business and Finance Outlook*, OECD Publishing.
- OECD (2015), *OECD Investment Policy Reviews*, OECD Publishing.
- OECD (2014), *Annual Report on the OECD Guidelines for Multinational Enterprises*, OECD Publishing.

Statistical publications
- OECD (2010), *Measuring Globalisation: OECD Economic Globalisation Indicators*, OECD Publishing.

Methodological publications
- Kalinova, B., A. Palerm and S. Thomsen (2010), "OECD's FDI Restrictiveness Index: 2010 Update", *OECD Working Papers on International Investment*, No. 2010/03.
- OECD (2009), *OECD Benchmark Definition of Foreign Direct Investment, Fourth edition*, OECD Publishing.

Websites
- Foreign Direct Investment Statistics – OECD Data, Analysis and Forecasts, *www.oecd.org/investment/statistics*.
- OECD International Investment, *www.oecd.org/daf/investment*.

Outflows and inflows of foreign direct investment
Million US dollars

	Outflows of foreign direct investment						Inflows of foreign direct investment					
	2009	2010	2011	2012	2013	2014	2009	2010	2011	2012	2013	2014
Australia	16 409	19 803	1 716	6 737	1 580	2 114	31 668	36 442	58 906	58 970	56 946	47 742
Austria	10 999	9 585	21 933	13 114	15 565	6 074	9 269	2 576	10 625	3 990	5 719	6 428
Belgium	..	..	46 413	33 834	23 063	11 611	..	..	76 938	6 518	13 678	3 655
Canada	39 660	34 721	52 144	53 948	50 521	57 043	22 733	28 399	39 667	39 273	70 545	57 376
Chile	6 487	10 226	12 470	17 252	9 217	10 994	12 051	15 220	16 815	24 924	18 071	20 820
Czech Republic	950	1 168	-328	1 794	4 021	-529	2 929	6 147	2 323	8 000	3 641	5 908
Denmark	3 689	1 382	11 278	7 359	9 534	12 984	392	-9 167	11 488	418	-742	3 859
Estonia	1 375	159	-1 476	1 032	431	-230	1 840	1 453	978	1 558	546	507
Finland	..	..	..	..	-2 686	-926	..	..	..	..	-6 609	15 726
France	100 872	48 158	51 462	31 574	24 993	42 871	30 735	13 890	31 671	16 985	42 884	15 192
Germany	..	..	..	..	34 313	104 230	..	..	..	..	22 395	-6 175
Greece	2 055	1 558	1 774	678	-785	904	2 436	330	1 144	1 741	2 817	1 671
Hungary	1 852	1 173	4 713	11 717	1 963	3 472	1 998	2 195	6 315	14 427	3 333	7 107
Iceland	2 248	-2 368	18	-3 205	460	-237	79	245	1 107	1 025	397	441
Ireland	..	..	..	22 573	29 023	43 135	..	..	..	45 276	44 890	31 133
Israel	1 753	8 657	9 165	3 255	5 499	3 667	4 605	6 335	8 727	8 469	12 449	6 739
Italy	..	..	..	..	25 107	26 137	..	..	..	..	24 268	19 538
Japan	74 699	56 276	107 550	122 514	135 745	113 699	11 939	-1 252	-1 757	1 732	2 303	2 092
Korea	17 436	28 280	29 705	30 632	28 360	30 558	9 022	9 497	9 773	9 496	12 767	9 899
Luxembourg	..	..	..	..	25 278	20 541	..	..	..	..	15 368	16 740
Mexico	9 604	15 050	12 636	22 470	13 138	8 304	17 756	26 168	23 328	19 492	44 886	24 154
Netherlands	26 267	68 363	34 818	6 174	68 856	48 046	38 748	-7 185	24 391	20 121	39 026	36 568
New Zealand	-1 002	716	2 524	-457	524	71	701	-61	4 222	3 396	1 831	2 493
Norway	12 330	30 520	14 412	27 536	8 152	21 478	8 673	21 238	10 895	26 750	1 608	10 140
Poland	1 807	6 149	1 028	2 905	1 488	1 975	10 043	12 800	15 953	12 441	3 626	12 532
Portugal	814	-9 956	13 917	-9 869	-139	3 138	1 282	1 507	5 997	8 337	1 659	5 594
Slovak Republic	..	..	..	..	-313	-123	..	..	..	..	-604	-332
Slovenia	214	-19	200	-258	-214	264	-477	106	1 088	339	-151	1 061
Spain	..	..	..	..	11 771	31 613	..	..	..	..	27 551	20 314
Sweden	26 205	20 364	29 912	28 977	29 074	13 994	10 095	141	12 946	16 349	3 673	10 697
Switzerland	44 361	73 827	44 084	53 153	10 237	16 819	48 061	17 509	24 397	25 844	-22 553	21 942
Turkey	1 553	1 469	2 330	4 106	3 525	6 656	8 585	9 086	16 136	13 283	12 355	12 198
United Kingdom	28 993	48 075	95 577	20 769	-18 770	-81 854	89 796	58 180	42 196	55 626	47 589	52 478
United States	310 383	301 080	419 061	339 694	328 628	336 935	150 442	205 850	236 068	193 795	216 587	111 577
EU 28	366 450	469 427	518 169	274 887	295 255	302 289	361 905	372 419	417 592	270 749	304 812	269 570
OECD	893 448	1 050 081	1 208 354	943 898	877 161	895 428	686 406	736 942	856 034	688 385	722 749	587 814
Brazil	-4 552	16 426	3 850	8 017	13 352	26 042	31 481	53 345	71 539	76 111	80 843	96 895
China	43 890	57 954	48 421	64 963	72 971	80 418	131 057	243 703	280 072	241 214	290 928	289 097
India	16 096	15 968	12 608	8 553	1 766	9 951	35 581	27 397	36 499	23 996	28 153	33 870
Indonesia	2 249	2 664	7 713	5 422	6 652	7 077	4 878	13 771	19 241	19 138	18 817	23 039
Russian Federation	34 450	41 116	48 635	28 423	70 685	63 513	27 752	31 668	36 868	30 188	53 397	30 011
South Africa	1 322	-84	-229	2 885	6 646	6 939	8 614	4 014	3 783	4 403	8 296	5 714

StatLink ᴍꜱ http://dx.doi.org/10.1787/888933336132

FDI flows
As a percentage of GDP, 2014 or latest available year

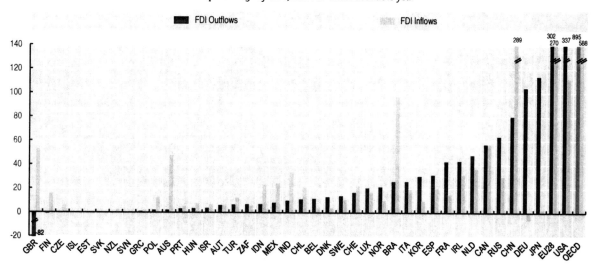

StatLink ᴍꜱ http://dx.doi.org/10.1787/888933334953

FOREIGN DIRECT INVESTMENT STOCKS

Foreign direct investment (FDI) is a key element in international economic integration. FDI creates direct, stable and long-lasting links between economies. It encourages the transfer of technology and know-how between countries, and allows the host economy to promote its products more widely in international markets. FDI is key to the creation of many global value chains by allowing firms to link and organise production across countries.

Definition

Foreign direct investment is a category of investment that reflects the objective of establishing a lasting interest by a resident enterprise in one economy in an enterprise that is resident in an economy other than that of the direct investor. The direct or indirect ownership of 10% or more of the voting power is evidence of such a relationship.

FDI positions relate to the stock of investments at a given point in time (e.g. end of year). FDI positions include equity (10% or more voting shares), reinvestment of earnings and inter-company debt.

Comparability

In 2014, the implementation of the latest international standards for compiling FDI statistics came into widespread use, which generally enhanced the comparability of FDI statistics across countries. However, some differences remain. For example, data for Brazil, India, Korea, South Africa and Switzerland are on an asset/liability basis while data for the other countries are on a directional basis. Implementation of the new standards also caused major changes to FDI statistics. Therefore, long historical series are not available for all countries.

Data for Austria, Belgium, Chile, Denmark, Hungary, Iceland, Luxembourg, Mexico, the Netherlands, Norway, Poland, Portugal and Spain exclude resident Special Purpose Entities.

The EU28 aggregate has an evolving composition: EU15 until end 2003; EU25 for 2004-06; and EU27 for 2007-12.

Overview

At the end of 2014, OECD FDI stocks of outward and inward FDI stood at USD 19.8 trillion and USD 16.6 trillion respectively, a level that almost doubled as compared to the 2005 positions (at USD 10.2 trillion and USD 8.5 trillion respectively). For many countries, 2014 shows a decrease of their stock of inward and outward FDI from 2013, a development due in most cases to movements in the US dollar, which is used for the conversions.

OECD investors account for around 80% of the global stock of outward FDI in 2014 as compared to 90% in 2005. The top three investing countries worldwide are the United States, Germany and the United Kingdom, accounting for 38% of global FDI outward stocks. OECD countries host 57% of the global stock of inward FDI in 2014 as compared to 73% in 2005. The top three hosts of FDI stocks worldwide in 2014 are the United States, China and the United Kingdom, which together represent 33% of the global stock of inward FDI.

Sources

- OECD (2015), *OECD International Direct Investment Statistics* (Database).

Further information

Analytical publications

- OECD (2015), *OECD Business and Finance Outlook*, OECD Publishing.
- OECD (2015), *OECD Investment Policy Reviews*, OECD Publishing.
- OECD (2014), *Annual Report on the OECD Guidelines for Multinational Enterprises*, OECD Publishing.

Statistical publications

- OECD (2010), *Measuring Globalisation: OECD Economic Globalisation Indicators*, OECD Publishing.

Methodological publications

- Kalinova, B., A. Palerm and S. Thomsen (2010), "OECD's FDI Restrictiveness Index: 2010 Update", *OECD Working Papers on International Investment*, No. 2010/03.
- OECD (2009), *OECD Benchmark Definition of Foreign Direct Investment, Fourth edition*, OECD Publishing.

Websites

- Foreign Direct Investment Statistics – OECD Data, Analysis and Forecasts, *www.oecd.org/investment/statistics*.
- OECD International Investment, *www.oecd.org/daf/investment*.

Outward and inward FDI stocks

Million US dollars

	Outward direct investment stocks						Inward direct investment stocks					
	2005	2010	2011	2012	2013	2014	2005	2010	2011	2012	2013	2014
Australia	205 368	449 768	418 814	476 426	456 993	448 171	247 748	527 096	554 931	614 542	568 094	568 863
Austria	75 497	181 636	193 133	209 533	231 840	216 555	83 767	160 614	152 760	164 696	178 828	175 592
Belgium	..	..	..	419 640	465 528	439 972	..	..	..	486 226	482 946	456 670
Canada	692 287	986 049	881 244	958 321	1 113 589	1 134 132	638 650	994 749	872 772	962 090	951 698	937 970
Chile	..	48 084	59 376	73 005	82 499	79 536	..	151 058	157 090	180 974	195 350	197 015
Czech Republic	3 610	14 923	13 214	17 368	20 627	15 978	60 662	128 505	120 569	136 494	134 085	111 504
Denmark	88 076	165 369	176 071	183 985	190 661	173 748	74 650	96 985	98 406	98 293	94 486	95 219
Estonia	1 892	5 189	4 267	5 469	6 787	6 093	11 192	14 451	14 906	17 077	21 202	19 645
Finland	..	..	..	..	147 422	116 721	..	..	..	..	87 096	93 428
France	625 585	1 172 979	1 247 922	1 307 605	1 360 308	1 274 769	371 448	630 692	698 832	717 253	796 500	726 685
Germany	831 364	1 383 601	1 432 696	1 346 449	1 449 647	1 411 083	646 319	955 428	965 948	862 875	944 631	827 857
Greece	13 602	42 623	48 041	44 960	36 300	30 390	29 189	35 025	29 058	24 763	25 850	22 456
Hungary	8 637	22 315	26 357	37 717	38 533	39 063	61 110	90 851	85 331	104 009	108 410	98 899
Iceland	10 091	11 481	11 711	9 093	9 503	8 031	4 553	11 025	11 754	9 325	7 367	7 422
Ireland	..	..	..	412 011	538 755	632 617	..	..	..	364 569	392 921	376 925
Israel	23 114	68 973	70 783	71 172	75 374	78 016	30 811	60 220	64 496	74 703	87 972	98 698
Italy	..	..	..	..	533 906	483 703	..	..	..	..	364 965	338 747
Japan	386 581	831 110	955 854	1 037 700	1 118 009	1 169 077	100 899	214 890	225 785	205 754	170 713	169 436
Korea	38 683	144 032	172 413	202 875	238 812	258 553	104 879	135 500	135 178	157 876	180 860	182 037
Luxembourg	..	..	..	..	101 283	129 759	..	..	..	..	91 397	179 824
Mexico	60 882	110 014	114 265	148 204	136 523	134 058	234 149	363 769	338 975	366 564	391 879	339 155
Netherlands	..	..	..	..	1 124 797	1 028 876	..	..	..	..	739 835	679 540
New Zealand	11 758	16 053	19 007	19 529	18 740	18 998	44 094	57 365	64 444	71 472	75 209	76 651
Norway	..	..	..	..	198 677	230 721	..	..	..	..	196 448	226 632
Poland	1 776	16 407	18 928	26 102	27 725	24 938	86 338	187 602	164 424	198 953	229 167	205 581
Portugal	30 972	43 968	54 412	49 587	51 200	43 541	51 828	84 869	84 979	98 698	108 181	92 722
Slovak Republic	..	3 456	4 021	4 765	4 830	2 977	..	50 327	51 978	55 118	58 022	52 310
Slovenia	3 276	8 147	7 826	7 533	7 142	6 432	7 056	10 667	11 490	12 202	12 269	12 257
Spain	..	..	..	..	513 326	491 005	..	..	..	..	604 681	539 625
Sweden	207 836	374 399	379 286	389 229	419 443	377 351	171 902	347 163	349 058	373 444	389 169	317 945
Switzerland	492 889	1 283 706	1 364 894	1 473 863	1 465 278	1 462 971	252 731	888 695	976 866	1 050 518	1 033 833	1 106 015
Turkey	8 315	22 506	27 652	30 936	33 321	39 507	71 322	187 013	136 475	189 994	149 608	177 388
United Kingdom	1 177 335	1 574 643	1 625 966	1 593 820	1 579 928	1 513 222	779 085	1 057 145	1 145 700	1 428 091	1 490 033	1 744 230
United States	3 637 996	4 809 587	4 514 327	5 222 873	6 291 370	6 285 320	2 817 970	3 422 293	3 498 726	3 915 538	4 954 713	5 390 081
EU 28	4 579 580	7 914 578	8 156 983	8 706 214	8 985 817	8 579 340	3 875 487	6 294 556	6 513 898	7 451 316	7 833 471	7 599 959
OECD	10 256 966	16 788 538	16 879 735	18 542 367	20 088 674	19 805 885	8 551 507	13 156 368	13 385 731	15 047 058	16 318 416	16 645 025
Brazil	79 259	191 349	206 187	270 864	300 791	302 964	181 344	682 346	696 408	743 964	747 891	755 371
China	64 493	317 210	424 780	531 900	660 480	744 289	471 549	1 569 604	1 906 908	2 068 000	2 331 238	2 677 901
India	12 832	96 911	109 519	118 072	119 838	129 788	50 614	205 603	206 374	224 984	226 748	252 141
Indonesia	..	6 672	6 204	12 401	19 350	24 116	..	160 735	184 804	211 635	230 799	253 655
Russian Federation	..	..	315 742	332 836	385 328	307 200	..	..	408 942	438 195	471 481	272 243
South Africa	31 038	83 248	97 051	111 779	128 681	..	96 693	179 564	159 391	163 509	152 123	..

StatLink http://dx.doi.org/10.1787/888933336152

FDI stocks

As a percentage of GDP, 2014 or latest available year

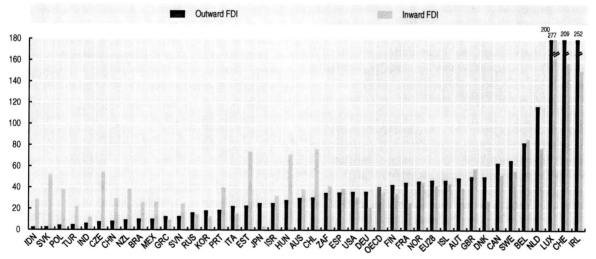

StatLink http://dx.doi.org/10.1787/888933334975

FDI REGULATORY RESTRICTIVENESS INDEX

Foreign direct investment (FDI) is a key element in international economic integration. FDI creates direct, stable and long-lasting links between economies. It encourages the transfer of technology and know-how between countries, and allows the host economy to promote its products more widely in international markets. FDI is also an additional source of funding for investment and, under the right policy environment, it can be an important vehicle for development.

Definition

The OECD FDI Regulatory Restrictiveness Index gauges the restrictiveness of a country's FDI rules through four types of restrictions: foreign equity restrictions; screening or approval mechanisms; restrictions on key foreign employment; and operational restrictions.

Comparability

The OECD FDI Regulatory Restrictiveness Index covers statutory restrictions in 22 sectors. The Index is currently available for 8 years: 1997, 2003, 2006, 2010-14. Restrictions are scored on a range from 0 (open) to 1 (closed). Absence of scores refers to the absence of restrictions. Implementation issues are not addressed and factors such as the degree of transparency or discretion in granting approvals are not taken into account.

For OECD and non-OECD countries adherents to the OECD *Declaration on International Investment and Multinational Enterprises*, the measures taken into account by the index are limited to statutory regulatory restrictions on FDI as reflected in countries' lists of exceptions to national treatment and measures notified for transparency under OECD instruments without assessing their actual enforcement. For the non-OECD countries, information is collected through *Investment Policy Reviews*. Information is updated on a yearly basis following the OECD Freedom of Investment monitoring of investment measures, and ad-hoc legal and regulatory documental research for the countries not covered.

Overview

The OECD FDI Regulatory Restrictiveness Index shows that there still remains significant variation across countries in terms of statutory restrictions on foreign direct investment. Countries in Asia and those with significant raw materials tend to be more restrictive. When used in combination with indicators measuring other aspects of the FDI climate, the Index can help to account for variations in countries' success in attracting FDI.

Seen from a broad perspective, countries continue to liberalise their requirements on international investment over time, albeit with occasional relapses. But worldwide, many service sectors remain partly off limits to foreign investors, holding back potential economy-wide productivity gains. Even within OECD countries, restrictions on foreign investment remain in key network sectors such as energy and transport. A key risk is that FDI restrictions limiting competition in service sectors end-up raising service input costs for other economic sectors and constraining productivity growth in the more dynamic downstream ones.

Sources
- OECD (2015), "*OECD FDI regulatory restrictiveness index*", OECD International Direct Investment Statistics (Database).

Further information
Analytical publications
- Nicolas, F., S. Thomsen and M. Bang (2013), "*Lessons from Investment Policy Reform in Korea*", OECD Working Papers on International Investment, No. 2013/02, OECD Publishing.
- OECD (2015), *OECD Investment Policy Reviews*, OECD Publishing.
- OECD (2014), *Southeast Asia Investment Policy Perspectives*, Paris.

Methodological publications
- Kalinova, B., A. Palerm and S. Thomsen (2010), "*OECD's FDI Restrictiveness Index: 2010 Update*", OECD Working Papers on International Investment, 2010/03, OECD Publishing.

Websites
- Monitoring investment and trade measures, *www.oecd.org/investment/g20.htm*.
- National Treatment for Foreign-Controlled Enterprises, *www.oecd.org/daf/inv/investment-policy/nationaltreatmentinstrument.htm*.
- OECD Codes of Liberalisation of Capital Movements and of Current Invisible Operations,*www.oecd.org/daf/fin/insurance/codes.htm*.

FDI Regulatory Restrictiveness Index
2014

	Total FDI Index	Primary sector	Manufacturing	Electricity	Distribution	Transport	Media	Communications	Financial services	Business services
Australia	0.127	0.078	0.075	0.075	0.075	0.260	0.200	0.400	0.133	0.078
Austria	0.106	0.150	-	1.000	-	0.182	-	-	0.002	0.322
Belgium	0.040	0.035	0.023	0.023	0.023	0.114	0.023	0.023	0.024	0.248
Canada	0.173	0.198	0.110	0.110	0.110	0.277	0.710	0.575	0.077	0.110
Chile	0.057	0.150	-	-	-	0.413	0.188	-	0.017	0.013
Czech Republic	0.010	0.025	-	-	-	0.075	-	-	0.010	-
Denmark	0.033	0.056	-	-	-	0.083	-	-	0.002	0.363
Estonia	0.018	0.023	-	-	-	0.150	-	-	0.002	-
Finland	0.019	0.015	0.009	0.084	0.009	0.092	0.009	0.009	0.011	0.046
France	0.045	0.155	-	-	-	0.150	0.048	-	0.054	0.003
Germany	0.023	0.069	-	-	-	0.200	0.025	-	0.005	-
Greece	0.032	0.079	-	-	-	0.150	0.113	-	0.020	0.056
Hungary	0.029	-	-	-	-	0.167	-	-	0.005	-
Iceland	0.167	0.241	0.112	0.562	0.112	0.204	0.112	0.112	0.119	0.112
Ireland	0.043	0.135	-	-	-	0.125	-	-	0.009	-
Israel	0.118	0.060	0.020	0.770	0.020	0.403	0.264	0.395	0.037	0.020
Italy	0.052	0.130	-	-	-	0.200	0.363	-	0.018	-
Japan	0.052	0.069	0.002	0.025	0.001	0.275	0.200	0.265	-	-
Korea	0.135	0.250	-	0.417	-	0.508	0.563	0.325	0.050	-
Luxembourg	0.004	-	-	-	-	0.075	-	-	0.002	-
Mexico	0.193	0.319	0.103	0.100	0.175	0.528	0.525	0.100	0.133	0.100
Netherlands	0.015	0.062	-	-	-	0.083	-	-	0.002	-
New Zealand	0.240	0.325	0.200	0.200	0.200	0.283	0.200	0.400	0.233	0.200
Norway	0.085	0.156	-	-	-	0.350	0.125	-	0.067	0.313
Poland	0.072	0.050	-	-	-	0.092	0.298	0.075	0.003	-
Portugal	0.007	0.006	-	-	-	0.083	-	-	0.017	-
Slovak Republic	0.049	-	-	-	-	0.075	-	-	0.002	-
Slovenia	0.007	-	-	-	-	0.150	-	-	0.002	-
Spain	0.021	0.011	-	-	-	0.075	0.225	-	0.002	0.113
Sweden	0.059	0.138	-	-	-	0.292	0.200	0.200	0.002	0.051
Switzerland	0.083	-	-	0.500	-	0.250	0.467	-	0.067	-
Turkey	0.059	0.013	-	-	-	0.383	0.200	-	-	0.125
United Kingdom	0.061	0.160	0.023	0.023	0.023	0.114	0.248	0.023	0.024	0.023
United States	0.089	0.181	-	0.197	-	0.550	0.250	0.110	0.042	-
EU 28	..	..	..	..	..	..				
OECD	0.068	0.098	0.020	0.120	0.022	0.218	0.163	0.089	0.035	0.067
Brazil	0.101	0.188	0.025	0.025	0.025	0.275	0.550	0.025	0.108	0.025
China	0.418	0.456	0.236	0.530	0.256	0.642	1.000	0.750	0.513	0.388
India	0.263	0.405	0.046	0.064	0.238	0.179	0.395	0.175	0.320	0.563
Indonesia	0.340	0.426	0.067	0.100	0.560	0.412	0.885	0.290	0.239	0.579
Russian Federation	0.181	0.157	0.095	0.030	0.050	0.350	0.350	0.100	0.432	0.175
South Africa	0.055	0.010	0.010	0.010	0.010	0.193	0.298	0.010	0.052	0.260

StatLink http://dx.doi.org/10.1787/888933336144

FDI regulatory restrictiveness index
2014

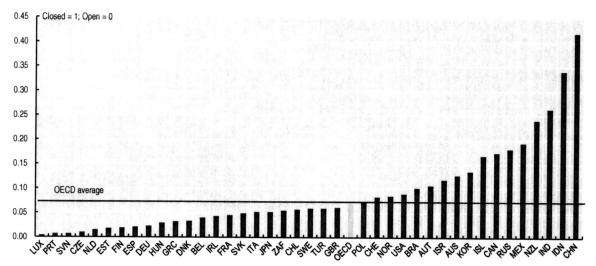

StatLink http://dx.doi.org/10.1787/888933334964

BALANCE OF PAYMENTS

The current account balance is the difference between current receipts from abroad and current payments to abroad. When the current account balance is positive, the country can use the surplus to repay foreign debts, to acquire foreign assets or to lend to the rest of the world. When the current account balance is negative, the deficit will be financed by borrowing from abroad or by liquidating foreign assets acquired in earlier periods.

Definition

Current account transactions consist of exports and imports of goods; exports and imports of services such as travel, international freight and passenger transport, insurance and financial services; primary income flows, consisting of compensation of employees (e.g. wages and salaries) and investment income (i.e. property income in *System of National Accounts*); and secondary income such as government transfers (i.e. international cooperation), worker's remittances and other transfers such as gifts, inheritances and prizes won from lotteries.

Investment income includes retained earnings (i.e. profits not distributed as dividends to the direct investor) of foreign subsidiaries. In general, earnings of direct investment enterprises are treated as if they were remitted abroad to the direct investor, with the part that is actually retained in the country where the direct investment enterprises are located shown as direct investment income reinvested earnings in the current account and as inward direct investment in the financial account.

Comparability

The data are taken from balance of payments statistics compiled according to the International Monetary Fund (IMF) *Balance of Payments Manual and International Investment Position* (BPM6) which was introduced in most countries in 2014. However, data for Mexico, Brazil, China, India, Indonesia, and South Africa are still presented according to the old BPM5. The IMF, OECD and other international organisations closely monitor balance of payments statistics reported by member countries through regular meetings of balance of payments compilers. As a result, there is relatively good comparability across countries.

Overview

The lead up to and the aftermath of the global financial and economic crisis had a clear impact on current account balances as a percentage of GDP of for a large number of countries between 2002, 2006, 2010 and 2014. An example of this rise and fall is Iceland, which saw its current account balance as a percentage of GDP fall from 1.1% in 2002 to negative 23.2% in 2006, due to the large inflow of capital seeking high interest rates and now sits at 3.2% in 2014. A number of other countries that exhibit a similar pattern are Estonia, Ireland, Portugal, Spain and the United States.

OECD countries that have recorded current account deficits throughout the period since 2002 are: Australia, Mexico, New Zealand, Poland, Turkey, the United Kingdom and the United States. This is partly due to the way in which earnings of direct investment enterprises are treated.

Turkey is the only OECD country that recorded a current account deficit of 5% of GDP or more on average over the three years to 2014 (negative 6.6%), although Turkey's current account deficit as a percentage of GDP has improved since 2011 when it reached negative 9.6%. Surpluses in excess of 5% of GDP were recorded by Denmark, Germany, Korea, Luxembourg, the Netherlands, Norway, Sweden, Slovenia and Switzerland.

Sources
- OECD (2015), *Main Economic Indicators*, OECD Publishing.

Further information

Analytical publications
- OECD (2008), *Export Credit Financing Systems in OECD Member Countries and Non-Member Economies*, OECD Publishing.

Methodological publications
- International Monetary Fund (IMF) (2009), *Balance of Payments and International Investment Position Manual*, 6th edition, IMF, Washington DC.
- OECD et al. (2010), *Manual on Statistics of International Trade in Services*, United Nations.

Online databases
- *Main Economic Indicators*.
- *OECD Economic Outlook: Statistics and Projections*.

Websites
- Sources & Methods of the OECD Economic Outlook, *www.oecd.org/economy/outlook/sources-and-methods.htm*.

Current account balance
As a percentage of GDP

	2002	2003	2004	2005	2006	2007	2008	2009	2010	2011	2012	2013	2014
Australia	-3.7	-5.4	-6.2	-5.9	-5.8	-6.7	-4.9	-4.6	-3.6	-3.0	-4.3	-3.4	-3.0
Austria	..	..	..	..	3.3	3.8	4.5	2.6	2.9	1.6	1.5	2.0	2.0
Belgium	..	3.5	3.3	2.1	1.9	2.0	-1.0	-1.1	1.8	-1.1	-0.1	-0.2	0.1
Canada	1.7	1.1	2.3	1.8	1.4	0.8	0.1	-2.9	-3.5	-2.7	-3.3	-3.0	-2.1
Chile	..	-0.9	2.4	1.6	4.7	4.3	-3.1	1.5	1.7	-1.1	-3.6	-3.7	-1.2
Czech Republic	-5.1	-5.7	-4.2	-1.0	-2.1	-4.3	-1.9	-2.3	-3.6	-2.1	-1.6	-0.5	0.6
Denmark	..	..	..	4.3	3.2	1.4	2.7	3.3	5.7	5.7	5.7	7.2	7.8
Estonia	-11.1	-12.9	-12.1	-8.7	-14.9	-15.1	-8.6	2.6	1.8	1.3	-2.4	-0.1	1.0
Finland	8.2	4.6	5.8	3.0	3.8	3.8	2.2	1.9	1.2	-1.8	-1.9	-1.7	-1.8
France	1.2	0.9	0.4	0.0	0.0	-0.3	-1.0	-0.8	-0.8	-1.0	-1.5	-1.4	-0.8
Germany	1.9	1.4	4.5	4.6	5.7	6.7	5.6	5.7	5.6	6.1	6.8	6.4	7.4
Greece	..	..	..	..	..	..	-14.4	-10.9	-10.0	-9.9	-2.4	-2.1	-2.1
Hungary	-6.3	-8.0	-8.6	-7.0	-7.1	-7.1	-7.0	-0.8	0.3	0.8	1.8	4.0	3.9
Iceland	1.1	-5.0	-9.8	-15.7	-23.2	-14.2	-22.9	-9.8	-6.5	-5.4	-4.4	5.7	3.2
Ireland	-0.6	0.5	-1.6	-5.2	-5.8	-9.2	-9.3	-6.6	-3.2	-2.7	1.5	4.3	6.1
Israel	-0.9	0.6	1.5	3.0	4.6	4.1	1.1	3.5	3.6	2.3	1.5	3.0	4.3
Italy	-0.5	-0.8	-0.5	-0.9	-1.5	-1.4	-2.8	-1.9	-3.5	-3.1	-0.5	0.9	1.9
Japan	2.7	3.2	3.9	3.7	4.0	4.9	2.9	2.9	4.0	2.2	1.0	0.8	0.5
Korea	0.8	1.7	3.9	1.4	0.3	1.0	0.6	3.9	2.6	1.5	4.1	6.2	6.3
Luxembourg	9.4	6.6	12.0	11.1	10.0	9.8	7.3	7.7	7.0	5.8	5.8	4.7	5.1
Mexico	-2.0	-1.2	-0.9	-1.1	-0.8	-1.4	-1.9	-0.9	-0.5	-1.1	-1.4	-2.3	-1.9
Netherlands	..	..	6.8	6.1	7.9	6.0	4.1	5.8	7.3	9.1	10.8	11.0	10.8
New Zealand	-2.2	-2.4	-4.5	-7.0	-7.2	-6.8	-7.7	-2.3	-2.2	-2.8	-4.0	-3.1	-3.1
Norway	..	..	..	16.2	16.2	12.2	15.6	10.6	10.9	12.3	12.4	10.0	9.4
Poland	..	..	-5.4	-2.5	-3.9	-6.2	-6.5	-3.8	-5.5	-5.0	-3.4	-1.3	-1.3
Portugal	-8.5	-7.2	-8.3	-9.9	-10.7	-9.7	-12.1	-10.4	-10.2	-6.0	-2.1	1.4	0.6
Slovak Republic	..	..	..	..	..	..	-6.2	-3.5	-4.7	-5.0	0.9	1.8	0.1
Slovenia	0.9	-0.8	-2.7	-1.8	-1.8	-4.1	-5.3	-0.6	-0.1	0.2	2.6	5.6	7.0
Spain	-3.7	-3.9	-5.6	-7.5	-9.0	-9.6	-9.2	-4.3	-3.9	-3.2	-0.3	1.4	0.8
Sweden	4.5	6.6	6.3	6.5	8.3	8.9	8.6	5.9	6.0	6.9	6.6	7.3	6.8
Switzerland	8.6	12.7	14.5	13.4	14.2	10.0	2.2	7.1	14.0	6.8	9.9	10.7	7.1
Turkey	-0.3	-2.5	-3.6	-4.4	-6.0	-5.8	-5.3	-1.9	-6.1	-9.6	-6.2	-7.8	-5.8
United Kingdom	-2.1	-1.7	-1.8	-1.2	-2.3	-2.5	-3.6	-3.0	-2.8	-1.7	-3.3	-4.5	-5.1
United States	-4.2	-4.5	-5.2	-5.7	-5.8	-5.0	-4.7	-2.7	-3.0	-3.0	-2.8	-2.3	-2.2
EU 28	..	..	..	..	..	..	..	..	..	..	..	..	..
OECD	..	..	..	..	..	..	-1.7	-0.5	-0.4	-0.6	-0.4	-0.1	0.0
Brazil	-1.3	0.7	1.7	1.6	1.2	0.2	-1.6	-1.3	-2.1	-2.0	-2.3	-3.4	-3.9
China	2.4	2.6	3.6	5.9	8.5	10.1	9.3	4.9	4.0	1.9	2.3		
India	1.4	1.5	0.2	-1.2	-1.0	-0.6	-2.5	-2.0	-3.2				
Indonesia	3.7	3.2	0.6	0.1	2.7	2.2	0.0	1.8	0.7	0.2	-2.7	-3.1	
Russian Federation	..	7.8	9.7	11.1	9.7	5.6	6.2	3.8	4.6	5.0	3.5	1.7	3.1
South Africa	0.8	-1.0	-2.9	-3.3	-5.1	-6.6	-6.8	-3.9	-2.8	..	..	..	..

StatLink ᴴᴱ▄ http://dx.doi.org/10.1787/888933336031

Current account balance
As a percentage of GDP

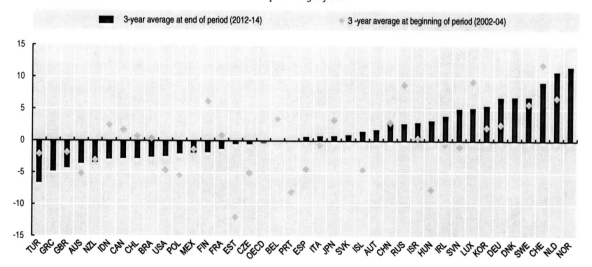

StatLink ᴴᴱ▄ http://dx.doi.org/10.1787/888933334849

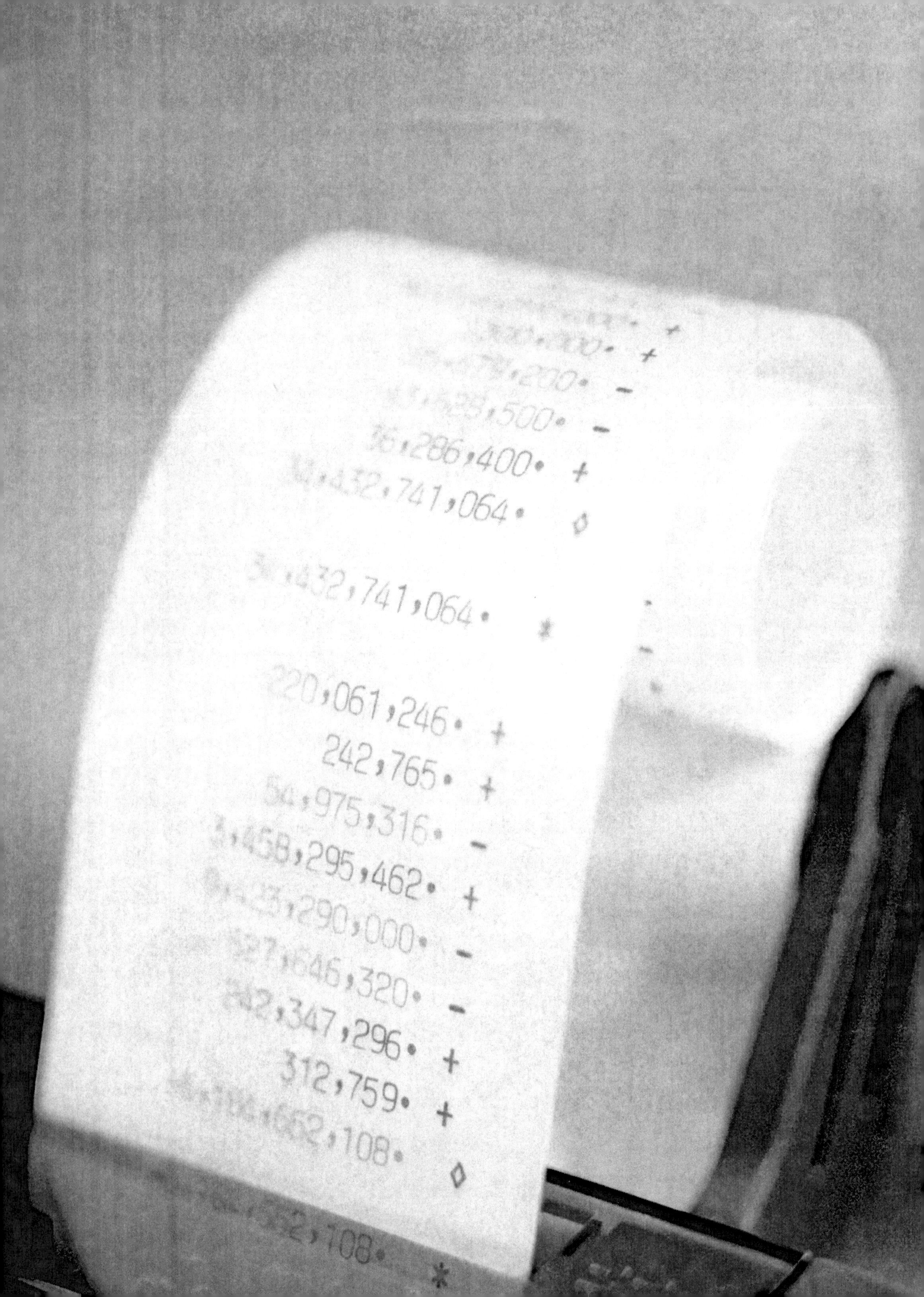
220,061,246• +
242,765• +
312,759• +

PRICES

INFLATION (CPI)

Consumer price indices have a long history in official statistics. They provide a measure of the erosion of living standards through price inflation and are probably one of the best known economic statistics used by the media and general public.

Definition

Consumer price indices (CPI) measure the change in the prices of a basket of goods and services that are typically purchased by specific groups of households. Consumer price indices cover virtually all households except for "institutional" households – people in prisons and military barracks, for example – and, in some countries, households in the highest income group.

The CPI for all items excluding food and energy provides a measure of underlying inflation, which is less affected by short-term fluctuations. The index for food covers food and non-alcoholic beverages but excludes purchases in restaurants. The index for energy covers all forms of energy, including fuels for motor vehicles, heating and other household uses.

Comparability

There are a number of differences in the ways that these indices are calculated. The most important ones concern the treatment of dwelling costs, the adjustments made for changes in the quality of goods and services, the frequency with which the basket weights are updated, and the index formulae used. In particular, country methodologies for the treatment of owner-occupied housing vary significantly. The European Harmonised Indices of Consumer Prices (HICPs) exclude owner-occupied housing as do national CPIs for Belgium, Chile, Estonia, France, Greece, Italy, Luxembourg, Poland, Portugal, Slovenia, Spain, Turkey, the United Kingdom and most of the countries outside the OECD area. For the United Kingdom, the national CPI is the same as the HICP. The European Union and euro area CPI refer to the HICP published by Eurostat and cover the 28 and 19 countries respectively for the entire period of the time series.

Overview

The annual average inflation rate from 2012-14 has been below 2.5% in all OECD countries except Chile, Iceland, Mexico and Turkey. The CPI for the OECD total dropped from 2.5% in the 3-year average from 2002-04 to 1.9% in the 3-year average from 2012-14. Over the entire period from 2002 to 2014, most OECD countries experienced substantial declines in inflation. By contrast, Japan experienced a substantial increase of inflation after many years of negative and flat rates while Mexico, Turkey, and Iceland all experienced periods or years of high inflation during this period.

Annual inflation rates have been higher for countries outside the OECD area.

Energy prices have been volatile during the whole period (2000-14) and have recorded large swings, with spikes in 2000, 2005, 2008 and 2011 and sharp declines in 2002, 2007 and 2014. Food prices have risen by less than total consumer prices in 2000 and 2010 but for the most recent period, 2014, they have risen faster. When excluding these more volatile items, the underlying consumer price index (i.e. all items excluding food and energy) points to a progressive decline in inflation rates from 2000 to 2010 followed by a slight increase from 2010 onwards.

Sources
- OECD (2015), *Main Economic Indicators*, OECD Publishing.

Further information

Analytical publications
- OECD (2015), *OECD Economic Outlook*, OECD Publishing.
- Brook, A.M. *et al.* (2004), "Oil Price Developments: Drivers, Economic Consequences and Policy Responses", *OECD Economics Department Working Papers*, No. 412.

Methodological publications
- OECD *et al.* (2004), *Consumer Price Index Manual: Theory and Practice*, ILO, Geneva.

Websites
- OECD Main Economic Indicators, *www.oecd.org/std/mei*.

Inflation (CPI)

Annual growth in percentage

	All items			All items non-food, non-energy			Food			Energy		
	2000	2010	2014	2000	2010	2014	2000	2010	2014	2000	2010	2014
Australia	4.5	2.9	2.5	4.4	2.8	2.6	0.3	1.1	2.8	16.3	8.5	1.2
Austria	2.3	1.8	1.6	1.7	1.4	2.0	0.6	0.5	2.0	10.7	7.6	-2.0
Belgium	2.5	2.2	0.3	1.8	1.5	1.6	0.9	1.7	-0.4	14.4	9.5	-6.2
Canada	2.7	1.8	1.9	1.7	1.3	1.6	1.1	0.9	2.5	16.2	6.6	3.5
Chile	3.8	1.4	4.7	3.1	0.5	3.9	1.1	2.2	7.0	22.0	7.1	6.2
Czech Republic	3.8	1.5	0.4	3.3	1.1	0.4	1.0	1.5	2.0	15.1	3.8	-4.2
Denmark	2.9	2.3	0.6	2.1	1.9	0.9	2.5	0.4	-0.9	11.8	9.0	-0.2
Estonia	4.0	3.0	-0.1	3.9	0.8	1.0	2.4	3.0	0.0	8.0	12.3	-4.0
Finland	3.0	1.2	1.0	2.6	1.2	1.5	1.1	-3.4	0.2	12.6	10.6	-1.7
France	1.7	1.5	0.5	0.5	0.9	0.9	2.2	0.8	-0.8	12.2	9.6	-1.1
Germany	1.4	1.1	0.9	0.9	0.7	1.4	-0.7	1.2	1.0	13.9	4.0	-2.1
Greece	3.2	4.7	-1.3	2.2	3.4	-1.2	1.9	0.1	-1.7	17.2	28.8	-1.8
Hungary	9.8	4.9	-0.2	8.4	3.7	2.3	9.2	2.8	-0.8	17.3	10.8	-6.8
Iceland	5.1	5.4	2.0	4.7	4.7	2.7	4.1	4.2	0.5	11.9	15.5	-1.3
Ireland	5.6	-0.9	0.2	5.6	-1.2	0.8	3.1	-4.6	-2.2	13.6	9.6	-1.5
Israel	1.1	2.7	0.5	0.4	2.6	0.9	2.3	2.5	-1.4	9.5	3.9	-0.3
Italy	2.5	1.5	0.2	2.1	1.6	0.9	1.6	0.2	0.1	11.6	3.5	-3.0
Japan	-0.7	-0.7	2.7	-0.5	-1.2	1.9	-2.3	-0.3	4.2	2.7	2.7	6.5
Korea	2.3	2.9	1.3	1.8	1.8	1.7	0.9	6.4	0.3	9.6	6.5	-0.4
Luxembourg	3.2	2.3	0.6	2.2	1.6	1.3	2.0	0.9	0.6	19.8	10.2	-4.6
Mexico	9.5	4.2	4.0	10.4	4.2	3.2	5.4	3.4	4.8	16.8	5.4	8.4
Netherlands	2.3	1.3	1.0	1.9	1.7	1.5	0.2	-0.1	-0.1	14.9	-0.3	-1.7
New Zealand	2.6	2.3	1.2	2.4	1.9	1.4	1.1	1.0	0.3	11.0	7.0	1.2
Norway	3.1	2.4	2.0	2.5	0.9	3.1	1.9	0.2	3.1	11.3	15.5	-4.0
Poland	9.9	2.6	0.1	9.3	1.5	0.7	9.7	2.8	-1.0	13.4	6.2	-1.1
Portugal	2.9	1.4	-0.3	2.9	1.0	0.1	2.1	-0.2	-1.3	6.0	9.5	-1.4
Slovak Republic	12.0	1.0	-0.1	11.5	3.1	0.7	5.2	1.6	-0.8	41.8	-2.8	-1.8
Slovenia	8.9	1.8	0.2	7.3	0.2	0.7	-13.8	1.0	-0.3	25.2	13.2	-1.4
Spain	3.4	1.8	-0.2	2.9	0.6	0.0	2.1	-0.8	-0.3	13.3	12.5	-0.8
Sweden	0.9	1.2	-0.2	-0.3	-0.4	0.6	0.0	1.4	0.4	7.2	6.8	-2.6
Switzerland	1.6	0.7	0.0	1.2	0.2	0.0	1.6	-1.1	0.9	18.0	9.2	-1.0
Turkey	54.9	8.6	8.9	58.0	7.2	8.6	46.6	10.6	12.6	56.4	10.5	2.5
United Kingdom	0.8	3.3	1.5	0.1	2.9	1.6	-0.5	3.4	-0.2	7.0	6.1	0.1
United States	3.4	1.6	1.6	2.4	1.0	1.7	2.2	0.3	2.4	16.9	9.5	-0.3
Euro area	2.2	1.6	0.4	1.0	1.0	0.8	1.2	0.4	-0.1	13.4	7.4	-1.9
EU 28	3.5	2.1	0.6	1.2	1.3	0.9	3.9	1.0	-0.2	12.7	7.2	-1.6
OECD	4.0	1.9	1.7	3.4	1.3	1.8	2.3	1.1	2.1	14.7	7.8	0.5
Brazil	7.0	5.0	6.3	..	..	..	5.1	6.1	7.6	..	..	..
China	0.4	3.3	2.0	..	..	..	-2.6	7.2	3.1	..	..	..
India	4.0	12.0	6.4	..	..	..	..	..	..	..	..	..
Indonesia	3.7	5.1	6.4	..	..	..	-4.8	9.4	6.8	..	..	..
Russian Federation	20.8	6.9	7.8	..	..	..	17.8	7.0	10.3	..	..	..
South Africa	5.3	4.1	6.1	..	4.2	5.5	7.8	1.2	8.0	..	14.6	7.2

StatLink ⟹ http://dx.doi.org/10.1787/888933336052

CPI: all items

Average annual growth in percentage

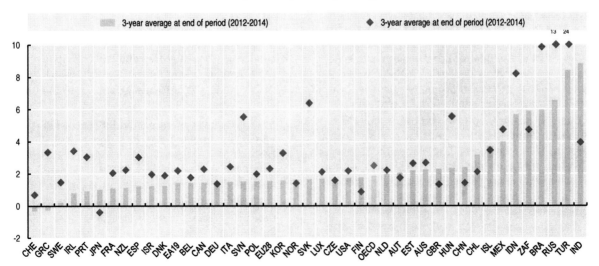

StatLink ⟹ http://dx.doi.org/10.1787/888933334865

PRODUCER PRICE INDICES

A variety of price indices may be used to measure inflation in an economy. These include consumer price indices (CPI), price indices relating to specific goods and/or services, GDP deflators and producer price indices (PPI). Whereas CPIs are designed to measure changes over time in average retail prices of a fixed basket of goods and services taken as representing the consumption habits of households, PPIs aim to provide measures of average movements of prices applied by the producers of various commodities. They are often seen as advanced indicators of price changes throughout the economy, including changes in the prices of consumer goods and services.

Definition

Producer price indices measure the rate of change in prices of products sold as they leave the producer. They exclude any taxes, transport and trade margins that the purchaser may have to pay. Manufacturing covers the production of semi-processed goods and other intermediate goods as well as final products such as consumer goods and capital equipment. The indexes shown here are weighted averages of monthly price changes in the manufacturing sector.

Comparability

The precise ways in which PPIs are defined and constructed depend on their intended use. In this context, national practices may differ and these differences may affect cross-country comparability. This is especially the case for aspects such as the weighting and aggregation systems, the treatment of quality differences, the sampling and collection of individual prices, the frequency with which the weights are updated, and in the index formulae used. Differences may also arise concerning the scope of the manufacturing sector and the statistical unit used for measurement. In some countries, for example, indices may reflect price changes in the output of the manufacturing sector as opposed to manufactured products.

While the PPI series for most countries refer to domestic sales of manufacturing goods, those for Australia, Canada, Chile, New Zealand and the United States include prices applied for foreign sales (i.e. "total market").

Overview

In the 3-year average from 2012-14, producer prices in the OECD area as a whole increased at an annual rate of around 0.9%, a lower rate than recorded in the 3-year average from 2002-04 (2.1%).

Producer prices have been, however, volatile during the whole period (2002-14), and have recorded swings, with peaks in 2008 and 2011 and decreases in 2002, 2009 and 2013. The effect of the financial and economic crisis is particularly noteworthy, with nearly all OECD countries recording negative growth in producer prices in 2009, with the OECD average at minus 4.0% for that year.

Since then the picture has been less clear in producer prices with some OECD countries seeing large increases in 2011 followed by large drops in 2012 and 2013 (Greece, Hungary and the Netherlands), while some have recorded low or continued negative growth (Switzerland and Sweden). The year 2014 shows also diverging patterns among OECD countries, with, on one side, large increases recorded in Turkey and Chile and to a smaller extent in Sweden, Australia, Canada, Japan and Mexico, and a slowdown in producer price inflation rates recorded in New Zealand, the United Kingdom, Belgium and Estonia.

Sources
• OECD (2015), *Main Economic Indicators*, OECD Publishing.

Further information

Analytical publications
• Brook, A.M. *et al.* (2004), "Oil Price Developments: Drivers, Economic Consequences and Policy Responses", *OECD Economics Department Working Papers*, No. 412.
• OECD (2015), *OECD Economic Outlook*, OECD Publishing.

Methodological publications
• International Monetary Fund (IMF) *et al.* (2004), *Producer Price Index Manual: Theory and Practice*, IMF, Washington, DC.
• OECD (2011), *Producer price Indices - Comparative Methodological Analysis*, OECD, Paris.
• OECD (2007), *Eurostat-OECD Methodological Guide for Developing Producer Price Indices for Services*, OECD Publishing.

Online databases
• *Main Economic Indicators: Producer prices.*

Websites
• OECD Main Economic Indicators, *www.oecd.org/std/mei.*

PPI: domestic manufacturing

Annual growth in percentage

	2002	2003	2004	2005	2006	2007	2008	2009	2010	2011	2012	2013	2014
Australia	0.2	0.5	3.9	6.0	7.9	2.3	8.3	-5.4	1.9	3.4	-0.5	1.1	3.1
Austria	-1.4	0.3	2.2	3.7	1.8	3.4	3.4	-2.2	4.4	5.0	1.5	0.1	-0.4
Belgium	0.1	0.9	4.2	6.0	5.5	3.6	5.7	-4.9	6.3	6.8	2.8	-0.2	-2.5
Canada	0.1	-1.2	3.2	1.6	2.3	1.5	4.4	-3.5	1.5	6.9	1.1	0.4	2.5
Chile	..	..	..	2.9	5.0	6.0	15.9	-3.3	5.5	4.6	0.3	2.6	8.6
Czech Republic	-1.3	-0.4	5.8	2.0	0.6	3.5	3.1	-5.5	1.5	5.7	2.3	0.2	1.0
Denmark	1.0	0.0	1.0	3.0	3.4	4.9	5.7	-1.2	3.2	4.6	3.1	1.3	-0.5
Estonia	-1.0	-0.6	3.4	2.3	4.8	10.1	7.6	-3.9	2.1	5.7	2.9	2.7	0.3
Finland	-1.9	-1.5	-0.2	3.8	5.0	4.7	7.2	-6.7	5.2	6.2	2.7	0.3	-0.5
France	-0.1	0.7	2.0	2.7	3.3	2.7	5.0	-6.2	2.3	5.2	2.0	-0.1	-1.3
Germany	0.2	0.6	1.7	2.4	2.3	2.3	3.1	-3.4	2.5	4.2	1.5	0.0	-0.4
Greece	2.1	2.1	3.8	6.4	7.9	3.5	9.7	-7.2	6.9	8.6	3.7	-2.1	-2.8
Hungary	2.0	3.7	7.3	4.3	5.7	4.3	8.6	-0.1	5.7	8.6	5.2	1.1	0.6
Iceland	..	..	..	..	17.5	1.8	31.0	11.3	11.8	9.2	1.1	-4.4	-0.7
Ireland	2.1	0.8	0.4	1.9	3.5	2.2	5.9	-3.6	1.6	6.2	2.8	1.3	-0.5
Israel	3.9	4.3	5.4	6.2	5.7	3.5	9.6	-6.3	4.0	7.7	4.4	0.4	-1.4
Italy	0.8	1.4	3.3	3.1	4.0	3.4	5.0	-5.6	3.6	4.9	1.9	0.0	-0.7
Japan	-2.4	-1.4	0.3	0.8	1.9	1.3	4.1	-4.8	-0.3	1.1	-1.7	0.5	2.8
Korea	-1.6	1.7	7.6	3.1	0.1	0.8	12.1	-1.8	4.3	9.0	-0.4	-3.0	-2.1
Luxembourg	0.9	3.3	14.8	0.1	9.0	7.6	12.9	-19.2	8.3	5.6	0.0	0.2	-0.2
Mexico	3.2	6.6	8.6	4.5	6.0	5.0	8.6	5.4	4.7	6.5	5.5	0.2	2.4
Netherlands	-0.6	1.3	3.6	4.5	4.8	6.1	7.5	-9.6	6.6	10.8	4.0	-1.0	-2.1
New Zealand	0.0	-1.7	2.8	5.6	6.5	4.0	14.9	-4.8	4.3	5.7	-2.1	3.1	0.6
Norway	-0.4	1.4	3.1	3.5	3.0	4.4	7.8	0.3	3.2	6.5	2.8	2.0	1.4
Poland	-1.7	0.8	8.0	1.4	1.9	3.6	3.4	-2.6	2.9	8.6	3.3	-0.8	-1.9
Portugal	0.4	0.4	2.9	3.4	3.4	1.5	5.0	-5.5	3.5	6.0	1.9	-0.8	-2.1
Slovak Republic	2.5	-0.1	2.5	1.3	1.5	0.2	2.0	-5.9	0.0	4.1	1.3	-0.3	-1.8
Slovenia	4.9	2.9	4.2	3.3	2.4	4.4	5.2	-2.0	2.1	4.1	1.1	0.4	-0.5
Spain	0.6	1.4	3.7	4.7	5.0	3.4	6.0	-5.5	4.1	6.5	2.7	0.0	-1.4
Sweden	0.6	-0.9	1.8	4.0	3.9	3.3	3.9	1.0	0.3	1.3	-0.2	-2.0	1.7
Switzerland	..	..	2.0	2.0	2.7	2.8	4.4	-2.8	0.5	0.1	-0.5	-0.1	-0.7
Turkey	48.3	20.8	13.1	7.6	9.3	5.6	11.8	-0.6	6.0	13.3	5.5	4.5	11.4
United Kingdom	-0.3	1.1	2.2	4.0	3.1	3.0	9.5	-2.3	4.1	7.4	2.2	1.1	-1.4
United States	-0.7	2.5	4.3	5.5	4.0	3.8	7.9	-4.9	5.0	7.8	2.1	0.4	0.8
Euro area	0.3	0.9	2.5	3.1	3.4	3.0	4.6	-5.0	3.3	5.3	2.0	-0.1	-0.9
EU 28	0.2	1.0	2.9	3.3	3.4	3.1	5.1	-4.6	3.3	5.6	2.1	0.0	-0.9
OECD	0.8	1.8	3.7	4.0	3.7	3.2	6.8	-4.0	3.7	6.3	1.8	0.3	0.7
Brazil	..	..	..	..	..	..	..	..	..	..	..	..	..
China	..	..	..	..	..	..	..	..	..	..	..	..	..
India	..	..	..	..	..	..	..	..	..	..	..	..	..
Indonesia	..	..	..	..	..	..	..	..	..	..	..	..	..
Russian Federation	8.0	16.0	19.4	13.8	11.1	13.2	21.1	-5.1	11.5	14.0	3.8	2.2	5.6
South Africa	13.3	4.6	2.0	3.7	6.4	9.8	15.2	0.7	1.9	5.7	6.6	6.0	7.4

StatLink http://dx.doi.org/10.1787/888933336516

PPI: domestic manufacturing

Average annual growth in percentage

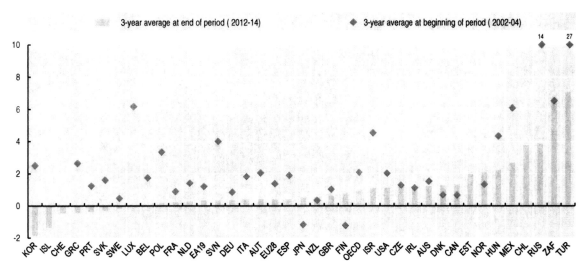

StatLink http://dx.doi.org/10.1787/888933335389

LONG-TERM INTEREST RATES

Long-term interest rates are one of the determinants of business investment. Low long-term interest rates encourage investment in new equipment; investment is, in turn, a major source of economic growth.

Definition

Long-term interest rates as measured here refer to government bonds with a residual maturity of about ten years. They are not the interest rates at which the loans were issued, but the interest rates implied by the prices at which these government bonds are traded on financial markets. For example if a bond was initially bought at a price of 100 with an interest rate of 9%, but it is now trading at a price 90, the interest rate shown here will be 10% ([9/90] × 100).

Long-term interest are, where possible, averages of daily rates. In all cases, they refer to bonds whose capital repayment is guaranteed by governments.

Long-term interest rates are mainly determined by three factors: the price that lenders charge for postponing consumption; the risk that the borrower may not repay the capital; and the fall in the real value of the capital that the lender expects to occur because of inflation during the lifetime of the loan. Interest rates refer to government borrowing and the risk factor is assumed to be very low. To an important extent the interest rates are driven by expected inflation rates.

Comparability

Comparability of these data is considered to be high. There may be differences, however, in the size of government bonds outstanding, and in the extent to which these rates are representatives of financial conditions in various countries.

Overview

Long-term interest rates peaked in 1981 for most OECD countries (for example, French government bonds reached 16.3%) but since then, rates have consistently and gradually decreased to hit historic low levels in 2014. For example, in 2014 long-term interest rates in the euro area fell to a low of 2.3%, while both Japan and Switzerland saw their long-term interest rates fall below 1%, (0.5% and 0.7% respectively).

From the end of the nineties to the start of the global financial crisis, the spread for 10-year bonds of European countries, vis-a-vis German bonds was small (around 0.1%). After 2008, in Greece, Ireland and Portugal spreads rose to 21.0 (2012), 7.0 (2011) and 9.1 (2012) respectively. The spreads also increased for Italy and Spain but to a lesser extent.

In 2014 there were only three OECD countries with long-term interest rates above 6%, namely Greece (6.9%), Iceland (6.4%) and Mexico (6.0%). Non-member countries for which data is available recorded higher rates e.g. 8.5% in Russia and 8.3% in South Africa.

Sources
• OECD (2015), *Main Economic Indicators*, OECD Publishing.

Further information

Analytical publications
• OECD (2015), *OECD Economic Outlook*, OECD Publishing.
• OECD (2014), *OECD Journal: Financial Market Trends*, OECD Publishing.
• OECD (2014), *OECD Sovereign Borrowing Outlook*, OECD Publishing.
• OECD (2008), *Understanding Economic Statistics: An OECD Perspective*, OECD Publishing.

Methodological publications
• OECD (1998), *Main Economic Indicators – Sources and Methods: Interest Rates and Share Price Indices*, OECD Publishing.

Websites
• Main Economic Indicators, *www.oecd.org/std/mei*.

Long-term interest rates

Percentage

	2002	2003	2004	2005	2006	2007	2008	2009	2010	2011	2012	2013	2014
Australia	5.84	5.37	5.59	5.34	5.59	5.99	5.82	5.04	5.37	4.88	3.38	3.70	3.66
Austria	4.96	4.14	4.13	3.39	3.80	4.30	4.36	3.94	3.23	3.32	2.37	2.01	1.49
Belgium	4.89	4.15	4.06	3.37	3.81	4.33	4.40	3.82	3.35	4.18	2.96	2.37	1.74
Canada	5.29	4.81	4.58	4.07	4.21	4.27	3.61	3.23	3.24	2.78	1.87	2.26	2.23
Chile	..	..	..	6.05	6.16	6.09	7.10	5.71	6.27	6.03	5.47	5.35	4.69
Czech Republic	4.88	4.12	4.82	3.54	3.80	4.30	4.63	4.84	3.88	3.71	2.78	2.11	1.58
Denmark	5.06	4.31	4.30	3.40	3.81	4.29	4.28	3.59	2.93	2.73	1.40	1.75	1.33
Estonia	..	..	..	..	..	..	..	..	..	..	..	..	..
Finland	4.98	4.14	4.11	3.35	3.78	4.29	4.29	3.74	3.01	3.01	1.88	1.86	1.45
France	4.86	4.13	4.10	3.41	3.80	4.30	4.23	3.65	3.12	3.32	2.54	2.20	1.67
Germany	4.78	4.07	4.04	3.35	3.76	4.22	3.98	3.22	2.74	2.61	1.50	1.57	1.16
Greece	5.12	4.27	4.26	3.59	4.07	4.50	4.80	5.17	9.09	15.75	22.50	10.05	6.93
Hungary	7.09	6.77	8.29	6.60	7.12	6.74	8.24	9.12	7.28	7.64	7.89	5.92	4.81
Iceland	7.96	6.65	7.49	8.64	8.83	9.42	11.07	8.26	6.09	5.98	6.19	5.79	6.37
Ireland	4.99	4.13	4.06	3.32	3.79	4.33	4.55	5.23	5.99	9.58	5.99	3.83	2.26
Israel	9.23	8.88	7.56	6.36	6.31	5.55	5.92	5.06	4.68	4.98	4.40	3.80	2.89
Italy	5.03	4.30	4.26	3.56	4.05	4.49	4.68	4.31	4.04	5.42	5.49	4.32	2.89
Japan	1.26	1.00	1.49	1.35	1.74	1.67	1.47	1.33	1.15	1.10	0.84	0.69	0.52
Korea	6.59	5.05	4.73	4.95	5.15	5.35	5.57	5.17	4.77	4.20	3.45	3.28	3.19
Luxembourg	4.68	3.32	2.84	2.41	3.30	..	..	..	2.95	2.92	1.83	1.83	1.34
Mexico	10.13	8.98	9.54	9.42	8.39	7.79	8.31	7.96	6.90	6.67	5.60	5.68	6.01
Netherlands	4.89	4.12	4.10	3.37	3.78	4.29	4.23	3.69	2.99	2.99	1.93	1.96	1.45
New Zealand	6.53	5.87	6.07	5.88	5.78	6.27	6.08	5.46	5.60	4.95	3.69	4.09	4.30
Norway	6.38	5.05	4.37	3.75	4.08	4.77	4.46	4.00	3.53	3.14	2.10	2.58	2.52
Poland	7.36	5.78	6.90	5.22	5.23	5.48	6.07	6.12	5.78	5.96	5.00	4.03	3.52
Portugal	5.01	4.18	4.14	3.44	3.91	4.42	4.52	4.21	5.40	10.24	10.55	6.29	3.75
Slovak Republic	6.94	4.99	5.03	3.52	4.41	4.49	4.72	4.71	3.87	4.42	4.55	3.19	2.07
Slovenia	..	6.40	4.68	3.81	3.85	4.53	4.61	4.38	3.83	4.97	5.81	5.81	3.27
Spain	4.96	4.12	4.10	3.39	3.78	4.31	4.36	3.97	4.25	5.44	5.85	4.56	2.72
Sweden	5.30	4.64	4.43	3.38	3.70	4.17	3.89	3.25	2.89	2.61	1.59	2.12	1.72
Switzerland	3.20	2.66	2.74	2.10	2.52	2.93	2.90	2.20	1.63	1.47	0.65	0.95	0.69
Turkey	..	..	..	..	..	..	..	..	..	..	..	..	..
United Kingdom	4.89	4.53	4.88	4.41	4.50	5.01	4.59	3.65	3.62	3.14	1.92	2.39	2.57
United States	4.61	4.02	4.27	4.29	4.79	4.63	3.67	3.26	3.21	2.79	1.80	2.35	2.54
Euro area	4.92	4.16	4.14	3.44	3.86	4.33	4.36	4.03	3.78	4.31	3.05	3.01	2.28
Brazil	..	..	..	..	..	..	..	..	..	..	..	..	..
China	..	..	..	..	..	..	..	..	..	..	..	..	..
India	..	..	..	..	..	..	..	..	..	..	..	..	..
Indonesia	..	..	..	..	..	..	..	..	..	..	..	..	..
Russian Federation	15.82	9.12	8.29	8.11	6.98	6.72	7.52	9.87	7.83	8.06	8.15	7.33	8.46
South Africa	11.50	9.62	9.53	8.07	7.94	7.99	9.10	8.70	8.62	8.52	7.90	7.72	8.25

StatLink ㎏ *http://dx.doi.org/10.1787/888933336351*

Long-term interest rates

Percentage

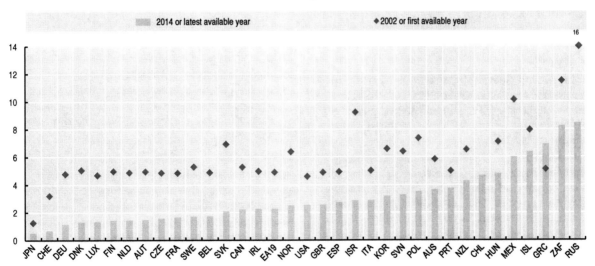

StatLink ㎏ *http://dx.doi.org/10.1787/888933335187*

RATES OF CONVERSION

To compare a single country's real GDP over a period of years, it is necessary to remove movements that are due to price changes. In the same way, in order to compare the real GDPs of a group of countries at a single point in time, it is necessary to remove any differences in their GDPs that are due to differences in their price levels. Price indices are used to remove the effects of price changes in a single country over time; purchasing power parities (PPPs) are used to remove the effects of the different levels of prices within a group of countries at a point in time.

Market exchange rates are sometimes used to convert national GDPs into a common currency. However, comparisons of GDP based on exchange rates do not reflect well the real volumes of goods and services in the different countries. For many of the low-income countries, for example, the differences between GDP converted using market exchange rates and GDP converted using PPPs are considerable. In general, the use of market exchange rates understates the real GDP of low-income countries and overstates the real GDP of high-income countries.

Definition

PPPs are currency converters that equalise price levels between countries. PPPs have been calculated by comparing the prices in OECD countries of a common basket of about 2 500 goods and services. Countries are not required to price all the items in the common basket because some of the items may be hard to find in certain countries. However, the common basket has been drawn up in such a way that each country can collect prices for a wide range of the goods and services that are representative of their markets.

The goods and services to be priced cover all those that enter into final expenditure: household consumption, government services, capital formation and net exports. Prices for the different items are weighted by their shares in total final expenditure to obtain the PPPs for GDP shown here.

Comparative price level indices are the ratios of PPPs to market exchange rates. At the level of GDP they provide a measure of the differences in the general price levels of countries.

Comparability

PPPs for the OECD and Russia have been calculated jointly by the OECD and Eurostat using standard procedures. In consultation with their member countries, OECD and Eurostat keep their methodology under review and improvements are made regularly. PPPs for non-OECD countries, with the exception of Russia, are calculated within the framework of the International Comparison Programme (ICP). There are six regions in the ICP programme, of which five – Africa, Asia-Pacific, the Commonwealth of Independent States (CIS), Latin America and Caribbean and Western Asia – are regions overseen by the ICP Global Office at the World Bank.

Overview

Over the period 2002-14, there were significant differences between changes in PPPs and changes in market exchange rates; even when the two indicators moved in the same direction, changes differed in their magnitude.

Price level indices are PPPs estimates for 2014 divided by market exchange rates for the same year, with the OECD set equal to 100. In general, there is a positive correlation between GDP levels and price levels. Australia, Norway and Switzerland, three OECD countries with high per capita income, also recorded the highest price levels in 2014, exceeding the average OECD level by 40% or more, while India had price levels of around 30% of the OECD average. Changes in price level indices should however be interpreted with caution as they are highly dependent on changes in exchange rates.

Sources

- OECD (2013), "*PPP benchmark results 2011*", OECD National Accounts Statistics (Database).
- For Brazil, China, Indonesia and South Africa, World development indicators (2014), World Bank, *http://data.worldbank.org/data-catalog/world-development-indicators*.

Further information

Analytical publications

- OECD (2008), *Understanding Economic Statistics: An OECD Perspective*, OECD Publishing.

Online databases

- OECD (2015), *OECD National Accounts Statistics* (Database).

Statistical publications

- OECD (2014), *National Accounts at a Glance*, OECD Publishing.

Websites

- Prices and Purchasing Power Parities (PPP), *www.oecd.org/std/ppp*.

Purchasing power parities and indices of price levels

| | Purchasing power parities | | | | | | Indices of price levels | | | | | |
| | National currency units per US dollar | | | | | | OECD = 100 | | | | | |
	2009	2010	2011	2012	2013	2014	2009	2010	2011	2012	2013	2014
Australia	1.443	1.505	1.511	1.522	1.522	1.536	111	135	148	155	146	140
Austria	0.844	0.841	0.835	0.839	0.844	0.835	116	109	110	106	112	112
Belgium	0.858	0.854	0.840	0.843	0.850	0.838	117	111	111	106	112	112
Canada	1.204	1.221	1.240	1.246	1.252	1.261	104	116	119	122	121	115
Chile	353.070	357.334	348.017	350.295	354.907	370.814	62	68	68	71	71	66
Czech Republic	13.899	13.954	13.398	13.430	13.393	13.332	72	71	72	67	68	65
Denmark	7.833	7.755	7.599	7.664	7.673	7.586	144	135	135	130	136	137
Estonia	0.524	0.524	0.524	0.539	0.551	0.564	72	68	69	68	73	76
Finland	0.903	0.911	0.908	0.918	0.932	0.939	124	118	120	116	123	126
France	0.861	0.857	0.844	0.853	0.854	0.829	118	111	112	108	113	111
Germany	0.809	0.796	0.784	0.786	0.794	0.787	111	103	104	99	105	106
Greece	0.697	0.702	0.700	0.688	0.645	0.626	95	91	93	87	85	84
Hungary	125.553	125.461	124.821	127.936	129.279	132.000	61	59	59	56	58	57
Iceland	124.992	131.845	134.752	136.698	138.204	140.228	100	105	110	107	113	121
Ireland	0.892	0.843	0.832	0.832	0.832	0.841	122	109	110	105	110	113
Israel	3.964	3.971	3.945	3.964	4.006	4.006	99	104	105	101	111	113
Italy	0.779	0.780	0.769	0.764	0.762	0.758	107	101	102	96	101	102
Japan	115.497	111.633	107.454	104.628	104.090	105.270	122	124	128	129	106	100
Korea	824.761	840.569	854.586	860.249	860.219	857.261	64	71	73	75	78	82
Luxembourg	0.907	0.922	0.894	0.898	0.915	0.900	124	119	118	113	121	121
Mexico	7.432	7.670	7.673	7.929	8.042	8.023	54	59	59	59	63	61
Netherlands	0.841	0.849	0.830	0.830	0.829	0.825	115	110	110	105	110	111
New Zealand	1.470	1.494	1.486	1.481	1.468	1.469	90	105	112	118	120	123
Norway	8.956	9.014	8.985	8.903	9.204	9.455	140	146	152	150	156	152
Poland	1.864	1.820	1.828	1.834	1.822	1.828	59	59	59	55	57	59
Portugal	0.633	0.632	0.620	0.593	0.589	0.588	87	82	82	75	78	79
Slovak Republic	0.511	0.510	0.518	0.519	0.513	0.503	70	66	69	65	68	67
Slovenia	0.644	0.641	0.630	0.615	0.608	0.604	88	83	83	78	80	81
Spain	0.709	0.717	0.704	0.688	0.680	0.676	97	93	93	87	90	91
Sweden	8.915	8.995	8.853	8.824	8.807	8.950	115	122	130	128	135	132
Switzerland	1.519	1.509	1.433	1.397	1.379	1.370	137	142	153	146	148	151
Turkey	0.912	0.941	0.992	1.051	1.112	1.199	58	61	56	57	58	55
United Kingdom	0.656	0.691	0.700	0.695	0.699	0.708	101	104	107	108	109	118
United States	1.000	1.000	1.000	1.000	1.000	1.000	98	98	95	98	100	101
EU 28	0.752	0.763	0.755	0.760	0.755	0.755	103	99	100	96	100	101
Brazil	1.311	1.402	1.471	1.517	1.608	1.667	65	78	84	76	74	72
China	3.147	3.316	3.506	3.514	3.521	3.655	45	48	52	55	57	60
India	13.182	14.194	15.109	15.915	16.762	17.689	27	30	31	29	28	29
Indonesia	3 181.203	3 402.693	3 606.566	3 699.950	3 803.351	3 941.790	30	37	39	39	36	34
Russian Federation	14.019	15.815	17.346	18.043	18.425	19.066	44	51	56	57	58	50
South Africa	4.322	4.598	4.774	4.901	5.110	5.342	50	61	62	59	53	50

StatLink http://dx.doi.org/10.1787/888933336563

Indices of price levels

OECD = 100, 2014

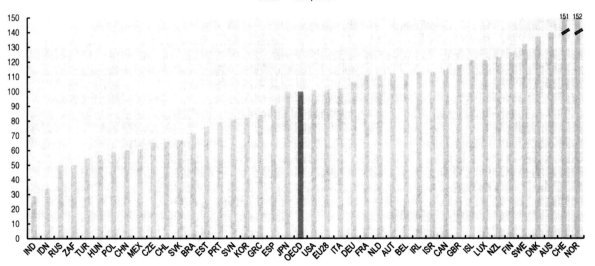

StatLink http://dx.doi.org/10.1787/888933335476

REAL EFFECTIVE EXCHANGE RATES

Effective exchange rates are a summary measure of the changes in the exchange rates of a country vis-à-vis its trading partners. They provide a broad interpretation of a country's price competitiveness, which is, in turn, a major determinant of the success of different countries in raising exports and productivity, fostering innovation and improving living standards.

Definition

Nominal effective exchange rate indices are calculated by comparing, for each country, the change in its own exchange rate against the US dollar to a weighted average of changes in its competitors' exchange rates, also against the US dollar. Changes in the competitor exchange rates are weighted using a matrix measuring the importance of bilateral trade flows in the current year.

The indicator of real effective exchange rates, i.e. relative consumer price indices, takes into account not only changes in market exchange rates but also variations in relative prices using consumer prices.

The change in a country's relative consumer prices between two years is obtained by comparing the change in the country's consumer price index converted into US dollars at market exchange rates to a weighted average of changes in its competitors' consumer price indices, also expressed in US dollars. The weighted average of competitors' prices is based on a matrix for the current year expressing the importance of bilateral trade.

Comparability

The index is constructed using a common procedure that assures a high degree of comparability both across countries and over time.

A rise in the index represents a deterioration in that country's competitiveness. Real effective exchange rates are a major short-run determinant of any country's capacity to compete. Note that the index only shows changes in the international competitiveness of each country over time. Differences between countries in the levels of the indices have no significance.

Real effective exchange rates try to eliminate the weakness in the nominal effective exchange rates - namely that potential competitiveness gains from exchange rate depreciations can be eroded by domestic inflation - by correcting effective nominal exchange rates for differences in inflation rates. Consumer prices are usually used to make the correction because they are readily available. However, this implicitly assumes that the relative price of domestic tradable goods as compared with foreign tradables evolves in parallel to the relative consumer prices, which is often not the case.

Overview

From around 2009 to 2012, France, Germany, Italy, Japan, the United Kingdom and the United States saw virtually no change in their real effective exchange rate. However since 2012, while rates for France, Germany, Italy and the United States have remained stable, Japan has seen a major gain in its international competitiveness, as measured by the drop in its real effective exchange rate, while the United Kingdom has seen its international competitiveness deteriorate.

Commodity exporting countries also saw an improvement in international competitiveness in the last few years (Australia, Canada, Chile and Norway) along with the Czech Republic, Sweden and Turkey. Iceland, Korea and New Zealand, on the other hand, all recorded drops in their international competitiveness over the last few years.

For non-OECD countries, with the exception of China, all have seen their international competitiveness improve; and in the case of Indonesia and South Africa quite substantially since 2010.

Sources
• OECD (2015), *OECD Economic Outlook*, OECD Publishing.

Further information

Analytical publications
• OECD (2015), *OECD Economic Surveys*, OECD Publishing.

Statistical publications
• OECD (2015), *Main Economic Indicators*, OECD Publishing.

Online databases
• *OECD Economic Outlook: Statistics and Projections.*

Websites
• Sources & Methods of the OECD Economic Outlook, *www.oecd.org/eco/sources-and-methods.*

Real effective exchange rates

Based on consumer price indices, 2010 = 100

	2002	2003	2004	2005	2006	2007	2008	2009	2010	2011	2012	2013	2014
Australia	69.6	78.6	85.1	87.6	87.4	92.9	91.0	88.2	100.0	106.9	108.4	103.7	99.0
Austria	99.1	102.3	103.4	102.5	101.7	102.1	102.2	103.0	100.0	100.4	98.8	100.8	102.6
Belgium	94.1	99.0	100.9	100.7	100.2	100.9	103.5	103.6	100.0	100.9	98.7	100.2	100.6
Canada	73.8	81.6	85.7	90.8	95.9	98.7	96.0	92.0	100.0	101.5	101.1	97.6	92.0
Chile	89.0	83.0	88.7	94.3	98.7	97.1	98.5	94.9	100.0	101.1	103.7	103.1	94.2
Czech Republic	79.7	78.1	79.0	83.3	87.5	89.9	102.9	99.0	100.0	102.0	98.8	96.6	91.5
Denmark	95.0	100.1	101.0	99.8	99.4	99.9	101.4	104.4	100.0	99.4	96.8	97.7	98.9
Estonia	86.5	89.6	91.2	91.4	92.2	95.8	101.7	103.4	100.0	101.2	100.1	102.9	104.8
Finland	103.1	107.8	107.6	104.2	102.6	103.6	105.1	106.7	100.0	99.6	96.9	98.6	101.4
France	97.7	103.0	104.8	103.4	102.7	103.1	103.8	104.0	100.0	99.3	96.3	97.4	97.8
Germany	100.3	105.3	106.7	104.5	103.5	104.8	104.8	105.7	100.0	99.0	95.7	97.8	99.0
Greece	88.0	93.5	95.8	95.9	96.6	98.0	99.8	101.4	100.0	100.7	96.8	95.9	95.5
Hungary	87.4	89.5	95.4	96.9	92.1	102.5	105.2	99.2	100.0	99.8	96.8	96.0	92.5
Iceland	125.4	132.2	135.7	153.4	143.1	148.7	116.4	95.0	100.0	101.0	101.5	105.4	113.1
Ireland	89.4	98.2	100.7	100.4	102.1	107.1	112.0	107.9	100.0	100.2	95.7	97.2	96.9
Israel	102.9	96.8	90.3	87.7	87.2	87.7	97.7	95.5	100.0	101.1	96.2	102.3	103.6
Italy	96.6	102.5	104.3	102.8	102.3	102.8	103.6	104.9	100.0	99.9	97.9	99.5	100.1
Japan	105.1	105.7	107.0	100.5	90.8	83.2	89.8	100.5	100.0	101.2	99.9	80.2	76.0
Korea	107.0	108.2	109.8	122.7	131.1	129.1	105.0	93.1	100.0	100.0	99.7	103.7	109.9
Luxembourg	94.3	98.0	99.4	99.1	99.7	100.6	101.6	102.3	100.0	100.5	99.0	100.4	100.8
Mexico	123.4	109.7	105.1	108.9	108.9	108.9	107.6	105.5	100.0	100.1	97.3	102.7	101.8
Netherlands	98.6	104.2	105.0	103.5	102.2	102.5	103.0	104.8	100.0	99.4	96.9	99.8	101.0
New Zealand	82.3	94.2	101.2	106.7	99.0	106.0	98.9	92.6	100.0	103.8	106.6	109.4	113.1
Norway	98.8	98.3	94.0	97.3	96.9	96.9	97.5	95.5	100.0	100.7	100.3	98.6	93.8
Poland	99.6	89.0	88.1	97.8	99.4	102.6	111.7	94.8	100.0	98.2	95.7	96.0	97.1
Portugal	97.9	102.1	103.2	102.3	102.8	103.5	103.6	102.9	100.0	100.8	99.5	99.6	99.3
Slovak Republic	61.2	69.5	76.2	77.7	81.6	90.0	97.5	104.7	100.0	100.9	100.4	101.8	102.5
Slovenia	95.8	99.3	99.5	98.4	98.4	99.9	102.2	103.7	100.0	99.0	97.2	98.8	99.5
Spain	91.0	95.9	98.1	98.5	99.8	101.3	103.4	103.4	100.0	100.5	98.2	99.9	99.8
Sweden	104.2	110.8	111.3	106.4	105.7	106.8	104.3	94.4	100.0	105.8	105.3	106.4	101.3
Switzerland	98.5	99.1	98.1	95.9	93.1	88.8	92.3	96.3	100.0	109.7	105.6	103.7	104.8
Turkey	73.7	78.2	80.9	89.6	88.8	96.1	97.0	91.3	100.0	88.4	91.7	90.3	86.1
United Kingdom	127.5	121.7	126.3	123.9	124.4	126.0	109.7	99.5	100.0	100.6	105.0	103.6	111.3
United States	124.1	116.8	111.8	110.0	109.2	104.3	100.3	104.8	100.0	95.3	97.7	97.8	100.1
Brazil	55.8	53.7	55.9	69.2	77.6	83.6	87.9	87.9	100.0	104.8	94.8	89.9	88.6
China	95.8	89.4	86.7	85.7	87.1	90.1	97.9	102.0	100.0	102.2	108.0	114.6	117.4
India	88.5	87.0	86.0	88.1	87.2	93.5	88.9	90.2	100.0	99.1	94.6	93.7	96.4
Indonesia	81.1	87.0	83.0	81.7	94.8	94.3	90.4	89.5	100.0	99.8	96.1	92.0	85.7
Russian Federation	66.3	67.2	72.5	80.4	88.7	93.0	99.3	91.1	100.0	104.0	105.9	107.5	97.1
South Africa	74.1	97.1	103.8	104.0	98.5	91.6	80.0	87.3	100.0	98.1	92.3	81.8	77.0

StatLink http://dx.doi.org/10.1787/888933336329

Real effective exchange rates based on consumer price indices

2010 = 100

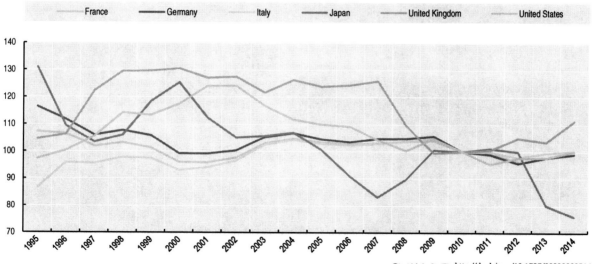

StatLink http://dx.doi.org/10.1787/888933335141

ENERGY AND TRANSPORTATION

ENERGY SUPPLY

Basic supply and demand data for all fuels are required to compare the contribution that each fuel makes to the economy and their interrelationships through the conversion of one fuel into another.

Definition

Energy supply refers to total primary energy supply (TPES). TPES equals production plus imports minus exports minus international bunkers plus or minus stock changes. The International Energy Agency (IEA) energy balance methodology is based on the calorific content of the energy commodities and a common unit of account. The unit of account adopted is the tonne of oil equivalent (toe) which is defined as 10^7 kilocalories (41.868 gigajoules). This quantity of energy is, within a few per cent, equal to the net heat content of one tonne of crude oil. The difference between the "net" and the "gross" calorific value for each fuel is the latent heat of vaporisation of the water produced during combustion of the fuel. For coal and oil, net calorific value is about 5% less than gross, for most forms of natural and manufactured gas the difference is 9-10%, while for electricity there is no difference. The IEA balances are calculated using the physical energy content method to calculate the primary energy equivalent.

Comparability

Data quality is not homogeneous for all countries and regions. In some countries, data are based on secondary sources, and where incomplete or unavailable, the IEA has made estimates. In general, data are likely to be more accurate for production and trade than for international bunkers or stock changes. Moreover, statistics for biofuels and waste are less accurate than those for traditional commercial energy data.

Overview

Between 1971 and 2013, the world's total primary energy supply more than doubled, reaching 13 541 Mtoe (million tonnes of oil equivalent). This equates to a compound growth rate of 2.2% per year. By comparison, world population grew on average by 1.5% and gross domestic product by 3.0% per year in real terms over the same period.

Energy supply growth was fairly constant over the period, except in 1974-75 and in the early 1980s as a consequence of the first two oil shocks, and in the early 1990s following the dissolution of the Soviet Union. With the economic crisis in 2008/2009, world energy supply declined by 1% in 2009. However, energy supply rebounded in 2010, increasing by 5% and kept growing by 3% in 2013.

The share of OECD in world primary energy supply decreased from 61% in 1971 to 39% in 2013. Strong economic development in Asia led to a large increase in the share of non-OECD Asia (including China) in world energy supply, from 13% to 35% over the same period. By contrast, the combined share of non-OECD Europe and Eurasia (which includes the Former Soviet Union) decreased significantly in the late 1980s and early 1990s.

Sources
- International Energy Agency (IEA) (2015), *Energy Balances of OECD Countries*, IEA, Paris.
- IEA (2015), *Energy Balances of Non-OECD Countries*, IEA, Paris.

Further information

Analytical publications
- IEA (2015), *Coal Information*, IEA, Paris.
- IEA (2015), *Energy Policies of IEA Countries* (series), IEA, Paris.
- IEA (2015), *Energy Technology Perspectives*, IEA, Paris.
- IEA (2015), *Natural Gas Information*, IEA, Paris
- IEA (2015), *Oil Information*, IEA, Paris.
- IEA (2015), *Renewables Information*, IEA, Paris.
- IEA (2015), *World Energy Outlook*, IEA, Paris.

Online databases
- IEA World Energy Statistics and Balances.

Websites
- International Energy Agency, *www.iea.org*.

Total primary energy supply
Million tonnes of oil equivalent (Mtoe)

	1971	1990	2004	2005	2006	2007	2008	2009	2010	2011	2012	2013	2014
Australia	51.6	86.4	112.7	113.5	118.2	122.2	126.7	127.2	124.5	126.0	126.3	129.1	128.7
Austria	18.8	24.8	32.7	33.8	33.8	33.4	33.6	32.0	34.1	33.1	33.1	33.2	32.1
Belgium	39.7	48.3	59.0	58.8	58.2	57.3	59.0	56.8	61.0	57.6	54.4	56.4	54.0
Canada	141.4	208.6	267.6	270.3	267.1	267.4	265.1	249.9	251.4	257.0	252.3	253.2	257.6
Chile	8.7	14.0	27.5	28.4	29.5	30.6	30.3	29.5	30.9	33.6	37.2	38.7	38.8
Czech Republic	45.4	49.6	45.5	44.9	46.0	46.0	45.0	42.1	44.4	42.8	42.6	42.0	41.5
Denmark	18.5	17.4	19.4	18.9	20.3	19.8	19.2	18.4	19.5	18.0	17.3	17.5	16.4
Estonia	..	9.8	5.3	5.2	5.1	5.7	5.5	4.9	5.6	5.6	5.5	6.1	6.1
Finland	18.2	28.4	37.2	34.3	37.4	36.9	35.4	33.4	36.6	35.2	33.9	33.0	34.2
France	158.6	224.0	269.8	271.1	267.0	263.8	265.0	253.6	261.7	251.8	252.4	253.3	242.1
Germany	305.1	351.2	339.5	337.0	346.4	327.9	331.5	310.5	326.9	310.7	311.8	317.7	303.6
Greece	8.7	21.4	29.7	30.3	30.2	30.2	30.4	29.4	27.6	26.8	26.6	23.4	22.5
Hungary	19.0	28.8	26.1	27.6	27.3	26.7	26.5	24.9	25.7	25.0	23.5	22.6	22.6
Iceland	0.9	2.3	3.1	3.1	3.9	4.6	5.2	5.4	5.4	5.8	5.7	5.9	5.8
Ireland	6.7	9.9	14.5	14.6	14.6	15.0	14.8	14.3	14.4	13.2	13.2	13.1	12.8
Israel	5.7	11.5	19.2	18.4	20.3	20.8	22.9	21.5	23.2	23.1	24.3	23.9	23.4
Italy	105.4	146.6	181.6	183.6	181.2	179.0	175.4	164.4	170.0	166.9	161.3	155.4	146.2
Japan	267.5	439.3	522.6	520.5	519.8	515.2	495.4	472.3	498.9	462.0	452.0	454.7	441.2
Korea	17.0	92.9	208.3	210.3	213.7	222.2	227.1	229.3	250.0	260.5	263.5	263.8	265.3
Luxembourg	4.1	3.4	4.3	4.4	4.3	4.2	4.2	4.0	4.2	4.2	4.1	4.0	3.8
Mexico	43.0	122.5	160.8	168.7	170.9	175.5	180.8	175.3	176.3	183.6	188.7	191.3	189.4
Netherlands	50.9	65.7	79.1	78.4	76.8	79.4	79.6	78.2	83.4	77.4	78.6	77.4	72.3
New Zealand	6.8	12.8	17.3	16.9	16.9	17.1	17.4	17.5	18.4	18.3	19.3	19.5	20.1
Norway	13.3	21.1	26.5	26.8	27.2	27.6	32.2	31.3	33.9	28.0	29.7	32.7	30.1
Poland	86.1	103.1	91.0	92.1	96.8	96.3	97.8	94.1	100.4	101.0	97.7	97.6	94.9
Portugal	6.3	16.8	25.8	26.5	25.2	25.3	24.7	24.4	23.5	22.9	21.7	21.8	21.1
Slovak Republic	14.3	21.3	18.4	18.8	18.6	17.9	18.3	16.7	17.8	17.4	16.7	17.2	15.4
Slovenia	..	5.7	7.1	7.3	7.3	7.3	7.7	7.0	7.3	7.3	7.0	6.9	6.8
Spain	42.6	90.1	139.0	141.9	141.8	143.8	139.1	127.9	127.8	125.7	125.5	116.7	113.9
Sweden	36.0	47.2	52.6	51.6	50.2	50.1	49.6	45.4	50.9	49.8	50.2	49.3	46.7
Switzerland	16.4	24.4	26.1	25.9	27.1	25.8	26.8	27.0	26.2	25.4	25.6	26.7	25.2
Turkey	19.5	52.7	80.7	84.2	93.2	100.0	98.7	97.8	105.3	112.2	116.9	116.5	119.4
United Kingdom	208.7	205.9	221.6	222.7	219.0	211.1	207.7	195.8	202.4	187.7	192.9	191.0	177.8
United States	1 587.5	1 915.1	2 307.8	2 318.8	2 296.8	2 337.0	2 277.1	2 164.8	2 215.4	2 191.2	2 139.8	2 188.4	2 206.0
EU 28	..	1 644.8	1 782.2	1 787.4	1 793.4	1 763.7	1 755.9	1 655.5	1 721.5	1 658.1	1 646.2	1 625.6	..
OECD	3 372.3	4 522.7	5 479.3	5 509.4	5 512.1	5 543.1	5 475.5	5 226.8	5 404.8	5 306.6	5 251.2	5 299.6	5 237.6
Brazil	69.8	140.2	210.0	215.3	222.8	235.5	248.6	240.5	265.9	270.0	281.7	293.7	..
China	391.1	870.7	1 639.0	1 775.3	1 937.9	2 043.4	2 087.9	2 253.4	2 469.1	2 801.2	2 907.9	3 009.5	..
India	152.2	306.6	498.0	517.7	544.5	573.7	600.4	662.1	692.7	716.4	752.0	775.5	..
Indonesia	35.1	98.6	176.7	179.8	184.0	183.2	186.8	200.0	209.4	205.3	211.8	213.6	..
Russian Federation	..	879.2	647.4	651.7	670.7	672.6	688.5	647.0	689.7	723.0	741.0	730.9	..
South Africa	45.4	91.0	128.5	128.3	127.3	136.3	146.9	144.0	141.8	142.7	140.3	141.3	..
World	5 522.5	8 768.2	11 203.3	11 480.9	11 807.0	12 082.9	12 220.9	12 135.7	12 789.0	13 133.7	13 327.9	13 541.3	..

StatLink ⟨⟩ http://dx.doi.org/10.1787/888933336800

Total primary energy supply by region
Million tonnes of oil equivalent (Mtoe)

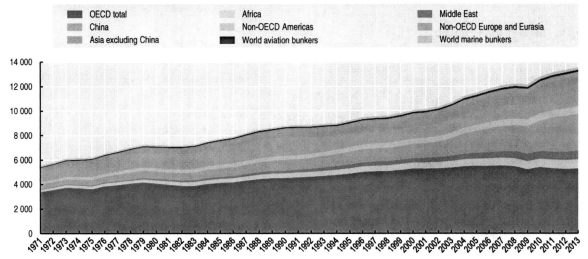

StatLink ⟨⟩ http://dx.doi.org/10.1787/888933335733

ENERGY INTENSITY

A common way to measure and compare the energy intensity of different countries, and how this changes over time, is to look at the ratio of energy supply to GDP. Energy intensity is sometimes also used as proxy of energy efficiency. However, this use can be misleading as energy intensity depends on numerous elements beyond energy efficiency such as climate, output composition, outsourcing of goods produced by energy-intensive industries, etc.

Definition

Energy intensity refers to total primary energy supply (TPES) per thousand US dollars of GDP. The ratios are calculated by dividing each country's annual TPES by each country's annual GDP expressed in constant 2005 prices and converted to US dollars using purchasing power parities (PPPs) for the year 2005.

TPES consists of primary energy production adjusted for net trade, bunkers and stock changes. Production of secondary energy (e.g. oil/coal products, electricity from fossil fuels, etc.) is not included since the "energy equivalent" of the primary fuels used to create the secondary products or electric power has already been counted. TPES is expressed in tonnes of oil equivalent.

Comparability

Care should be taken when comparing energy intensities between countries and over time since different national circumstances (e.g. density of population, country size, average temperatures and economic structure) will affect the ratios. A decrease in the TPES/GDP ratio may reflect a restructuring of the economy and the transfer of energy-intensive industries such as iron and steel out of the country. The harmful effects of such outsourcing may increase the global damage to the environment if the producers abroad use less energy efficient techniques.

Overview

Sharp improvements in the efficiency of key end uses, shifts to electricity, some changes in manufacturing output and consumer behaviour have occurred in many OECD countries since 1971. As a consequence, energy supply per unit of GDP fell significantly, particularly in the 1979-1990 period.

Contributing to the trend were higher fuel prices, long-term technological progress, government energy efficiency programmes and regulations.

Globally the ratio of energy supply to GDP (TPES/GDP) fell less than the ratio of energy consumption to GDP (total final consumption/GDP), because of increased use of electricity. The main reason for this divergence is that losses in electricity generation outweighed intensity improvements achieved in end uses such as household appliances.

Among OECD countries, the ratio of energy consumption to GDP varies considerably. Apart from energy prices, winter weather is a key element in these variations, as are raw materials processing techniques, the distance goods must be shipped, the size of dwellings, the use of private rather than public transport and other lifestyle factors.

Sources
- International Energy Agency (IEA) (2015), *Energy Balances of OECD Countries*, IEA, Paris.
- IEA (2015), *Energy Balances of Non-OECD Countries*, IEA, Paris.

Further information

Analytical publications
- IEA (2015), *Energy Technology Perspectives*, IEA, Paris.
- IEA (2015), *Energy Policies of IEA Countries* (series), IEA, Paris.
- IEA (2015), *Tracking Clean Energy Progress 2015*, IEA, Paris.
- IEA (2015), *World Energy Outlook*, IEA, Paris.
- IEA (2013), *Transition to Sustainable Buildings: Strategies and Opportunities to 2050*, IEA, Paris.

Online databases
- IEA World Energy Statistics and Balances.

Websites
- International Energy Agency, *www.iea.org*.

Total primary energy supply per unit of GDP

Tonnes of oil equivalent (toe) per thousand 2005 US dollars of GDP calculated using PPPs

	1971	1990	2000	2005	2006	2007	2008	2009	2010	2011	2012	2013	2014
Australia	0.21	0.20	0.18	0.16	0.16	0.16	0.16	0.16	0.15	0.15	0.15	0.14	0.14
Austria	0.16	0.12	0.11	0.12	0.12	0.11	0.11	0.11	0.11	0.11	0.11	0.11	0.10
Belgium	0.26	0.19	0.19	0.17	0.16	0.16	0.16	0.16	0.17	0.15	0.15	0.15	0.14
Canada	0.34	0.27	0.25	0.23	0.22	0.22	0.22	0.21	0.20	0.20	0.19	0.19	0.19
Chile	0.18	0.16	0.15	0.14	0.14	0.13	0.13	0.13	0.12	0.13	0.13	0.13	0.13
Czech Republic	0.37	0.28	0.22	0.20	0.19	0.18	0.17	0.17	0.17	0.16	0.16	0.16	0.16
Denmark	0.21	0.13	0.11	0.10	0.11	0.10	0.10	0.10	0.11	0.10	0.09	0.09	0.09
Estonia	..	0.60	0.30	0.23	0.21	0.21	0.22	0.23	0.25	0.24	0.22	0.24	0.23
Finland	0.30	0.24	0.22	0.20	0.21	0.20	0.19	0.20	0.21	0.20	0.19	0.19	0.20
France	0.19	0.16	0.14	0.14	0.14	0.13	0.13	0.13	0.13	0.12	0.12	0.12	0.12
Germany	0.23	0.17	0.13	0.13	0.13	0.12	0.12	0.12	0.12	0.11	0.11	0.11	0.10
Greece	0.08	0.12	0.12	0.11	0.10	0.10	0.10	0.10	0.10	0.11	0.11	0.10	0.10
Hungary	0.24	0.21	0.18	0.16	0.15	0.15	0.15	0.15	0.15	0.14	0.14	0.13	0.12
Iceland	0.29	0.34	0.36	0.29	0.35	0.38	0.42	0.46	0.48	0.50	0.48	0.48	0.46
Ireland	0.22	0.15	0.10	0.09	0.08	0.08	0.08	0.09	0.09	0.08	0.08	0.08	0.07
Israel	0.15	0.13	0.12	0.11	0.11	0.11	0.12	0.11	0.11	0.10	0.11	0.10	0.10
Italy	0.14	0.11	0.11	0.11	0.10	0.10	0.10	0.10	0.10	0.10	0.10	0.10	0.09
Japan	0.19	0.13	0.14	0.13	0.13	0.13	0.12	0.13	0.13	0.12	0.11	0.11	0.11
Korea	0.20	0.20	0.20	0.18	0.17	0.17	0.17	0.17	0.18	0.18	0.17	0.17	0.17
Luxembourg	0.51	0.21	0.13	0.14	0.13	0.12	0.12	0.12	0.12	0.12	0.12	0.11	0.10
Mexico	0.11	0.14	0.12	0.13	0.12	0.12	0.12	0.13	0.12	0.12	0.12	0.12	0.12
Netherlands	0.20	0.16	0.13	0.13	0.12	0.12	0.12	0.12	0.13	0.12	0.12	0.12	0.11
New Zealand	0.15	0.20	0.20	0.16	0.16	0.15	0.16	0.16	0.16	0.16	0.17	0.16	0.16
Norway	0.19	0.15	0.13	0.12	0.12	0.12	0.14	0.14	0.15	0.12	0.12	0.13	0.12
Poland	0.36	0.33	0.20	0.18	0.17	0.16	0.16	0.15	0.15	0.15	0.14	0.14	0.13
Portugal	0.08	0.10	0.11	0.11	0.11	0.11	0.10	0.10	0.10	0.10	0.10	0.10	0.09
Slovak Republic	0.33	0.33	0.26	0.21	0.19	0.17	0.16	0.16	0.16	0.15	0.14	0.15	0.13
Slovenia	..	0.17	0.16	0.15	0.15	0.14	0.14	0.14	0.14	0.14	0.14	0.14	0.13
Spain	0.10	0.12	0.12	0.12	0.11	0.11	0.11	0.10	0.10	0.10	0.10	0.10	0.09
Sweden	0.24	0.21	0.18	0.17	0.16	0.15	0.15	0.14	0.15	0.15	0.15	0.14	0.13
Switzerland	0.09	0.10	0.09	0.09	0.09	0.08	0.08	0.09	0.08	0.08	0.08	0.08	0.07
Turkey	0.11	0.12	0.12	0.11	0.11	0.11	0.11	0.12	0.12	0.11	0.12	0.11	0.11
United Kingdom	0.23	0.15	0.12	0.11	0.10	0.10	0.10	0.09	0.10	0.09	0.09	0.09	0.08
United States	0.35	0.23	0.20	0.18	0.17	0.17	0.17	0.16	0.16	0.16	0.15	0.15	0.15
EU 28	..	0.16	0.14	0.13	0.13	0.12	0.12	0.12	0.12	0.11	0.11	0.11	..
OECD	0.25	0.18	0.16	0.15	0.15	0.14	0.14	0.14	0.14	0.14	0.13	0.13	0.13
Brazil	0.12	0.11	0.11	0.11	0.11	0.11	0.11	0.11	0.11	0.11	0.11	0.11	..
China	1.08	0.58	0.29	0.28	0.27	0.25	0.23	0.23	0.23	0.23	0.23	0.22	..
India	0.25	0.22	0.19	0.16	0.15	0.15	0.15	0.15	0.14	0.14	0.14	0.13	..
Indonesia	0.19	0.14	0.15	0.14	0.13	0.13	0.12	0.12	0.12	0.11	0.11	0.10	..
Russian Federation	..	0.47	0.49	0.38	0.37	0.34	0.33	0.34	0.34	0.34	0.34	0.33	..
South Africa	0.22	0.28	0.28	0.27	0.26	0.26	0.27	0.27	0.26	0.25	0.24	0.24	..
World	0.27	0.22	0.19	0.18	0.17	0.17	0.17	0.16	0.17	0.16	0.16	0.16	..

StatLink http://dx.doi.org/10.1787/888933336713

Total primary energy supply per unit of GDP

Tonnes of oil equivalent (toe) per thousand 2005 US dollars of GDP calculated using PPPs

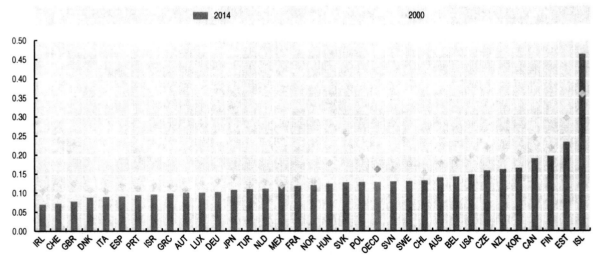

StatLink http://dx.doi.org/10.1787/888933335641

ELECTRICITY GENERATION

The amount of electricity generated by a country, and the breakdown of that production by type of fuel, reflects the natural resources, imported energy, national policies on security of energy supply, population size, electrification rate as well as the stage of development and rate of growth of the economy in each country.

Definition

Electricity generation includes fossil fuels, nuclear, hydro (excluding pumped storage), geothermal, solar, biofuels, etc. It includes electricity produced in electricity-only plants and in combined heat and power plants. Both main activity producer and autoproducer plants are included, where data are available. Main activity producers generate electricity for sale to third parties as their primary activity. Autoproducers generate electricity wholly or partly for their own use as an activity which supports their primary activity. Both types of plants may be privately or publicly owned.

Electricity generation is measured in terawatt hours, which expresses the generation of 1 terawatt (10^{12} watts) of electricity for one hour.

Overview

World electricity generation rose at an average annual rate of 3.6% from 1971 to 2013, greater than the 2.2% growth in total primary energy supply. This increase was largely due to more electrical appliances, the development of electrical heating in several developed countries and of rural electrification programmes in developing countries.

The share of electricity production from fossil fuels has gradually fallen, from 74% in 1971 to 67% in 2013. This decrease was due to a progressive move away from oil, which fell from 21% to 4%.

Oil for world electricity generation has been displaced in particular by dramatic growth in nuclear electricity generation, which rose from 2% in 1971 to 18% in 1996. However, the share of nuclear has been falling steadily since then and represented 11% in 2013.

The share of coal remained stable, at 40-41%, while that of natural gas increased from 13% in 1971 to 22% in 2013. The share of hydro-electricity decreased from 23% to 16% over the same time range.

Due to large development programmes in several OECD countries, the share of new and renewable energies, such as solar, wind, geothermal, biofuels and waste increased. However, these energy forms remain of limited importance: in 2013, they accounted for only around 6% of total electricity production for the world as a whole.

Comparability

Some countries, both OECD member and non-member countries, have trouble reporting electricity generation from autoproducer plants. In some non-member countries it is also difficult to obtain information on electricity generated by biofuels and waste. For example, electricity generated from waste biofuel in sugar refining remains largely unreported in a number of countries.

Sources
- International Energy Agency (IEA) (2015), *Energy Balances of OECD Countries*, IEA, Paris.
- IEA (2015), *Energy Balances of Non-OECD Countries*, IEA, Paris.

Further information

Analytical publications
- IEA (2015), *World Energy Outlook*, IEA, Paris.
- IEA (2013), *Electricity and a Climate-Constrained World, Data and Analyses*, IEA, Paris.
- OECD (2015), *Aligning Policies for a Low-carbon Economy*, OECD Publishing.
- OECD (2013), *Inventory of Estimated Budgetary Support and Tax Expenditures for Fossil Fuels 2013*, OECD Publishing.
- OECD (2013), *Taxing Energy Use, A Graphical Analysis*, OECD Publishing.
- Cooke, D. (2011), "Empowering Customer Choice in Electricity Markets", *IEA Energy Papers*, No. 2011/13.

Online databases
- IEA Electricity Information Statistics.
- IEA World Energy Statistics and Balances.

Websites
- International Energy Agency, *www.iea.org*.

Electricity generation
Terawatt hours (TWh)

	1975	1990	2004	2005	2006	2007	2008	2009	2010	2011	2012	2013	2014
Australia	73.6	154.3	229.6	228.3	232.7	243.0	243.1	248.7	252.2	253.2	250.0	249.0	248.2
Austria	34.9	49.3	61.9	64.1	62.1	62.6	64.5	66.3	67.9	62.3	68.7	64.5	61.6
Belgium	40.8	70.3	84.4	85.7	84.3	87.5	83.6	89.8	93.8	89.0	81.8	82.1	71.3
Canada	277.1	482.0	599.9	625.0	610.5	629.3	632.0	609.1	599.0	633.0	633.1	651.8	639.4
Chile	8.7	18.4	51.2	52.5	55.3	58.5	59.7	60.7	60.4	65.7	69.8	73.1	76.7
Czech Republic	45.9	62.3	83.8	81.9	83.7	87.8	83.2	81.7	85.3	86.9	86.8	86.2	85.1
Denmark	18.3	26.0	40.4	36.2	45.6	39.3	36.6	36.4	38.9	35.2	30.7	34.7	31.9
Estonia	..	17.2	10.3	10.2	9.7	12.2	10.6	8.8	13.0	12.9	12.0	13.3	12.4
Finland	26.2	54.4	85.8	70.6	82.3	81.2	77.4	72.1	80.7	73.5	70.4	71.3	68.0
France	185.3	417.2	568.7	571.4	569.6	564.1	569.0	530.8	564.4	556.4	560.9	567.4	557.2
Germany	383.8	547.7	611.1	615.8	632.7	633.7	634.4	590.0	626.6	607.2	623.7	627.4	608.8
Greece	16.1	34.8	58.8	59.4	60.2	62.7	62.9	61.1	57.4	59.2	60.8	57.1	47.6
Hungary	20.5	28.4	33.7	35.8	35.9	40.0	40.0	35.9	37.4	36.0	34.6	30.3	29.3
Iceland	2.3	4.5	8.6	8.7	9.9	12.0	16.5	16.8	17.1	17.2	17.5	18.1	18.1
Ireland	7.5	14.2	25.2	25.6	27.1	27.8	29.9	28.0	28.4	27.5	27.4	25.8	26.0
Israel	9.7	20.9	47.3	48.6	50.6	53.8	57.0	55.0	58.6	59.7	63.0	59.9	57.1
Italy	145.8	213.1	295.8	296.8	307.7	308.2	313.5	288.3	298.8	300.6	297.3	287.9	276.2
Japan	473.1	835.5	1 068.3	1 089.9	1 094.8	1 125.5	1 075.5	1 043.4	1 108.7	1 042.8	1 026.2	1 038.5	1 020.0
Korea	20.1	105.4	366.6	387.9	402.3	425.9	443.9	451.7	496.7	520.1	530.9	537.9	541.3
Luxembourg	1.1	0.6	3.4	3.3	3.5	3.2	2.7	3.2	3.2	2.7	2.8	1.8	1.9
Mexico	43.9	115.8	232.6	243.8	249.5	257.3	261.9	261.0	271.1	295.8	293.9	297.1	300.4
Netherlands	54.3	71.9	102.4	100.2	98.4	105.2	107.6	113.5	118.1	113.0	102.5	100.9	102.5
New Zealand	20.6	32.3	42.5	43.0	43.6	43.7	43.8	43.5	44.9	44.5	44.3	43.3	43.5
Norway	77.4	121.6	110.1	137.2	121.2	136.1	141.2	131.0	123.2	126.4	146.6	133.7	141.6
Poland	96.8	134.4	152.6	155.4	160.8	158.8	154.7	151.1	157.1	163.1	161.7	164.0	158.5
Portugal	10.7	28.4	44.8	46.2	48.6	46.9	45.5	49.5	53.7	51.9	45.6	50.5	52.0
Slovak Republic	13.4	25.5	30.5	31.4	31.3	27.9	28.8	25.9	27.5	28.3	28.3	28.5	26.5
Slovenia	..	12.4	15.3	15.1	15.1	15.0	16.4	16.4	16.2	15.9	15.5	15.8	17.2
Spain	82.1	151.2	276.7	289.4	295.6	301.8	311.0	291.9	298.3	291.5	293.9	279.3	273.9
Sweden	80.6	146.0	151.7	158.4	143.3	148.8	149.9	136.6	148.5	150.3	166.4	153.0	154.1
Switzerland	43.0	55.0	63.9	57.8	62.1	66.4	67.0	66.7	66.1	62.9	68.2	68.8	69.8
Turkey	15.6	57.5	150.7	162.0	176.3	191.6	198.4	194.8	211.2	229.4	239.5	240.2	250.4
United Kingdom	270.8	317.8	391.3	395.4	393.4	393.0	384.8	373.0	378.6	364.3	360.4	356.3	332.2
United States	2 011.2	3 202.8	4 148.1	4 268.9	4 275.0	4 323.9	4 343.0	4 165.4	4 354.4	4 326.6	4 270.8	4 286.9	4 310.9
EU 28	..	2 576.3	3 269.5	3 290.1	3 335.2	3 349.9	3 354.8	3 190.6	3 333.4	3 267.8	3 265.8	3 229.9	..
OECD	4 611.0	7 629.1	10 247.6	10 502.0	10 574.7	10 774.8	10 790.1	10 398.0	10 857.1	10 804.9	10 786.0	10 796.2	10 711.6
Brazil	78.9	222.8	387.5	403.0	419.3	445.1	463.1	466.1	515.7	531.8	552.7	570.3	..
China	198.3	621.3	2 204.8	2 502.5	2 869.8	3 287.5	3 482.0	3 742.0	4 197.3	4 704.9	4 984.7	5 436.6	..
India	85.9	292.7	684.0	715.7	773.8	823.6	848.4	917.3	979.4	1 074.5	1 123.0	1 193.5	..
Indonesia	3.0	32.7	120.2	127.5	133.1	142.2	149.3	156.8	169.8	183.3	193.1	215.6	..
Russian Federation	..	1 082.2	929.9	951.2	993.9	1 013.4	1 038.4	990.0	1 036.1	1 053.0	1 069.3	1 057.6	..
South Africa	74.9	165.4	240.9	242.1	250.9	260.5	255.5	246.8	256.6	259.6	254.9	253.2	..
World	6 518.7	11 826.1	17 519.3	18 282.2	18 990.6	19 826.3	20 216.6	20 161.6	21 460.3	22 158.7	22 656.6	23 321.6	..

StatLink ▮◉▮ http://dx.doi.org/10.1787/888933336794

World electricity generation by source of energy
Terawatt hours (TWh)

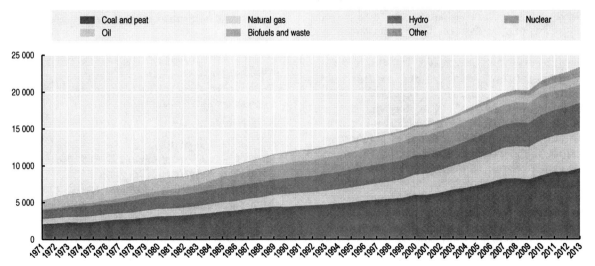

StatLink ▮◉▮ http://dx.doi.org/10.1787/888933335729

NUCLEAR ENERGY

Nuclear energy expanded rapidly in the 1970s and 1980s, but in the last 20 years only small numbers of new nuclear power plants have entered operation. The role of nuclear energy in reducing greenhouse gas emissions and in increasing energy diversification and security of supply has been increasingly recognised over the last few years, leading to renewed interest in building new nuclear plants in several countries. However, the accident at the Fukushima Daiichi nuclear power plant in Japan following a major earthquake and tsunami in March 2011 has led some countries to review their nuclear programmes. Belgium, Germany and Switzerland decided to hasten the phase out of nuclear power while others conducted safety checks of nuclear facilities causing a delay in nuclear development programmes. With successful completion of these safety reviews no other countries decided to exit nuclear power, development plans were resumed and, as a result, global nuclear capacity is expected to increase over the next few years.

Much of the future growth in nuclear capacity is expected to be in non-OECD economies. China in particular has begun a rapid expansion of nuclear capacity, with a total of 26 units under construction as of end 2014. India and Russia also have several new plants under construction. Among OECD countries, Finland, France, Japan, Korea, the Slovak Republic and the United States all presently have one or more nuclear plants under construction, while Turkey is finalising plans for the construction of its first two nuclear power plants (a total of four reactors each) and Poland is actively planning its first nuclear units. However, there remains uncertainty on the role of nuclear power in Japan where all 48 operational reactors were offline throughout 2014.

Definition

Nuclear electricity generation in terawatt hours (TWh) and the percentage share of nuclear in total electricity generation. Information on the number of nuclear power plants in operation and under construction as of December 2014.

Comparability

Some generation data are provisional and may be subject to revision. Generation data for Japan are for the fiscal year.

Overview

In 2014, nuclear energy provided 19.3% of total electricity supply in the OECD (and 11.1% of the world's electricity). However, the use of nuclear energy varies widely. In all, 18 of the 34 OECD countries currently use nuclear energy, with eight generating one-third or more of their total electricity from this source in 2014. Collectively, OECD countries produce about 80% of the world's nuclear energy. The remainder is produced in 12 non-OECD economies.

Analysis indicates that, as part of a scenario to limit global temperature rise to two degrees, nuclear generating capacity should rise from about 370 GW at present to around 1 100 GW by 2050, supplying almost 20% of global electricity. This would be a major contribution to cutting the emissions of greenhouse gases from the electricity supply sector. However, uncertainties remain concerning the successful construction and operation of the next generation of nuclear plants, public and political acceptance of nuclear energy in the wake of the Fukushima Daiichi accident, and the extent to which other low-carbon energy sources are successfully developed. Presently the current level of development of nuclear energy is lagging behind these projections, with recent annual capacity additions only a third of what is required to meet the two degree scenario objectives by 2025.

Sources

- Nuclear Energy Agency (NEA) (2015), *Nuclear Energy Data*, OECD Publishing.
- Data for non-OECD countries provided by the *International Atomic Energy Agency (IAEA)*.

Further information

Analytical publications

- International Energy Agency (IEA) (2015), *Energy Technology Perspectives*, IEA, Paris.
- IEA (2015), *Technology Roadmap: Nuclear Energy*, IEA, Paris.
- NEA, International Atomic Energy Agency (2014), *Uranium 2014: Resources, Production and Demand*, OECD Publishing.
- International Energy Agency (IEA) (2013), *Tracking Clean Energy Progress 2013*, IEA, Paris.
- NEA (2015), *Nuclear Development (series)*, OECD Publishing.

Websites

- Nuclear Energy Agency, *www.oecd-nea.org*.

Nuclear electricity generation and nuclear plants

	2014		Number as of 31 December 2014	
	Terawatt hours	As a percentage of total electricity generation	Plants connected to the grid	Plants under construction
Australia	-	-	-	-
Austria	-	-	-	-
Belgium	32.0	50.0	7	-
Canada	100.9	16.0	19	-
Chile	-	-	-	-
Czech Republic	28.6	33.3	6	-
Denmark	-	-	-	-
Estonia	-	-	-	-
Finland	22.2	33.9	4	1
France	415.9	76.9	58	1
Germany	91.7	15.8	9	-
Greece	-	-	-	-
Hungary	14.7	49.0	4	-
Iceland	-	-	-	-
Ireland	-	-	-	-
Israel	-	-	-	-
Italy	-	-	-	-
Japan	0.0	0.0	48	4
Korea	150.4	30.1	23	5
Luxembourg	-	-	-	-
Mexico	9.3	4.4	2	-
Netherlands	3.5	3.5	1	-
New Zealand	-	-	-	-
Norway	-	-	-	-
Poland	-	-	-	-
Portugal	-	-	-	-
Slovak Republic	14.5	57.5	4	2
Slovenia	6.1	37.4	1	-
Spain	54.8	20.4	8	-
Sweden	62.2	41.2	10	-
Switzerland	26.4	37.9	5	-
Turkey	-	-	-	-
United Kingdom	57.8	16.6	16	-
United States	797.0	20.2	99	5
EU 28	833.6	26.9	131	4
OECD	1 888.0	19.3	324	18
Brazil	14.5	2.9	2	1
China	123.8	2.4	23	26
India	33.2	3.5	21	6
Indonesia	-	-	-	-
Russian Federation	169.1	18.6	34	9
South Africa	14.8	6.2	2	-
World	2 410.4	11.1	438	70

StatLink ⟶ http://dx.doi.org/10.1787/888933336434

Nuclear electricity generation
As a percentage of total electricity generation, 2014

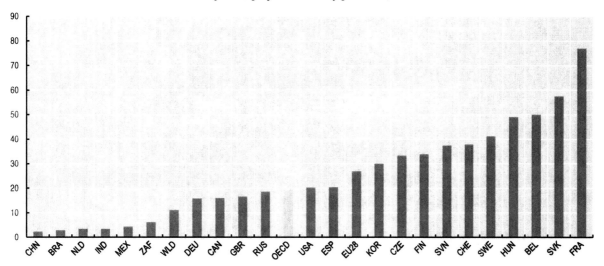

StatLink ⟶ http://dx.doi.org/10.1787/888933335278

RENEWABLE ENERGY

More and more governments are recognising the importance of promoting sustainable development and combating climate change when setting out their energy policies. Higher energy use has contributed to higher greenhouse gas emissions and higher concentration of these gases in the atmosphere. One way to reduce greenhouse gas emissions, while diversifying the energy portfolio, is to replace energy from fossil fuels by energy from renewables.

Definition

Data refer to the contribution of renewables to total primary energy supply (TPES) in OECD countries and the emerging economies (Brazil, China, India, Indonesia, South Africa and Russia). Renewables include the primary energy equivalent of hydro (excluding pumped storage), geothermal, solar, wind, tide and wave. It also includes energy derived from solid biofuels, biogasoline, biodiesels, other liquid biofuels, biogases, and the renewable fraction of municipal waste. Biofuels are defined as fuels derived directly or indirectly from biomass (material obtained from living or recently living organisms). Included here are wood, vegetal waste (including wood waste and crops used for energy production), ethanol, animal materials/wastes and sulphite lyes. Municipal waste comprises wastes produced by the residential, commercial and public service sectors that are collected by local authorities for disposal in a central location for the production of heat and/or power.

Both renewable and non-renewable shares of waste are included under "Biofuels and waste".

Overview

In OECD countries, total renewables supply grew on average by 2.7% per year between 1971 and 2014 as compared to 1.0% per year for total primary energy supply. Annual growth for hydro (1.1%) was lower than for other renewables such as geothermal (4.9%) and biofuels and waste (2.9%). Due to a very low base in 1971, solar and wind experienced the most rapid growth in OECD countries, especially where government policies have stimulated expansion of these energy sources.

For the OECD as a whole, the contribution of renewables to energy supply increased from 4.8% in 1971 to 9.2% in 2014. The contribution of renewables varied greatly by country. On the high end, renewables represented 89.3% of energy supply in Iceland and 43.5% in Norway. On the low end, renewables contributed less than 5% to the energy supply for Japan, Korea, Luxembourg and the Netherlands.

In 2013 renewables contributed 40% to the energy supply of Brazil, 34% in Indonesia, 26% in India, 11% in China, 11% in South Africa and 3% in Russia.

Comparability

Biofuels and waste data are often based on small sample surveys or other incomplete information. Thus, the data give only a broad impression of developments and are not strictly comparable between countries. In some cases, complete categories of vegetal fuel are omitted due to lack of information.

Sources
- International Energy Agency (IEA) (2015), *Energy Balances of OECD Countries*, IEA, Paris.
- IEA (2015), *Energy Balances of Non-OECD Countries*, IEA, Paris.

Further information
Analytical publications
- IEA (2015), *Energy Policies of IEA Countries* (series), IEA, Paris.
- IEA (2015), *Energy Technology Perspectives*, IEA, Paris.
- IEA (2015), *Medium-Term Renewable Energy Market Report*, IEA, Paris.
- IEA (2015), *World Energy Outlook*, IEA, Paris.
- IEA (2012), *Solar Heating and Cooling*, IEA Technology Roadmaps, IEA, Paris.
- IEA (2011), *Deploying Renewables, Best and Future Policy Practice*, IEA, Paris.
- IEA (2011), *Harnessing Variable Renewables: A Guide to the Balancing Challenge*, IEA, Paris.
- IEA (2009), *Cities, Towns and Renewable Energy: Yes In My Front Yard*, IEA, Paris.
- Nuclear Energy Agency (NEA) (2012), *Nuclear Energy and Renewables* , NEA, Paris.
- OECD (2012), *OECD Green Growth Studies: Linking Renewable Energy to Rural Development*, OECD Publishing.

Statistical publications
- IEA (2015), *Renewables Information*, IEA, Paris.

Online databases
- IEA World Energy Statistics and Balances.

Websites
- International Energy Agency, *www.iea.org*.

Contribution of renewables to energy supply

As a percentage of total primary energy supply

	1970	1990	2004	2005	2006	2007	2008	2009	2010	2011	2012	2013	2014
Australia	8.47	5.87	5.79	5.69	5.63	5.62	5.57	4.42	4.71	4.92	5.63	6.03	6.60
Austria	13.59	20.29	19.74	21.00	22.09	24.09	25.27	27.87	27.30	26.58	30.53	30.08	30.84
Belgium	0.05	1.00	1.64	1.97	2.35	2.93	3.41	4.22	4.59	5.37	6.16	6.19	6.63
Canada	15.29	16.11	15.58	16.95	16.71	17.24	17.38	18.06	17.63	18.24	18.11	18.87	18.34
Chile	..	27.84	24.22	25.10	25.33	23.52	24.49	26.13	22.13	23.13	29.96	31.29	32.39
Czech Republic	..	1.85	3.82	3.97	4.20	4.65	4.92	5.76	6.26	6.99	7.53	8.52	8.52
Denmark	1.63	5.94	13.72	15.02	14.25	16.20	16.88	17.95	20.12	22.23	24.39	25.09	27.77
Estonia	..	1.92	11.29	11.29	10.44	10.57	11.77	14.73	15.05	14.85	15.60	13.97	14.53
Finland	27.89	19.34	23.34	23.58	23.27	23.49	25.85	24.12	25.54	25.96	29.38	29.99	29.65
France	9.31	6.80	5.83	5.86	5.91	6.38	7.13	7.52	8.11	7.27	8.36	9.21	8.64
Germany	1.34	1.51	4.30	5.11	5.94	7.24	7.04	7.88	8.43	9.43	10.34	10.50	11.13
Greece	8.82	5.15	5.28	5.43	5.89	5.72	5.63	6.35	7.74	8.03	9.25	11.21	10.86
Hungary	2.79	2.59	3.64	4.32	4.51	5.11	6.01	7.38	7.61	7.56	7.57	8.27	8.48
Iceland	45.65	71.36	75.88	76.31	80.26	83.78	86.80	87.82	88.47	89.75	89.67	89.60	89.34
Ireland	1.15	1.69	1.95	2.51	2.89	3.18	3.89	4.64	4.60	5.88	6.05	6.51	7.43
Israel	..	3.15	3.83	3.99	3.67	3.64	4.71	4.97	4.99	4.96	4.79	4.90	5.12
Italy	5.61	4.42	6.60	6.26	6.82	6.62	7.65	9.61	10.67	11.96	14.80	16.97	17.78
Japan	2.53	3.45	3.27	3.15	3.33	3.17	3.23	3.34	3.83	4.18	4.14	4.45	4.86
Korea	..	1.08	0.46	0.51	0.55	0.59	0.60	0.66	0.72	0.74	0.86	1.01	1.06
Luxembourg	0.20	0.54	1.17	1.64	1.76	3.05	3.17	3.16	3.04	3.00	3.37	3.94	4.36
Mexico	..	12.24	10.26	10.45	10.03	9.99	10.09	9.52	9.91	9.40	8.82	7.94	9.07
Netherlands	..	1.12	2.15	2.75	2.98	3.02	3.51	4.03	3.75	4.28	4.36	4.28	4.60
New Zealand	30.01	32.91	31.40	31.50	32.07	32.20	32.92	35.65	38.67	40.03	37.45	38.76	39.14
Norway	37.53	54.09	39.91	48.36	42.51	46.37	41.50	38.84	34.41	42.86	46.62	38.48	43.45
Poland	1.30	1.53	4.75	4.87	4.85	5.01	5.69	6.66	7.25	7.87	8.83	8.77	9.41
Portugal	21.61	19.53	14.71	13.13	16.75	17.69	17.54	19.65	23.24	22.49	20.65	24.43	24.63
Slovak Republic	..	1.54	3.98	4.30	4.48	5.28	5.12	6.75	7.42	7.45	8.16	8.19	8.89
Slovenia	..	9.12	11.52	10.61	10.52	10.05	11.02	14.26	14.42	13.49	14.73	16.47	18.59
Spain	6.32	6.88	6.34	5.92	6.46	6.96	7.59	9.83	11.78	11.80	12.86	14.91	14.80
Sweden	17.20	24.43	25.00	28.75	28.66	30.55	31.49	34.84	33.39	33.20	36.93	34.67	34.38
Switzerland	18.35	14.91	16.46	16.01	15.50	17.78	17.84	17.82	19.00	18.08	20.69	20.27	21.22
Turkey	34.35	18.32	13.36	12.03	11.12	9.60	9.43	10.14	11.04	10.00	10.40	12.07	9.32
United Kingdom	0.19	0.50	1.48	1.79	1.95	2.18	2.64	3.16	3.36	4.09	4.33	5.30	6.42
United States	3.68	5.02	4.39	4.54	4.77	4.67	5.07	5.44	5.60	6.09	6.03	6.45	6.51
EU 28	..	4.34	6.27	6.58	6.97	7.52	8.04	9.10	9.82	10.19	11.35	12.10	..
OECD	..	5.93	5.98	6.24	6.44	6.59	6.98	7.45	7.75	8.17	8.60	9.02	9.17
Brazil	..	46.74	42.28	42.92	43.31	44.40	44.46	45.80	43.94	42.74	40.72	39.49	..
China	..	24.27	14.44	13.68	12.77	12.46	12.73	12.20	11.59	10.39	10.67	10.81	..
India	..	45.54	33.38	32.96	32.09	31.16	30.19	27.92	27.36	27.33	26.41	26.31	..
Indonesia	..	46.55	35.69	35.02	34.84	35.44	36.22	34.84	33.30	34.56	33.56	33.95	..
Russian Federation	..	3.01	2.92	2.87	2.81	2.88	2.58	2.83	2.57	2.45	2.41	2.61	..
South Africa	..	11.54	10.52	10.71	11.03	10.32	9.75	10.11	10.46	10.55	10.84	10.96	..
World	..	12.74	12.36	12.44	12.43	12.49	12.74	13.12	13.01	12.99	13.23	13.51	..

StatLink http://dx.doi.org/10.1787/888933336553

OECD renewable energy supply

Thousand tonnes of oil equivalent (ktoe)

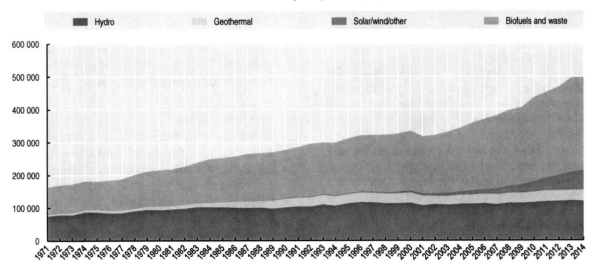

StatLink http://dx.doi.org/10.1787/888933335468

OIL PRODUCTION

The Middle East and North Africa are exceptionally well-endowed with energy resources, holding about 67% of the world's proven conventional oil reserves at the end of 2014. Current oil production is relatively low in comparison to these reserves and further development of them will be critical to meeting global energy needs in the coming decades. Unconventional oil (e.g. oil shale and sands, liquid supplies based on coal and biomass, and liquids arising for the chemical processing of natural gas) is also expected to play an increasing role in meeting world demand.

Definition

Crude oil production refers to the quantities of oil extracted from the ground after the removal of inert matter or impurities. Crude oil is a mineral oil consisting of a mixture of hydrocarbons of natural origin, being yellow to black in colour, of variable density and viscosity.

Refinery production refers to the output of secondary oil products from an oil refinery. Crude oil includes all primary oils – crude oil, natural gas liquids, and other hydrocarbons, for example synthetic crude oil from tar sands, shale oil, etc.

Comparability

In general, data on oil production are of high quality. In some instances, information has been based on secondary sources or estimated by the International Energy Agency (IEA).

Overview

World crude oil production has increased by 57% over the 43 years from 1971 to 2014. In 2014, production reached 3 858 million tonnes or about 76 million barrels per day. Growth was not constant over the period as production declined in the aftermath of two oil shocks in the early and late 1970s.

In 2014, the Middle East region's share of oil production was 31% of the world total. However, both the level of production and its share in the world total varied significantly over the period, from 39% of the world total in 1974 to 19% in 1985. Increased production in the 1980s and 1990s put the OECD on par with the Middle East during that period, but by 2014, the share of OECD oil production had fallen to 23%.

In 2014, OECD crude oil production rose by 7% year-on-year, driven by strong growth in North America. In the rest of the world, most of the growth happened outside of OPEC countries (minus 0.1% for OPEC and 1% for rest of the world).

The United States has overtaken Saudi Arabia and Russia as the world's leading producer of crude oil. Canada also remained in the top-five with production levels close to the ones of China. In the rest of the OECD, production by all major oil producers except Norway declined from 2013 to 2014.

With the increase in the production of United States and Canada, the five top oil-producing countries represented together nearly half (48%) of world production. OPEC member countries represented 40% of total oil production and OECD members 25%.

Sources
- International Energy Agency (IEA) (2015), *Energy Balances of OECD Countries*, IEA, Paris.
- IEA (2015), *Energy Balances of Non-OECD Countries*, IEA, Paris.
- IEA (2015), *Oil Information*, IEA, Paris.

Further information

Analytical publications
- IEA (2015), *Energy Policies of IEA Countries*, IEA, Paris.
- IEA (2015), *Energy Technology Perspectives*, IEA, Paris.
- IEA (2015), *Medium-Term Gas Market Report*, IEA, Paris.
- IEA (2015), *Medium-Term Oil Market Report*, IEA, Paris.
- IEA (2015), *World Energy Outlook*, IEA, Paris.
- OECD (2014), *Chemicals Used in Oil Well Production*, Series on Emission Scenario Documents, No. 31, OECD Publishing.

Online databases
- IEA World Energy Statistics and Balances.

Websites
- International Energy Agency, *www.iea.org*.
- Oil Market Report, *www.oilmarketreport.org*.

Production of crude oil

Thousand tonnes of oil equivalent (ktoe)

	1971	1990	2004	2005	2006	2007	2008	2009	2010	2011	2012	2013	2014
Australia	14 826	29 026	28 534	25 673	23 216	25 912	23 855	24 510	23 906	23 092	23 043	20 093	18 582
Austria	2 628	1 208	1 077	980	998	997	995	1 056	1 026	972	933	886	925
Belgium	-	-	-	-	-	-	-	-	-	-	-	-	-
Canada	72 408	94 147	149 294	146 228	153 665	157 146	155 262	153 349	161 138	170 764	183 664	195 251	212 268
Chile	1 766	1 166	390	355	348	592	602	721	611	641	532	539	418
Czech Republic	35	218	579	588	440	429	343	306	269	341	319	258	260
Denmark	-	6 113	19 783	19 018	17 294	15 579	14 414	13 252	12 486	11 237	10 250	8 918	8 350
Estonia	-	-	-	-	-	-	-	-	-	-	-	-	-
Finland	-	-	83	89	90	24	14	59	43	38	46	42	42
France	2 499	3 471	1 527	1 357	1 225	1 196	1 336	1 173	1 125	1 088	988	1 012	921
Germany	7 724	4 709	4 437	4 603	4 563	4 536	4 247	3 851	3 315	3 454	3 373	3 374	3 136
Greece	-	837	122	92	87	74	57	73	105	89	86	64	58
Hungary	1 990	2 273	1 591	1 418	1 359	1 214	1 245	1 207	1 090	968	1 030	880	818
Iceland	-	-	-	-	-	-	-	-	-	-	-	-	-
Ireland	-	-	-	-	-	-	-	-	-	-	-	-	-
Israel	5 830	13	2	2	7	4	6	6	4	20	12	12	12
Italy	1 254	4 468	5 616	6 260	6 103	6 308	5 719	4 962	5 620	5 608	5 629	5 748	5 982
Japan	852	696	699	750	742	808	767	748	695	698	620	549	516
Korea	-	-	437	534	571	581	536	692	698	707	718	605	609
Luxembourg	-	-	-	-	-	-	-	-	-	-	-	-	-
Mexico	25 654	152 756	198 747	193 675	187 341	176 984	166 861	156 254	154 961	153 327	152 190	150 058	144 799
Netherlands	1 748	4 069	2 973	2 338	2 083	2 857	2 434	2 029	1 684	1 701	1 786	1 936	2 053
New Zealand	-	1 966	1 169	1 084	1 061	2 086	2 933	2 771	2 745	2 382	2 121	1 855	2 068
Norway	287	83 659	146 590	135 281	125 850	121 770	116 694	110 526	99 371	96 340	87 327	82 051	84 179
Poland	396	175	917	892	813	733	788	697	744	676	700	983	971
Portugal	-	-	-	-	-	-	-	-	-	-	-	-	-
Slovak Republic	163	77	219	261	226	259	232	203	210	223	189	227	250
Slovenia	-	3	-	-	-	-	-	-	-	-	-	-	-
Spain	127	1 168	260	169	142	145	129	107	125	102	145	375	311
Sweden	-	3	-	-	-	-	-	-	-	-	-	-	-
Switzerland	-	-	-	-	-	-	-	-	-	1	-	-	-
Turkey	3 529	3 613	2 224	2 231	2 134	2 109	2 134	2 373	2 478	2 342	2 310	2 370	2 436
United Kingdom	237	95 248	99 633	88 467	80 010	79 872	74 612	70 898	64 368	53 223	46 275	42 206	41 334
United States	549 436	432 545	339 085	322 545	317 808	317 454	312 911	335 501	346 692	360 705	407 368	475 946	534 593
EU 28	-	134 586	145 818	133 715	122 181	120 159	112 293	105 326	97 300	84 694	76 417	71 664	70 086
OECD	693 389	923 627	1 005 989	954 889	928 175	919 670	889 125	887 324	885 509	890 739	931 655	996 238	1 065 891
Brazil	8 662	33 393	78 800	86 943	92 405	94 187	97 335	104 057	109 591	112 833	112 660	110 145	122 207
China	40 120	138 306	175 942	181 427	184 855	186 423	190 561	189 619	203 157	203 034	207 644	210 101	211 855
India	7 460	35 323	39 150	37 679	39 345	39 533	39 002	39 404	43 139	43 694	43 334	43 036	42 701
Indonesia	44 947	74 589	54 476	53 445	50 207	47 632	49 222	48 215	48 442	46 147	44 486	42 181	40 338
Russian Federation	..	526 252	458 466	468 708	478 130	490 038	488 530	493 641	506 541	514 864	521 251	524 196	531 095
South Africa	-	-	1 621	853	811	175	150	430	494	494	252	214	214
World	2 552 306	3 240 983	3 995 826	4 046 002	4 070 191	4 045 004	4 079 918	3 994 336	4 076 661	4 119 083	4 195 257	4 215 637	4 300 002

StatLink http://dx.doi.org/10.1787/888933336469

Production of crude oil by region

Thousand tonnes of oil equivalent (ktoe)

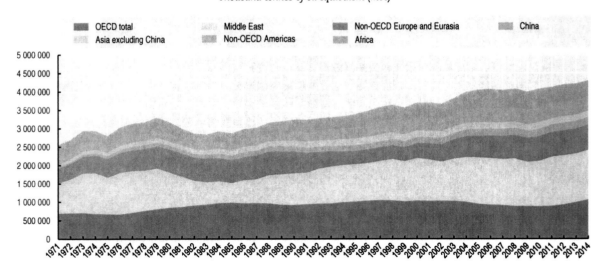

Legend: OECD total · Middle East · Non-OECD Europe and Eurasia · China · Asia excluding China · Non-OECD Americas · Africa

StatLink http://dx.doi.org/10.1787/888933335324

OIL PRICES

The price of crude oil, from which oil products such as gasoline are derived, is influenced by a number of factors beyond the traditional movements of supply and demand, notably geopolitics. Some of the lowest cost reserves are located in sensitive areas of the world. In addition, technological advances can have a significant influence on crude oil prices, for example by making new oil fields profitable to exploit or by providing substitute energy sources such as biofuels. So far though, the transport sector, driving global oil demand, remains heavily dependent on oil products. Therefore, demand for oil and consequently oil prices are closely linked to economic cycles.

There is not one price for crude oil but many. World crude oil prices are established, always in US dollars, in relation to three market traded benchmarks (West Texas Intermediate [WTI], Brent [or North Sea], and Dubai), and are often seen quoted at premiums or discounts to these prices.

Overview

The 1973 Arab oil embargo had a major price impact with Arabian Light prices surging from USD 1.84/barrel in 1972 to USD 10.98 in 1974. The next spike came with the 1981 Iranian revolution, when prices rose to a high of nearly USD 40/barrel. Prices declined gradually after this crisis. They dropped considerably in 1986 when Saudi Arabia substantially increased its oil production. The first Gulf crisis in 1990 brought a new peak. In 1997, crude oil prices declined due to the impact of the Asian financial crisis.

Prices increased again in 1999 with OPEC target reductions and tightening stocks. A dip occurred in 2001 and 2002, but the expectation of war in Iraq raised prices to over USD 30/barrel in the first quarter of 2003. Prices remained high in the latter part of 2003 and in 2004. Crude oil prices increased dramatically in late August 2005 after Hurricane Katrina hit the US coast of the Gulf of Mexico. Prices increased throughout 2006 and into 2007 as the demand for oil in emerging economies, especially China, put pressure on the supply/demand balance, averaging 24 per cent higher than in the previous year.

Early in 2008, prices crossed the symbolic USD 100/barrel threshold and by July reached just under USD 150/barrel, bringing the price of oil to a record high in nominal and real terms. From early 2009 prices plummeted to USD 40/barrel as the impact of high prices and the onset of the global financial crisis sharply curbed oil demand, though by year-end they had risen to between USD 70 and 80/barrel.

Crude oil prices increased steadily throughout 2010 and 2011, and, with the post-recession demand rebound, tightening stocks and low spare capacity, reached a peak of USD 122/barrel in March 2012. These high prices led to a period of significant over supply. After fluctuating around the USD 105/barrel mark until August 2014, prices halved to USD 50/barrel in January 2015. Following a rebound to USD 60/barrel in June 2015, prices were at USD 40/barrel by the end of the year.

Definition

Crude oil import prices come from the IEA's Crude Oil Import Register. Information is collected from national agencies according to the type of crude, by geographic origin and by quality of crude. Average prices are obtained by dividing value by volume as recorded by customs administrations for each tariff position. Values are recorded at the time of import and include cost, insurance and freight (c.i.f.) but exclude import duties. The nominal crude oil spot price from 2003 onwards is for Dubai and from 1970 to 2002 for Arabian Light. These nominal spot prices are expressed in US dollars per barrel of oil. The real price was calculated using the deflator for GDP at market prices and rebased with reference year 1970 = 100.

Comparability

Average crude oil import prices depend on the quality of the crude oil imported. High quality crude oils such as UK Forties, Norwegian Oseberg and Venezuelan Light can be significantly more expensive than lower quality crude oils such as Canadian Heavy and Venezuelan Extra Heavy. High quality crudes command a higher premium because, amongst other factors, they are easier, being less corrosive, to transport and process, and produce higher yields of quality oil products. For any given country, the mix of crude oils imported each month will directly influence the average monthly price.

Sources

- International Energy Agency (IEA) (2015), *Energy Prices and Taxes*, IEA, Paris.

Further information

Analytical publications

- IEA (2015), *Energy Policies of IEA Countries*, IEA, Paris.
- IEA (2015), *Medium-Term Gas Market Report*, IEA, Paris.
- IEA (2015), *Medium-Term Oil Market Report*, IEA, Paris.
- IEA (2015), *World Energy Outlook*, IEA, Paris.

Online databases

- IEA Energy Prices and Taxes Statistics.

Websites

- International Energy Agency, *www.iea.org*.
- Oil Market Report, *www.oilmarketreport.org*.

Crude oil import prices

US dollars per barrel, average unit value, c.i.f.

	1980	1990	2004	2005	2006	2007	2008	2009	2010	2011	2012	2013	2014
Australia	31.81	24.21	40.93	56.71	66.71	77.13	107.83	63.40	82.60	115.66	117.78	114.19	107.05
Austria	33.66	24.58	38.21	53.15	64.44	71.86	103.05	60.69	80.00	110.92	112.50	110.63	103.81
Belgium	29.93	21.11	35.35	50.06	61.06	70.35	96.01	61.77	79.65	110.50	110.83	108.45	98.49
Canada	30.21	24.15	38.13	52.37	64.33	70.04	101.41	60.29	79.14	110.80	110.61	108.60	98.60
Chile	..	..	..	..	..	..	..	..	..	..	..	..	..
Czech Republic	..	..	34.82	51.28	62.05	68.54	97.71	60.77	79.04	110.42	112.33	110.26	102.13
Denmark	33.56	23.18	38.78	54.40	66.92	74.94	96.48	62.87	80.40	112.77	107.90	107.25	100.19
Estonia	..	..	..	..	..	..	..	..	..	..	..	..	..
Finland	..	..	36.09	51.12	63.37	70.48	94.79	61.01	79.10	109.23	110.47	107.57	97.53
France	..	..	37.61	52.74	63.69	72.22	97.63	61.64	79.78	111.79	112.01	109.56	99.40
Germany	33.96	23.17	36.65	52.30	63.29	71.60	96.70	61.18	78.49	110.63	112.21	109.62	99.76
Greece	31.81	22.42	34.53	50.33	60.97	69.93	93.60	60.10	78.97	109.41	111.92	107.61	95.55
Hungary	..	..	..	..	..	..	..	..	..	..	..	..	..
Iceland	..	..	..	..	..	..	..	..	..	..	..	..	..
Ireland	31.15	25.55	39.24	55.24	66.38	74.16	100.39	62.61	80.95	113.92	115.64	110.46	99.87
Israel	..	..	..	..	..	..	..	..	..	..	..	..	..
Italy	31.84	23.23	36.60	51.33	62.50	70.20	96.67	60.69	79.29	110.23	112.18	109.98	99.09
Japan	33.11	22.64	36.59	51.57	64.03	70.09	100.98	61.29	79.43	109.30	114.75	110.61	104.16
Korea	..	..	36.15	50.19	62.82	70.01	98.11	61.12	78.72	108.63	113.24	108.59	101.24
Luxembourg	..	..	..	..	..	..	..	..	..	..	..	..	..
Mexico	..	..	..	..	..	..	..	..	..	..	..	..	..
Netherlands	32.80	21.83	35.02	50.00	61.47	68.74	97.89	60.54	78.55	109.19	111.54	108.55	99.22
New Zealand	32.77	21.97	41.71	56.07	67.36	73.84	105.80	65.85	80.62	112.38	117.70	113.43	105.96
Norway	33.17	18.46	39.20	53.08	58.83	70.16	80.22	69.08	81.06	111.18	108.23	109.07	101.61
Poland	..	..	..	..	..	..	94.02	60.83	77.89	109.58	109.97	107.71	96.28
Portugal	35.45	22.75	37.89	51.94	62.77	70.23	98.83	62.49	79.13	112.33	112.21	109.74	100.22
Slovak Republic	..	..	..	..	..	69.97	90.49	59.37	78.72	108.90	109.83	107.29	95.63
Slovenia	..	..	..	..	..	..	..	..	..	..	..	..	..
Spain	32.25	21.88	36.03	50.54	60.99	68.66	94.86	59.78	77.84	108.50	109.48	106.77	97.07
Sweden	32.22	23.02	36.47	51.78	62.50	70.13	95.09	60.58	79.00	110.67	112.36	109.10	97.75
Switzerland	34.68	24.23	38.73	55.81	66.76	74.92	101.03	63.27	80.92	112.51	111.30	110.35	101.91
Turkey	..	23.11	34.90	50.65	61.48	68.59	98.07	61.27	78.26	109.81	111.70	108.37	99.71
United Kingdom	31.22	22.92	37.75	53.79	65.00	73.80	99.34	62.39	80.60	113.49	112.62	110.27	100.07
United States	33.39	21.07	35.86	48.82	59.17	66.77	94.97	58.83	76.02	102.43	101.16	97.25	89.43
EU 28	..	..	..	..	..	..	..	..	..	..	..	..	..
OECD	..	..	..	..	..	..	..	..	..	..	..	..	..
Brazil	..	..	..	..	..	..	..	..	..	..	..	..	..
China	..	..	..	..	..	..	..	..	..	..	..	..	..
India	..	..	..	..	..	..	..	..	..	..	..	..	..
Indonesia	..	..	..	..	..	..	..	..	..	..	..	..	..
Russian Federation	..	..	..	..	..	..	..	..	..	..	..	..	..
South Africa	..	..	..	..	..	..	..	..	..	..	..	..	..

StatLink ᵃᵉᵇ http://dx.doi.org/10.1787/888933336456

Crude oil spot prices

US dollars per barrel

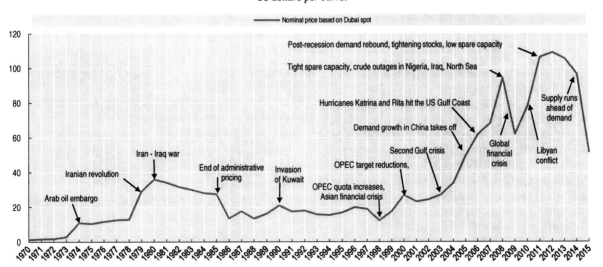

StatLink ᵃᵉᵇ http://dx.doi.org/10.1787/888933335315

GOODS TRANSPORT

There is an increasing demand for data on the transport sector to assess its various impacts on the economy, the environment and societies. However comparability of transport data between countries is not always possible worldwide due to the lack of harmonised definitions and methods. The Glossary for Transport Statistics (4th edition) provides common definitions to all member states of the European Union, the International Transport Forum and the United Nations Economic Commission for Europe.

Definition

Goods transport data refer to the total movement of goods using inland transport modes (rail, road, inland waterways and pipelines) on a given network. Data are expressed in tonne-kilometres which represents the transport of one tonne over one kilometre. The distance to be taken into consideration is the distance actually run.

Comparability

The International Transport Forum collects, on an annual basis from all its member countries, data on transport statistics. Data are collected from Transport Ministries, national statistics offices and other institution designated as official data sources.

Transport is classified as national if both loading and unloading take place in the same country. If one of them occurs in another country then the transport is considered as international. The statistics on international road transport, based on the nationality concept are different for statistics for other modes that are based on the territoriality concept.

Statistics based on the territoriality concept reflect the goods and the vehicles entering or leaving a country irrespective of the nationality of the transporting vehicle. Statistics based on the nationality concept only reflect the vehicles registered in the reporting country.

Although there are clear definitions for all the terms used in transport statistics, countries might have different methodologies to calculate tonne-kilometre. Methods could be based on traffic or mobility surveys, use very different sampling methods and estimating techniques which could affect the comparability of their statistics.

The aggregate "EU28" does not include Cyprus, and for OECD neither Chile nor Israel are included.

In case of missing data for a country, the ITF can calculate estimates based generally on the growth rates of the relevant region to calculate aggregated trends.

Overview

If global freight volumes transported by sea and air rebounded strongly, following the 2008 economic crisis and the collapse of world trade for rail and road freight the recovery has been slower, reflecting domestic economic performance more than trade.

After having been hit severely by the economic crisis, OECD rail freight transport volumes continued to recover and remain above their pre-crisis levels. If OECD rail freight volumes increased by 1.1% in 2014 when compared to the previous year, in the European Union, rail freight volume stagnated (0.3%) during the same period to a level slightly over 405 billion ton-kilometres. This is still 8% below their level in 2008. In Russia, rail freight volumes continued to increase in 2014 (4.7%) with more than 2.3 billion ton-kilometres, a level that is 8.7 % above pre-crisis volumes.

Road freight transport suffered in 2009 and recovery in road freight has been slow. Road transport data for 2014 show an overall stagnation when compared to 2013 levels however volumes remain above their 2008 levels (3.4% for the OECD). The increase in activity, expressed in ton-kilometres, was 0.3 % for both the OECD and the EU in 2014 when compared with the previous year. However road freight activity in the emerging economies continued to increase throughout the 2008-14 period.

Sources
- International Transport Forum (ITF) (2015), *Goods transport* (Database).

Further information

Analytical publications
- ITF (2015), *ITF Transport Outlook 2015*, ITF, Paris.
- OECD (2012), *Strategic Transport Infrastructure Needs to 2030*, OECD Publishing.
- OECD, ITF (2010), *Improving Reliability on Surface Transport Networks*, OECD Publishing.

Statistical publications
- ITF (2015), *Key Transport Statistics*, ITF, Paris.
- ITF (2013), *Spending on transport infrastructure 1995-2011*, ITF, Paris.
- ITF (2012), *Trends in the Transport Sector*, ITF, Paris.

Methodological publications
- ITF, Statistical Office of the European Communities and United Nations Economic Commission (2010), *Illustrated Glossary for Transport Statistics 4th Edition*, OECD Publishing.

Websites
- International Transport Forum, *www.internationaltransportforum.org*.

Inland goods transport

Billion tonne-kilometres

	2002	2003	2004	2005	2006	2007	2008	2009	2010	2011	2012	2013	2014
Australia	294.2	311.1	326.5	348.0	359.1	376.4	404.6	418.7	444.0	479.6	517.5	551.6	588.4
Austria	45.8	45.0	45.7	44.5	49.9	49.8	50.0	43.4	45.7	46.7	45.0	45.6	47.5
Belgium	70.5	67.7	65.6	62.1	62.1	60.7	57.0	50.7	50.9	50.5	..	..	..
Canada	403.0	434.8	497.5	507.9	520.9	523.5	513.0	479.4	523.8	561.1	591.0	604.5	..
Chile	..	..	..	..	..	..	..	..	..	..	..	..	..
Czech Republic	63.2	64.8	63.4	61.4	69.2	67.4	69.5	60.5	68.5	71.8	68.1	71.5	71.4
Denmark	18.1	18.2	17.9	18.2	18.3	18.2	16.8	15.6	16.4	17.9	17.6	17.4	17.8
Estonia	14.1	16.1	17.3	16.5	16.0	14.9	13.0	11.2	12.2	12.2	10.9	10.7	9.6
Finland	37.8	41.1	42.5	41.6	40.9	40.4	41.9	36.6	40.2	36.4	34.9	34.0	33.1
France	266.5	265.0	270.3	261.5	270.2	278.3	264.4	225.1	230.0	237.3	221.3	216.8	210.6
Germany	440.9	444.3	470.1	486.4	516.8	538.6	536.9	474.9	499.0	507.8	491.9	496.6	..
Greece	15.0	15.2	16.1	16.5	17.2	18.2	17.7	17.5	20.7	20.8	20.7	19.4	19.6
Hungary	31.5	33.0	36.7	41.9	48.4	53.9	53.5	50.1	50.5	51.1	50.7	53.2	55.3
Iceland	0.7	0.7	0.7	0.7	0.8	0.8	0.8	0.8	0.8	0.8	0.8	0.8	0.8
Ireland	14.9	16.3	17.7	18.5	17.9	19.3	17.4	12.1	11.0	10.0	10.0	9.2	9.9
Israel		..	..	..	..	..	..	..	..	..	..	..	..
Italy	193.9	176.4	192.3	205.3	189.9	187.2	198.7	184.7	191.7	165.0	148.5	149.3	..
Japan	334.2	344.7	350.1	357.8	369.7	378.1	368.7	355.2	266.6	254.0	230.4	235.2	..
Korea	102.8	109.4	111.7	111.0	119.6	116.1	113.0	108.4	112.3	114.5	118.6	129.0	..
Luxembourg	10.4	10.5	10.9	9.6	9.7	9.9	10.2	8.9	9.3	9.4	7.2	7.7	..
Mexico	244.5	249.3	254.2	276.4	283.1	299.6	301.9	280.8	299.1	306.6	312.8	313.1	..
Netherlands	81.3	83.9	89.8	88.9	89.1	90.7	91.7	80.5	94.3	95.0	93.1	91.6	91.7
New Zealand	20.5	21.1	23.1	23.2	23.2	23.8	25.5	21.6	24.0	24.7	25.5	25.9	..
Norway	19.0	20.4	22.7	23.7	23.9	24.1	25.2	23.6	24.3	23.8	24.3	25.8	26.4
Poland	150.1	160.3	188.5	196.2	216.7	238.6	248.8	259.0	288.2	297.0	305.4	331.5	335.8
Portugal	32.3	29.5	43.7	45.6	48.0	49.5	41.9	37.9	37.3	40.2	32.5	39.2	..
Slovak Republic	25.9	27.5	28.9	32.7	33.0	37.7	39.5	35.3	36.7	37.9	38.1	39.5	41.0
Slovenia	5.0	5.3	5.4	5.6	5.7	6.2	6.2	4.9	5.7	5.9	5.3	5.7	6.2
Spain	204.6	212.3	241.1	254.1	262.6	278.9	262.4	227.5	226.1	223.5	215.6	208.7	212.3
Sweden	51.0	51.6	53.5	56.4	57.7	59.6	60.9	52.5	56.2	56.3	59.3	59.6	60.1
Switzerland	25.5	25.8	27.1	27.6	29.0	29.1	29.6	27.6	28.2	29.1	28.3	29.2	..
Turkey	205.8	179.0	178.2	181.7	192.9	204.1	229.1	231.9	241.5	259.4	265.2	261.9	261.8
United Kingdom	183.9	186.4	194.3	199.2	200.0	204.7	193.0	170.3	182.8	185.5	..	..	..
United States	7 250.9	7 297.5	7 373.6	7 475.7	7 556.7	7 584.5	7 882.9	7 122.5	7 441.4	7 730.3	..	..	..
EU 28	2 082.6	2 108.0	2 266.4	2 342.1	2 424.6	2 516.7	2 482.4	2 213.8	2 329.5	2 344.7	2 286.2	..	..
OECD	10 857.4	10 964.0	11 277.1	11 496.3	11 718.0	11 882.9	12 185.6	11 129.7	11 579.4	11 962.0	12 287.6	..	..
Brazil	..	..	..	..	..	..	..	..	..	..	..	..	..
China	2 890.2	3 149.6	3 711.8	4 162.8	4 616.8	5 261.7	7 733.0	8 248.3	9 566.0	10 979.5	12 022.8	16 815.1	..
India	..	..	..	1 176.1	1 335.5	1 471.5	1 581.6	1 739.6	1 881.1	2 018.6	2 092.7	..	..
Indonesia	..	..	..	..	..	..	..	..	..	..	..	..	..
Russian Federation	2 657.9	2 925.4	3 192.4	3 295.2	3 390.1	3 523.1	3 509.1	3 220.9	3 387.6	3 529.9	3 739.6	3 750.3	3 840.1
South Africa	..	..	..	..	..	..	..	..	..	..	..	..	..

StatLink http://dx.doi.org/10.1787/888933336731

Inland goods transport

Average annual growth rate in percentage, 2004-14 or latest available period

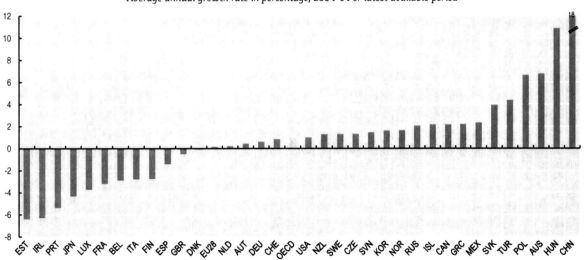

StatLink http://dx.doi.org/10.1787/888933335666

PASSENGER TRANSPORT

Although some studies have suggested a saturation of passenger travel by car in some developed countries, the demand for passenger mobility continues to increase worldwide. There is a need for good and comprehensive data on passenger mobility in order to develop sustainable passenger mobility systems. Comparability of transport data between countries is not always possible worldwide due to the lack of harmonised definitions and methods. The Glossary for Transport Statistics (4th edition) provides common definitions to all member states of the European Union, the International Transport Forum and the United Nations Economic Commission for Europe.

Definition

Passenger transport data refer to the total movement of passengers using rail or road (passenger cars, buses or coaches) transport modes. Data are expressed in passenger-kilometres which represents the transport of one passenger over one kilometre. The distance to be taken into consideration is the distance actually run.

Comparability

Although there are clear definitions for all the terms used in transport statistics, countries might have different methodologies to calculate passenger-kilometres. Methods could be based on traffic or mobility surveys, use very different sampling methods and estimating techniques which could affect the comparability of their statistics.

If passenger transport by rail or by regular buses and coaches can be estimated fairly easily, passengers transport by passenger car or by un-schedule coaches are much more difficult to track down. Some countries do not report passenger car transport at all, others carry out different types of surveys to estimate passenger travel on their territory. There is no common methodology for this and since no method provides a complete vision of passenger movements, data are not always comparable between countries.

The aggregate "EU28" does not include Cyprus, and for OECD neither Chile nor Israel are included.

In case of missing data for a country, estimates are based generally on the growth rates of the relevant region. These estimates are used solely to calculate aggregated trends in graphic representations and are not shown at the individual country level.

Overview

The economic crisis had a relatively small impact on rail passenger transport. If rail passenger-kilometres fell in 2009 in the OECD and the EU, volumes have recovered since then and in 2014 they are above pre-crisis levels by 3.9% and 6.3% respectively. However there are marked differences between countries. Indeed, some European countries showed a decrease in their rail passenger traffic in 2014, notably in the Netherlands (minus 8.4%), Slovenia (minus 8.3%) and Poland (minus 4.7%). A few countries resisted the otherwise downward trend; Ireland (8.0%), Portugal (5.6%), the United Kingdom (4.4%) and the Czech Republic (2.6%). Outside Europe, rail passenger-kilometres for Russia dropped by 6.1% in 2014 when compared to the previous year. Rail passenger-kilometres continues to show strong growth in China (8.0%) and India (6.9%) which account for nearly 70% of the estimated global rail passenger transport.

However, there continue to be marked differences in the EU. In France and Germany, passenger-kilometres have remained consistently above their pre-crisis levels. Passenger transport by rail in the United Kingdom has experienced continuous growth in volumes whereas passenger traffic in Italy, which had deteriorated since the economic crisis, shows an increase in trend since 2013, but still remains below pre-crisis levels.

Data on passenger-kilometres travelled in passenger cars are less detailed and less up to date in many countries. Within the EU, the decline was on average 0.5% in the 15 countries where data are available for 2014. In the United States, passenger travel by car fell 0.6% in 2013 when compared to 2012.

Sources

- International Transport Forum (ITF) (2015), "*Passenger transport*" (Database).

Further information

Analytical publications
- ITF (2015), *ITF Transport Outlook 2015*, ITF, Paris.
- OECD (2014), *OECD Tourism Trends and Policies*, OECD Publishing.
- OECD (2012), *Strategic Transport Infrastructure Needs to 2030*, OECD Publishing.
- OECD and ITF (2010), *Improving Reliability on Surface Transport Networks*, OECD Publishing.

Statistical publications
- ITF (2012), *Trends in the Transport Sector*, ITF, Paris.

Methodological publications
- ITF, Statistical Office of the European Communities and United Nations Economic Commission (2010), *Illustrated Glossary for Transport Statistics 4th Edition*, OECD Publishing.

Websites
- International Transport Forum, *www.internationaltransportforum.org*.

Inland passenger transport

Billion passenger-kilometres

	2002	2003	2004	2005	2006	2007	2008	2009	2010	2011	2012	2013	2014
Australia	272.4	279.0	291.0	291.8	287.8	292.0	294.9	294.8	296.7	300.0	302.8	304.9	306.7
Austria	8.3	8.2	8.3	8.5	9.3	9.6	10.8	10.7	10.3	10.9	11.3	11.9	12.1
Belgium	132.2	133.0	135.5	136.1	137.6	140.7	139.1	140.6	140.3	144.2	140.1	..	..
Canada	494.6	486.4	489.8	514.2	511.6	504.9	494.0	494.4	..	..	..	..	..
Chile	..	..	..	..	..	..	..	..	..	..	..	..	..
Czech Republic	81.6	83.3	82.7	83.9	86.1	88.0	88.6	88.3	81.0	81.5	80.5	81.3	84.1
Denmark	69.2	69.9	71.5	71.7	72.5	74.2	74.3	73.6	73.2	73.5	74.1	74.6	73.7
Estonia	2.8	2.8	2.9	3.2	3.4	3.2	3.0	2.6	2.5	2.5	2.7	2.8	2.9
Finland	69.3	70.6	71.9	72.9	73.5	75.1	75.0	75.7	76.2	76.9	76.8	76.7	76.9
France	912.2	917.7	923.3	919.2	924.2	938.6	934.8	937.3	946.2	952.5	955.4	964.2	970.5
Germany	1 001.9	996.5	1 024.4	1 016.2	1 024.0	1 026.9	1 033.4	1 041.9	1 046.8	1 057.8	1 061.1	1 066.1	..
Greece	43.6	43.6	44.3	44.3	44.1	44.5	43.8	43.6	43.5	43.1	43.1	..	..
Hungary	75.2	76.4	78.1	76.5	79.2	79.2	79.3	78.6	76.5	76.3	76.5	76.6	77.9
Iceland	4.6	4.7	4.9	5.1	5.5	5.7	5.6	5.6	5.6	5.4	5.5	5.6	5.9
Ireland	..	..	..	..	..	..	..	..	..	..	..	..	..
Israel	..	..	..	..	..	..	..	..	..	..	..	..	..
Italy	854.6	854.5	865.1	828.1	829.5	829.5	828.3	869.7	847.8	814.6	726.7	771.7	..
Japan	1 337.7	1 339.2	1 333.0	1 324.2	1 313.6	1 324.6	1 310.5	1 292.5	1 100.7	953.4	964.7	..	..
Korea	296.9	289.8	242.9	255.4	260.4	260.9	364.3	366.3	437.2	426.4	425.6	426.3	..
Luxembourg	..	..	..	..	..	..	..	..	..	..	..	..	..
Mexico	393.3	399.1	410.1	423.0	437.1	450.0	464.0	437.3	452.9	466.5	481.7	485.8	..
Netherlands	175.1	176.2	181.5	179.6	179.5	182.2	178.5	172.7	166.7	173.1	173.4	..	..
New Zealand	..	..	..	..	..	..	..	..	..	..	..	..	..
Norway	60.6	60.9	61.7	61.3	62.3	64.0	65.2	65.8	65.8	66.8	67.7	68.5	70.7
Poland	208.6	212.6	216.6	219.6	223.8	229.8	240.5	245.3	248.4	256.1	265.7	267.7	..
Portugal	99.5	100.1	101.4	101.3	101.1	101.7	101.0	..	..	..	..	..	..
Slovak Republic	35.9	35.3	34.4	35.7	35.9	35.9	35.3	34.0	34.3	34.7	34.7	34.8	35.1
Slovenia	25.4	25.6	26.0	26.3	26.9	28.4	28.9	29.8	29.6	29.6	29.6	..	..
Spain	383.8	392.3	404.0	412.6	412.4	424.3	427.4	430.6	415.0	412.6	398.1	392.2	384.3
Sweden	123.9	124.7	125.1	125.6	125.9	129.0	128.4	128.7	128.3	129.9	130.6	128.7	136.2
Switzerland	96.2	97.3	98.5	100.1	101.4	103.2	104.7	107.4	109.4	111.0	112.8	114.6	..
Turkey	168.5	170.2	179.5	187.2	192.9	214.7	211.2	217.8	232.4	248.1	263.5	272.0	280.5
United Kingdom	752.7	753.5	755.5	752.3	758.2	762.8	759.9	755.8	742.0	740.3	742.1	737.2	..
United States	5 640.7	5 680.6	5 765.9	5 788.2	5 695.1	5 855.6	5 663.2	5 007.5	5 009.6	5 057.1	5 127.7	5 166.9	..
EU 28	5 018.3	5 041.7	5 121.1	5 093.8	5 132.3	5 187.9	5 195.4	5 242.2	5 194.1	5 179.7	5 099.3	..	..
OECD	13 721.7	13 783.8	13 928.4	13 962.8	13 913.7	14 177.5	14 086.9	13 453.6	13 326.0	13 239.7	13 272.7	..	..
Brazil	..	..	..	..	..	..	..	..	..	..	..	..	..
China	1 277.5	1 248.4	1 446.1	1 535.4	1 675.3	1 872.3	2 025.5	2 139.0	2 378.3	2 637.3	2 828.0	2 184.7	..
India	3 330.0	3 611.2	4 044.7	4 867.6	5 240.8	5 630.0	6 034.0	6 459.5	6 918.5	7 397.5	7 923.0	8 434.0	9 010.0
Indonesia	..	..	..	..	..	..	..	..	..	..	..	..	..
Russian Federation	323.3	323.4	332.7	314.2	313.5	323.8	327.8	292.8	279.4	278.1	277.7	263.3	257.3
South Africa	..	..	..	..	..	..	..	..	..	..	..	..	..

StatLink http://dx.doi.org/10.1787/888933336749

Inland passenger transport

Average annual growth rate in percentage, 2004-14 or latest available period

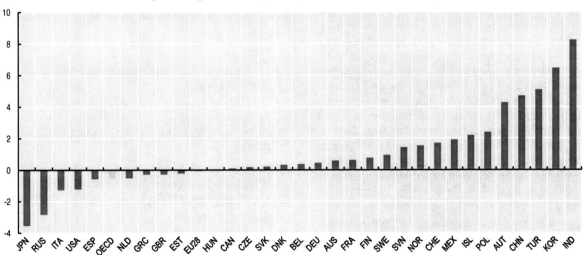

StatLink http://dx.doi.org/10.1787/888933335675

ROAD FATALITIES

The number of road motor vehicles is high amongst member countries of the International Transport Forum and reducing road accidents is a concern for all governments. Such concern becomes more challenging with increasing needs for more mobility.

Definition

A road vehicle is a vehicle running on wheels and intended for use on roads, it includes bicycles and road motor vehicles. A road motor vehicle is a road vehicle fitted with an engine whence it derives its sole means of propulsion, and which is normally used for carrying persons or goods or for drawing, on the road, vehicles used for the carriage of persons or goods. They include buses, coaches, trolley buses, goods road vehicles and passenger road motor vehicles. Although tramways (street-cars) are rail borne vehicles they are integrated into the urban road network and considered as road motor vehicles.

Road fatality means any person killed immediately or dying within 30 days as a result of a road injury accident. Suicides involving the use of a road motor vehicle are excluded.

Comparability

Road motor vehicles are attributed to the countries where they are registered while deaths are attributed to the countries in which they occur.

Fatalities per million inhabitants express the mortality rate, or an overall risk of being killed in traffic for a citizen.

Overview

The first ten years of the 21st century saw record road safety performance in most countries of the International Transport Forum (ITF). Following three consecutive years of record improvements in 2008, 2009 and 2010, the number of people killed in road accidents continued to fall in 2014 recording a drop of 1.2% in OECD countries (excluding Chile and Israel). However, in 2014 one third of ITF countries reported an increase in road fatalities when compared to 2013, Russia (10.9%), the United Kingdom (4.7%), France (3.5%) and Germany (1.1%) Countries used to good road safety performance might report an increase in road fatalities; this could be explained by the difficulty in improving further an already good level of safety performance.

These overall positive developments should not hide the economic costs and human tragedies behind the data. While high-income countries look back on a record decade in reducing road fatalities, 90% of global road deaths occur in low and middle income countries and estimates put annual world road fatalities above 1.3 million, with 50 million serious injuries.

It can be compared with other causes of death in a country (heart diseases, cancer, HIV, etc.), however when comparing countries road fatality risks, this indicator loses its relevance if countries do not have the same level of motorisation. Fatalities per vehicle-kilometre provides a better measure of fatality risk on road networks, even if it does not take into account non-motorised vehicles such as bicycles, but there is currently no harmonisation in the methodology to calculate distances travelled, and not all countries collect this indicator.

The numbers of vehicles entering the existing stock is usually accurate, but information on the numbers of vehicles withdrawn from use is less certain. Therefore it can only be used to compare safety performance between countries with similar traffic and car use characteristics. In addition it does not take into account non-motorised vehicles such as bicycles.

Sources
- International Transport Forum (ITF) (2015), "*Road traffic Injury Accidents*" (Database).
- ITF (2015), *Quarterly Transport Statistics* (Database).

Further information

Analytical publications
- ITF (2015), *IRTAD Road Safety Annual Report*, OECD Publishing.
- ITF (2011), *Reporting on Serious Road Traffic Casualties*, ITF, Paris.
- OECD, ITF (2013), *Cycling, Health and Safety*, OECD Publishing.

Statistical publications
- ITF (2015), *Key Transport Statistics*, ITF, Paris.
- ITF (2012), *Trends in the Transport Sector*, OECD Publishing.

Methodological publications
- ITF, Statistical Office of the European Communities and United Nations Economic Commission (2010), *Illustrated Glossary for Transport Statistics 4th Edition*, OECD Publishing.

Websites
- International Transport Forum, *www.internationaltransportforum.org*.

Road fatalities
Per million inhabitants

	2002	2003	2004	2005	2006	2007	2008	2009	2010	2011	2012	2013	2014
Australia	87	81	79	80	77	77	68	69	61	57	57	51	49
Austria	118	115	107	93	88	83	82	76	66	62	63	54	50
Belgium	131	117	112	104	101	100	88	87	77	78	69	65	..
Canada	93	88	85	90	88	84	73	66	66	59	60	55	..
Chile	..	..	..	..	..	..	..	..	..	..	..	..	..
Czech Republic	140	142	136	126	104	119	104	86	77	74	71	62	65
Denmark	86	80	68	61	56	74	74	55	46	39	30	34	..
Estonia	162	120	125	125	151	146	99	75	59	76	66	61	59
Finland	80	73	72	72	64	72	65	52	51	54	47	47	41
France	124	97	89	84	74	72	66	66	61	61	56	50	51
Germany	83	80	71	65	62	60	55	51	45	49	45	41	42
Greece	149	146	151	149	149	144	139	130	113	103	89	79	72
Hungary	141	131	128	127	129	123	99	82	74	64	61	60	63
Iceland	101	79	79	64	102	48	38	53	25	38	28	46	12
Ireland	96	84	92	95	85	77	62	52	46	41	35	41	42
Israel	..	..	..	..	..	..	..	..	..	..	..	..	..
Italy	122	115	106	100	97	88	80	72	69	65	63	56	54
Japan	76	70	67	63	57	52	47	46	45	43	41	40	..
Korea	152	151	137	132	131	127	120	119	111	105	108	101	94
Luxembourg	139	117	109	101	91	96	72	96	63	64	64	83	..
Mexico	46	43	42	43	44	48	47	42	43	37	38	..	..
Netherlands	66	67	54	50	50	48	46	44	39	40	39	34	34
New Zealand	103	114	106	98	94	100	86	89	86	65	70	57	65
Norway	68	61	56	48	52	49	53	44	43	34	29	37	29
Poland	152	148	150	143	137	146	143	120	103	110	94	88	84
Portugal	161	148	123	119	92	92	84	70	89	84	68	61	61
Slovak Republic	116	122	113	112	113	123	113	71	65	60	65	46	54
Slovenia	134	121	137	129	131	145	106	84	67	69	63	61	52
Spain	129	128	110	88	92	85	67	59	53	44	41	36	36
Sweden	63	59	53	49	49	51	43	39	28	34	30	27	28
Switzerland	70	74	69	55	49	51	47	45	42	40	42	33	30
Turkey	63	60	66	67	68	72	60	61	56	52	51	49	46
United Kingdom	60	61	56	55	54	50	43	38	30	31	28	28	29
United States	150	148	146	147	143	137	123	110	107	104	107	103	102
EU 28	110	104	97	92	88	86	79	70	63	61	56	51	..
OECD	107	103	99	96	93	90	81	74	70	68	66	..	..
Brazil	..	..	..	..	..	..	..	..	..	..	..	..	..
China	..	..	83	76	68	62	55	51	49	46	44	43	..
India	79	79	83	84	92	99	102	106	112	117	112	110	110
Indonesia	..	..	..	..	..	..	..	..	..	..	..	..	..
Russian Federation	229	246	240	237	229	233	210	194	186	196	195	188	208
South Africa	..	..	..	..	..	..	..	..	..	..	..	..	..

StatLink ⏩ http://dx.doi.org/10.1787/888933336538

Road fatalities
2014 or latest available year

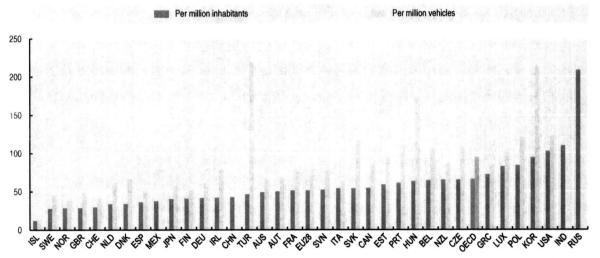

Per million inhabitants   Per million vehicles

StatLink ⏩ http://dx.doi.org/10.1787/888933335413

LABOUR

EMPLOYMENT RATES

Employment rates are a measure of the extent of utilisation of available labour resources. In the short term, these rates are sensitive to the economic cycle, but in the longer term they are significantly affected by government policies with regard to higher education and by policies that facilitate employment of women and disadvantaged groups.

Definition

Employment rates are calculated as the ratio of the employed to the working age population. Employment is generally measured through household labour force surveys. According to the ILO Guidelines, employed persons are defined as those aged 15 or over who report that they have worked in gainful employment for at least one hour in the previous week or who had a job but were absent from work during the reference week. Those not in employment consist of persons who are classified as either unemployed or inactive, in the sense that they are not included in the labour force for reasons of experiencing difficulty to find a job, study, incapacity or the need to look after young children or elderly relatives or personal choice.

The working age population refers to persons aged 15 to 64.

Comparability

All OECD countries use the ILO Guidelines for measuring employment. Operational definitions used in national labour force surveys may vary slightly from country to country. Employment levels are also likely to be affected by changes in the survey design, the survey scope and the survey conduct. Despite these changes, employment rate are fairly consistent over time.

There are series breaks due to a major redesign of the national labour force survey in Chile between 2009 and 2010, in Israel between 2011 and 2012 and in Turkey between 2013 and 2014. For Israel there was a change from a quarterly to a monthly survey as well as a change in concept from "civilian" to "total" labour force.

Overview

In 2014, the OECD employment rate was 65.7%, 0.6 percentage point higher than in 2013. Among OECD countries, employment rates ranged from a bit less than 50% in Greece and Turkey to more than 80% in Iceland.

Employment rates for men are higher than those for women in all OECD countries with an average OECD difference of 15.7 percentage points in 2014. However, there are large cross country differences in the employment gaps, which range from less than 5 percentage points in Finland, Sweden, Norway and Iceland (which are also the only four countries where the employment rate for women is above 70%), to more than 20 percentage points in Korea, Chile, Mexico and Turkey (the country with the lowest women's employment rate, at 29.5% in 2014). The employment gap has closed by 3.3 percentage points since 2005 in the OECD area due to an increase in women's employment rates, while those of men declined since the onset of the crisis in late 2007 and in particular in countries hard hit by the crisis. However, compared to 2013, the gap was stable in 2014

Since 2005, the employment rate for women has increased in about three quarters of countries. By contrast, over the same period, almost two-thirds of countries have registered decreasing men's employment rates.

Sources
• OECD (2015), OECD Employment Outlook, OECD Publishing.

Further information

Analytical publications
• Jaumotte, F. (2003), "Female Labour Force Participation", OECD Economics Department Working Papers, No. 376.
• OECD (2015), How's Life? Measuring Well-being, OECD Publishing.
• OECD (2015), OECD Skills Outlook, OECD Publishing.
• OECD (2011), Divided We Stand, Why Inequality Keeps Rising, OECD Publishing.

Statistical publications
• OECD (2014), OECD Labour Force Statistics, OECD Publishing.

Online databases
• OECD Employment and Labour Market Statistics.

Websites
• Employment policies and data, www.oecd.org/employment/emp.
• Labour statistics, www.oecd.org/employment/labour-stats.

Employment rates by gender
Share of persons of working age in employment

	Women				Men				Total			
	2000	2010	2013	2014	2000	2010	2013	2014	2000	2010	2013	2014
Australia	61.3	66.1	66.4	66.1	76.9	78.6	77.6	77.1	69.1	72.4	72.0	71.6
Austria	59.6	65.7	66.9	66.9	77.4	76.0	76.0	75.3	68.5	70.8	71.4	71.1
Belgium	51.5	56.5	57.2	58.0	69.5	67.5	66.4	65.8	60.5	62.0	61.8	61.9
Canada	65.6	68.8	69.7	69.4	76.2	74.1	75.2	75.2	70.9	71.5	72.4	72.3
Chile	..	46.7	51.0	51.7	..	72.1	73.8	72.8	..	59.3	62.3	62.2
Czech Republic	56.9	56.3	59.6	60.7	73.2	73.5	75.7	77.0	65.0	65.0	67.7	69.0
Denmark	71.6	71.1	70.1	69.8	80.8	75.6	75.0	75.8	76.3	73.4	72.6	72.8
Estonia	57.4	60.8	65.7	66.3	63.4	61.7	71.4	73.0	60.3	61.3	68.5	69.6
Finland	64.2	66.9	67.8	68.0	70.1	69.4	69.9	69.5	67.2	68.2	68.9	68.7
France	..	59.8	60.4	60.4	..	68.4	67.9	67.3	..	64.0	64.1	63.8
Germany	..	66.1	69.0	69.5	..	76.0	78.0	78.1	..	71.1	73.5	73.8
Greece	41.7	48.0	39.9	41.1	71.5	70.4	57.9	58.0	56.5	59.1	48.8	49.4
Hungary	49.7	50.2	52.6	55.9	63.1	59.9	63.7	67.8	56.2	55.0	58.1	61.8
Iceland	..	76.2	79.0	79.3	..	80.1	83.2	84.0	..	78.2	81.1	81.6
Ireland	53.9	55.8	55.9	56.7	76.3	63.5	65.1	66.9	65.2	59.7	60.5	61.7
Israel	50.9	56.9	63.0	64.2	61.4	63.4	71.2	71.5	56.1	60.2	67.1	67.9
Italy	39.6	46.1	46.5	46.8	68.0	67.5	64.7	64.7	53.7	56.8	55.5	55.7
Japan	56.8	60.4	62.5	63.7	81.1	80.7	80.8	81.6	69.0	70.6	71.7	72.7
Korea	50.0	52.6	53.9	54.9	73.1	73.9	74.9	75.7	61.5	63.3	64.4	65.3
Luxembourg	..	57.2	59.1	60.5	..	73.1	72.2	72.6	..	65.2	65.7	66.6
Mexico	..	43.2	45.0	44.2	..	77.8	78.3	78.1	..	59.7	60.8	60.4
Netherlands	63.5	69.3	69.0	68.1	82.1	80.0	78.2	78.2	73.0	74.7	73.6	73.1
New Zealand	63.1	66.5	67.7	69.1	77.8	78.2	78.3	79.7	70.3	72.2	72.8	74.2
Norway	73.7	73.3	73.5	73.4	81.3	77.3	77.3	77.0	77.5	75.3	75.4	75.2
Poland	48.9	52.6	53.4	55.2	61.2	65.3	66.6	68.2	55.0	59.0	60.0	61.7
Portugal	60.5	61.0	57.9	59.7	76.6	69.7	63.5	65.8	68.4	65.3	60.6	62.6
Slovak Republic	51.5	52.3	53.3	54.3	62.2	65.2	66.4	67.7	56.8	58.8	59.9	61.0
Slovenia	58.4	62.6	59.2	60.0	67.2	69.7	67.1	67.6	62.9	66.2	63.3	63.9
Spain	41.3	52.8	50.3	51.2	71.2	64.8	59.2	60.7	56.3	58.9	54.8	56.0
Sweden	..	69.7	72.5	73.1	..	74.6	76.3	76.6	..	72.2	74.4	74.9
Switzerland	..	72.5	74.4	75.2	..	84.6	84.7	84.5	..	78.6	79.6	79.9
Turkey	..	26.2	29.7	29.5	..	66.7	69.5	69.5	..	46.3	49.5	49.5
United Kingdom	64.7	64.5	65.8	67.1	77.8	74.4	75.4	76.8	71.2	69.4	70.5	71.9
United States	67.8	62.4	62.3	63.0	80.6	71.1	72.6	73.5	74.1	66.7	67.4	68.1
EU 28	..	58.2	58.8	59.6	..	70.1	69.4	70.1	..	64.1	64.1	64.8
OECD	..	56.5	57.4	57.9	..	72.6	73.1	73.6	..	64.5	65.1	65.7
Brazil	..	..	..	..	..	..	..	..	..	..	..	..
China	..	..	..	..	..	..	..	..	..	..	..	..
India	..	..	..	..	..	..	..	..	..	..	..	..
Indonesia	..	..	..	..	..	..	..	..	..	..	..	..
Russian Federation	59.3	63.3	64.4	64.8	67.6	71.6	73.6	74.3	63.3	67.3	68.8	69.3
South Africa	39.0	35.3	36.9	36.9	53.2	48.7	48.7	48.9	45.7	41.8	42.7	42.8

StatLink ⟲ http://dx.doi.org/10.1787/888933336088

Employment rates: total
Share of persons of working age in employment

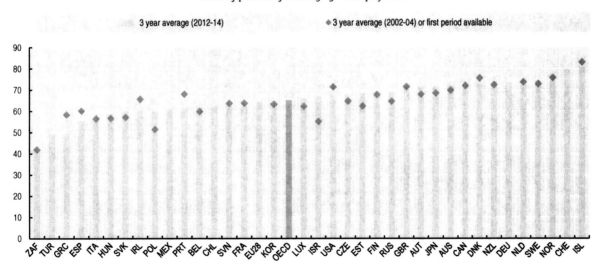

3 year average (2012-14)　　◆ 3 year average (2002-04) or first period available

StatLink ⟲ http://dx.doi.org/10.1787/888933334907

EMPLOYMENT RATES BY AGE GROUP

Labour markets differ in how employment opportunities are allocated among people of different ages. Employment rates for people of different ages are significantly affected by government policies with regard to higher education, pensions and retirement age.

Definition

The employment rate for a given age group is measured as the number of employed people of a given age as a ratio of the total number of people in that same age group.

Employment is generally measured through national labour force surveys. In accordance with the ILO Guidelines, employed persons are those aged 15 or over who report that they have worked in gainful employment for at least one hour in the previous week or who had a job but were absent from work in the reference week. Those not in employment consist of persons who are classified as either unemployed or inactive, in the sense that they are not included in the labour force for reasons of experiencing difficulty to find a job, study, incapacity or the need to look after young children or elderly relatives or personal choice.

Employment rates are shown for three age groups: persons aged 15 to 24 are those just entering the labour market following education; persons aged 25 to 54 are those in their prime working lives; persons aged 55 to 64 are those who are approaching retirement.

Comparability

Employment levels are likely to be affected by changes in the survey design, the survey scope, the survey conduct and adjustments to the population controls based on census results and intercensal population estimates between censuses. Despite these changes, the employment rates shown here are fairly consistent over time.

There are series breaks due to a major redesign of the national labour force survey in Chile between 2009 and 2010, in Israel between 2011 and 2012 and in Turkey between 2013 and 2014. For Israel there was a change from a quarterly to a monthly survey as well as a change in concept from "civilian" to "total" labour force.

Overview

Employment rates for people aged 25 to 54 (prime-age) are relatively similar between OECD countries, with rates in all countries except Turkey ranging between 62.4% and 86.9% in 2014. Eight countries have prime-age rates below the OECD average whereas the rates are 6 or more percentage points above the average in eleven countries. Cross country differences are larger when looking at the youngest age group (aged 15-24) where, in 2014, employment rates ranged between less than 25% in eight countries – Greece, Italy, Spain, Luxembourg, the Slovak Republic, Portugal, Belgium and Hungary – to over 60% in just two countries – Switzerland and Iceland. Employment rates for the oldest age group (aged 55-64) also vary considerably, between 70% or more in five countries – Switzerland, Norway, Sweden, New Zealand and Iceland – to less than 40% in three countries – Turkey, Greece and Slovenia.

As a consequence of the financial crisis, compared to 2005, prime-age employment rates have fallen quite significantly in a few countries, by more than 5 percentage points in Greece, Spain and Ireland and by 2 to 5 percentage points in Italy, Portugal, Denmark, Iceland, and the United States. The employment rates for older workers increased by 5.6 percentage points on average in the OECD area, between 2005 and 2014, with the largest increases of more than 12 percentage points recorded in Germany, Poland, Austria, Italy, the Netherlands, the Slovak Republic, Chile and Israel.

Sources
- OECD (2015), *OECD Employment Outlook*, OECD Publishing.
- For non-member countries: National sources.

Further information

Analytical publications
- OECD (2015), *Ageing and Employment Policies*, OECD Publishing.
- OECD (2012), *Better Skills, Better Jobs, Better Lives: A Strategic Approach to Skills Policies*, OECD Publishing.
- OECD (2010), *Off to a Good Start? Jobs for Youth*, OECD Publishing.

Statistical publications
- OECD (2014), *OECD Labour Force Statistics*, OECD Publishing.

Online databases
- *OECD Employment and Labour Market Statistics.*

Websites
- Ageing and Employment Policies, *www.oecd.org/employment/emp/ageingandemploymentpolicies.htm*.
- Employment policies and data, *www.oecd.org/employment/emp*.
- Labour statistics, *www.oecd.org/employment/labour-stats*.
- Youth employment and unemployment, *www.oecd.org/employment/emp/action-plan-youth.htm*.

Employment rates by age group

As a percentage of population in that age group

	Persons 15-24 in employment				Persons 25-54 in employment				Persons 55-64 in employment			
	2000	2005	2010	2014	2000	2005	2010	2014	2000	2005	2010	2014
Australia	61.7	63.3	60.5	57.7	76.2	78.8	79.5	78.8	46.0	53.5	60.6	61.5
Austria	52.6	51.6	52.8	52.1	82.6	81.6	83.3	83.5	28.9	30.0	41.2	45.1
Belgium	29.1	27.5	25.2	23.2	77.4	78.3	80.0	79.1	26.3	31.8	37.4	42.7
Canada	56.2	57.7	54.9	55.6	79.9	81.3	80.5	81.2	48.1	54.8	58.1	60.4
Chile	..	25.4	30.5	30.1	..	67.5	72.0	74.9	..	51.0	58.0	64.2
Czech Republic	36.4	27.5	25.2	27.1	81.6	82.0	82.2	83.8	36.3	44.5	46.5	54.0
Denmark	66.0	62.3	58.1	53.8	84.1	84.5	82.8	82.0	55.7	59.5	58.5	63.2
Estonia	30.2	30.7	25.4	33.3	74.5	79.2	74.9	80.9	45.0	55.7	53.8	64.0
Finland	41.1	40.5	38.8	41.4	80.9	81.7	81.6	80.5	41.7	52.7	56.3	59.1
France	..	30.4	30.1	27.9	..	80.8	82.0	79.8	..	38.6	39.7	46.9
Germany	..	41.9	46.3	46.1	..	77.4	81.5	83.5	..	45.5	57.7	65.6
Greece	27.6	25.0	20.1	13.3	70.5	74.0	73.2	62.4	38.9	42.0	42.4	34.1
Hungary	33.5	21.8	18.3	23.5	73.0	73.7	72.5	79.3	22.2	33.0	33.6	41.8
Iceland	..	70.5	61.7	69.2	..	87.7	82.9	85.1	..	84.3	79.8	83.6
Ireland	50.4	48.7	31.5	28.4	75.3	78.0	70.3	72.6	45.3	51.6	50.2	53.0
Israel	28.2	26.6	27.0	44.5	70.4	70.6	73.9	78.2	46.7	52.4	59.8	65.1
Italy	26.5	25.7	20.3	15.6	68.0	72.3	71.1	67.9	27.7	31.4	36.5	46.2
Japan	42.8	40.9	38.5	40.3	78.7	79.2	80.7	82.2	62.8	63.9	66.0	68.6
Korea	29.4	29.9	23.0	25.8	72.2	73.4	73.8	75.7	57.8	58.7	60.9	65.6
Luxembourg	..	24.9	21.2	20.4	..	80.7	82.3	83.8	..	31.7	39.7	42.6
Mexico	..	44.6	42.5	41.2	..	68.9	69.1	70.1	..	53.2	53.5	55.0
Netherlands	68.7	65.2	63.0	58.8	81.7	82.9	84.7	81.7	38.2	46.1	53.7	59.9
New Zealand	54.2	56.3	49.4	51.7	78.2	81.5	79.9	81.7	56.8	69.5	73.2	76.2
Norway	57.7	53.4	51.5	50.2	85.4	83.3	84.7	83.9	65.2	65.5	68.6	72.2
Poland	24.5	22.5	26.4	25.8	70.9	69.6	77.2	78.4	28.4	27.2	34.1	42.5
Portugal	42.2	35.3	27.9	22.4	81.8	80.7	79.2	77.4	50.7	50.4	49.5	47.8
Slovak Republic	29.0	25.6	20.7	21.8	74.7	75.3	75.8	76.8	21.4	30.3	40.6	44.8
Slovenia	32.8	34.0	34.1	26.8	82.6	83.8	83.7	81.9	22.8	30.7	35.1	35.4
Spain	32.5	38.5	25.0	16.7	68.4	74.8	70.0	67.4	37.0	43.1	43.6	44.3
Sweden	..	39.0	38.8	42.8	..	83.5	84.0	85.4	..	69.5	70.5	74.0
Switzerland	..	59.9	62.5	61.7	..	85.1	85.8	86.9	..	65.1	68.0	71.6
Turkey	..	..	30.0	33.5	..	..	55.4	58.8	..	..	29.6	31.4
United Kingdom	56.7	54.3	46.8	48.1	80.2	81.3	79.8	82.1	50.7	56.8	57.2	61.0
United States	59.7	53.9	45.0	47.6	81.5	79.3	75.1	76.7	57.8	60.8	60.3	61.3
EU 28	..	36.0	33.9	32.4	..	77.0	77.7	77.4	..	42.3	46.2	51.8
OECD	..	42.5	39.0	39.7	..	75.8	75.2	76.0	..	51.7	54.0	57.3
Brazil	..	43.6	46.0	43.4	..	..	..	..	..	..	..	..
China	..	..	..	..	..	..	..	..	..	..	..	..
India	..	..	..	..	..	..	..	..	..	..	..	..
Indonesia	..	..	..	..	..	..	..	..	..	..	..	..
Russian Federation	34.6	33.1	34.2	33.4	80.2	82.9	83.6	85.7	34.8	45.9	46.7	47.4
South Africa	..	..	12.8	12.3	..	..	56.8	57.5	..	..	37.9	40.6

StatLink ⬛⬛ http://dx.doi.org/10.1787/888933336076

Employment rates for age group 15-24

Persons in employment as a percentage of population in that age group

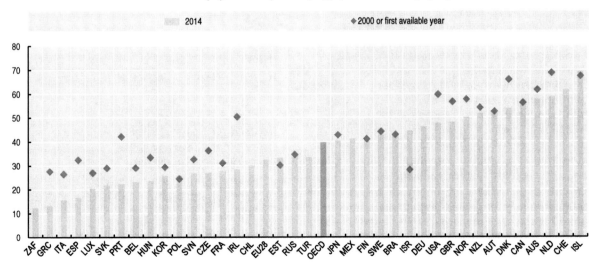

StatLink ⬛⬛ http://dx.doi.org/10.1787/888933334898

PART-TIME EMPLOYMENT

Opportunities for part-time work are especially important for people who do not want to work full-time because of family circumstances, such as parents (often woman) with young children and those caring for the elderly. Indeed, recent surveys in a large number of OECD countries show that most people who work part-time do so by choice. This suggests that countries with little part-time employment could foster increased employment by policies that promote the availability of part-time jobs.

Definition

Part-time employment refers to persons who usually work less than 30 hours per week in their main job. This definition has the advantage of being comparable across countries as national definitions of part-time employment vary greatly from one country to another. Part-time workers include both employees and the self-employed.

Overview

The incidence of part-time employment for the OECD area as a whole was 16.7% in 2014. But this incidence differed significantly across countries. In Australia, the Netherlands and Switzerland, over 25% of all those in employment were working part-time, while this share was under 10% in seven Eastern European countries and below 5% in the Czech Republic, Hungary, and the Slovak Republic. In Russia this rate is also low at 4% and at 8% in South Africa.

In recent years, part-time work has accounted for a substantial share of overall employment growth in many OECD countries. For the OECD as a whole, the incidence of part-time employment increased by close to 3 percentage points between 2002 and 2014, while overall employment rates declined since the onset of the jobs crisis in late 2007. Part-time employment rates grew by 5 percentage points or more in Austria, Japan, Mexico and the Netherlands but also in Greece, Italy, Spain and Ireland that were hard hit by the crisis. The largest increase in part-time employment rates occurred in Austria (9.2 percentage points) which benefited from an overall increase in employment rates of women over the 2002-14 period. In Iceland and Poland as well as in Russia, part-time employment declined, by more than 3 percentage points in 2002-14.

The growth of part-time employment has been especially important for groups that are often under-represented in the labour force such as women – over 5 percentage points in Austria, Greece, Italy, Japan, Korea, Slovenia and Spain; youth – over 20 percentage points in Denmark, Ireland, Slovenia and Spain; and older workers – over 5 percentage points in Austria, Ireland, Italy, Mexico and Spain.

Employment is generally measured through household labour force surveys. According to the ILO Guidelines, employed persons are those aged 15 or over who report that they have worked in gainful employment for at least one hour in the previous week or who had a job but were absent from work in the reference week. The rates shown here refer to the number of persons who usually work less than 30 hours per week in their main job as a percentage of the total number of those in employment.

Comparability

All OECD countries use the ILO Guidelines for measuring employment. Operational definitions used in national labour force surveys may, however, vary slightly across countries. Employment levels are also likely to be affected by changes in the survey design, the survey scope and the survey conduct. Despite these changes, employment rates are fairly consistent over time. Information on the number of hours usually worked is mostly collected in household labour force surveys. Part-time rates are considered to be of good comparability.

There are two series breaks due a major redesign of the national labour force survey in Chile between 2009 and 2010 and in Israel between 2011 and 2012. For Israel there was a change from a quarterly to a monthly survey as well as a change in concept from "civilian" to "total" labour force.

Sources
- OECD (2015), *OECD Employment Outlook*, OECD Publishing.
- For non-member countries: National sources.

Further information

Analytical publications
- OECD (2015), *How's Life?*, OECD Publishing.
- OECD (2007), *Babies and Bosses – Reconciling Work and Family Life*, OECD Publishing.

Statistical publications
- OECD (2014), *OECD Labour Force Statistics*, OECD Publishing.

Online databases
- *OECD Employment and Labour Market Statistics*.

Websites
- Employment policies and data, *www.oecd.org/employment/emp*.
- Labour statistics, *www.oecd.org/employment/labour-stats*.

Incidence of part-time employment

As a percentage of total employment

	2002	2003	2004	2005	2006	2007	2008	2009	2010	2011	2012	2013	2014
Australia	24.0	24.3	23.8	24.0	23.9	23.7	23.8	24.6	24.8	24.7	24.6	24.9	25.2
Austria	13.3	13.7	15.3	16.4	17.0	17.3	17.8	18.7	19.2	19.0	19.4	19.9	20.9
Belgium	17.6	18.3	18.5	18.5	18.7	18.1	18.3	18.2	18.3	18.8	18.7	18.2	18.1
Canada	18.8	19.0	18.5	18.4	18.2	18.3	18.6	19.3	19.6	19.3	19.0	19.1	19.3
Chile	5.2	5.7	6.6	7.2	7.7	8.0	9.1	10.5	17.4	17.2	16.7	16.5	17.0
Czech Republic	2.9	3.2	3.1	3.3	3.3	3.5	3.5	3.9	4.3	3.9	4.3	4.9	4.8
Denmark	15.5	16.2	17.0	17.3	17.9	17.3	17.8	18.8	19.2	19.2	19.4	19.2	19.7
Estonia	7.2	7.8	7.2	6.9	6.8	6.8	6.3	8.5	8.8	8.9	8.2	8.0	7.6
Finland	11.0	11.3	11.3	11.2	11.4	11.7	11.5	12.2	12.5	12.7	13.0	13.0	13.3
France	13.8	13.0	13.3	13.2	13.2	13.3	12.9	13.3	13.6	13.6	13.7	14.0	14.2
Germany	18.8	19.6	20.1	21.5	21.8	22.0	21.8	21.9	21.7	22.3	22.2	22.6	22.3
Greece	5.4	5.6	5.9	6.4	7.4	7.7	7.9	8.5	8.9	9.1	9.8	10.3	11.2
Hungary	2.6	3.2	3.3	3.2	2.7	2.8	3.1	3.5	3.7	4.8	4.8	4.6	4.2
Iceland	20.1	16.0	16.6	16.4	16.0	15.9	15.1	17.5	18.4	17.0	17.3	17.4	16.7
Ireland	18.4	18.9	18.9	19.3	19.3	19.9	20.9	23.8	24.9	25.7	25.0	24.2	23.4
Israel	15.5	15.3	15.2	15.1	15.2	14.8	14.7	14.8	14.0	13.7	15.0	14.4	14.7
Italy	11.6	11.7	14.8	14.7	15.0	15.3	16.0	15.9	16.4	16.7	17.8	18.5	18.8
Japan	17.7	18.2	18.1	18.3	18.0	18.9	19.6	20.3	20.2	20.6	20.5	21.9	22.7
Korea	7.6	7.7	8.4	9.0	8.8	8.9	9.3	9.9	10.7	13.5	10.2	11.1	10.5
Luxembourg	12.5	13.3	13.2	13.9	12.7	13.1	13.4	16.4	15.8	16.0	15.5	15.3	15.5
Mexico	13.5	13.4	15.1	16.8	17.0	17.6	17.6	17.9	18.9	18.2	19.4	19.0	18.7
Netherlands	33.9	34.5	35.0	35.6	35.4	35.9	36.1	36.7	37.1	37.2	37.8	38.7	38.5
New Zealand	22.5	22.1	21.8	21.6	21.2	21.9	22.1	22.4	21.8	22.1	22.3	21.6	21.5
Norway	20.6	21.0	21.1	20.8	21.1	20.4	20.3	20.4	20.1	20.0	19.8	19.5	18.8
Poland	11.7	11.5	12.0	11.7	10.8	10.1	9.3	8.7	8.7	8.3	8.0	7.7	7.1
Portugal	9.7	10.0	9.8	9.6	9.4	10.0	9.9	9.8	9.6	11.7	12.5	12.0	11.0
Slovak Republic	1.6	2.2	2.6	2.4	2.4	2.4	2.6	2.9	3.7	4.0	3.8	4.3	4.9
Slovenia	4.9	5.0	7.5	7.4	7.8	7.8	7.5	8.3	9.4	8.6	7.9	8.6	9.6
Spain	7.6	7.8	8.3	10.8	10.7	10.5	10.9	11.6	12.2	12.7	13.6	14.7	14.7
Sweden	13.8	14.1	14.4	13.5	13.4	14.4	14.4	14.6	14.5	14.3	14.3	14.3	14.2
Switzerland	24.8	25.1	24.8	25.1	25.5	25.4	25.9	26.5	26.1	25.9	26.0	26.4	26.9
Turkey	6.6	6.0	6.1	5.6	7.6	8.1	8.5	11.1	11.5	11.7	11.8	12.3	10.6
United Kingdom	23.1	23.4	23.4	23.0	23.2	22.9	23.0	23.9	24.6	24.7	25.0	24.6	24.1
United States	13.1	13.2	13.2	12.8	12.6	12.6	12.8	14.1	13.5	12.6	13.4	12.3	12.3
EU 28	14.8	14.9	15.5	15.9	16.0	16.0	16.0	16.4	16.7	17.0	17.3	17.6	17.4
OECD	14.4	14.6	15.0	15.2	15.2	15.4	15.6	16.4	16.6	16.5	16.9	16.8	16.7
Brazil	17.9	18.0	18.2	19.0	19.2	18.3	18.0	17.8	..	16.0	16.2	16.4	..
China	..	..	..	..	..	..	..	..	..	..	..	..	..
India	..	..	..	..	..	..	..	..	..	..	..	..	..
Indonesia	..	..	..	..	..	..	..	..	..	..	..	..	..
Russian Federation	3.8	5.3	5.4	5.6	5.3	5.1	5.0	4.7	4.3	4.1	4.1	4.3	4.0
South Africa	..	..	..	..	..	..	7.9	8.1	7.7	7.4	7.7	8.3	8.0

StatLink ᴀᴦ🔲 http://dx.doi.org/10.1787/888933336520

Incidence of part-time employment

As a percentage of total employment

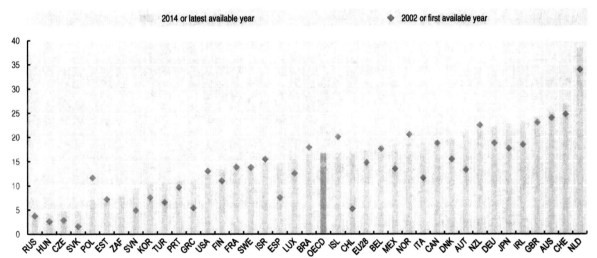

▨ 2014 or latest available year   ◆ 2002 or first available year

StatLink ᴀᴦ🔲 http://dx.doi.org/10.1787/888933335407

SELF-EMPLOYMENT

Self-employment may be seen either as a survival strategy for those who cannot find any other means of earning an income or as evidence of entrepreneurial spirit and a desire to be one's own boss. Self-employment rates reflect these various motives.

Definition

Employment is generally measured through national labour force surveys. According to the ILO Guidelines, employed persons are defined as those aged 15 or over who report that they have worked in gainful employment for at least one hour in the previous week or who had a job but were absent from work in the reference week.

Self-employed persons include employers, own-account workers, members of producers' co-operatives, and unpaid family workers. People in the last of these groups do not have a formal contract to receive a fixed amount of income at regular intervals, but they share in the income generated by the enterprise; unpaid family workers are particularly important in farming and retail trade. Note that all persons who work in corporate enterprises, including company directors, are considered to be employees.

Rates are the percentages of the self-employed in total employment.

Comparability

All OECD countries use ILO Guidelines for measuring employment. Operational definitions used in national labour force surveys may, however, vary slightly across countries. Only unincorporated self-employed are included in self-employed in Australia, Canada and the United States. Employment levels are also likely to be affected by changes in the survey design, questions sequencing and/or the ways in which surveys are conducted. Despite this, self-employment rates are likely to be fairly consistent over time.

Overview

In 2014, the share of self-employed workers in total employment ranged from under 7% in Luxembourg and the United States to well over 30% in Brazil, Greece, Mexico and Turkey. In general, self-employment rates are highest in countries with low per capita income although Italy, with a self-employment rate of around 25%, is an exception. Ireland and Spain also combine high per capita incomes and high self-employment rates.

Over the period 2000-14, self-employment rates have fallen in more than two thirds of countries and by 2.4 percentage points in the OECD area. These falls have mostly occurred prior to the onset of the global financial crisis in late 2007. However the Czech Republic, the Netherlands, Slovenia and the United Kingdom saw moderate to strong increases and the Slovak Republic even had an increase exceeding 7 percentage points, albeit from low levels. Conversely, and starting from a higher level, there have been sharp declines in self-employment rates of 3 percentage points or more in Turkey, Korea, Greece, Portugal, Poland, Mexico and Italy but also in Australia, Hungary, Iceland, Japan, New Zealand, and Switzerland.

Levels and changes in total self-employment rates conceal significant differences between men and women. In 2014, only Mexico and Turkey recorded self-employment rates for women higher than those for men with many of them working as unpaid family workers. In the case of Turkey, almost 40% of all working women are self-employed, albeit down from 64.7% in 2000.

Sources

- OECD (2014), OECD Labour Force Statistics, OECD Publishing.
- For non-member countries: National sources.

Further information

Analytical publications

- OECD (2015), Financing SMEs and Entrepreneurs, OECD Publishing.
- OECD (2015), OECD Employment Outlook, OECD Publishing.
- OECD (2014), OECD Studies on SMEs and Entrepreneurship, OECD Publishing.
- OECD (2005), OECD SME and Entrepreneurship Outlook 2005, OECD Publishing.

Statistical publications

- OECD (2014), Entrepreneurship at a Glance, OECD Publishing.

Online databases

- OECD Employment and Labour Market Statistics.

Websites

- Employment policies and data, www.oecd.org/employment/ emp.
- Labour statistics, www.oecd.org/employment/labour-stats.
- SMEs and entrepreneurship, www.oecd.org/industry/smes.

Self-employment rates

As a percentage of total employment by gender

	Women				Men				Total			
	2000	2012	2013	2014	2000	2012	2013	2014	2000	2012	2013	2014
Australia	10.3	8.4	8.1	..	16.0	12.4	12.2	..	13.5	10.6	10.3	..
Austria	12.3	10.5	10.6	10.5	14.0	15.4	15.6	15.8	13.3	13.1	13.2	13.3
Belgium	13.5	10.5	10.7	12.3	17.5	17.6	18.8	18.3	15.8	14.3	15.1	15.5
Canada	9.2	8.0	8.1	8.0	11.8	9.7	9.5	9.4	10.6	8.9	8.8	8.8
Chile	24.5	24.8	25.1	25.6	32.4	25.3	25.7	26.0	29.8	25.1	25.4	25.9
Czech Republic	10.2	13.5	13.5	12.9	19.1	22.3	21.3	22.1	15.2	18.5	17.9	18.1
Denmark	5.7	5.6	5.6	..	12.1	12.3	12.1	..	9.1	9.1	9.0	..
Estonia	6.0	5.1	5.9	5.7	11.4	12.6	12.4	12.5	8.8	8.9	9.2	9.1
Finland	9.2	8.9	8.8	9.4	17.8	18.2	18.0	18.5	13.7	13.6	13.5	14.1
France	7.3	7.5	7.6	7.6	10.9	12.3	12.6	12.6	9.3	10.0	10.2	10.2
Germany	7.9	8.4	8.1	8.0	13.4	14.4	14.0	13.6	11.0	11.6	11.2	11.0
Greece	39.0	31.1	31.9	29.8	43.7	40.4	40.4	39.4	42.0	36.6	36.9	35.4
Hungary	10.5	8.7	8.2	7.8	19.1	14.5	14.0	13.7	15.2	11.8	11.3	11.0
Iceland	11.0	8.8	8.4	7.8	24.0	15.9	16.7	16.8	18.0	12.5	12.7	12.5
Ireland	8.6	7.5	8.1	7.9	25.9	24.8	24.9	25.5	18.8	16.7	17.1	17.4
Israel	9.3	8.7	9.0	9.1	18.3	16.2	15.8	15.6	14.2	12.7	12.6	12.5
Italy	22.0	18.3	18.3	18.5	32.3	30.2	30.1	29.7	28.5	25.2	25.1	24.9
Japan	18.3	10.7	10.4	..	15.5	12.6	12.4	..	16.6	11.8	11.5	..
Korea	38.4	26.0	25.3	24.6	35.7	29.8	29.0	28.4	36.8	28.2	27.4	26.8
Luxembourg	6.9	..	..	..	7.7	..	..	..	7.4	6.1	6.2	..
Mexico	35.2	35.1	33.8	32.7	36.4	32.8	32.5	31.7	36.0	33.7	33.0	32.1
Netherlands	9.4	11.5	12.1	..	12.6	18.4	19.2	..	11.2	15.2	15.9	..
New Zealand	14.5	12.4	11.7	11.8	25.7	20.4	18.8	18.3	20.6	16.6	15.4	15.3
Norway	4.8	4.1	4.4	4.3	9.8	9.4	9.3	9.8	7.4	6.9	7.0	7.2
Poland	24.8	19.2	18.4	17.7	29.5	25.0	24.5	24.3	27.4	22.4	21.8	21.4
Portugal	24.5	17.7	17.5	14.9	27.5	26.5	26.4	24.6	26.1	22.2	22.1	19.9
Slovak Republic	4.6	9.9	9.8	9.9	10.8	19.8	20.2	19.7	8.0	15.5	15.6	15.4
Slovenia	13.0	12.8	13.6	16.0	18.6	19.2	19.6	20.7	16.1	16.2	16.9	18.6
Spain	16.6	12.7	13.1	13.0	22.2	21.3	22.1	21.7	20.2	17.4	17.9	17.7
Sweden	5.7	5.9	6.2	6.2	14.5	14.6	14.5	14.1	10.3	10.5	10.6	10.3
Switzerland	12.3	10.3	10.2	10.0	13.9	10.4	10.5	10.0	13.2	10.4	10.4	10.0
Turkey	64.7	45.7	43.4	39.8	46.5	33.5	32.7	31.5	51.4	37.1	35.9	34.0
United Kingdom	8.3	9.6	9.6	..	16.7	19.0	18.7	..	12.8	14.6	14.4	..
United States	6.1	5.6	5.6	5.4	8.6	7.8	7.5	7.4	7.4	6.8	6.6	6.5
EU 28	14.8	12.4	12.3	..	20.9	20.2	20.0	..	18.3	16.6	16.5	..
OECD	15.1	13.2	13.0	12.8	19.6	18.0	17.7	17.5	17.7	15.9	15.6	15.4
Brazil	..	27.1	26.8	..	..	34.3	34.4	..	..	31.2	31.2	..
China	..	..	..	..	..	..	..	..	..	..	..	..
India	..	..	..	..	..	..	..	..	..	..	..	..
Indonesia	..	..	..	..	..	..	..	..	..	..	..	..
Russian Federation	9.7	6.0	6.4	6.3	10.5	7.8	8.1	8.1	10.1	6.9	7.3	7.2
South Africa	..	..	..	..	..	..	..	..	..	..	..	..

StatLink http://dx.doi.org/10.1787/888933336573

Self-employment rates: total

As a percentage of total employment

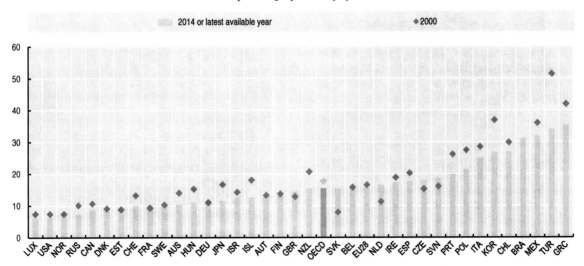

StatLink http://dx.doi.org/10.1787/888933335485

EMPLOYMENT BY REGION

Inequalities in economic performance across regions partly reflect the extent to which each region is able to utilise its available labour resources, and especially to increase job opportunities for under-represented groups.

Definition

Employed persons are all persons who during the reference week of the survey worked at least one hour for pay or profit, or were temporarily absent from such work. The employment rate is the number of employed persons as a percentage of the working age (15-64) population.

Comparability

As for other regional statistics, comparability is affected by differences in the meaning of the word "region". This results in significant differences in terms of geographic area and population both within and among countries. To address this issue, the OECD has classified regions within each country based on two levels: territorial level 2 (TL2, large regions) and territorial level 3 (TL3, small regions). Labour market data for Canada refers to a different regional grouping, labelled non-official grids (NOG) comparable to

TL3. For Brazil, China, Russia and South Africa only large regions have been defined.

Data on employment growth refer to period 2000-14 for all countries, except for Germany and Slovenia, the first available year is 2001, and 2004 for Turkey. Data on employment increase contributed by the top 10% regions include only countries with average positive growth of employment over 2000-14. Greece and Japan are excluded. Denmark is excluded due to lack of data on comparable years.

Data on regional employment growth refer to small regions (TL3), except for Iceland, Israel, Mexico, Poland, Portugal, Slovenia and Russia where it is large regions (TL2).

Data on female employment refer to large regions (TL2).

Overview

Differences in employment opportunities within countries are often larger than across countries. In almost half of the countries, differences in regional employment growth rates across regions were above 2 percentage points over the period 2000-14. Regional differences in employment in OECD countries were the largest in Austria, Poland, Italy, and the United States, and among the emerging economies, Russia.

A small number of regions drive employment creation at the national level. On average, almost half of overall employment creation in OECD countries between 2000 and 2014 was accounted for by just 10% of regions. The regional contribution to national employment creation was particularly concentrated in certain countries. In Greece, Japan, Australia and the United States, more than two-third of employment growth was spurred by 10% of regions.

Comparing the periods before and after the peak of the recent economic crisis, respectively 2000-07 and 2009-14, the regional concentration of employment creation has increased in 20 of the 30 countries, resulting in higher differences in employment among regions.

In one fourth of OECD regions, the difference between employment rates for men and women is higher than 20 percentage points. In 2014, OECD countries with the highest regional disparities of difference in gender employment rates were Mexico, Turkey, Chile, the United States and Israel.

Sources
- OECD (2013), *OECD Regions at a Glance*, OECD Publishing.

Further information

Analytical publications
- OECD (2014), *OECD Regional Outlook*, OECD Publishing.
- OECD (2012), *Promoting Growth in All Regions*, OECD Publishing.
- OECD (2009), *Regions Matter: Economic Recovery, Innovation and Sustainable Growth*, OECD Publishing.

Online databases
- OECD Regional Database.

Websites
- Regional Development, *www.oecd.org/regional/regional-policy*.
- Regions at a Glance Interactive, *http://rag.oecd.org*.

Differences in annual employment growth across regions
Percentage, 2014

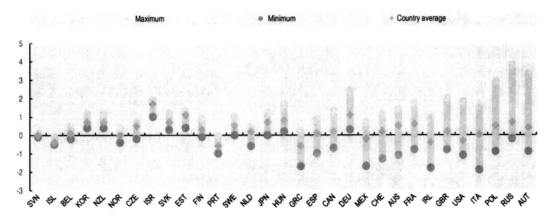

StatLink ⟪⟫ http://dx.doi.org/10.1787/888933335430

Share of national employment growth due to the 10% of most dynamic regions
Percentage

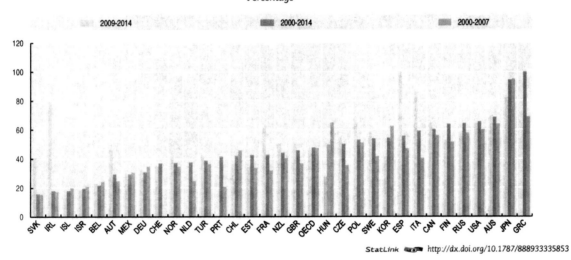

StatLink ⟪⟫ http://dx.doi.org/10.1787/888933335853

Regional disparities in the employment rate gender difference (men-women)
Percentage point, 2014

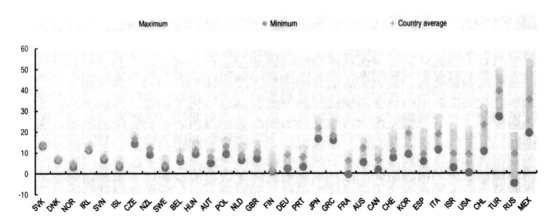

StatLink ⟪⟫ http://dx.doi.org/10.1787/888933335978

HOURS WORKED

Lower hours worked is one of the forms in which the benefits of productivity growth have been shared by people. Hours worked is also one of the ways that labour markets adjust during business cycles. In recent years, governments of several OECD countries have also pursued policies to make it easier for parents to reconcile work and family life, and some of these policies have tended to reduce working time.

Definition

The average number of hours worked per year is calculated as the total number of hours actually worked over the year divided by the average number of people in employment. The data cover employees and self-employed workers; they include both full-time and part-time employment.

Employment is generally measured through household labour force surveys. In accordance with the ILO Guidelines, employed persons are defined as those aged 15 years or over who report that they have worked in gainful employment for at least one hour in the previous week or were temporarily absent from work.

Overview

Over the period from 2002 to 2014, average hours worked per employed person have fallen in almost all OECD countries except Norway, the Slovak Republic and Sweden. This decline is more pronounced in two-thirds of countries than the decline in the previous decade, while annual hours worked remained stable in Belgium, the Netherlands, Sweden, the Slovak Republic and the United Kingdom.

For the OECD as a whole, the average hours worked per employed person fell from 1 819 annual hours in 2002 to 1 770 in 2014; this is equivalent to a reduction of more than one hour per week over a year with 45 work weeks. Sharp reductions in annual hours worked over this period occurred in about one-third of OECD countries where they fell by 80 or more hours, with a further decline of 150 or more hours in Korea (minus 340), Chile (minus 260), albeit from high levels, Austria, Hungary, Iceland, Israel, Estonia, Turkey, Italy and Ireland. Most of the decline in hours worked materialised following the onset of the global crisis in ten countries - some hard hit by the crisis, such as Estonia, Greece, Hungary, and Italy, but also Austria, Chile, Korea, Israel, Switzerland and Turkey.

Although one should exercise caution when comparing levels across countries, actual hours worked are significantly above the OECD average, by 200 or more hours, in Mexico, Korea, Greece and Chile and significantly below the OECD average, by 200 or less hours, in Germany, the Netherlands, Norway, Denmark, France, Slovenia and Switzerland.

Estimates of the hours actually worked are based on national labour force surveys in many countries, while others use establishment surveys, administrative records or a combination of sources. Actual hours worked include regular work hours of full-time and part-time workers, over-time (paid and unpaid), hours worked in additional jobs, and time not worked because of public holidays, annual paid leave, illness, maternity and parental leave, strikes and labour disputes, bad weather, economic conditions and several other minor reasons.

Comparability

Data are based on a range of sources of varying reliability. Annual working hours reported for 34 OECD countries and Russia are provided by national statistical offices and are estimated using the best available sources. These national data are intended for comparisons of trends in productivity and labour inputs (or total hours) and are not fully suitable for inter-country comparisons of the level of hours worked per worker because of differences in their sources and other uncertainties about their international comparability.

Sources
- OECD (2015), *OECD Employment Outlook*, OECD Publishing.

Further information

Analytical publications
- OECD (2015), *How's Life?*, OECD Publishing.

Methodological publications
- OECD (2009), *Productivity Measurement and Analysis*, OECD Publishing.
- OECD (2004), "Recent Labour Market Developments and Prospects: Clocking In (and Out): Several Facets of Working Time", *OECD Employment Outlook 2004*, OECD Publishing.

Online databases
- OECD Employment and Labour Market Statistics.

Websites
- Productivity statistics, *www.oecd.org/statistics/productivity*.
- Online OECD employment database, *www.oecd.org/employment/database*.

Average hours actually worked

Hours per year per person in paid employment

	2002	2003	2004	2005	2006	2007	2008	2009	2010	2011	2012	2013	2014
Australia	1 731	1 736	1 736	1 730	1 720	1 711	1 717	1 690	1 692	1 699	1 678	1 663	1 664
Austria	1 792	1 784	1 787	1 764	1 746	1 736	1 729	1 673	1 665	1 670	1 649	1 629	..
Belgium	1 582	1 578	1 572	1 565	1 575	1 579	1 572	1 554	1 560	1 572	1 573	1 576	..
Canada	1 754	1 740	1 760	1 747	1 745	1 741	1 734	1 702	1 703	1 700	1 713	1 708	1 704
Chile	2 250	2 235	2 232	2 157	2 165	2 128	2 095	2 074	2 068	2 047	2 024	2 015	1 990
Czech Republic	1 816	1 806	1 817	1 817	1 799	1 784	1 790	1 779	1 800	1 806	1 776	1 763	1 776
Denmark	1 487	1 482	1 481	1 474	1 479	1 456	1 450	1 446	1 436	1 455	1 443	1 438	1 436
Estonia	1 973	1 978	1 986	2 008	2 001	1 998	1 968	1 831	1 875	1 919	1 886	1 866	1 859
Finland	1 714	1 705	1 707	1 697	1 693	1 691	1 685	1 661	1 668	1 662	1 650	1 643	1 645
France	1 487	1 484	1 513	1 507	1 484	1 500	1 507	1 489	1 494	1 496	1 490	1 474	1 473
Germany	1 431	1 425	1 422	1 411	1 425	1 424	1 418	1 373	1 390	1 393	1 374	1 363	1 371
Greece	2 093	2 091	2 083	2 136	2 125	2 111	2 106	2 081	2 019	2 131	2 058	2 060	2 042
Hungary	2 005	1 978	1 986	1 987	1 984	1 979	1 982	1 963	1 958	1 976	1 889	1 880	1 858
Iceland	2 012	1 973	1 979	1 970	1 958	1 932	1 934	1 849	1 834	1 878	1 853	1 846	1 864
Ireland	1 904	1 887	1 875	1 883	1 879	1 865	1 844	1 812	1 801	1 801	1 806	1 815	1 821
Israel	1 993	1 974	1 942	1 931	1 919	1 931	1 931	1 927	1 918	1 920	1 910	1 867	1 853
Italy	1 827	1 816	1 815	1 812	1 813	1 818	1 807	1 776	1 777	1 773	1 734	1 733	1 734
Japan	1 798	1 799	1 787	1 775	1 784	1 785	1 771	1 714	1 733	1 728	1 745	1 734	1 729
Korea	2 464	2 424	2 392	2 351	2 346	2 306	2 246	2 232	2 187	2 090	2 163	2 079	2 124
Luxembourg	1 663	1 658	1 614	1 597	1 608	1 544	1 584	1 628	1 643	1 607	1 615	1 649	1 643
Mexico	2 271	2 277	2 271	2 281	2 281	2 262	2 260	2 253	2 242	2 250	2 226	2 237	2 228
Netherlands	1 435	1 427	1 448	1 434	1 430	1 430	1 430	1 422	1 421	1 422	1 426	1 421	1 425
New Zealand	1 826	1 823	1 830	1 815	1 795	1 774	1 761	1 740	1 755	1 746	1 734	1 752	1 762
Norway	1 414	1 401	1 421	1 423	1 420	1 426	1 430	1 407	1 415	1 421	1 420	1 408	1 427
Poland	1 979	1 984	1 983	1 994	1 985	1 976	1 969	1 948	1 940	1 938	1 929	1 918	1 923
Portugal	1 894	1 887	1 893	1 895	1 883	1 900	1 887	1 887	1 890	1 867	1 849	1 852	1 857
Slovak Republic	1 754	1 698	1 742	1 769	1 774	1 791	1 793	1 780	1 805	1 793	1 789	1 772	1 763
Slovenia	1 614	1 616	1 627	1 590	1 562	1 551	1 566	1 569	1 580	1 557	1 537	1 550	1 561
Spain	1 765	1 756	1 742	1 726	1 716	1 704	1 713	1 720	1 710	1 717	1 704	1 699	1 689
Sweden	1 595	1 582	1 605	1 605	1 599	1 612	1 617	1 609	1 635	1 632	1 618	1 607	1 609
Switzerland	1 614	1 627	1 657	1 652	1 643	1 633	1 623	1 615	1 613	1 607	1 592	1 576	1 568
Turkey	1 943	1 943	1 918	1 936	1 944	1 911	1 900	1 881	1 877	1 864	1 855	1 832	..
United Kingdom	1 684	1 674	1 674	1 673	1 669	1 677	1 659	1 651	1 652	1 625	1 654	1 669	1 677
United States	1 810	1 800	1 802	1 799	1 800	1 797	1 791	1 767	1 777	1 786	1 789	1 788	1 789
EU 28	..	..	..	..	..	..	..	..	..	..	..	..	..
OECD	1 819	1 812	1 813	1 807	1 808	1 802	1 794	1 700	1 776	1 773	1 773	1 770	1 770
Brazil	..	..	..	..	..	..	..	..	..	..	..	..	..
China	..	..	..	..	..	..	..	..	..	..	..	..	..
India	..	..	..	..	..	..	..	..	..	..	..	..	..
Indonesia	..	..	..	..	..	..	..	..	..	..	..	..	..
Russian Federation	1 982	1 993	1 993	1 989	1 998	1 999	1 997	1 974	1 976	1 979	1 982	1 980	1 985
South Africa	..	..	..	..	..	..	..	..	..	..	..	..	..

StatLink *http://dx.doi.org/10.1787/888933336245*

Average hours actually worked

Hours per year per person in paid employment

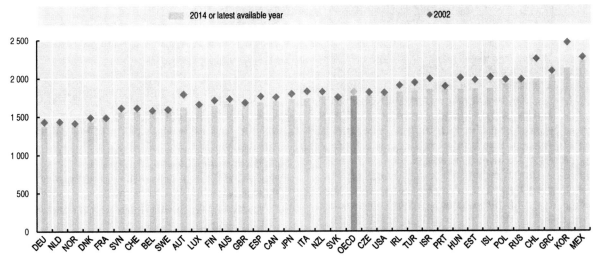

StatLink *http://dx.doi.org/10.1787/888933335059*

UNEMPLOYMENT RATES

The unemployment rate is one measure of the extent of labour market slack, as well as being an important indicator of economic and social well-being. Breakdowns of unemployment by gender show how women are faring compared to men.

Definition

Unemployed persons are defined as those who report that they are without work, that they are available for work and that they have taken active steps to find work in the last four weeks. The ILO Guidelines specify what actions count as active steps to find work; these include answering vacancy notices, visiting factories, construction sites and other places of work, and placing advertisements in the press as well as registering with labour offices.

The unemployment rate is defined as the number of unemployed persons as a percentage of the labour force, where the latter consists of the unemployed plus those in paid or self-employment.

Overview

When looking at total unemployment rates averaged over the three years ending 2014, countries can be divided into three groups: a low unemployment group with rates below 5% (Korea, Norway, Japan, Switzerland and Mexico); a middle group with unemployment rates between 5% and 10%; and a high unemployment group with unemployment rates of 10% and above (Italy, Ireland, the Slovak Republic, Portugal, South Africa, Spain and Greece).

In almost two thirds of countries, unemployment rates decreased in 2014, with marked declines (by more than 1.5 percentage point) in Hungary, Portugal, Ireland and Spain.

The breakdown of unemployment by gender shows that, in line with the overall rate, OECD unemployment rates for both men and women was significantly higher in 2014 than in 2008. The unemployment rate for men, which had been lower than the rate for women in 2008, rose considerably faster and by 2009 was higher than the rate for women. This is first explained by the fact that job losses over the early stages of the crisis were particularly severe in sectors which traditionally have been occupied by men – namely construction, manufacturing and mining and quarrying. Between 2009 and 2010, the rise in the overall OECD unemployment rates decelerated faster for men, and between 2010 and 2014, the men to women unemployment ratio has decreased in about two third of the countries. However, in 2014, the rate for men was still higher than the rate for women in about half of the countries.

When unemployment is high, some persons become discouraged and stop looking for work; they are then excluded from the labour force. This implies that the unemployment rate may fall, or stop rising, even though there has been no underlying improvement in the labour market.

Comparability

All OECD countries use the ILO Guidelines for measuring unemployment in their national labour force surveys. The operational definitions used in national labour force surveys may, however, vary slightly across countries. Unemployment levels are also likely to be affected by changes in the survey design and the survey conduct. Despite these limits, unemployment rates are of good international comparability and fairly consistent over time.

Unemployment rates differ from rates derived from registered unemployed at labour offices that are often published in individual countries. Data on registered unemployment have limited international comparability, as the rules for registering at labour offices vary from country to country.

There are series breaks due to a major redesign of the national labour force survey in Chile between 2009 and 2010, in Israel between 2011 and 2012 and in Turkey between 2013 and 2014. For Israel there was a change from a quarterly to a monthly survey as well as a change in concept from "civilian" to "total" labour force.

Sources

* OECD (2015), *Main Economic Indicators*, OECD Publishing.
* For non-member countries: National sources.

Further information

Analytical publications

* OECD (2015), *OECD Employment Outlook*, OECD Publishing.
* Venn, D. (2012), "Eligibility Criteria for Unemployment Benefits", *OECD Social, Employment and Migration Working Papers*, No. 131.

Statistical publications

* OECD (2014), *OECD Labour Force Statistics*, OECD Publishing.
* OECD (2014), *Society at a Glance: OECD Social Indicators*, OECD Publishing.

Online databases

* *OECD Employment and Labour Market Statistics.*

Websites

* Employment policies and data, *www.oecd.org/employment/emp*.
* Labour statistics, *www.oecd.org/employment/labour-stats*.

Unemployment rates
As a percentage of labour force

	Women				Men				Total			
	2000	2008	2013	2014	2000	2008	2013	2014	2000	2008	2013	2014
Australia	6.1	4.6	5.6	6.2	6.5	4.0	5.7	6.0	6.3	4.2	5.7	6.1
Austria	3.8	4.4	5.3	5.4	3.3	3.9	5.4	5.8	3.5	4.1	5.3	5.6
Belgium	8.7	7.6	8.2	7.9	5.8	6.5	8.6	9.0	7.0	7.0	8.4	8.5
Canada	6.7	5.6	6.6	6.4	7.0	6.6	7.5	7.4	6.8	6.1	7.1	6.9
Chile	10.3	9.5	6.9	6.9	9.3	6.8	5.3	6.0	9.7	7.8	5.9	6.4
Czech Republic	10.5	5.6	8.3	7.4	7.4	3.5	5.9	5.1	8.8	4.4	7.0	6.1
Denmark	5.2	3.7	7.3	6.8	4.1	3.2	6.7	6.4	4.6	3.4	7.0	6.6
Estonia	13.3	5.1	8.2	6.8	15.9	5.7	9.1	7.9	14.6	5.4	8.6	7.4
Finland	10.6	6.7	7.5	7.9	9.1	6.1	8.8	9.3	9.8	6.4	8.2	8.7
France	..	7.4	9.8	10.0	..	6.7	10.0	10.5	..	7.1	9.9	10.3
Germany	8.1	7.7	4.9	4.6	7.5	7.4	5.5	5.3	7.8	7.5	5.2	5.0
Greece	17.2	11.5	31.3	30.2	7.5	5.1	24.5	23.6	11.4	7.8	27.5	26.5
Hungary	5.6	8.0	10.1	7.9	7.1	7.7	10.2	7.6	6.4	7.8	10.2	7.7
Iceland	..	2.6	5.1	4.8	..	3.3	5.6	5.0	..	2.9	5.4	4.9
Ireland	4.2	4.9	10.7	9.4	4.4	7.5	15.0	12.8	4.3	6.4	13.0	11.3
Israel	9.2	6.5	6.3	5.9	8.4	5.7	6.2	5.9	8.8	6.1	6.2	5.9
Italy	14.5	8.5	13.1	13.8	8.1	5.5	11.5	11.9	10.6	6.7	12.1	12.7
Japan	4.5	3.9	3.7	3.4	4.9	4.1	4.3	3.8	4.7	4.0	4.0	3.6
Korea	3.7	2.6	2.9	3.5	5.0	3.6	3.3	3.6	4.4	3.2	3.1	3.5
Luxembourg	..	6.0	6.4	5.8	..	4.3	5.4	5.9	..	5.1	5.8	5.9
Mexico	..	4.1	5.0	4.9	..	3.8	4.9	4.8	2.5	3.9	4.9	4.8
Netherlands	3.8	3.0	7.3	7.7	2.3	2.5	7.2	7.1	2.9	2.8	7.2	7.4
New Zealand	6.0	4.3	7.0	6.6	6.3	4.1	5.6	5.1	6.2	4.2	6.2	5.8
Norway	3.2	2.4	3.2	3.2	3.4	2.7	3.6	3.7	3.3	2.5	3.4	3.5
Poland	18.1	8.0	11.1	9.6	14.4	6.4	9.7	8.5	16.1	7.1	10.3	9.0
Portugal	5.0	8.8	16.4	14.3	3.2	6.5	16.0	13.5	4.0	7.6	16.2	13.9
Slovak Republic	18.6	10.9	14.5	13.6	18.9	8.4	14.0	12.8	18.8	9.5	14.2	13.2
Slovenia	7.1	4.8	10.9	10.5	6.5	4.0	9.4	8.9	6.7	4.4	10.1	9.7
Spain	20.5	12.8	26.7	25.4	9.6	10.1	25.6	23.6	13.9	11.2	26.1	24.4
Sweden	..	6.6	7.9	7.7	..	5.9	8.2	8.2	..	6.2	8.1	8.0
Switzerland	..	..	4.5	4.7	..	..	4.3	4.4	..	..	4.4	4.5
Turkey	..	10.0	10.6	11.8	..	9.6	7.9	9.0	..	9.7	8.7	9.9
United Kingdom	5.0	5.1	7.0	5.8	6.1	6.1	8.0	6.4	5.6	5.6	7.5	6.1
United States	4.1	5.4	7.1	6.1	3.9	6.1	7.6	6.3	4.0	5.8	7.4	6.2
EU 28	..	7.4	10.9	10.3	..	6.6	10.8	10.1	..	7.0	10.8	10.2
OECD	..	6.0	7.9	7.5	..	5.8	7.8	7.3	..	5.9	7.9	7.3
Brazil	..	..	..	..	..	..	..	..	12.7	7.9	5.4	4.9
China	..	..	..	..	..	..	..	..	..	..	..	..
India	..	..	..	..	..	..	..	..	..	..	..	..
Indonesia	..	..	..	..	..	..	..	..	6.1	8.4	6.0	5.8
Russian Federation	10.4	6.1	5.2	4.8	10.6	6.6	5.8	5.5	10.5	6.4	5.5	5.2
South Africa	26.5	25.9	26.7	27.2	20.4	19.9	23.1	23.3	23.3	22.5	24.7	25.1

StatLink http://dx.doi.org/10.1787/888933336753

Unemployment rates: total
As a percentage of labour force

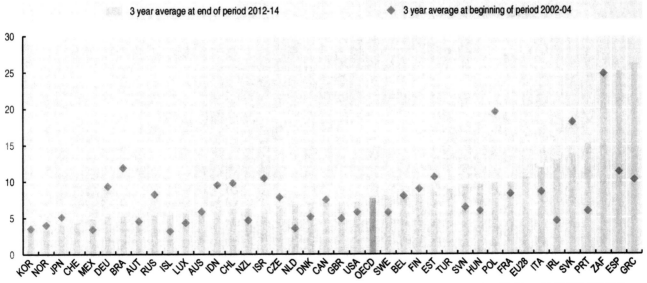

3 year average at end of period 2012-14   3 year average at beginning of period 2002-04

StatLink http://dx.doi.org/10.1787/888933335684

LONG-TERM UNEMPLOYMENT

Long-term unemployment is of particular concern to the people affected and to policy makers. Apart from the mental and material stress caused to the unemployed and their families, high rates of long-term unemployment indicate that labour markets are operating inefficiently.

Rates of long-term unemployment are generally lower in countries that have enjoyed high GDP growth rates in recent years. Lower rates of long-term unemployment may also occur at the onset of an economic downturn due to rising inflow of newly unemployed persons, as witnessed during the first years of the recent global economic crisis. Subsequently, long-term unemployment may gradually begin to unfold in the case of a prolonged economic and jobs crisis as is currently the case in a number of OECD countries.

Definition

Long-term unemployment is defined as referring to people who have been unemployed for 12 months or more. Ratios are the proportion of these long-term unemployed among all unemployed, hereafter called long-term unemployment rates. Lower duration limits (e.g. six months or more) are sometimes considered in national statistics on the subject.

Unemployment is defined in all OECD countries in accordance with the ILO Guidelines. Unemployment is usually measured by national labour force surveys and refer to persons who report that they have worked in gainful employment for less than one hour in the previous week, who are available for work and who have taken actions to seek employment in the previous four weeks. The ILO Guidelines specify the kinds of actions that count as seeking work.

Comparability

All OECD countries use the ILO Guidelines for measuring unemployment. Operational definitions used in national labour force surveys may vary slightly across countries. Unemployment levels may also be affected by changes in the survey design and the survey conduct. Despite these caveats long-term unemployment rates are fairly consistent over time.

In comparing rates of long-term unemployment, it is important to bear in mind differences in institutional arrangements between countries. Rates of long-term unemployment will generally be higher in countries where unemployment benefits are relatively generous and are available for long periods of unemployment. In countries where benefits are low and of limited duration, unemployed persons will more quickly lower their wage expectations or consider taking jobs that are in other ways less attractive than those which they formerly held.

Overview

In 2014, more than one-third of the unemployed were long-term unemployed in the OECD area. The rates varied from 10% or less in Korea and Mexico, to 50% or more in Estonia, Ireland and Italy and more than two-thirds of the unemployed in Greece and the Slovak Republic. For at least the last ten years, the share of long-term unemployed has remained stubbornly high in Germany despite a rising trend in employment rates since 2005.

Over the period 2002-14, long-term unemployment rates increased by almost 8 percentage points for the OECD as a whole. Country patterns differ depending on how deeply national labour markets were affected by the global financial and the Euro area sovereign debt crisis. Since 2002, sharp rises, of 5 percentage points or more, were recorded in 14 countries, exceeding 10 percentage points in the Netherlands, Portugal, Spain, Switzerland, the United Kingdom and the United States, with a dramatic increase of more than 20 percentage points in Greece, Ireland and Portugal. Falls of over 5 per cent occurred in just four countries, with Poland recording the steepest fall of over 10 percentage points. More recently, long-term unemployment has actually increased since 2011 in a number of European countries, notably in Italy, Slovenia, Portugal and Greece.

In Russia and South Africa, long-term unemployment declined markedly since 2002 by more than 10 percentage points. In South Africa however, close to 58% of unemployed people were still long-term unemployed in 2014.

Sources
• OECD (2014), *OECD Labour Force Statistics*, OECD Publishing.
• For non-member countries: National sources.

Further information

Analytical publications
• OECD (2015), *OECD Employment Outlook*, OECD Publishing.

Online databases
• *OECD Employment and Labour Market Statistics.*

Websites
• Employment policies and data, *www.oecd.org/employment/emp*.
• Labour statistics, *www.oecd.org/employment/labour-stats*.

Long-term unemployment

Persons unemployed for 12 months or more as a percentage of total unemployed

	2002	2003	2004	2005	2006	2007	2008	2009	2010	2011	2012	2013	2014
Australia	22.4	21.5	20.6	18.2	18.1	15.4	14.9	14.7	18.6	18.9	19.0	19.1	21.8
Austria	19.2	24.5	27.9	25.5	28.0	27.2	24.3	21.7	25.4	26.3	24.9	24.6	27.2
Belgium	48.8	45.3	49.0	51.7	51.2	50.4	47.6	44.2	48.8	48.3	44.7	46.0	49.9
Canada	9.6	10.0	9.5	9.6	8.7	7.5	7.3	8.0	12.1	13.6	12.7	12.9	12.9
Chile	..	..	..	..	..	..	..	..	..	..	..	..	..
Czech Republic	50.7	49.9	51.8	53.6	55.2	53.4	50.2	31.2	43.3	41.6	43.4	44.9	44.5
Denmark	19.1	20.4	21.5	23.4	20.8	16.1	13.5	9.5	20.2	24.4	28.0	25.5	25.2
Estonia	54.8	46.9	51.1	54.2	48.6	49.8	31.2	27.3	45.3	57.3	54.7	44.5	45.3
Finland	24.4	24.7	23.4	24.9	24.8	23.0	18.2	16.6	23.6	22.6	21.7	21.2	23.1
France	32.7	39.3	40.6	41.1	41.9	40.2	37.4	35.2	40.2	41.5	40.4	40.4	42.7
Germany	47.8	50.0	51.8	53.0	56.4	56.6	52.5	45.5	47.4	47.9	45.4	44.7	44.3
Greece	51.1	54.7	52.9	51.9	54.1	49.7	47.1	40.4	44.6	49.3	59.1	67.1	73.5
Hungary	44.8	42.2	45.1	46.1	46.3	47.5	47.3	42.4	50.3	48.8	46.6	49.8	48.9
Iceland	11.1	8.1	11.2	13.3	7.3	8.0	4.1	6.9	21.3	27.8	27.9	21.9	13.6
Ireland	30.1	32.8	34.9	33.4	31.6	30.0	26.5	29.1	49.1	59.3	61.7	60.6	59.2
Israel	13.5	18.0	24.2	25.3	27.3	24.9	22.7	20.3	22.4	20.2	13.3	12.7	10.6
Italy	59.6	58.1	49.0	49.8	49.6	47.5	45.7	44.6	48.5	52.0	53.2	56.9	61.4
Japan	30.8	33.5	33.7	33.3	33.0	32.0	33.3	28.5	37.6	39.4	38.5	41.2	37.6
Korea	2.5	0.6	1.1	0.8	1.1	0.6	2.7	0.5	0.3	0.4	0.3	0.4	..
Luxembourg	27.4	24.7	21.0	26.4	29.5	28.7	32.4	23.1	29.3	28.8	30.3	30.4	27.4
Mexico	0.9	0.9	1.1	2.1	2.1	2.3	1.4	1.7	2.0	1.9	1.8	1.4	1.2
Netherlands	26.5	27.7	34.2	40.2	43.0	39.4	34.4	24.8	27.6	33.6	33.7	35.9	40.2
New Zealand	14.8	13.6	11.7	9.8	7.6	6.0	4.3	6.4	8.9	8.9	13.3	12.2	13.6
Norway	6.4	6.4	9.2	9.5	14.5	8.8	6.0	7.7	9.5	11.6	8.7	9.2	11.8
Poland	48.4	49.7	47.9	52.2	50.4	45.9	29.0	25.2	25.5	31.6	34.8	36.5	36.2
Portugal	34.5	35.0	44.4	48.3	50.4	47.2	47.4	44.2	52.2	48.4	48.8	56.4	59.6
Slovak Republic	59.8	61.2	60.6	68.1	73.1	70.8	66.0	50.9	59.3	64.0	63.7	66.6	66.8
Slovenia	55.6	52.8	51.4	47.3	49.3	45.7	42.2	30.1	43.3	44.2	47.9	51.0	54.5
Spain	33.4	33.5	31.9	24.4	21.6	20.4	18.0	23.8	36.6	41.6	44.4	49.7	52.8
Sweden	20.9	17.8	18.9	..	..	12.8	12.1	12.8	17.3	18.2	17.5	17.0	16.8
Switzerland	21.8	26.1	33.5	39.0	39.1	40.8	34.3	30.1	33.1	38.8	35.3	33.2	37.7
Turkey	29.4	24.4	39.2	39.4	35.7	30.3	26.9	25.3	28.6	26.5	24.9	24.4	20.6
United Kingdom	21.7	21.4	20.5	21.0	22.3	23.7	24.1	24.5	32.6	33.5	34.7	36.2	35.7
United States	8.5	11.8	12.7	11.8	10.0	10.0	10.6	16.3	29.0	31.3	29.3	25.9	23.0
EU 28	43.1	42.9	41.8	44.5	44.5	41.6	36.2	32.6	39.1	42.0	43.6	46.4	48.6
OECD	27.3	28.5	29.4	31.9	31.3	28.5	24.9	23.6	31.5	33.5	34.1	35.1	35.2
Brazil	..	..	..	..	..	..	..	..	..	..	..	..	..
China	..	..	..	..	..	..	..	..	..	..	..	..	..
India	..	..	..	..	..	..	..	..	..	..	..	..	..
Indonesia	..	..	..	..	..	..	..	..	..	..	..	..	..
Russian Federation	38.9	37.6	39.2	39.0	42.3	40.6	35.2	28.7	30.0	32.9	30.9	31.0	28.1
South Africa	68.5	68.4	65.1	63.7	59.5	57.7	50.2	50.1	56.7	59.7	58.5	57.8	57.8

StatLink http://dx.doi.org/10.1787/888933336367

Long-term unemployment

Persons unemployed for 12 months or more as a percentage of total unemployed

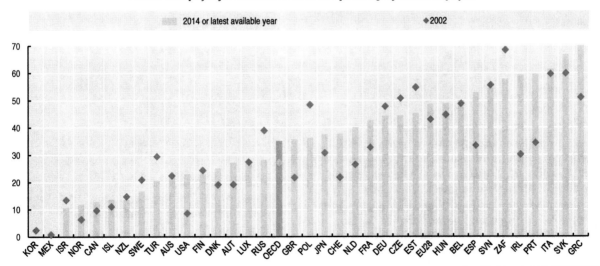

StatLink http://dx.doi.org/10.1787/888933335196

UNEMPLOYMENT BY REGION

The unemployment rate is an important indicator of economic and social well-being. Breakdowns by region show that large international differences hide even larger differences among regions within each country.

Definition

Unemployed persons are defined as those who are without work, who are available for work and have taken active steps to find work in the last four weeks. The unemployment rate is defined as the ratio between unemployed persons and the labour force, where the latter is composed of unemployed and employed persons.

The long-term unemployment rate is defined as the ratio of those unemployed for 12 months or more out of the total labour force. The incident of long-term unemployment is defined as the ratio of the long-term unemployed out of the total unemployed. The youth unemployment rate is defined as the ratio between the unemployed persons aged between 15 and 24 and the labour force in the same age class.

The Gini index is a measure of inequality among all regions of a given country. The index takes on values between 0 and 1, with zero interpreted as no disparity. It assigns equal weight to each region regardless of its size; therefore differences in the values of the index among countries may be partially due to differences in the average size of regions.

While in the study of income inequality individuals are the obvious unit of analysis, there is no such straightforward parallel in regional economics. The size of regions varies significantly both within and between countries so that the degree of geographic concentration and territorial disparity depends on the very definition of a region. Typically, as the size of a region increases, territorial differences tend to be averaged out and disparities to decrease.

Comparability

Comparability of regional statistics is affected by differences in the meaning of the word "region". This results in significant differences in terms of geographic area and population both within and among countries. To address this issue, the OECD has classified regions within each country based on two levels: territorial level 2 (TL2, large regions) and territorial level 3 (TL3, small regions). Labour market data for Canada refers to a different regional grouping, labelled non-official grids (NOG), which is comparable to the small regions. For Brazil, China, India, Russia and South Africa only large regions have been defined.

Data on unemployment, youth and long-term unemployment refer to large (TL2) regions.

Data on unemployment refer to period 2007-14 for all countries.

Data on youth unemployment rate refer to 2014, except 2013 for Israel. New Zealand is not included due to lack of data on comparable years. No regional data for Iceland and Korea exist.

Data on the long-term unemployment refer to 2014 for all countries. Austria and New Zealand are not included due to lack of data on comparable years. No regional data for Iceland, Japan, Korea, Mexico and the United States exist.

Overview

Regional disparities in unemployment have decreased mainly in countries (as measured by the Gini index) where the economic downturn has affected all regions evenly, such as Portugal, Greece, Spain, and Italy.

Youth unemployment is of particular concern in Spain, Italy, Greece, Portugal and Poland where regional differences are high and some regions display a youth unemployment rate above 40%.

Long-term unemployment rates also show large regional variations not only in dual economies such as Italy, but also in Spain, the United States, the Slovak Republic and the United Kingdom.

Sources
• OECD (2013), *OECD Regions at a Glance*, OECD Publishing.

Further information

Analytical publications
• OECD (2014), *OECD Regional Outlook*, OECD Publishing.
• OECD (2012), *Promoting Growth in All Regions*, OECD Publishing.

Online databases
• OECD Regional Database.

Websites
• Regional Statistics and Indicators, *www.oecd.org/regional/regional-policy/regionalstatisticsandindicators.htm*.
• Regions at a Glance Interactive, *http://rag.oecd.org*.

Gini index of regional unemployment rates

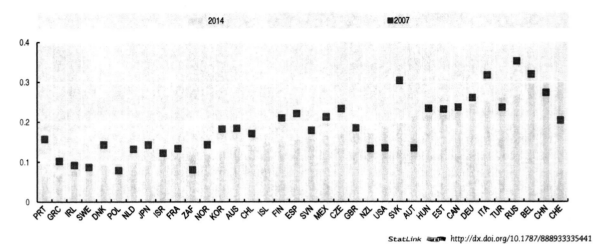

StatLink http://dx.doi.org/10.1787/888933335441

Regional variation of the youth unemployment rate
Percentage, 2014

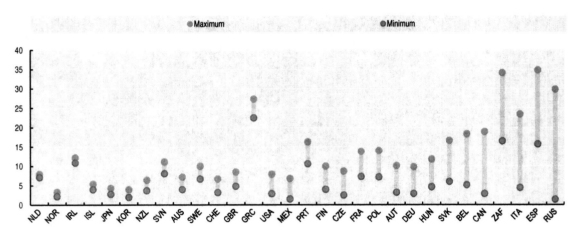

StatLink http://dx.doi.org/10.1787/888933335862

Regional variation in incidence of long-term unemployment
Ratio, 2014

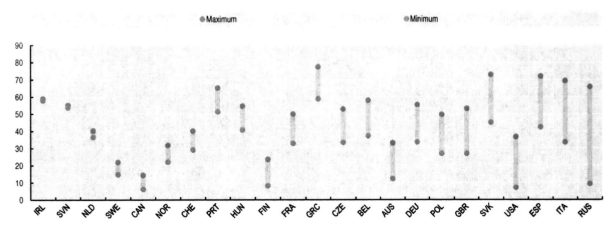

StatLink http://dx.doi.org/10.1787/888933335981

ENVIRONMENT AND SCIENCE

WATER AND WASTE

ABSTRACTIONS OF FRESHWATER
MUNICIPAL WASTE

AIR AND CLIMATE

EMISSIONS OF CARBON DIOXIDE
SULPHUR AND NITROGEN EMISSIONS
GREENHOUSE GAS EMISSIONS
REGIONAL QUALITY OF AIR

RESEARCH AND DEVELOPMENT

EXPENDITURE ON R&D
RESEARCHERS
PATENTS

ABSTRACTIONS OF FRESHWATER

Freshwater resources are of major environmental, economic and social importance. Their distribution varies widely among and within countries. If a significant share of a country's water comes from transboundary rivers, tensions between countries can arise. In arid regions, freshwater resources may at times be limited to the extent that demand for water can be met only by going beyond sustainable use. Freshwater abstractions, particularly for public water supply, irrigation, industrial processes and cooling of electric power plants, exert a major pressure on water resources, with significant implications for their quantity and quality. Main concerns relate to overexploitation and inefficient use of water and to their environmental and socio-economic consequences.

Definition

Water abstractions refer to freshwater taken from ground or surface water sources, either permanently or temporarily, and conveyed to the place of use. If the water is returned to a surface water source, abstraction of the same water by the downstream user is counted again in compiling total abstractions: this may lead to double counting.

Mine water and drainage water are included, whereas water used for hydroelectricity generation (which is considered an *in situ* use) is normally excluded.

Data are for gross abstractions of freshwater taken from ground or surface waters and per capita

Comparability

Information on the use of water resources can be derived from water resource account. It is available for most OECD countries, but often incomplete. The definitions and estimation methods employed may vary considerably from country to country and over time. In general, data availability and quality are best for water abstractions for public supply. For some countries the data refer to water permits and not to actual abstractions. OECD totals are estimates based on linear interpolations to fill missing values, and exclude Chile. Data for the United Kingdom refer to England and Wales only.

Overview

Over the last century, the estimated growth in global water demand was more than double the rate of population growth, with agriculture being the largest user of water.

In the 1980s, some countries stabilised their abstractions through more efficient irrigation techniques, the decline of water-intensive industries, increased use of more efficient technologies and reduced losses in pipe networks. Since the mid-1990s, OECD-wide trends in water abstractions have been generally stable. In some countries this is due to increased use of alternative water sources, including water reuse and desalination.

The use of irrigation water in the OECD area declined slightly compared to agricultural production, but in about half of the countries it increased driven by expansion in the irrigated area. In semi-arid areas in North America and the Mediterranean region, groundwater sustains an increasing share of irrigation. Water stress levels vary greatly among and within countries. Most face seasonal or local water quantity problems, and several have extensive arid or semi-arid regions where water availability is a constraint on economic development. In more than one-third of OECD countries, freshwater resources are under medium to high stress. In a few countries water resources are abundant and population density is low.

Sources
- OECD (2016), "Water", *OECD Environment Statistics* (database).
- OECD (2015), *Environment at a Glance*, OECD Publishing.

Further information
Analytical publications
- Love, P. (2013), *Water*, OECD Insights, OECD Publishing.
- OECD (2015), *Water Resources Allocation: Sharing Risks and Opportunities*, OECD Publishing.
- OECD (2015), *OECD Studies on Water*, OECD Publishing.
- OECD (2012), *OECD Environmental Outlook*, OECD Publishing.
- OECD (2009), *Managing Water for All: An OECD Perspective on Pricing and Financing*, OECD Studies on Water, OECD Publishing.
- United Nations WWAP (World Water Assessment Programme) (2015), *The United Nations World Water Development Report 2015: Water for a Sustainable World*, Paris, UNESCO.

Websites
- Environmental indicators, modelling and outlooks, *www.oecd.org/env/indicators-modelling-outlooks*.
- The water challenge: OECD's response, *www.oecd.org/water*.

Water abstractions

	Water abstractions per capita m³ per capita						Total abstractions millions m³					
	1985	1990	1995	2000	2005	2013 or latest available year	1985	1990	1995	2000	2005	2013 or latest available year
Australia	925	..	1 337	..	958	629	14 600	..	24 071	..	19 336	14 060
Austria	473	496	434	..	..	..	3 580	3 807	3 449	..	..	..
Belgium	..	..	814	735	610	572	..	..	8 248	7 536	6 389	6 176
Canada	..	..	1 612	..	1 301	1 025	..	..	47 250	..	41 955	35 351
Chile	..	..	..	..	..	..	..	..	..	..	..	..
Czech Republic	356	350	266	187	190	157	3 679	3 623	2 743	1 918	1 949	1 650
Denmark	333	245	169	136	119	117	1 705	1 261	887	726	644	652
Estonia	..	2 049	1 239	1 066	1 168	1 227	..	3 215	1 780	1 471	1 578	1 631
Finland	816	471	506	..	..	..	4 000	2 347	2 586	..	..	..
France	631	665	..	554	554	472	34 887	37 687	..	32 715	33 872	30 006
Germany	..	..	531	..	..	404	..	..	43 374	..	..	33 036
Greece	553	774	731	909	870	..	5 496	7 862	7 770	9 924	9 654	..
Hungary	588	607	579	648	489	509	6 267	6 293	5 976	6 621	4 929	5 051
Iceland	464	655	617	580	558	..	112	167	165	163	165	..
Ireland	..	..	..	..	193	167	..	..	..	..	799	757
Israel	..	382	327	275	249	176	..	1 780	1 812	1 727	1 728	1 340
Italy	..	..	..	..	..	..	..	..	..	..	..	..
Japan	720	719	708	685	653	639	87 209	88 906	88 881	86 972	83 427	81 454
Korea	455	480	525	..	607	..	18 580	20 570	23 670	..	29 198	..
Luxembourg	183	..	138	..	..	80	67	..	57	..	..	43
Mexico	..	..	780	698	714	690	..	..	73 672	70 428	76 508	81 651
Netherlands	..	..	..	707	640	..	..	..	..	11 546	10 724	
New Zealand	..	..	..	..	..	1 191	..	..	..	..	..	5 201
Norway	488	..	..	..	619	..	2 025	..	..	..	2 864	..
Poland	441	399	338	314	302	295	16 408	15 164	12 924	11 994	11 521	11 242
Portugal	200	..	..	..	..	..	2 003	..	..	..	..	..
Slovak Republic	399	399	258	217	169	118	2 061	2 116	1 386	1 171	907	637
Slovenia	..	..	..	..	461	554	..	..	..	..	923	1 156
Spain	1 204	..	845	907	876	809	46 250	..	33 288	36 525	38 029	37 349
Sweden	356	347	309	303	291	287	2 970	2 968	2 725	2 688	2 631	2 690
Switzerland	409	397	365	357	337	249	2 646	2 665	2 571	2 564	2 507	1 983
Turkey	387	500	542	648	620	642	19 400	28 073	33 482	43 650	44 684	46 956
United Kingdom	..	..	..	..	174	129	..	..	..	..	10 324	8 214
United States	1 953	1 852	1 750	1 710	1 634	1 583	464 737	462 250	466 118	482 558	482 972	489 528
EU 28	..	..	..	..	..	..	..	..	..	..	..	..
OECD	988	949	928	901	872	860	..	..	..	..	..	..
Brazil	..	..	..	..	305	424	..	..	..	..	56 019	83 300
China	..	..	..	..	426	442	..	..	..	..	561 100	608 660
India	..	..	..	..	..	..	..	..	..	..	..	..
Indonesia	..	..	..	..	..	..	..	..	..	..	..	..
Russian Federation	..	..	..	..	518	463	..	..	..	..	74 366	66 296
South Africa	..	..	..	..	..	..	..	..	..	..	..	..

StatLink http://dx.doi.org/10.1787/888933336789

Water abstractions
m³/capita, 2013 or latest available year

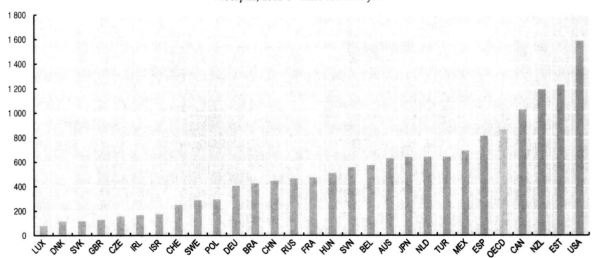

StatLink http://dx.doi.org/10.1787/888933335712

MUNICIPAL WASTE

The amount of municipal waste generated in a country is related to the rate of urbanisation, the types and patterns of consumption, household revenue and lifestyles. While municipal waste is only one part of total waste generated in each country, its management and treatment often absorbs more than one third of the public sector's financial efforts to abate and control pollution.

The main concerns raised by municipal waste are the potential impacts from inappropriate waste management on human health and the environment (soil and water contamination, air quality, land use and landscape).

Definition

Municipal waste is waste collected by or on behalf of municipalities. It includes household waste originating from households (i.e. waste generated by the domestic activity of households) and similar waste from small commercial activities, office buildings, institutions such as schools and government buildings, and small businesses that treat or dispose of waste at the same facilities used for municipally collected waste.

The kilogrammes of municipal waste per capita produced each year – or "waste generation intensities" – provide one broad indicator of the potential environmental and health pressures from municipal waste. They should be complemented with information on waste management practices and costs, and on consumption levels and patterns.

Comparability

The definition of municipal waste, the type of waste covered and the surveying methods used to collect information vary from country to country and over time. Breaks in time series exist for: Denmark, Estonia, Greece,

Hungary, Ireland, Italy, Korea, Luxembourg, Mexico, Norway, Poland, the Slovak Republic, Slovenia and Turkey.

The main problems in terms of data comparability relate to the coverage of household like waste from commerce and trade, and of separate waste collections that may include hazardous waste from households such as waste batteries or waste electric and electronic equipment (WEEE) and waste collected by the private sector in the framework of extended producer responsibility schemes.

In some cases the reference year refers to the closest available year.

Data for Estonia exclude packaging waste separately collected for recycling and thus under-estimate the amount of municipal waste generated.

Sources
- OECD (2015), *Environment at a Glance: OECD Indicators*, OECD Publishing.
- OECD (2015), "Municipal Waste", *OECD Environment Statistics* (Database).

Further information

Analytical publications
- OECD (2015), *Material Resources, Productivity and the Environment*, OECD Green Growth Studies, OECD Publishing.
- OECD (2013), *Greening Household Behaviour: Overview from the 2011 Survey*, OECD Studies on Environmental Policy and Household Behaviour, OECD Publishing.
- OECD (2012), *Sustainable Materials Management: Making Better Use of Resources*, OECD Publishing.
- OECD (2004), *Addressing the Economics of Waste*, OECD Publishing.

Methodological publications
- OECD (2009), *Guidance Manual for the Control of Transboundary Movements of Recoverable Wastes*, OECD Publishing.
- OECD (2008), *Guidance Manual on Environmentally Sound Management of Waste*, OECD Publishing.

Websites
- Resource productivity and waste, *www.oecd.org/environment/waste*.

Overview

During the 1990s, municipal waste generated in the OECD area has risen (19%), mostly in line with private consumption expenditure and GDP. As of the early 2000s, this rise has been slowing down. Today, the quantity of municipal waste generated exceeds an estimated 650 million tonnes (522 kg per capita). The amount and composition of municipal waste vary widely among OECD countries, being related to levels and patterns of consumption, the rate of urbanisation, lifestyles, and national waste management practices.

More and more waste is being diverted from landfills and incinerators and fed back into the economy through recycling. Landfill nonetheless remains the major disposal method in many OECD countries.

Municipal waste generation

	Generation intensities kg per capita							Total amount generated thousand tonnes
	1980	1985	1990	1995	2000	2005	2013 or latest available year	2013 or latest available year
Australia	680	..	..	..	694	..	647	14 035
Austria	..	..	417	437	539	575	580	4 883
Belgium	280	310	345	455	476	483	438	4 905
Canada	..	..	..	..	..	..	..	
Chile	204	225	249	282	329	353	385	6 517
Czech Republic	..	..	..	302	334	289	307	3 228
Denmark	399	475	..	521	610	662	751	4 192
Estonia	..	..	..	371	459	435	293	386
Finland	..	..	..	413	502	477	493	2 682
France	..	..	..	476	514	530	530	34 828
Germany	..	..	628	623	642	565	614	49 780
Greece	259	302	295	301	407	437	504	5 585
Hungary	..	..	530	460	446	461	378	3 738
Iceland	..	..	..	426	462	517	347	112
Ireland	188	..	..	513	601	736	587	2 693
Israel	..	..	..	..	631	590	607	4 894
Italy	249	265	353	454	509	540	484	29 595
Japan	375	348	407	416	432	413	354	45 359
Korea	..	514	715	387	361	367	358	17 881
Luxembourg	352	357	585	587	654	678	661	355
Mexico	..	..	..	323	305	330	360	42 103
Netherlands	..	478	497	539	598	599	525	8 845
New Zealand	..	..	..	..	..	..	..	..
Norway	547	592	555	637	620	430	501	2 518
Poland	283	298	292	287	320	319	297	11 295
Portugal	203	..	301	387	440	452	429	4 598
Slovak Republic	..	..	..	302	317	273	304	1 645
Slovenia	..	..	..	596	513	494	409	853
Spain	..	..	..	476	614	592	455	20 931
Sweden	302	317	374	386	428	477	458	4 399
Switzerland	448	527	611	602	659	664	712	5 708
Turkey	270	359	..	441	454	435	407	30 920
United Kingdom	..	..	473	498	577	591	494	30 890
United States	605	634	757	740	783	779	725	227 604
EU 28	..	..	..	..	..	..	..	..
OECD	..	..	502	521	554	554	522	656 169
Brazil	..	..	..	..	336	328	295	57 900
China	..	..	..	..	..	..	..	..
India	..	..	..	..	..	..	..	..
Indonesia	..	..	..	..	..	..	..	..
Russian Federation	..	294	..	..	354	402	563	80 564
South Africa	..	..	..	..	..	..	..	..

StatLink http://dx.doi.org/10.1787/888933336776

Municipal waste generation
kg per capita, 2013 or latest available year

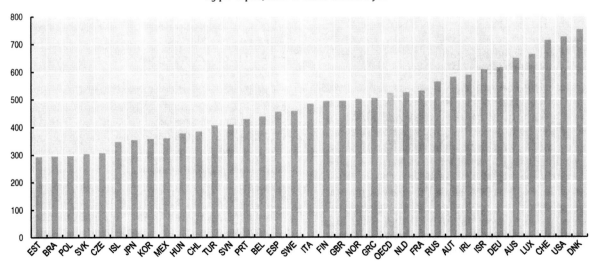

StatLink http://dx.doi.org/10.1787/888933335704

EMISSIONS OF CARBON DIOXIDE

Carbon dioxide (CO_2) makes up the largest share of man-made greenhouse gases. The addition of man-made greenhouse gases to the atmosphere disturbs the earth's radiative balance (i.e. the balance between the solar energy that the earth absorbs and radiates back into space). This is leading to an increase in the earth's surface temperature and to related effects on climate, sea level and world agriculture.

Definition

Emissions refer to CO_2 from burning oil, coal, natural gas and waste materials for energy use. Carbon dioxide also enters the atmosphere from deforestation and from some industrial processes such as cement production. However, emissions of CO_2 from these other sources represent a smaller share of global emissions, and are not included. The 2006 IPCC Guidelines for National Greenhouse Gas Inventories provide a fuller, technical definition of how CO_2 emissions have been estimated.

Comparability

These emissions estimates are affected by the quality of the underlying energy data. For example, some countries, both OECD and non-OECD members, have trouble reporting information on bunker fuels and may not be able to accurately split fuel consumption between domestic and international transport. Since emissions from bunkers are excluded from the national totals, this affects the comparability of the estimates across countries. On the other hand, since these estimates have been made using the same method and emission factors for all countries, in general, the comparability across countries is quite good.

Overview

Global emissions of carbon dioxide have more than doubled since 1971, increasing on average 2% per year. In 1971, the current OECD countries were responsible for 67% of world CO_2 emissions. As a consequence of rapidly rising emissions in the developing world, the OECD contribution to the total fell to 37% in 2013. By far, the largest increase in non-OECD countries occurred in Asia, where China's emissions of CO_2 from fuel combustion have risen, on average, by 6% per annum between 1971 and 2013. Driven primarily by increased use of coal, CO_2 emissions from fuel combustion in China increased over tenfold between 1971 and 2013.

Two significant downturns in OECD CO_2 emissions occurred following the oil shocks of the mid-1970s and early 1980s. Emissions from the economies in transition declined in the 1990s, helping to offset the OECD increases between 1990 and the present. However, this decline did not stabilise global emissions as emissions in developing countries continued to grow. With the economic crisis in 2008/2009, world CO_2 emissions declined by 2% in 2009. However, growth in CO_2 emissions have rebounded, with emissions increasing by 1% in 2012 and 2% in 2013.

Disaggregating the emissions estimates shows substantial variations within individual sectors. Between 1971 and 2013, the combined share of electricity and heat generation and transport shifted from one-half to two-thirds of the total. The share of the respective fuels in overall emissions also changed significantly during the period. The share of oil decreased from 48% to 34%, while the share of natural gas increased from 15% to 20% and that of coal in global emissions increased from 38% to 46%. Fuel switching, including the penetration of nuclear, and the increasing use of other non-fossil energy sources only reduced the CO_2/total primary energy supply ratio by 6% over the past 40 years.

Sources

- International Energy Agency (2015), CO2 Emissions from Fuel Combustion, IEA, Paris.

Further information

Analytical publications

- IEA (2015), Energy Technology Perspectives, IEA, Paris.
- IEA (2015), World Energy Outlook, IEA, Paris.
- IEA (2014), Energy, Climate Change and Environment: 2014 Insights, IEA, Paris.
- IEA (2013), Electricity and a Climate-Constrained World: Data and Analyses, IEA, Paris.
- OECD (2013), Aligning Policies for a Low-Carbon Economy, OECD Publishing.
- OECD (2013), Effective Carbon Prices, OECD Publishing.
- OECD (2013), Inventory of Estimated Budgetary Support and Tax Expenditures for Fossil Fuels 2013, OECD Publishing.
- OECD (2013), Taxing Energy Use, A Graphical Analysis, OECD Publishing.

Methodological publications

- Intergovernmental Panel on Climate Change (IPCC) (2006), 2006 IPCC Guidelines for National Greenhouse Gas Inventories, prepared by the National Greenhouse Gas Inventories Programme, Eggleston H.S., Buendia L., Miwa K., Ngara T. and Tanabe K. (eds), IGES, Japan.

Online databases

- IEA CO2 Emissions from Fuel Combustion Statistics.
- OECD Environment Statistics.

CO$_2$ emissions from fuel combustion
Million tonnes

	1971	1990	2003	2004	2005	2006	2007	2008	2009	2010	2011	2012	2013
Australia	143	260	354	367	371	376	386	389	394	385	385	387	389
Austria	49	56	73	74	75	73	70	71	65	70	68	65	65
Belgium	118	106	112	111	107	104	100	104	93	102	94	89	89
Canada	340	419	534	526	536	524	554	539	504	515	524	524	536
Chile	21	29	49	53	54	56	63	67	64	69	75	77	82
Czech Republic	154	150	121	122	118	119	121	116	109	111	110	106	101
Denmark	55	51	57	52	48	56	52	49	47	47	42	37	39
Estonia	..	36	17	17	17	16	19	18	15	19	18	16	19
Finland	40	54	71	67	55	66	64	56	53	62	54	49	49
France	423	346	368	369	370	361	353	349	333	340	310	312	316
Germany	978	940	821	805	787	799	767	775	720	759	731	745	760
Greece	25	70	94	94	95	94	98	94	90	83	82	77	69
Hungary	60	66	57	55	55	54	53	52	47	48	46	42	40
Iceland	1	2	2	2	2	2	2	2	2	2	2	2	2
Ireland	22	30	42	42	44	45	44	44	39	39	35	36	34
Israel	14	33	61	61	59	62	64	64	64	68	68	75	68
Italy	289	389	445	455	456	449	441	429	384	392	384	367	338
Japan	751	1 049	1 188	1 189	1 196	1 183	1 221	1 137	1 076	1 126	1 178	1 217	1 235
Korea	53	232	438	460	458	465	477	489	502	551	574	575	572
Luxembourg	16	11	10	11	11	11	11	11	10	11	11	10	10
Mexico	94	260	358	364	382	391	405	399	396	414	428	434	452
Netherlands	128	145	167	169	163	161	162	164	158	168	157	157	156
New Zealand	14	22	33	32	34	34	33	33	30	36	30	31	31
Norway	23	27	35	36	36	35	36	36	35	38	36	36	35
Poland	287	345	293	297	296	308	307	302	291	310	303	297	292
Portugal	14	38	57	58	61	56	55	53	53	48	47	46	45
Slovak Republic	39	55	37	36	37	36	36	35	33	35	33	31	32
Slovenia	..	14	15	15	15	16	16	17	15	15	15	15	14
Spain	119	203	303	319	334	325	338	310	276	262	265	260	236
Sweden	82	52	54	52	49	47	45	43	41	46	42	39	38
Switzerland	39	41	43	43	44	43	41	43	42	43	39	40	42
Turkey	42	127	203	207	216	240	265	265	257	265	285	303	284
United Kingdom	621	548	532	533	531	533	521	508	459	477	439	462	449
United States	4 288	4 802	5 609	5 688	5 702	5 602	5 686	5 512	5 120	5 355	5 219	5 032	5 120
EU 28	..	4 024	3 939	3 940	3 916	3 922	3 868	3 790	3 499	3 611	3 465	3 425	3 340
OECD	9 342	11 006	12 653	12 781	12 816	12 742	12 907	12 573	11 819	12 306	12 132	11 990	12 038
Brazil	87	184	292	310	311	314	330	348	324	370	390	422	452
China	831	2 184	4 117	4 788	5 360	5 881	6 276	6 338	6 618	7 095	8 420	8 519	8 977
India	182	534	954	1 034	1 086	1 157	1 266	1 342	1 513	1 597	1 660	1 780	1 869
Indonesia	25	134	312	319	322	343	358	355	370	383	390	416	425
Russian Federation	..	2 163	1 494	1 488	1 482	1 537	1 533	1 554	1 440	1 529	1 604	1 551	1 543
South Africa	157	244	348	375	372	374	391	423	399	409	395	408	420
World	13 995	20 623	24 992	26 177	27 048	27 856	28 783	28 871	28 322	29 838	31 293	31 491	32 190

StatLink http://dx.doi.org/10.1787/888933336022

World CO$_2$ emissions from fuel combustion, by region
Million tonnes

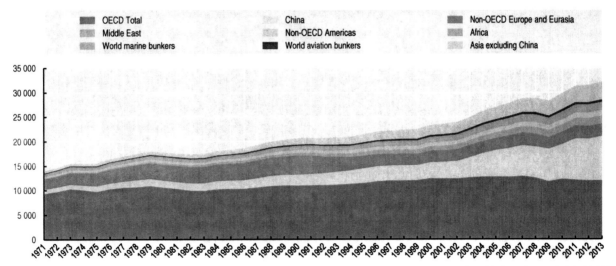

StatLink http://dx.doi.org/10.1787/888933334826

SULPHUR AND NITROGEN EMISSIONS

Atmospheric pollutants from energy transformation and energy consumption, but also from industrial processes, are the main contributors to regional and local air pollution and raise concerns as to their effects on human health and ecosystems.

In the atmosphere, emissions of sulphur and nitrogen compounds are transformed into acidifying substances. When these substances reach the ground, acidification of soil, water and buildings arises. Soil acidification is one important factor causing forest damage; acidification of the aquatic environment may severely impair the life of plant and animal species.

Nitrogen oxides (NO_X) also contribute to ground-level ozone formation and are responsible for eutrophication, reduction in water quality and species richness. High concentrations of NO_X cause respiratory illnesses.

Definition

Total emissions refer to emissions from human activities of sulphur oxides (SO_X) and nitrogen oxides (NO_X).

It should be kept in mind that SO_X and NO_X emissions provide only a partial view of air pollution problems. They should be supplemented with information on the acidity of rain and snow, and the exceedance of critical loads in soil and water, which reflect the actual acidification of the environment, and with information on population exposure to air pollutants.

Comparability

International data on SO_X and NO_X emissions are available for almost all OECD countries. The details of estimation methods for emissions such as emission factors and reliability, extent of sources and pollutants included in estimation, etc., may differ from one country to another.

Overview

SO_X emissions have continued to decrease since 2000 for the OECD as a whole as a combined result of changes in energy demand through energy savings and fuel substitution, pollution control policies and technical progress.

NO_X emissions have continued to decrease in the OECD overall since 2000, but less than SO_X emissions. This is mainly due to changes in energy demand, pollution control policies and technical progress. In the late 2000s, the slowdown in economic activity following the 2008 economic crisis further contributed to reduce emissions. However, these results have not compensated in all countries for steady growth in road traffic, fossil fuel use and other activities generating NO_X.

The high emission levels of SO_X for Iceland are due to SO_X emissions from geothermal energy which represented 80% of total emissions in 2012.

OECD totals do not include Chile and Mexico.

Sources
- OECD (2014), "Air emissions by source", *OECD Environment Statistics* (database).
- OECD (2015), *Environment at a Glance*, OECD Publishing.
- United Nations Framework Convention on Climate Change (UNFCCC), "National Inventory Submissions", National Reports.

Further information

Analytical publications
- OECD (2014), *The Cost of Air Pollution: Health Impacts of Road Transport*, OECD Publishing.
- OECD (2012), "Review of the Implementation of the OECD Environmental Strategy for the First Decade of the 21st Century", OECD, Paris.

Online databases
- *OECD Environment Statistics.*

Websites
- Environmental indicators, modelling and outlooks, *www.oecd.org/environment/indicators-modelling-outlooks.*

Sulphur and nitrogen oxides emissions
Thousand tonnes

	Sulphur oxides						Nitrogen oxides					
	2007	2008	2009	2010	2011	2012	2007	2008	2009	2010	2011	2012
Australia	2 440.2	2 618.1	2 594.6	2 381.0	2 356.4	2 333.9	1 659.9	1 667.9	1 657.8	1 669.8	1 678.0	1 706.7
Austria	24.7	22.4	17.0	18.6	18.0	17.2	217.4	204.8	189.0	193.1	182.5	178.3
Belgium	123.8	96.1	74.5	59.9	52.7	48.0	261.2	230.5	204.9	212.2	198.2	189.7
Canada	1 968.2	1 789.9	1 538.3	1 375.2	1 286.9	1 287.7	2 273.4	2 183.9	2 075.9	2 061.7	1 964.2	1 861.7
Chile	..	..	..	..	..	..	..	..	..	..	..	..
Czech Republic	216.5	174.3	173.5	170.3	169.0	157.9	283.2	261.1	251.4	239.1	225.9	210.6
Denmark	25.5	20.0	14.9	14.9	14.0	12.5	172.0	154.3	136.1	131.8	124.6	115.4
Estonia	88.0	69.4	54.8	83.2	72.7	40.6	38.5	35.7	30.2	36.7	35.8	32.3
Finland	82.0	68.3	58.7	66.6	60.7	52.0	182.7	167.7	153.5	165.5	155.2	145.6
France	424.2	359.3	311.2	287.8	246.3	232.4	1 269.4	1 168.3	1 086.1	1 065.9	999.7	981.5
Germany	453.9	454.2	406.6	430.4	423.8	427.1	1 476.7	1 402.1	1 303.3	1 324.9	1 289.1	1 269.3
Greece	537.9	445.2	425.6	265.4	262.2	244.9	414.1	392.2	379.5	319.4	296.0	258.6
Hungary	36.4	36.6	30.9	32.3	35.3	31.8	163.0	160.2	153.6	151.5	137.3	122.4
Iceland	58.0	74.2	68.7	73.4	80.2	83.9	26.3	24.4	24.8	22.4	20.9	20.5
Ireland	54.5	45.2	32.4	26.3	24.7	23.2	120.9	108.8	87.0	80.1	71.8	73.8
Israel	198.9	183.8	167.8	164.0	174.2	..	201.4	196.3	183.9	186.1	182.0	..
Italy	339.8	284.6	232.8	214.2	193.9	177.7	1 112.5	1 042.0	970.3	951.6	927.8	849.2
Japan	1 031.8	990.0	957.0	951.2	942.2	936.8	1 957.3	1 870.4	1 778.3	1 730.2	1 675.2	1 626.9
Korea	402.5	418.0	387.7	401.7	434.0	..	1 187.8	1 044.9	1 014.1	1 061.1	1 040.0	..
Luxembourg	2.4	2.2	2.2	2.2	1.7	2.0	51.6	49.7	43.3	45.6	47.6	45.4
Mexico	..	2 241.2	..	..	..	..	..	3 206.9	..	..	..	..
Netherlands	59.3	50.0	36.7	33.5	33.5	33.8	287.9	279.0	254.7	253.5	237.7	227.3
New Zealand	82.2	86.4	74.3	73.5	74.2	78.2	160.5	161.9	151.8	150.6	152.8	157.9
Norway	20.1	20.0	15.4	19.5	18.4	16.7	201.6	190.4	179.8	182.0	174.2	166.2
Poland	1 229.2	1 007.3	868.2	935.6	897.5	853.3	860.3	829.9	809.4	862.1	845.9	817.3
Portugal	162.9	114.1	79.0	70.2	64.5	59.2	241.6	215.6	204.4	189.1	179.0	170.1
Slovak Republic	70.6	69.4	64.1	69.4	68.5	58.5	95.6	93.6	84.2	88.6	85.2	81.0
Slovenia	14.6	12.8	10.5	9.8	10.9	10.2	49.3	54.1	46.9	46.1	46.2	45.1
Spain	1 135.9	512.8	459.9	424.9	459.5	407.9	1 368.7	1 179.5	1 043.9	965.7	958.9	928.0
Sweden	32.4	30.2	29.5	32.0	29.2	27.8	164.4	155.9	147.1	148.7	139.5	131.8
Switzerland	13.2	13.7	11.8	12.5	10.6	10.8	84.7	81.6	76.8	75.3	70.5	69.3
Turkey	2 646.2	2 560.2	2 663.8	2 558.8	2 652.7	2 739.1	1 038.6	989.5	967.5	938.1	1 115.7	1 087.7
United Kingdom	588.0	490.3	397.3	415.0	385.4	426.4	1 467.7	1 317.6	1 147.0	1 113.1	1 040.4	1 057.0
United States	10 562.9	9 302.1	8 223.8	7 016.9	5 853.1	4 694.5	16 334.5	15 252.7	14 316.1	13 497.2	13 045.1	12 257.9
EU 28	..	..	..	..	..	..	..	..	..	..	..	..
OECD	25 126.7	22 421.3	20 483.5	18 690.4	17 406.8	16 052.8	35 424.5	33 166.3	31 152.8	30 158.8	29 342.9	28 108.0
Brazil	..	..	..	..	..	..	..	..	..	..	..	..
China	..	..	..	..	..	..	..	..	..	..	..	..
India	..	..	..	..	..	..	..	..	..	..	..	..
Indonesia	..	..	..	..	..	..	..	..	..	..	..	..
Russian Federation	4 709.0	4 675.0	4 512.0	4 512.0	4 462.0	4 431.0	3 764.0	3 809.0	3 669.0	3 735.0	3 649.0	3 452.0
South Africa	..	..	..	..	..	..	..	..	..	..	..	..

StatLink ⬛ http://dx.doi.org/10.1787/888933336620

Sulphur and nitrogen oxides emissions
Kilograms per capita, 2012 or latest available year

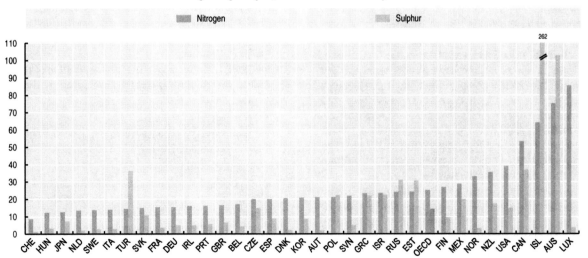

StatLink ⬛ http://dx.doi.org/10.1787/888933335546

GREENHOUSE GAS EMISSIONS

Emissions of greenhouses gases (GHG) from human activities disturb the radiative energy balance of the earth's atmosphere system. They exacerbate the natural greenhouse effect, leading to temperature changes and other consequences for the earth's climate.

Climate change is of concern mainly as regards its impact on ecosystems (biodiversity), human settlements and agriculture, and on the frequency and scale of extreme weather events. It could have significant consequences for human well-being and socio-economic activities.

Definition

Emissions refer to the sum of six GHGs that have direct effects on climate change and are considered responsible for a major part of global warming: carbon dioxide (CO_2), methane (CH_4), nitrous oxide (N_2O), chlorofluorocarbons (CFCs), hydrofluorocarbons (HFCs), perfluorocarbons (PFCs) and sulphur hexafluoride (SF_6).

They show total gross emissions expressed in CO_2 equivalents as well as emission intensities per capita. They refer to GHG emitted within the national territory; CO_2 emissions and removals from land use change and forestry are excluded as are international transactions of emission reduction units or certified emission reductions.

Comparability

Data on GHG emissions are reported annually to the Secretariat of the United Nations Framework Convention on Climate Change (UNCCC) with 1990 as a base year but not by all OECD countries. They display a good level of comparability. The high per capita emissions of Luxembourg result from the lower taxation of road fuels compared to neighbouring countries, which attracts drivers to refuel in the country.

The OECD total does not include Israel.

Sources

- OECD (2015), *Environment at a Glance*, OECD Publishing.
- OECD (2014), "Greenhouse gas emissions by source", *OECD Environment Statistics* (Database).
- United Nations Framework Convention on Climate Change (UNFCCC) (2013), *Greenhouse Gas Inventory Data* (Database).

Further information

Analytical publications

- OECD (2015), *Aligning Policies for a Low-Carbon Economy*, OECD Publishing.
- OECD (2015), *The Economic Consequences of Climate Change*, OECD Publishing.
- OECD (2012), "Review of the Implementation of the OECD Environmental Strategy for the First Decade of the 21st Century", OECD, Paris.

Statistical publications

- International Energy Agency (IEA) (2015), *CO2 Emissions from Fuel Combustion: Highlights 2015*, OECD Publishing.

Methodological publications

- Intergovernmental Panel on Climate Change (IPCC) (2006), *2006 IPCC Guidelines for National Greenhouse Gas Inventories*, prepared by the National Greenhouse Gas Inventories Programme, Eggleston H.S., Buendia L., Miwa K., Ngara T. and Tanabe K. (eds), IGES, Hayama, Japan.

Online databases

- CO2 Emissions from Fuel Combustion.

Websites

- Climate change, *www.oecd.org/environment/cc*.

Overview

Emissions of greenhouse gas emissions have been declining in recent years in almost all OECD countries. They fell by almost 5% since 2008 in the OECD area. This is partly due to a slowdown in economic activity following the 2008 economic crisis, but also to a strengthening of climate policies and changing patterns of energy consumption. CO_2 remains predominant and determines the overall trend. Together with CH_4 and N_2O, it accounts for about 98% of GHG emissions. The other gases account for about 2%, but their emissions are growing.

Individual OECD countries' contributions to the additional greenhouse effect, and their rates of progress, vary significantly. These differences partly reflect different national circumstances, such as composition and rate of economic growth, population growth, energy resource endowment, and the extent to which the countries have taken steps to reduce emissions from various sources.

Greenhouse gas emissions

Thousand tonnes CO_2 equivalent

	1990	1995	2000	2005	2006	2007	2008	2009	2010	2011	2012
Australia	414 974	436 864	489 813	523 479	529 885	537 931	544 574	541 178	540 211	541 543	543 648
Austria	78 086	79 744	80 277	92 581	89 711	86 967	86 882	80 148	84 808	82 761	80 059
Belgium	142 952	150 327	145 857	142 063	138 342	133 440	135 823	123 209	130 611	120 146	116 520
Canada	590 908	639 072	721 362	735 829	727 850	749 289	731 081	689 313	699 302	701 212	698 626
Chile	49 897	59 286	74 488	82 005	83 285	92 828	93 970	90 933	91 576	..	..
Czech Republic	196 146	151 774	146 330	145 965	147 021	147 246	142 185	134 206	137 008	135 277	131 466
Denmark	70 020	77 280	69 955	65 589	73 470	68 920	65 404	62 511	63 007	58 052	53 118
Estonia	40 615	20 064	17 157	18 421	17 837	20 949	19 546	16 189	19 892	20 484	19 188
Finland	70 329	70 768	69 188	68 624	79 900	78 249	70 126	66 003	74 397	66 861	60 966
France	560 384	556 875	564 597	563 577	551 868	542 721	537 953	514 380	522 156	495 982	496 221
Germany	1 248 049	1 117 580	1 040 367	994 460	1 002 426	976 584	979 803	912 606	946 388	928 695	939 083
Greece	104 927	109 718	126 579	135 311	131 794	134 637	130 758	124 110	117 878	114 728	110 985
Hungary	97 603	78 475	76 504	78 376	77 485	75 651	73 328	66 976	67 638	66 034	61 981
Iceland	3 538	3 315	3 903	3 859	4 391	4 619	5 022	4 779	4 646	4 441	4 468
Ireland	55 246	58 903	68 216	69 656	69 166	68 371	68 020	62 312	61 895	57 750	58 531
Israel	..	..	72 439	73 312	74 656	76 870	77 954	74 111	76 924	78 452	..
Italy	519 055	530 333	551 237	574 262	563 373	555 078	540 620	490 113	499 359	486 601	460 083
Japan	1 234 320	1 335 888	1 340 523	1 350 321	1 332 533	1 364 258	1 280 903	1 205 673	1 256 095	1 306 518	1 343 118
Korea	295 683	442 840	511 187	569 466	575 193	591 429	605 407	609 167	667 755	697 708	..
Luxembourg	12 901	10 177	9 762	13 095	12 946	12 361	12 188	11 684	12 250	12 125	11 839
Mexico	458 754	487 432	564 970	614 648	643 362	670 204	699 201	688 927	701 360	..	..
Netherlands	211 850	223 161	213 023	209 448	205 559	204 199	203 314	197 787	209 286	195 064	191 669
New Zealand	60 641	64 465	70 899	78 287	78 186	76 222	75 764	73 101	73 491	74 393	76 048
Norway	50 409	50 242	54 058	54 469	54 288	56 006	54 425	51 809	54 347	53 294	52 733
Poland	466 372	441 103	396 104	398 827	414 148	415 449	406 081	387 700	407 475	405 741	399 268
Portugal	60 767	71 399	84 100	87 686	82 647	80 269	78 032	74 854	70 634	69 317	68 752
Slovak Republic	73 227	53 232	48 947	50 264	50 318	48 395	49 001	44 690	45 382	44 698	42 710
Slovenia	18 444	18 549	18 953	20 314	20 526	20 672	21 384	19 373	19 411	19 463	18 911
Spain	283 749	322 108	380 004	431 393	423 789	432 112	398 444	359 659	347 181	345 887	340 809
Sweden	72 714	74 152	68 563	66 913	66 778	65 233	63 014	59 097	65 072	60 754	57 604
Switzerland	52 890	51 576	51 775	54 209	53 846	51 910	53 653	52 366	54 095	49 973	51 449
Turkey	188 434	238 820	298 091	330 740	350 881	382 378	368 734	371 149	403 495	424 091	439 874
United Kingdom	778 805	726 758	693 693	678 253	675 547	666 079	646 736	593 380	609 147	566 269	584 304
United States	6 219 524	6 597 665	7 075 609	7 228 293	7 150 744	7 287 750	7 090 753	6 642 320	6 854 728	6 716 993	6 487 847
EU 28	..	..	..	..	..	..	..	..	..	..	..
OECD	14 756 908	15 279 204	16 086 790	16 480 697	16 434 113	16 625 965	16 258 947	15 352 402	15 858 726	15 674 979	15 505 620
Brazil	573 079	660 104	756 664	863 895	881 670	881 782	910 098	890 515	954 325	991 691	1 027 739
China	..	..	..	7 465 862	..	..	..	..	..	..	..
India	..	..	1 523 767	..	..	..	..	..	..	..	..
Indonesia	266 818	..	554 334	..	..	..	..	..	..	..	..
Russian Federation	3 363 342	2 207 676	2 053 321	2 135 398	2 201 494	2 206 100	2 245 851	2 130 321	2 221 342	2 284 293	2 295 045
South Africa	347 349	..	..	..	..	..	..	..	..	..	..

StatLink ⟶ http://dx.doi.org/10.1787/888933336230

Greenhouse gas emissions

Tonnes per capita

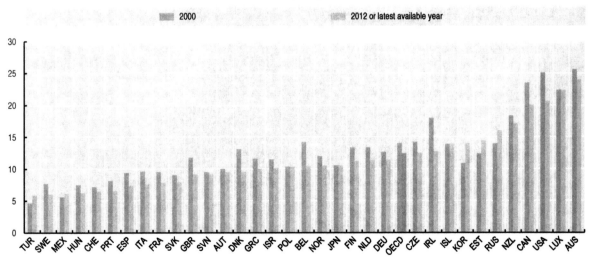

StatLink ⟶ http://dx.doi.org/10.1787/888933335043

REGIONAL QUALITY OF AIR

The impact of outdoor air pollution on people's health is sizeable. Fine particulate matters (or PM2.5, 2.5 microns and smaller), a mixture of sulphates, nitrates, ammonia, sodium chloride, carbon, mineral dust and water suspended in the air, can cause respiration and cardiovascular morbidity or mortality from lung cancer, cardiovascular and respiratory diseases.

Definition

Average exposure to air pollution (PM2.5) is estimated at city, regional and national levels using the satellite-based data. The satellite-based data are weighted with data on population distributed at circa $1km^2$ resolution. Subsequently, the exposure to air pollution is calculated by taking the weighted average value of PM2.5 for the $1km^2$ grid cells present in each territory (country, region or city), with the weight given by the estimated population count in each cell.

Comparability of regional statistics is affected by differences in the meaning of the word "region". This results in significant differences in terms of geographic area and population both within and among countries. To address this issue, the OECD has classified regions within each country based on two levels: territorial level 2 (TL2, large regions) and territorial level 3 (TL3, small regions).

Metropolitan areas are defined as the functional urban areas (FUA) with population above 500 000. The functional urban areas are defined as densely populated municipalities (urban cores) and adjacent municipalities with high levels of commuting towards the densely populated urban cores (hinterland). Functional urban areas can extend across administrative boundaries, reflecting the economic geography of where people actually live and work.

Comparability

Air pollution in regions refers here to small regions.

The functional urban areas have not been identified in Iceland, Israel, New Zealand and Turkey. The FUA of Luxembourg does not appear in the figures since it has a population below 500 000 inhabitants.

Overview

OECD estimates show a wide variation in PM2.5 exposure levels across regions within countries, with the largest exposures in Mexico, Italy, Chile and Turkey. In 58% of OECD regions, representing 64% of the total OECD population, the levels of air pollution were higher than World Health Organization recommendations. Critically high values are found in some regions in Korea, Turkey, Mexico, Italy and Israel, among the OECD countries, and China and India. For example, Mexico shows a national average exposure to PM2.5 of 11.5 $\mu g/m^3$, however half of the population live in regions with air pollution levels higher than the national average.

More than one-third of urban population in the OECD area breathes a cleaner air than the rest of the population. At the country level, the share of urban population exposed to lower levels of air pollution than the rest of the country varies from 100% in Estonia to 10% in Spain. In the Czech Republic, Denmark, Finland, Hungary, Ireland, Norway, Slovenia and the Slovak Republic the entire urban population is exposed to pollution levels above the national average.

Cities' characteristics and local efforts to reduce air pollution paint a differentiated geography of urban air quality also within countries. For example, the average exposure to PM2.5 in Cuernavaca (Mexico), Milan (Italy) and Kumamoto (Japan) is three times higher than in other cities of these countries. All cities in Canada, Finland, Chile, Estonia, Norway, Ireland and Australia have relatively low level of air pollution.

Sources
- OECD (2013), *OECD Regions at a Glance*, OECD Publishing.

Further information

Analytical publications
- OECD (2012), *Redefining "Urban": A New Way to Measure Metropolitan Areas*, OECD Publishing.
- Piacentini, M. et K. Rosina (2012), *Measuring the Environmental Performance of Metropolitan Areas with Geographic Information Sources*, OECD Regional Development Working Papers, No. 2012/05, OECD Publishing.

Online databases
- Metropolitan areas.

Websites
- Regions at a Glance interactive, *http://rag.oecd.org*.
- Regional statistics and indicators, *www.oecd.org/governance/regional-policy/regionalstatisticsandindicators.htm*.

Regional disparities in average exposure to air pollution

Regions with the lowest and highest exposure to PM2.5 levels, 2011

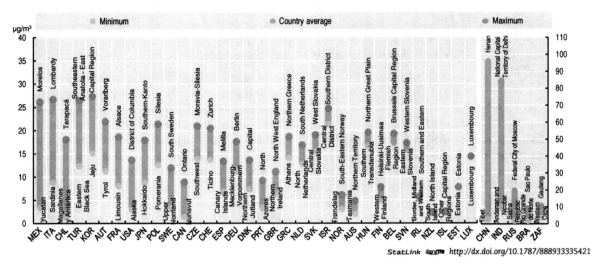

StatLink http://dx.doi.org/10.1787/888933335421

Share of urban population with exposure to PM2.5 below the national average

2011

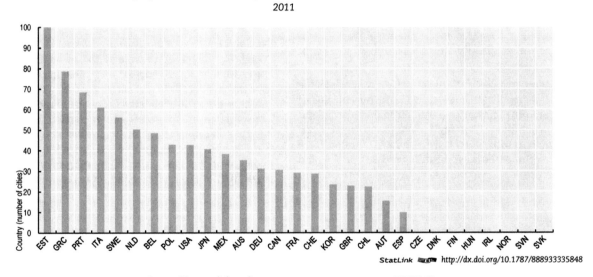

StatLink http://dx.doi.org/10.1787/888933335848

Urban disparities in average exposure to PM2.5

Cities with the lowest and highest exposure to PM2.5 levels in each country, 2011

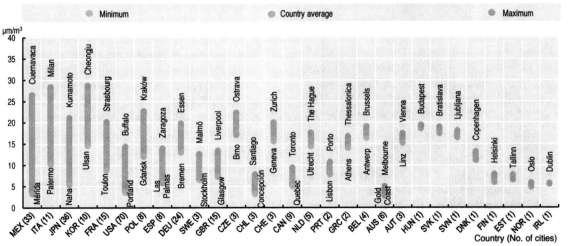

StatLink http://dx.doi.org/10.1787/888933335960

EXPENDITURE ON R&D

Expenditure on research and development (R&D) is a key indicator of countries' innovative efforts. Research and development comprise creative work undertaken on a systematic basis in order to increase the stock of knowledge (including knowledge of man, culture and society) and the use of this knowledge to devise new applications.

Definition

Research and development covers three activities: basic research; applied research; and experimental development. Basic research is experimental or theoretical work undertaken primarily to acquire new knowledge of the underlying foundation of phenomena and observable facts, without any particular application or use in view. Applied research is also original investigation undertaken in order to acquire new knowledge; it is, however, directed primarily towards a specific practical aim or objective. Experimental development is systematic work, drawing on existing knowledge gained from research and/or practical experience, which is directed to producing new materials, products or devices, to installing new processes, systems and services, or to improving substantially those already produced or installed.

The main aggregate used for international comparisons is gross domestic expenditure on R&D (GERD). This consists of the total expenditure (current and capital) on R&D carried out by all resident companies, research institutes, university and government laboratories, etc. It includes R&D funded from abroad but excludes domestic funds for R&D performed outside the domestic economy. GERD is expressed in constant 2010 dollars (adjusted for purchasing power parity) and as a share of GDP (R&D intensity).

Comparability

R&D data have been compiled according to the 2002 guidelines of the *Frascati Manual* which have now been superseded by the 2015 edition. The revised definitions are in the course of being implemented and are not expected to revise significantly the major indicators. Estimates of the resources allocated to R&D are affected by national characteristics such as the periodicity and coverage of national R&D surveys across institutional sectors and industries (and the inclusion of firms and organisations of different sizes); and the use of different sampling and estimation methods.

Data for Israel exclude defence. Those for Korea, prior to 2007, exclude social sciences and the humanities. For the United States, R&D capital expenditures are excluded (except for the government sector) and depreciation charges of the business enterprises are included.

The latest update to the *System of National Accounts* (SNA), the 2008 SNA, recognised the role of R&D as an activity leading to the creation of an intellectual asset. One implication of this is that the level of GDP has been revised upwards and the R&D intensity ratio has been reduced, as the numerator has stayed constant and the denominator increased. Users should be careful when comparing the R&D intensity of countries that have and have not capitalised R&D in their national accounts. Likewise, they should avoid comparing previously published measures of R&D intensity and more recent ones.

Overview

Among OECD countries, the United States has the highest level of gross domestic expenditure on R&D (GERD), with 40% of the total OECD GERD in 2013, followed by Japan (14%) and Germany (9%). Since 2000, real R&D expenditure has been growing fastest in Estonia (average annual growth rate of 12.5%), Turkey (9.7%), Korea (9.4%) and Slovenia (7%). Outside the OECD area, China's average annual real growth in R&D spending has been 17.2%, making it the world's second largest R&D performer and ahead of Japan since 2009.

In 2013, R&D amounted to 2.4% of GDP for the OECD as a whole. Denmark, Finland, Israel, Japan, Korea and Sweden were the only OECD countries whose R&D-to-GDP ratio exceeded 3%.

Over the last decade, R&D intensity grew in the EU (from 1.7% to 1.9%), in Japan (from 3.1% to 3.5%) and in the United States (from 2.6% to 2.7%). Estonia, Portugal, Slovenia and Turkey were the fastest growing OECD countries. In the same period, R&D intensity in China increased from 1.1% to 2.1% and surpassed the EU for the first time in 2012.

Sources
• OECD (2015), *Main Science and Technology Indicators*, OECD Publishing.

Further information

Analytical publications
• OECD (2015), *Frascati Manual 2015: Guidelines for Collecting and Reporting Data on Research and Experimental Development*, OECD Publishing.
• OECD (2015), *OECD Science, Technology and Industry Scoreboard*, OECD Publishing.
• OECD (2014), *OECD Science, Technology and Industry Outlook*, OECD Publishing.

Methodological publications

Online databases
• OECD Science, Technology and R&D Statistics.

Websites
• Main Science and Technology Indicators (supplementary material), *www.oecd.org/sti/msti*.
• Research and Development Statistics, *www.oecd.org/sti/rds*.

Gross domestic expenditure on R&D

Million US dollars, 2010 constant prices and PPPs

	2001	2002	2003	2004	2005	2006	2007	2008	2009	2010	2011	2012	2013
Australia	..	12 206	..	13 773	..	17 031	..	20 174	..	20 546	20 653	..	..
Austria	6 093	6 424	6 825	6 981	7 818	8 039	8 545	9 223	8 969	9 586	9 662	10 485	10 754
Belgium	7 540	7 161	6 996	7 145	7 172	7 469	7 828	8 231	8 272	8 766	9 358	9 770	9 963
Canada	23 380	23 499	23 857	24 959	25 401	25 663	25 673	25 303	25 333	25 029	24 946	24 436	23 673
Chile	..	..	..	..	..	..	892	1 113	1 037	1 028	1 162	1 265	1 398
Czech Republic	2 362	2 399	2 589	2 709	2 942	3 313	3 699	3 615	3 593	3 796	4 507	5 129	5 474
Denmark	5 073	5 353	5 527	5 468	5 537	5 771	6 091	6 684	7 005	6 812	6 959	7 045	7 089
Estonia	150	163	188	222	263	351	363	405	382	444	712	687	562
Finland	5 693	5 897	6 097	6 361	6 567	6 849	7 222	7 712	7 476	7 653	7 666	7 101	6 781
France	44 884	46 165	45 371	46 088	45 888	46 997	47 513	48 490	50 530	50 730	52 155	53 196	53 493
Germany	71 846	72 750	73 457	73 239	73 809	77 602	79 820	85 650	84 767	87 822	93 726	96 756	96 069
Greece	1 572	..	1 691	1 715	1 894	1 942	2 064	2 359	2 134	1 927	1 967	1 890	2 119
Hungary	1 674	1 883	1 831	1 801	2 013	2 227	2 183	2 254	2 436	2 473	2 625	2 744	3 078
Iceland	280	281	275	..	311	351	338	338	338	..	314	..	263
Ireland	1 711	1 815	1 988	2 178	2 333	2 473	2 659	2 921	3 192	3 166	3 082	3 160	..
Israel	6 669	6 588	6 286	6 563	7 145	7 752	8 807	8 926	8 611	8 673	9 372	9 993	10 236
Italy	21 201	22 066	21 634	21 793	21 874	23 162	24 492	24 898	24 697	25 152	25 022	25 548	24 835
Japan	123 563	125 578	128 853	131 447	140 618	147 337	152 878	151 532	138 627	140 607	145 528	146 330	154 515
Korea	23 896	24 934	26 543	29 986	32 316	36 635	40 952	43 839	46 549	52 173	58 427	64 268	68 149
Luxembourg	..	..	578	596	606	678	702	707	698	641	618	506	515
Mexico	5 058	5 639	5 689	6 011	6 352	6 154	6 274	6 971	7 094	7 864	7 651	8 077	9 505
Netherlands	11 993	11 689	11 960	12 259	12 450	12 689	12 660	12 564	12 395	12 822	14 383	14 527	14 638
New Zealand	1 197	..	1 370	..	1 432	..	1 575	..	1 679	..	1 722	..	1 693
Norway	3 592	3 680	3 829	3 791	3 958	4 178	4 571	4 802	4 828	4 744	4 899	5 054	5 168
Poland	3 395	3 103	3 104	3 367	3 550	3 684	4 015	4 476	5 072	5 723	6 223	7 478	7 428
Portugal	2 061	1 960	1 877	1 997	2 090	2 676	3 231	4 161	4 413	4 363	4 071	3 695	3 617
Slovak Republic	531	500	526	494	519	542	566	616	597	816	903	1 114	1 157
Slovenia	656	668	595	682	732	840	834	984	1 013	1 163	1 378	1 426	1 417
Spain	11 201	12 428	13 654	14 311	15 663	17 454	19 075	20 578	20 359	20 336	19 756	18 608	17 960
Sweden	12 630	..	12 189	11 931	12 263	13 255	12 752	13 610	12 611	12 585	12 952	13 145	13 396
Switzerland	..	..	..	9 346	..	..	..	10 875	..	..	..	12 250	..
Turkey	4 053	4 208	4 069	4 774	5 901	6 192	8 070	8 154	9 086	9 853	10 921	11 964	12 774
United Kingdom	33 572	34 389	34 831	34 443	35 873	37 387	39 153	39 035	38 605	38 139	38 787	37 633	38 116
United States	338 685	333 151	342 931	347 142	361 066	377 207	395 494	415 342	411 369	410 093	420 072	419 722	433 380
EU 28	249 178	254 184	256 513	259 025	265 325	279 139	289 692	303 718	302 976	308 607	320 503	325 744	325 568
OECD	797 175	801 542	819 758	835 994	872 322	916 577	960 528	998 381	985 019	998 864	1 033 905	1 048 576	1 076 732
Brazil	..	..	..	..	..	..	..	..	..	..	..	..	..
China	46 018	56 499	65 854	78 656	94 305	111 357	127 816	147 563	186 611	213 010	243 035	282 481	317 848
India	..	..	..	..	..	..	..	..	..	..	..	..	..
Indonesia	..	..	..	..	..	..	..	..	..	..	..	..	..
Russian Federation	22 623	25 097	27 753	26 629	26 276	28 551	32 234	31 745	35 078	33 094	33 298	35 522	35 937
South Africa	3 126	..	3 545	3 964	4 429	4 867	5 040	5 232	4 847	4 405	4 529	4 614	..

StatLink ▄▄ http://dx.doi.org/10.1787/888933336203

Gross domestic expenditure on R&D

As a percentage of GDP

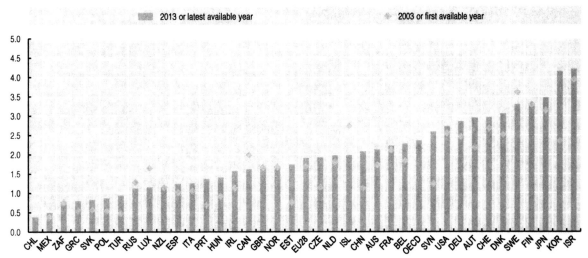

StatLink ▄▄ http://dx.doi.org/10.1787/888933335027

RESEARCHERS

On average, in OECD countries, labour costs account for half of the R&D expenditure. Researchers represent around 60% of total R&D personnel on average in the OECD.

Definition

Researchers are professionals engaged in the conception and creation of new knowledge, products, processes, methods and systems, as well as those who are directly involved in the management of projects for such purposes. They include researchers working in both civil and military research in government, universities and research institutes as well as in the business sector.

Researchers are part of human resources devoted to R&D. Other categories of R&D personnel are technicians (and equivalent staff) who participate in R&D by performing scientific and technical tasks, and other supporting staff (skilled and unskilled craftsmen, secretarial and clerical staff participating in R&D projects).

The number of researchers is measured in full-time equivalents (i.e. a person working half-time on R&D is counted as 0.5 person-year) and expressed per thousand people employed in each country. The number of researchers includes staff engaged in R&D during the course of one year.

Overview

In the OECD area, around 4.4 million persons were employed as researchers in 2013. There were about 7.8 researchers per thousand of employed persons, compared with 5.4 per thousand employed in 1995, and this has steadily increased over the last two decades.

The Nordic countries as well as Korea and Israel top the table for the numbers of researchers per thousand persons employed, with Israel the highest in the OECD, recording 17.4 researchers per thousand persons employed in 2012. Conversely, researchers per thousand of employed people are low in Chile and Mexico. Other countries with low rates, below 5.0 researchers per thousand of employed people, include Italy, Poland and Turkey.

In 2012, in the OECD, about 2.6 million researchers were engaged in the business sector. This represents approximately 60% of the total although there are differences across countries: two out of three researchers work in the business sector in the United States, about three out of four in Japan and Korea, but less than one out of two in the EU. Chile, Mexico, and South Africa have a low intensity of business researchers (less than one per 1 000 employees in industry). In these countries, the business sector plays a much smaller role in the national R&D system than the higher education and government sectors.

Comparability

The data on researchers have been compiled according to the 2002 guidelines of the *Frascati Manual* which have now been superseded by the 2015 edition. The revised definitions are in the course of being implemented and are not expected to revise significantly the major indicators. Comparability over time is affected to some extent by improvements in the coverage of national R&D surveys and by the efforts of countries to improve the international comparability of their data.

For the United States, the total numbers of researchers are OECD estimates and exclude military personnel in the government sector. For China, from 2009 researcher data are collected according to the *Frascati Manual* definition of researcher.

Sources
- OECD (2015), *Main Science and Technology Indicators*, OECD Publishing.

Further information

Analytical publications
- OECD (2015), *OECD Science, Technology and Industry Scoreboard*, OECD Publishing.
- OECD (2014), *OECD Science, Technology and Industry Outlook*, OECD Publishing.

Methodological publications
- OECD (2015), *Frascati Manual 2015: Guidelines for Collecting and Reporting Data on Research and Experimental Development*, OECD Publishing.

Online databases
- OECD *Science, Technology and R&D Statistics*.

Websites
- Main Science and Technology Indicators (supplementary material), *www.oecd.org/sti/msti*.
- Research and Development Statistics, *www.oecd.org/sti/rds*.

Researchers

Per thousand employed, full-time equivalent

	2001	2002	2003	2004	2005	2006	2007	2008	2009	2010	2011	2012	2013
Australia	..	7.8	..	8.3	..	8.5	..	8.6	..	..	..	..	..
Austria		6.4		6.8	7.3	7.4	7.9	8.4	8.5	8.9	8.9	9.3	9.4
Belgium	7.7	7.4	7.4	7.7	7.8	8.1	8.3	8.2	8.6	9.1	9.4	9.6	9.8
Canada	7.5	7.4	7.7	8.0	8.3	8.4	8.9	9.0	8.8	9.1	9.2	8.8	..
Chile	..	..	..	..	..	..	0.9	0.9	0.7	0.8	0.8	0.9	0.8
Czech Republic	3.1	3.1	3.3	3.4	4.9	5.3	5.5	5.7	5.6	5.8	6.1	6.6	6.7
Denmark	7.1	9.3	9.1	9.6	10.2	10.3	10.5	12.3	13.0	13.6	14.2	14.9	14.9
Estonia	4.5	5.2	5.0	5.6	5.4	5.5	5.7	6.2	7.5	7.4	7.7	7.7	7.3
Finland	15.8	16.4	17.7	17.3	16.4	16.5	15.6	16.0	16.3	16.7	15.9	15.9	15.7
France	6.8	7.1	7.4	7.7	7.7	7.9	8.2	8.4	8.7	9.1	9.2	9.6	9.8
Germany	6.6	6.7	6.9	6.9	6.9	7.1	7.2	7.4	7.8	8.0	8.1	8.4	8.5
Greece	3.3	..	3.5	..	4.2	4.2	4.4	..	..	..	5.6	6.2	7.5
Hungary	3.5	3.5	3.6	3.6	3.8	4.2	4.1	4.5	5.0	5.3	5.7	5.9	6.1
Iceland	11.7	..	12.2	..	13.4	14.2	12.5	12.9	14.9	..	13.5	..	..
Ireland	5.1	5.3	5.5	5.9	5.9	5.9	5.9	6.8	7.2	7.5	8.2	8.6	..
Israel	..	..	..	..	..	..	..	..	..	..	15.7	17.4	..
Italy	2.8	3.0	2.9	3.0	3.4	3.5	3.7	3.8	4.1	4.2	4.3	4.5	4.9
Japan	10.0	9.7	10.1	10.0	10.4	10.4	10.4	10.0	10.1	10.2	10.2	10.0	10.2
Korea	6.3	6.4	6.8	6.9	7.9	8.6	9.5	10.0	10.4	11.1	11.9	12.8	12.8
Luxembourg	..	..	6.7	6.8	7.2	6.4	6.6	6.5	6.8	7.3	8.2	6.6	6.8
Mexico	0.6	0.8	0.9	1.0	1.1	0.9	0.9	0.9	1.0	0.8	0.8	..	..
Netherlands	5.4	5.2	5.2	5.8	5.7	6.2	5.8	5.7	5.3	6.1	6.9	8.3	8.8
New Zealand	5.7	..	6.5	..	6.3	..	6.9	..	7.5	..	7.4	..	7.9
Norway	8.5	..	8.9	8.9	9.0	9.3	9.6	9.8	10.1	10.2	10.4	10.4	10.4
Poland	4.0	4.1	4.3	4.4	4.4	4.1	4.1	3.9	3.9	4.2	4.1	4.3	4.6
Portugal	3.5	3.7	4.0	4.1	4.2	4.9	5.6	8.0	8.1	8.5	9.2	9.3	9.7
Slovak Republic	4.7	4.5	4.7	5.2	5.2	5.5	5.7	5.6	6.0	7.0	6.9	6.9	6.7
Slovenia	4.9	5.0	4.1	4.3	5.7	6.2	6.4	7.0	7.6	8.0	9.3	9.5	9.4
Spain	4.6	4.7	5.1	5.3	5.5	5.6	5.8	6.1	6.7	6.9	6.8	6.9	6.9
Sweden	10.5	..	11.0	11.2	12.7	12.6	10.1	11.0	10.6	11.0	10.6	10.7	13.3
Switzerland	..	..	..	6.0	..	..	..	5.5	..	..	..	7.5	..
Turkey	1.2	1.2	1.7	1.7	2.0	2.1	2.4	2.5	2.7	2.8	3.0	3.3	3.5
United Kingdom	6.5	7.1	7.7	8.0	8.6	8.7	8.6	8.5	8.8	8.8	8.6	8.7	8.7
United States	7.3	7.5	8.0	7.8	7.6	7.7	7.6	8.1	8.8	8.5	8.8	8.7	..
EU 28	5.4	5.6	5.8	6.0	6.2	6.3	6.4	6.6	6.8	7.1	7.2	7.5	7.7
OECD	6.3	6.4	6.7	6.7	6.9	7.0	7.0	7.2	7.5	7.5	7.7	7.8	..
Brazil	..	..	..	..	..	..	..	..	..	..	..	..	..
China	1.0	1.1	1.2	1.2	1.5	1.6	1.9	2.1	1.5	1.6	1.7	1.8	1.9
India	..	..	..	..	..	..	..	..	..	..	..	..	..
Indonesia	..	..	..	..	..	..	..	..	..	..	..	..	..
Russian Federation	7.8	7.4	7.3	7.1	6.8	6.7	6.6	6.4	6.4	6.3	6.3	6.2	6.2
South Africa	1.2	..	1.2	1.5	1.4	1.4	1.4	1.3	1.4	1.4	1.4	1.5	..

StatLink http://dx.doi.org/10.1787/888933336548

Researchers

Per thousand employed, full-time equivalent, 2013 or latest available year

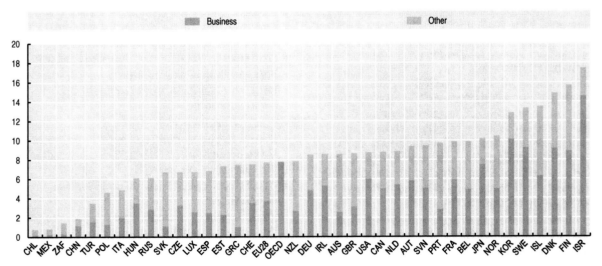

StatLink http://dx.doi.org/10.1787/888933335457

PATENTS

Patent-based indicators provide a measure of the output of a country's R&D, i.e. its inventions. The methodology used for counting patents can however influence the results, as simple counts of patents filed at a national patent office are affected by various kinds of limitations (such as weak international comparability) and highly heterogeneous patent values. To overcome these limits, the OECD has developed triadic patent families, which are designed to capture all important inventions and to be internationally comparable.

Definition

A patent family is defined as a set of patents registered in various countries (i.e. patent offices) to protect the same invention. Triadic patent families are a set of patents filed at three of these major patent offices: the European Patent Office, the Japan Patent Office and the United States Patent and Trademark Office.

Triadic patent family counts are attributed to the country of residence of the inventor and to the date when the patent was first registered.

Triadic patent families are expressed as numbers and per million inhabitants.

Comparability

The concept of triadic patent families has been developed in order to improve the international comparability and quality of patent-based indicators. Indeed, only patents registered in the same set of countries are included in the family: home advantage and influence of geographical location are therefore eliminated. Furthermore, patents included in the triadic family are typically of higher economic value: patentees only take on the additional costs and delays of extending the protection of their invention to other countries if they deem it worthwhile.

Overview

Although the volume of triadic patent families remained relatively steady over time, with more than 50 500 triadic patent families filed in 2013, there has been a significant shift in the origin of patented inventions. The share of triadic patent families originating from Europe (26.2%), Japan (26.6%) and the United States (27.0%) report a loss of 1 to 4 percentage points compared to the levels observed in 2003. Asian countries are increasingly contributing to patent families: the most spectacular growth among OECD countries has been observed by Korea, whose share of all triadic patent families increased from 3.8% in 2003 to 5.8% in 2013. Strong rises are also observed for China and India, with an average growth in the number of triadic patents of more than 17% and 12% a year respectively seen between 2003 and 2013.

When triadic patent families are expressed relative to the total population, Switzerland, Japan, Germany, Sweden and Denmark were the five most inventive countries in 2013, with the highest values recorded in Switzerland (148) and Japan (125). Ratios for Austria, Belgium, Finland, Israel, Korea, the Netherlands and the United States are also above the OECD average (40).

Sources
• OECD (2015), OECD Patent Statistics (Database).

Further information

Analytical publications
• Haščič, I. and M. Migotto (2015), "Measuring Environmental innovation using patent data", OECD Environment Working Papers, No. 2015/89.
• OECD (2015), OECD Science, Technology and Industry Scoreboard, OECD Publishing.
• OECD (2014), OECD Science, Technology and Industry Outlook, OECD Publishing.

Methodological publications
• Dernis, H. and M. Khan (2004), "Triadic Patent Families Methodology", OECD Science, Technology and Industry Working Papers, No. 2004/2.
• OECD (2009), OECD Patent Statistics Manual, OECD Publishing.
• Squicciarini, M., H. Dernis and C. Criscuolo (2013), "Measuring Patent Quality: Indicators of Technological and Economic Value", OECD Science, Technology and Industry Working Papers, No. 2013/03.

Websites
• Intellectual Property (IP) statistics and analysis, www.oecd.org/innovation/intellectual-property-statistics-and-analysis.htm.

Triadic patent families
Number

	2001	2002	2003	2004	2005	2006	2007	2008	2009	2010	2011	2012	2013
Australia	466	491	498	524	482	365	346	317	351	305	301	299	304
Austria	339	349	346	353	408	355	376	343	367	389	419	458	500
Belgium	438	473	464	565	541	478	430	457	479	474	490	487	471
Canada	635	681	669	736	715	667	682	690	678	554	545	562	564
Chile	9	6	3	7	6	9	7	9	11	15	16	16	15
Czech Republic	20	23	23	24	25	28	23	28	17	14	29	32	38
Denmark	281	287	312	369	390	317	316	345	258	302	340	347	364
Estonia	3	1	6	0	3	7	4	3	3	3	5	5	5
Finland	417	318	350	396	390	293	259	253	224	226	230	240	241
France	2 809	2 753	2 757	2 968	3 051	2 885	2 782	2 887	2 722	2 472	2 606	2 539	2 484
Germany	7 242	6 890	6 747	6 997	7 143	6 532	5 809	5 473	5 561	5 352	5 396	5 440	5 465
Greece	11	12	20	15	24	22	14	16	15	5	9	9	8
Hungary	42	37	50	60	59	48	59	31	50	37	40	41	40
Iceland	5	14	6	5	7	8	10	5	2	3	3	3	3
Ireland	61	67	86	96	97	76	93	84	85	64	70	74	75
Israel	387	323	363	422	501	421	349	369	377	350	367	389	414
Italy	917	929	900	974	964	822	729	759	737	700	688	696	705
Japan	16 630	16 830	17 909	18 712	17 717	17 992	17 722	15 726	15 330	16 042	16 423	16 220	15 970
Korea	1 157	1 570	2 195	2 570	2 750	2 350	1 982	1 828	2 108	2 460	2 668	2 887	3 154
Luxembourg	28	15	23	27	21	24	15	20	20	24	24	22	20
Mexico	14	14	21	19	19	27	19	17	15	14	15	16	17
Netherlands	1 364	1 870	1 987	1 974	1 761	1 478	1 065	1 127	1 052	819	961	930	916
New Zealand	57	81	76	80	73	72	56	72	55	44	45	48	50
Norway	113	132	120	134	142	123	106	87	129	116	118	121	122
Poland	15	20	16	24	18	18	25	37	32	61	71	81	92
Portugal	9	8	12	12	16	21	42	29	17	16	21	22	26
Slovak Republic	4	4	6	1	2	3	4	5	2	8	11	11	11
Slovenia	8	17	16	14	22	8	12	16	17	16	15	16	16
Spain	213	225	207	293	292	269	258	269	255	236	254	249	244
Sweden	754	794	758	804	970	885	964	837	797	641	675	677	644
Switzerland	983	992	1 042	1 100	1 087	1 149	1 008	995	968	1 060	1 106	1 153	1 207
Turkey	12	10	11	17	16	17	9	27	28	34	38	41	42
United Kingdom	2 294	2 231	2 202	2 098	2 169	2 091	1 799	1 699	1 724	1 681	1 693	1 715	1 770
United States	16 022	16 504	16 807	17 230	17 399	15 502	13 916	13 829	13 537	12 823	13 254	13 819	14 606
EU 28	17 287	17 356	17 340	18 101	18 411	16 678	15 106	14 738	14 460	13 558	14 067	14 111	14 162
OECD	53 762	54 969	57 009	59 618	59 281	55 359	51 292	48 690	48 023	47 362	48 945	49 661	50 604
Brazil	65	58	57	67	76	71	70	84	78	65	69	78	88
China	154	272	358	403	522	565	695	826	1 297	1 417	1 542	1 657	1 785
India	109	172	167	175	206	214	197	290	310	375	439	484	528
Indonesia	2	5	3	2	1	5	1	1	1	3	4	5	6
Russian Federation	83	80	79	70	91	75	78	59	87	89	102	111	119
South Africa	28	39	43	38	49	40	37	52	35	30	39	42	42
World	54 541	56 013	58 149	60 830	60 762	56 815	52 946	50 598	50 519	50 080	51 950	52 867	54 037

StatLink http://dx.doi.org/10.1787/888933336477

Triadic patent families
Number per million inhabitants, 2013

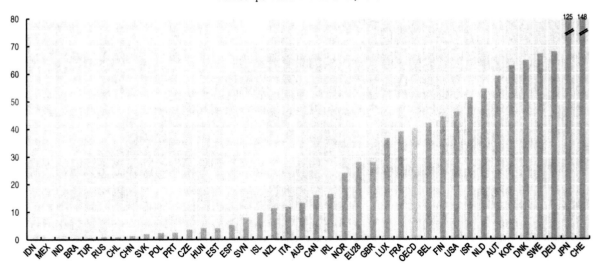

StatLink http://dx.doi.org/10.1787/888933335331

EDUCATION

INTERNATIONAL STUDENT ASSESSMENT

How effective are school systems in providing young people with a solid foundation in the knowledge and skills that will equip them for life and learning beyond school? The OECD Programme for International Student Assessment (PISA) assesses student knowledge and skills at age 15, i.e. toward the end of compulsory education. The PISA 2012 survey covers mathematics, reading, science and problem-solving. For the first time, PISA 2012 also included an assessment of the financial literacy of young people and an optional computer-based assessment of mathematics.

Definition

PISA is a triennial survey of 15-year-old students around the world. The survey examines how well students can extrapolate from what they have learned and can apply that knowledge in unfamiliar settings, both in and outside of school. The PISA survey covers 3 main subjects: mathematics, reading and science and in each round, one of these subjects is the major domain and the other two are minor domains. In PISA 2012 the major domain was mathematics.

For PISA, mathematical literacy means the capacity to formulate, employ and interpret mathematics in a variety of contexts to describe, predict and explain phenomena. It assists individuals in recognising the role that mathematics plays in the world and to make the well-founded judgements and decisions needed by constructive, engaged and reflective citizens. Reading literacy is the capacity to understand, use and reflect on written texts in order to achieve one's goals, develop one's knowledge and potential, and participate in society. Scientific literacy is the capacity to use scientific knowledge to identify questions, acquire new knowledge, explain scientific phenomena, and draw evidence-based conclusions about science-related issues.

Comparability

Leading experts in countries participating in PISA provide advice on the scope and nature of the assessments, with final decisions taken by the PISA Governing Board. Substantial efforts and resources are devoted to achieving cultural and linguistic breadth and balance in the assessment materials. Stringent quality assurance mechanisms are applied in the item development and translation, sampling, data collection, scoring and data management stages to ensure comparability of the results.

Around 510 000 15-year-old students in 65 participating countries or economies were assessed in PISA 2012. Because the results are based on probability samples, standard errors (S.E.) are normally shown in the tables.

Overview

The average score from the PISA 2012 results across OECD countries are 494 points for mathematics, 496 points for reading and 501 points for science. Korea has the highest score in mathematics, with a mean score of 554 points, while Japan shows the highest scores in reading and science, with mean scores of 538 and 547 respectively.

Marked gender differences in mathematics performance – in favour of boys – are observed in 27 countries presented. Only in Iceland do girls outperform boys in mathematics. Across OECD countries, boys outperform girls with an 11 score-point difference. By contrast, girls outperform boys in reading everywhere. Across OECD countries, the difference in favour of girls is about 38 score points. In science, boys outperform girls in eight countries, while in five countries girls outperform boys. Across OECD countries, the gender differences in science tend to be smaller than in mathematics and reading, with only one score point in favour of boys.

Sources
- OECD (2014), *PISA 2012 Results: What Students Know and Can Do: Student Performance in Mathematics, Reading and Science* (Volume I, Revised edition, February 2014), PISA, OECD Publishing.

Further information

Analytical publications
- OECD (2013), *PISA 2012 Results: Excellence Through Equity (Volume II): Giving Every Student the Chance to Succeed*, PISA, OECD Publishing.
- OECD (2013), *PISA 2012 Results: What Makes Schools Successful? (Volume IV): Resources, Policies and Practices*, PISA, OECD Publishing.

Statistical publications
- OECD (2015), *Education at a Glance. OECD Indicators*, OECD Publishing.

Methodological publications
- OECD (2014), *PISA 2012 Technical Report*, OECD, Paris.
- OECD (2013), *PISA 2012 Assessment and Analytical Framework: Mathematics, Reading, Science, Problem Solving and Financial Literacy*, PISA, OECD Publishing.

Online databases
- OECD PISA Database.

Websites
- Programme for International Student Assessment (PISA), *www.oecd.org/pisa*.

Mean scores by gender in PISA
2012

| | Mathematics scale | | | | Reading scale | | | | Science scale | | | |
| | Girls | | Boys | | Girls | | Boys | | Girls | | Boys | |
	Mean score	S.E.	Mean score	S.E.	Mean score	S.E.	Mean score	S.E.	Mean score	S.E.	Mean score	S.E.
Australia	498	2.0	510	2.4	530	2.0	495	2.3	519	2.1	524	2.5
Austria	494	3.3	517	3.9	508	3.4	471	4.0	501	3.4	510	3.9
Belgium	509	2.6	520	2.9	525	2.7	493	3.0	503	2.6	507	3.0
Canada	513	2.1	523	2.1	541	2.1	506	2.3	524	2.0	527	2.4
Chile	411	3.1	436	3.8	452	2.9	430	3.8	442	2.9	448	3.7
Czech Republic	493	3.6	505	3.7	513	3.4	474	3.3	508	3.5	509	3.7
Denmark	493	2.3	507	2.9	512	2.6	481	3.3	493	2.5	504	3.5
Estonia	518	2.2	523	2.6	538	2.3	494	2.4	543	2.3	540	2.5
Finland	520	2.2	517	2.6	556	2.4	494	3.1	554	2.3	537	3.0
France	491	2.5	499	3.4	527	3.0	483	3.8	500	2.4	498	3.8
Germany	507	3.4	520	3.0	530	3.1	486	2.9	524	3.5	524	3.1
Greece	449	2.6	457	3.3	502	3.1	452	4.1	473	3.0	460	3.8
Hungary	473	3.6	482	3.7	508	3.3	468	3.9	493	3.3	496	3.4
Iceland	496	2.3	490	2.3	508	2.5	457	2.4	480	2.9	477	2.7
Ireland	494	2.6	509	3.3	538	3.0	509	3.5	520	3.1	524	3.4
Israel	461	3.5	472	7.8	507	3.9	463	8.2	470	4.0	470	7.9
Italy	476	2.2	494	2.4	510	2.3	471	2.5	492	2.4	495	2.2
Japan	527	3.6	545	4.6	551	3.6	527	4.7	541	3.5	552	4.7
Korea	544	5.1	562	5.8	548	4.5	525	5.0	536	4.2	539	4.7
Luxembourg	477	1.4	502	1.5	503	1.8	473	1.9	483	1.7	499	1.7
Mexico	406	1.4	420	1.6	435	1.6	411	1.7	412	1.3	418	1.5
Netherlands	518	3.9	528	3.6	525	3.5	498	4.0	520	3.9	524	3.7
New Zealand	492	2.9	507	3.2	530	3.5	495	3.3	513	3.3	518	3.2
Norway	488	3.4	490	2.8	528	3.9	481	3.3	496	3.7	493	3.2
Poland	516	3.8	520	4.3	539	3.1	497	3.7	527	3.2	524	3.7
Portugal	481	3.9	493	4.1	508	3.7	468	4.2	490	3.8	488	4.1
Slovak Republic	477	4.1	486	4.1	483	5.1	444	4.6	467	4.2	475	4.3
Slovenia	499	2.0	503	2.0	510	1.8	454	1.7	519	1.9	510	1.9
Spain	476	2.0	492	2.4	503	1.9	474	2.3	493	1.9	500	2.3
Sweden	480	2.4	477	3.0	509	2.8	458	4.0	489	2.8	481	3.9
Switzerland	524	3.1	537	3.5	527	2.5	491	3.1	512	2.7	518	3.3
Turkey	444	5.7	452	5.1	499	4.3	453	4.6	469	4.3	458	4.5
United Kingdom	488	3.8	500	4.2	512	3.8	487	4.5	508	3.7	521	4.5
United States	479	3.9	484	3.8	513	3.8	482	4.1	498	4.0	497	4.1
EU 28	..	..	..	..	..	..	..	..	..	..	..	..
OECD	489	0.5	499	0.6	515	0.5	478	0.6	500	0.5	502	0.6
Brazil	383	2.3	401	2.2	425	2.2	394	2.4	404	2.3	406	2.3
China	..	..	..	..	..	..	..	..	..	..	..	..
India	..	..	..	..	..	..	..	..	..	..	..	..
Indonesia	373	4.3	377	4.4	410	4.3	382	4.8	383	4.1	380	4.1
Russian Federation	483	3.1	481	3.7	495	3.2	455	3.5	489	2.9	484	3.5
South Africa	..	..	..	..	..	..	..	..	..	..	..	..

StatLink ᴍ⬛ http://dx.doi.org/10.1787/888933336494

Performance in mathematics, reading and science, PISA 2012
Mean score

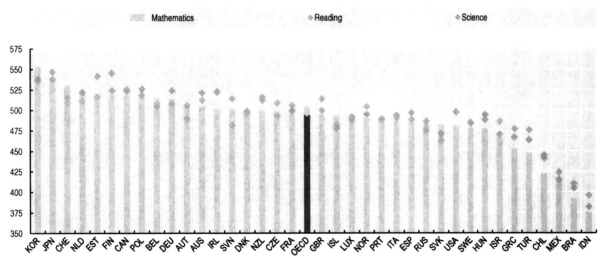

StatLink ᴍ⬛ http://dx.doi.org/10.1787/888933335359

STUDENTS, COMPUTERS AND LEARNING

Information and communication technology (ICT) has revolutionised many aspects of people's personal and professional lives. As computers and the Internet have reached a central role in everyday life, students who have not acquired basic skills in reading, writing and navigating through a complex digital landscape will find themselves unable to participate fully in the economic, social and cultural life around them. By analysing PISA 2012 data, it is possible to examine how students' access to ICT devices and their experience in using these technologies evolve in recent years.

Definition

The OECD Programme for International Student Assessment (PISA) is a triennial survey of 15-year-old students around the world. The survey examines how well students can extrapolate from what they have learned and can apply that knowledge in unfamiliar settings, both in and outside of school.

Additional questionnaire materials were developed and offered as international options to the participating countries and economies, including the information communication technology familiarity questionnaire. It consists of questions to students regarding their access to uses of, and attitudes towards computers.

Comparability

In PISA 2012, 29 OECD countries and 13 partner countries and economies chose to distribute the optional ICT familiarity component of the student questionnaire. In 2012, this component contained 12 questions, some of which were retained from the previous PISA survey (2009) to allow for comparisons across time. New questions focused on the age at first use of computers and the Internet; the amount of time spent on the Internet; and,

since mathematics was the major domain assessed in PISA 2012, on the use of computers during mathematics lessons.

Additional information on the availability and use of ICT at home and at school, as well as on school policies on using ICT, was collected through the main student and school questionnaires, and is available for the 65 participating countries and economies in PISA 2012.

Sources
- OECD (2015), *Students, Computers and Learning: Making the Connection*, PISA, OECD Publishing.

Further information

Analytical publications
- OECD (2015), *The ABC of Gender Equality in Education: Aptitude, Behaviour, Confidence*, PISA, OECD Publishing.
- OECD (2014), *PISA 2012 Results: Creative Problem Solving (Volume V): Students' Skills in Tackling Real-Life Problems*, PISA, OECD Publishing.
- OECD (2014), *PISA 2012 Results: What Students Know and Can Do (Volume I, Revised edition, February 2014): Student Performance in Mathematics, Reading and Science*, PISA, OECD Publishing.
- OECD (2013), *PISA 2012 Results: What Makes Schools Successful? (Volume IV): Resources, Policies and Practices*, PISA, OECD Publishing.

Statistical publications
- OECD (2015), *Education at a Glance: OECD Indicators*, OECD Publishing.

Methodological publications
- OECD (2014), *PISA 2012 Technical Report*, OECD, Paris.
- OECD (2013), *PISA 2012 Assessment and Analytical Framework: Mathematics, Reading, Science, Problem Solving and Financial Literacy*, PISA, OECD Publishing.

Online databases
- OECD PISA Database.

Websites
- Programme for International Student Assessment (PISA), *www.oecd.org/pisa*.

Overview

On average across OECD countries, students spent over 2 hours online each day in 2012. In that same year, 96% of 15-year-old students in OECD countries reported that they have a computer at home, 43% of students reported having three or more computes at home, and 72% reported that they use a desktop, laptop or tablet computer at school. But in Korea, only 42% of students reported that they use computers at school – and Korea is among the top performers in the digital reading and computer-based mathematics tests in the OECD Programme for International Student Assessment in 2012. By contrast, in countries where it is more common for students to use the Internet at school for schoolwork, students' performance in reading declined between 2000 and 2012, on average.

STUDENTS, COMPUTERS AND LEARNING

ICT equipment and use at school and at home

PISA 2012

	ICT use at or for school						Home ICT equipment			
	Number of 15-year-old students per school computer		Students using computers at school		Students browsing the Internet weekly for schoolwork (at school)		Students with at least one computer at home		Students with three or more computers at home	
	Mean	S.E.	%	S.E.	%	S.E.	%	S.E.	%	S.E.
Australia	0.9	0.0	93.7	0.3	80.8	0.6	99.0	0.1	64.6	0.5
Austria	2.9	0.5	81.4	1.0	48.0	1.3	99.5	0.1	45.3	1.1
Belgium	2.8	0.3	65.3	0.8	29.4	0.9	98.9	0.1	55.0	0.6
Canada	2.8	1.0	..	..	..	..	98.9	0.1	53.0	0.6
Chile	4.7	0.9	61.7	1.5	44.5	1.3	88.3	0.9	20.9	0.8
Czech Republic	1.6	0.1	83.2	1.0	47.6	1.1	98.1	0.3	36.9	0.9
Denmark	2.4	0.3	86.7	0.8	80.8	0.8	99.9	0.0	84.7	0.6
Estonia	2.1	0.1	61.0	1.0	28.9	1.0	98.5	0.2	37.3	0.7
Finland	3.1	0.1	89.0	0.6	34.9	1.1	99.8	0.1	56.1	0.7
France	2.9	0.2	..	..	..	..	99.0	0.1	45.0	0.9
Germany	4.2	1.3	68.7	1.3	28.9	1.0	99.4	0.1	54.0	0.9
Greece	8.2	1.1	65.9	1.3	44.9	1.1	94.6	0.4	18.4	0.7
Hungary	2.2	0.1	74.7	1.0	35.7	1.1	96.2	0.5	24.2	0.8
Iceland	4.1	0.0	81.9	0.6	28.9	0.7	99.3	0.1	70.7	0.9
Ireland	2.6	0.2	63.5	1.4	32.4	1.1	98.7	0.2	36.0	0.8
Israel	4.7	0.6	55.2	1.5	30.6	1.3	96.5	0.4	44.6	1.0
Italy	4.1	0.5	66.8	0.7	28.8	0.6	98.7	0.1	27.7	0.4
Japan	3.6	0.1	59.2	1.9	11.3	0.8	92.4	0.6	17.1	0.6
Korea	5.3	0.2	41.9	1.7	11.0	0.9	98.6	0.2	10.1	0.6
Luxembourg	2.2	0.0	..	..	..	..	99.1	0.1	56.6	0.7
Mexico	15.5	2.0	60.6	0.8	39.5	0.8	58.5	0.8	9.1	0.5
Netherlands	2.6	0.2	94.0	0.6	67.5	1.3	99.8	0.1	69.0	0.7
New Zealand	1.2	0.1	86.4	0.5	59.3	1.0	96.8	0.3	41.6	0.9
Norway	1.7	0.1	91.9	0.7	69.0	1.3	99.1	0.2	83.9	0.6
Poland	4.0	0.1	60.3	1.3	30.3	1.2	97.7	0.3	22.9	1.0
Portugal	3.7	0.3	69.0	1.2	38.1	1.1	97.1	0.3	36.6	1.1
Slovak Republic	2.0	0.2	80.2	0.9	43.1	1.3	94.4	0.6	26.4	0.8
Slovenia	3.3	0.0	57.2	0.8	41.6	0.7	99.7	0.1	43.4	0.8
Spain	2.2	0.1	73.2	0.9	51.1	1.0	97.9	0.2	37.9	0.7
Sweden	3.7	0.8	87.0	1.1	66.6	1.5	99.6	0.1	74.8	0.7
Switzerland	2.7	0.2	78.3	1.0	32.5	0.9	99.5	0.1	58.9	0.7
Turkey	44.9	9.7	48.7	1.7	28.0	1.2	70.7	1.1	4.1	0.5
United Kingdom	1.4	0.1	..	..	..	..	98.8	0.2	50.9	0.8
United States	1.8	0.2	..	..	..	..	94.5	0.5	37.6	1.3
EU 28	..	..	..	..	..	..	..	..	..	..
OECD	4.7	0.3	72.0	0.2	41.9	0.2	95.8	0.1	42.8	0.1
Brazil	22.1	2.7	..	..	..	..	73.5	0.7	9.4	0.5
China	..	..	..	..	..	..	..	..	..	..
India	..	..	..	..	..	..	..	..	..	..
Indonesia	16.4	2.2	..	..	..	..	25.8	2.0	1.9	0.8
Russian Federation	3.0	0.1	80.2	0.7	20.3	0.8	92.8	0.7	10.5	0.9
South Africa	..	..	..	..	..	..	..	..	..	..

StatLink http://dx.doi.org/10.1787/888933336342

Time spent on line in school and outside of school

Minutes per day, PISA 2012

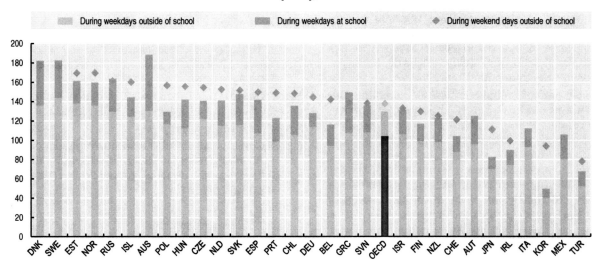

During weekdays outside of school   During weekdays at school   During weekend days outside of school

StatLink http://dx.doi.org/10.1787/888933335163

EARLY CHILDHOOD EDUCATION AND CARE

As family structures change, so do the relative ages of parents. More women and men are waiting until later in life to start a family. They do so for a number of reasons, including planning for greater financial security and emotional maturity, taking more time to find a stable relationship, and committing to their careers before turning their attention to having children. As younger and older parents are also more likely to be in the workforce today, there is a growing need for early childhood education. In addition, there is increasing awareness of the key role that early childhood education plays in the cognitive and emotional development of the young.

Enrolling children in early childhood education can also mitigate social inequalities and promote better student outcomes overall. Many of the inequalities found in education systems are already evident when children enter formal schooling and persist as they progress through the school system. Because inequalities tend to grow when school is not compulsory, earlier entrance into the school system may reduce these inequalities. In addition, pre-primary education helps to prepare children to enter and succeed in formal schooling.

Overview

In most OECD countries, education now begins for most children well before they are 5 years old. Four out of ten 2-year-olds are enrolled in early childhood education across OECD countries, as a whole, growing to almost three out of four (74%) for 3-year-olds. The highest enrolment rates of 3-year-olds in early childhood education are found in Belgium, Denmark, France, Iceland, Italy, New Zealand, Norway, Spain and the United Kingdom.

The ratio of children to teaching staff is an indicator of the resources devoted to early childhood education. The child-teacher ratio at the pre-primary level, excluding non-teaching staff (e.g. teachers' aides), ranges from more than 20 children per teacher in Chile, China, France, Indonesia and Mexico, to fewer than 10 in Estonia, Iceland, New Zealand, Russia, Slovenia, Sweden and the United Kingdom.

Sustained public funding is critical for supporting the growth and quality of early childhood education programmes. Public expenditure on pre-primary education is mainly used to support public institutions, but in some countries it also funds private institutions, to varying degrees. At the pre-primary level, annual expenditure, from both public and private sources, per child for both public and private institutions averages USD 8 008 in OECD countries. However, expenditure varies from USD 4 000 or less in Israel, Latvia and South Africa, to more than USD 10 000 in Australia, Iceland, Luxembourg, Sweden, the United Kingdom and the United States.

Definition

The *International Standard Classification of Education* (ISCED) level 0 refers to early childhood programmes that have an intentional education component. ISCED level 0 programmes target children below the age of entry into primary education (ISCED level 1). These programmes aim to develop cognitive, physical and socio-emotional skills necessary for participation and well-being in school and society.

Thanks to the new ISCED classification, level 0 covers now early childhood education for all ages, including very young children. Programmes are sub-classified into two categories, depending on the level of complexity of the educational content: early childhood educational development (code 01) and pre-primary education (code 02). Early childhood educational development programmes (code 01) are generally designed for children younger than 3. They were introduced as a new category in ISCED-2011 and were not covered by ISCED-97. Pre-primary education (code 02) corresponds exactly to level 0 in ISCED-97.

Comparability

There are many different early education systems and structures within OECD countries. Consequently, there is also a range of different approaches to identifying the boundary between early childhood education and childcare. These differences should be taken into account when drawing conclusions from international comparisons.

Sources
- OECD (2015), *Education at a Glance*, OECD Publishing.

Further information

Analytical publications
- OECD (2013), *PISA 2012 Results: What Makes Schools Successful (Volume IV): Resources, Policies and Practices*, PISA, OECD Publishing.
- OECD (2011), *Starting Strong III: A Quality Toolbox for Early Childhood Education and Care*, OECD Publishing.

Methodological publications
- OECD/Eurostat/UNESCO Institute for Statistics (2015), *ISCED 2011 Operational Manual: Guidelines for Classifying National Education Programmes and Related Qualifications*, OECD Publishing.

Online databases
- OECD Education Statistics.

Websites
- OECD Education at a Glance (supplementary material), *www.oecd.org/education/education-at-a-glance-19991487.htm*.

Early childhood educational development programmes and pre-primary education

	2013					2012					
	Pre-primary share of total early childhood enrolment	Early childhood educational development		Pre-primary education		Share of public expenditure			Annual expenditure by educational institutions for all services, USD per student		
	ISCED 02/ (ISCED 01 + ISCED 02)	Pupils/contact staff ratio	Pupils/teaching staff ratio	Pupils/contact staff ratio	Pupils/teaching staff ratio	Early childhood educational development	Pre-primary	All early childhood education	Early childhood educational development	Pre-primary	All early childhood education
		ISCED 01	ISCED 01	ISCED 02	ISCED 02	ISCED 01	ISCED 02	ISCED 01 + ISCED 02	ISCED 01	ISCED 02	ISCED 01 + ISCED 02
Australia	42	..	..	..	..	4	47	21	10 054	10 298	10 146
Austria	87	6	9	9	14	69	87	84	9 434	7 716	7 954
Belgium	..	..	..	..	16	..	96	..	..	6 975	..
Chile	80	9	13	19	27	..	..	82	..	..	4 599
Czech Republic	100	..	..	14	14	..	92	92	..	4 447	4 447
Denmark	63	..	..	..	..	..	..	81	..	..	10 911
Estonia	..	..	..	..	9	..	..	99	..	..	2 193
Finland	79	..	..	..	10	90	89	89	17 860	9 998	11 559
France	100	..	..	15	22	..	93	93	..	6 969	6 969
Germany	77	5	5	9	10	70	79	76	13 720	8 568	9 744
Greece	..	..	..	12	12	..	..	..	..	..	..
Hungary	..	..	..	11	11	..	92	..	..	4 539	..
Iceland	69	3	3	6	6	88	85	86	12 969	10 250	11 096
Israel	76	..	..	..	..	..	85	..	..	3 416	..
Italy	..	..	..	14	14	..	91	91	..	7 892	7 892
Japan	100	..	..	14	15	..	44	44	..	5 872	5 872
Korea	..	..	..	..	..	..	62	..	..	5 674	..
Luxembourg	100	..	..	11	11	..	99	..	..	19 719	..
Mexico	95	26	83	25	25	..	..	83	..	..	2 445
Netherlands	100	..	..	14	16	..	87	87	..	8 176	8 176
New Zealand	62	..	4	..	8	72	87	80	12 656	9 670	10 726
Norway	64	..	..	5	11	86	86	86	15 604	9 050	11 383
Poland	100	..	..	..	16	..	76	76	..	6 505	6 505
Portugal	..	..	..	..	17	..	61	..	..	5 713	..
Slovak Republic	100	..	..	13	13	..	83	83	..	4 694	4 694
Slovenia	70	6	6	9	9	75	79	78	11 665	7 472	8 726
Spain	77	..	9	..	15	62	73	70	7 924	6 182	6 588
Sweden	73	..	5	6	6	..	..	..	14 180	12 212	12 752
Switzerland	..	..	..	..	16	..	..	..	..	5 457	5 457
Turkey	..	..	..	..	17	..	..	..	..	..	..
United Kingdom	83	..	..	..	10	64	63	63	9 495	10 699	10 548
United States	..	..	..	10	12	..	75	..	..	10 042	..
OECD	81	9	14	12	14	68	80	78	12 324	8 008	7 886
Brazil	64	8	13	15	17	..	..	..	..	..	2 939
China	100	..	..	17	22	..	..	..	..	..	..
Indonesia	61	..	20	19	21	..	88	..	..	..	..
Russian Federation	84	..	..	4	10	..	..	89	..	..	4 887
South Africa	100	..	..	..	..	..	..	..	..	806	806

StatLink http://dx.doi.org/10.1787/888933336044

Enrolment rates at age 3 and 4 in early childhood education
2013

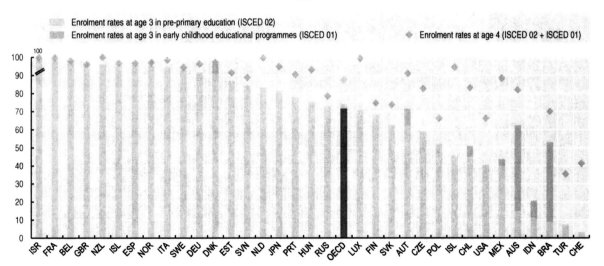

StatLink http://dx.doi.org/10.1787/888933334855

YOUTH INACTIVITY

Young people who are neither in employment nor in education or training (the "NEET" population) are at risk of becoming socially excluded – individuals with income below the poverty-line and lacking the skills to improve their economic situation.

Definition

The share refers to young people who are neither in education or training nor in employment, as a percentage of the total number of young people in the corresponding age group. Young people in education include those attending part-time as well as full-time education, but exclude those in non-formal education and in educational activities of very short duration. Employment is defined according to the ILO Guidelines and covers all those who have been in paid work for at least one hour in the reference week of the survey or were temporarily absent from such work.

Overview

On average across OECD countries, 17.9% of the 20-24 year-olds and 7.2% of the 15-19 year-olds were neither in school nor at work in 2014. For OECD countries as a whole, the proportion of the 20-24 year-olds who were not in education but employed fell from 48.2% to 36.2% between 2000 and 2014, while the percentage of individuals in education increased steadily. The proportion of 20-24 year-olds who were neither in employment nor in education or training (NEET) remained stable at around 17-19% between 2000 and 2014.

In 2014, Greece, Italy and Turkey were the only countries where more than 30% of 20-24 year-olds were NEET. Turkey has the highest proportion of NEET, but it is also the only country among these three to show a decrease in the percentage of NEET between 2005 and 2014, from 49.7% in 2005 to 36.3% in 2014. Germany's share of 20-24 year-old NEET (18.7%) was above the OECD average (17.4%) in 2005, but by 2014, that share fell back to 10.1%, well below the OECD average of 17.9%. In fact, the proportion of 20-24 year-old NEET in Germany is now one of the smallest among OECD countries along with those in Iceland (9.4%), Luxembourg (9.0%), the Netherlands (10.4%) and Norway (10.0%).

Women are more often neither in employment nor in education or training than men. Among 20-24 year olds, 19.4% of women and 16.4% of men were NEET in 2014, on average across OECD countries. In Mexico and Turkey, the gender difference in the shares of 20-24 year-olds who were NEET was around 30 percentage points.

Comparability

The length and the quality of the schooling individuals receive have an impact on students' transition from education to work; so do labour-market conditions, the economic environment and demographics. National traditions also play an important role. For example, in some countries, young people traditionally complete schooling before they look for work; in others, education and employment are concurrent. In some countries, there is little difference between how young women and men experience their transitions from school to work, while in other countries, significant proportions of young women raise families full-time after leaving the education system and do not enter employment. The ageing of the population in OECD countries should favour employment among young adults, as, theoretically, when older people leave the labour market, their jobs are made available to the young. However, during recessionary periods, high general unemployment rates make the transition from school to work substantially more difficult for young people, as those with more work experience are favoured over new entrants into the labour market. In addition, when labour-market conditions are unfavourable, younger people often tend to stay in education longer, because high unemployment rates drive down the opportunity costs of education.

Please note that data for Chile for 2010 refer to 2009 and data for Brazil, Chile and Korea for 2014 refer to 2013. In Israel, the proportion of NEETs in 2014 is not comparable with data from 2010 and previous years.

Sources
- OECD (2015), *Education at a Glance*, OECD Publishing.

Further information

Analytical publications
- OECD, *et al.* (2015), *African Economic Outlook 2013*, OECD Publishing.
- OECD (2015), *OECD Education Working Papers*, OECD Publishing.
- OECD (2013), *OECD Skills Outlook*, OECD Publishing.
- OECD (2010), *Jobs for Youth*, OECD Publishing.

Statistical publications
- OECD (2014), *Society at a Glance: OECD Social Indicators*, OECD Publishing.

Online databases
- *OECD Education Statistics.*

Websites
- OECD Education at a Glance (supplementary material), *www.oecd.org/education/education-at-a-glance-19991487.htm*.

Youth who are not in education nor in employment

As a percentage of persons in that age group

	Youth aged between 15 and 19				Youth aged between 20 and 24			
	2000	2005	2010	2014	2000	2005	2010	2014
Australia	6.8	7.4	8.1	7.2	13.3	11.6	11.2	13.2
Austria	..	7.0	5.5	7.2	..	12.7	13.0	12.0
Belgium	6.5	6.2	5.9	5.4	16.0	18.3	18.0	18.9
Canada	8.2	6.9	8.2	7.1	15.9	14.5	15.7	14.8
Chile	..	..	17.0	12.7	..	..	27.5	21.1
Czech Republic	7.9	5.3	3.8	3.2	20.3	16.6	13.6	12.3
Denmark	2.7	4.3	5.5	3.5	6.5	8.3	12.1	12.7
Estonia	..	5.2	6.1	7.0	..	16.3	22.4	16.1
Finland	..	5.2	5.1	5.5	..	13.0	15.8	15.6
France	7.0	6.3	7.9	7.9	17.6	17.8	20.6	18.3
Germany	5.7	4.4	3.7	2.9	16.9	18.7	13.7	10.1
Greece	9.3	11.7	7.5	10.5	25.9	21.6	21.6	31.3
Hungary	8.6	6.4	4.6	6.8	22.0	18.9	21.5	20.6
Iceland	..	..	6.2	5.5	..	6.6	12.2	9.4
Ireland	4.4	4.5	10.1	9.1	9.7	12.3	26.1	21.1
Israel	..	26.4	23.6	7.8	..	41.5	37.4	18.5
Italy	13.1	11.2	12.5	11.2	27.5	24.1	27.1	34.8
Japan	8.8	8.8	9.9	6.6	..	..	..	..
Korea	..	..	8.5	7.7	..	..	23.5	22.2
Luxembourg	..	2.2	6.3	2.4	8.2	9.3	7.5	9.0
Mexico	18.3	18.2	17.6	15.3	27.1	27.0	26.1	24.9
Netherlands	3.7	3.1	3.1	3.6	8.2	8.1	7.4	10.4
New Zealand	..	7.2	8.6	7.1	..	14.0	17.7	14.4
Norway	..	2.5	3.5	3.5	8.0	9.6	9.0	10.0
Poland	4.5	1.7	3.6	4.0	30.8	20.1	17.6	19.2
Portugal	7.7	8.4	7.4	6.1	11.0	14.1	16.4	23.9
Slovak Republic	26.3	6.3	4.6	5.7	33.1	25.2	22.1	18.6
Slovenia	..	4.9	3.2	4.6	..	13.0	9.3	13.4
Spain	8.0	10.9	12.8	12.1	15.0	19.1	27.0	29.0
Sweden	3.6	4.6	5.3	4.3	10.7	12.9	14.2	12.0
Switzerland	7.9	7.5	4.8	4.7	5.9	11.9	11.1	12.4
Turkey	31.2	36.1	25.6	21.0	44.2	49.7	43.7	36.3
United Kingdom	8.0	9.3	10.0	8.4	15.4	16.8	19.3	17.0
United States	7.0	6.1	7.6	7.6	14.4	15.5	19.4	17.5
EU 28	..	..	..	..	..	..	..	..
OECD	9.4	8.2	8.3	7.2	17.7	17.4	18.8	17.9
Brazil	..	..	..	15.7	..	..	..	24.0
China	..	..	..	..	..	..	..	..
India	..	..	..	..	..	..	..	..
Indonesia	..	..	..	..	..	..	..	..
Russian Federation	..	..	..	..	..	..	..	..
South Africa	..	..	..	..	..	..	..	..

StatLink http://dx.doi.org/10.1787/888933336606

Youth aged between 20 and 24 who are not in education nor in employment

As a percentage of persons in that age group, 2014

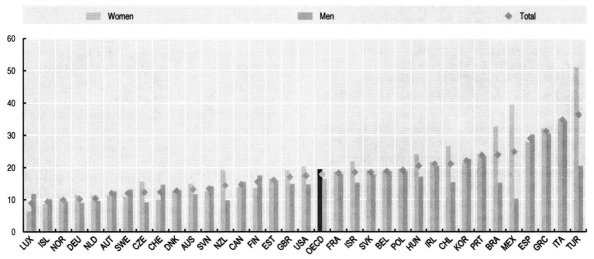

StatLink http://dx.doi.org/10.1787/888933335528

HOW MANY STUDENTS STUDY ABROAD?

As national economies become more interconnected, governments and individuals are looking to higher education to broaden students' horizons. By pursuing high level studies in countries other than their own students may expand their knowledge of other cultures and languages, and better equip themselves in an increasingly globalised labour market. Some countries, particularly in the European Union, have established policies and schemes that promote such mobility to foster intercultural contacts and help build social networks.

Definition

Students are classified as "international" if they left their country of origin for the purpose of study. Students are classified as "foreign" when they are not citizens of the country where they are enrolled. This includes international students as well as other students who are permanent residents, albeit not citizens, of the countries in which they are studying such as young people from immigrant families.

Comparability

Data on international and foreign students refer to the academic year 2012/2013, based on an annual joint data collection by UNESCO, the OECD and Eurostat.

Overview

OECD countries attract 73% of all students enrolled abroad in countries reporting data to the OECD and the UNESCO Institute for Statistics. Within the OECD area, EU countries host the largest proportion (35%) of international students. At the level of single countries, the United States hosted the largest number of all international students (19% of the total), followed by the United Kingdom (10%), Australia and France (6%), Germany (5%), Canada and Japan (both 3%) and, among the emerging economies with data on foreign students only, Russia (3%). The destinations of international students highlight the attractiveness of specific education systems, whether because of their academic reputation or because of subsequent immigration opportunities.

But they can also reflect language as well as cultural considerations, geographic proximity and the similarities between some education systems.

Students from Asia form the largest group of international students enrolled in countries reporting data: 53% or the total in all reporting destinations. In particular, students from China account for 22% of all international students enrolled in tertiary education in the OECD area, the highest share among all reporting countries.

The share of international students within total enrolment depends on the level of education. On average across OECD countries, international students represent 6% of the students enrolled in programmes at the bachelor's or equivalent level, but this proportion is 14% at the master's or equivalent level and 24% at the doctoral or equivalent level.

Trends in the number of foreign students worldwide, computed until 2012, reveal that this number has been steadily increasing. The number of students enrolled in a country of which they are not citizens increased by 50% (from 3 to 4.5 million) between 2005 and 2012.

Sources

- OECD (2015), *Education at a Glance*, OECD Publishing.

Further information

Analytical publications

- Keeley, B. (2009), *International Migration: The Human Face of Globalisation*, OECD Insights, OECD Publishing.
- OECD (2013), *Higher Education in Regional and City Development*, OECD Publishing.
- OECD (2013), *Higher Education Management and Policy*, OECD Publishing.
- OECD (2013), *How is international student mobility shaping up?*, OECD publishing.
- OECD (2008), *Tertiary Education for the Knowledge Society*, OECD Review of Tertiary Education, OECD Publishing.
- OECD (2004), *Internationalisation and Trade in Higher Education: Opportunities and Challenges*, OECD Publishing.

Online databases

- OECD Education Statistics.

Websites

- OECD Education at a Glance (supplementary material), *www.oecd.org/education/education-at-a-glance-19991487.htm*.

International student mobility and foreign students in tertiary education

As a percentage of all students (international plus domestic), 2013

	International students					Foreign students				
	Total tertiary education	Short-cycle tertiary programmes	Bachelor's or equivalent level	Master's or equivalent level	Doctoral or equivalent level	Total tertiary education	Short-cycle tertiary programmes	Bachelor's or equivalent level	Master's or equivalent level	Doctoral or equivalent level
Australia	18.0	12.2	14.0	37.9	33.0	..	..	..	..	..
Austria	16.8	1.5	19.7	19.3	27.5	..	..	..	..	..
Belgium	10.0	5.9	7.7	16.1	37.7	..	..	..	..	..
Canada	9.0	9.0	7.3	13.0	25.6	..	..	..	..	..
Chile	0.3	0.1	0.1	2.5	3.4	..	..	..	..	..
Czech Republic	..	..	..	..	..	9.4	4.2	8.1	11.4	12.8
Denmark	10.1	13.3	5.8	17.6	29.5	..	..	..	..	..
Estonia	2.9	..	2.2	4.0	7.2	..	..	..	..	..
Finland	7.1	0.0	5.0	11.5	16.8	..	..	..	..	..
France	9.8	4.2	7.6	13.1	39.9	..	..	..	..	..
Germany	7.1	0.0	4.4	11.7	7.1	..	..	..	..	..
Greece	..	..	..	..	..	..	..	..	..	..
Hungary	5.8	0.5	3.7	14.4	7.5	..	..	..	..	..
Iceland	6.5	20.6	5.9	5.6	19.8	..	..	..	..	..
Ireland	6.4	2.1	5.8	10.2	25.3	..	..	..	..	..
Israel	..	..	..	..	..	..	..	3.1	4.2	4.6
Italy	..	..	..	..	..	4.4	5.4	4.4	4.0	12.5
Japan	3.5	3.6	2.6	7.6	18.8	..	..	..	..	..
Korea	..	..	..	..	..	1.7	0.2	1.5	6.2	7.7
Luxembourg	43.5	15.5	24.4	67.1	84.1	..	..	..	..	..
Mexico	0.2	0.0	0.2	0.7	2.6	..	..	..	..	..
Netherlands	10.2	1.5	8.4	17.4	37.8	..	..	..	..	..
New Zealand	16.1	20.7	13.1	20.3	43.3	..	..	..	..	..
Norway	3.6	5.4	1.8	7.0	20.9	..	..	..	..	..
Poland	1.5	0.0	1.1	2.2	1.6	..	..	..	..	..
Portugal	3.9	..	2.6	4.7	15.0	..	..	..	..	..
Slovak Republic	4.9	0.5	3.7	6.3	8.6	..	..	..	..	..
Slovenia	2.6	0.9	2.3	3.6	7.6	..	..	..	..	..
Spain	2.9	5.5	0.8	4.9	16.2	..	..	..	..	..
Sweden	5.8	0.2	2.4	9.3	31.5	..	..	..	..	..
Switzerland	16.8	..	10.1	27.4	52.1	..	..	..	..	..
Turkey	..	..	..	..	..	1.1	0.3	1.1	3.7	4.5
United Kingdom	17.5	5.0	13.2	36.1	41.4	..	..	..	..	..
United States	3.9	1.8	3.2	8.2	32.4	..	..	..	..	..
EU 28	..	..	..	..	..	..	..	..	..	..
OECD	8.6	5.1	6.2	13.9	23.9	..	..	..	..	..
Brazil	..	..	..	..	..	..	0.3	0.2	..	..
China	..	..	..	..	..	0.3	0.0	0.4	1.0	2.4
India	..	..	..	..	..	..	..	..	..	..
Indonesia	..	..	..	..	..	..	..	..	..	..
Russian Federation	..	..	..	..	..	1.7	0.8	..	3.1	3.9
South Africa	..	..	..	..	..	..	..	..	..	..

StatLink http://dx.doi.org/10.1787/888933336638

Distribution of foreign and international students in tertiary education

2013

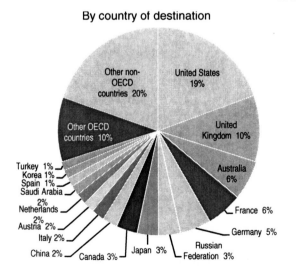

By country of destination

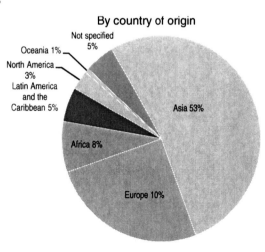

By country of origin

StatLink http://dx.doi.org/10.1787/888933335551

EDUCATIONAL ATTAINMENT

Educational attainment is a commonly used proxy for the stock of human capital – say, the skills available in the population and the labour force. As globalisation and technology continue to re-shape the needs of labour markets worldwide, the demand for individuals with a broader knowledge base and more specialised skills, e.g. advanced analytical capacities, and complex communication skills, continues to rise. As a result, more individuals are pursuing higher levels of education now than in previous generations, leading to significant shifts in attainment levels over time within countries.

Definition

Educational attainment refers to the highest level of education completed by a person, shown as a percentage of all persons in that age group. Below upper secondary education includes early childhood education, primary education or lower secondary education. Programmes at the lower secondary education level are designed to lay the foundation across a wide range of subjects. Programmes at the upper secondary level are more specialised and offer students more choices and diverse pathways for completing their secondary education. Tertiary education includes short-cycle tertiary education, bachelor's, master's, or doctoral or equivalent levels.

Comparability

The *International Standard Classification of Education* (ISCED 2011) is used to define the levels of education in a comparable way across countries. The ISCED 2011 *Operational Manual: Guidelines for Classifying National Education Programmes and Related Qualifications* describes ISCED 2011 education programmes and attainment levels and examples for each country.

Note that data for Brazil, Chile, France and Russia for 2014 refer to 2013 and for South Africa to year 2012. Data for Indonesia for 2014 refer to 2011 and data for 2010 refer to 2006. In the United Kingdom, data for upper secondary attainment include completion of a sufficient volume and standard of programmes that would be classified individually as completion of intermediate upper secondary programmes (18% of the adults are under this group).

Sources
- OECD (2015), *Education at a Glance*, OECD Publishing.

Further information

Analytical publications
- OECD (2016), *Trends Shaping Education*, OECD Publishing.
- OCDE (2015), *Reviews of National Policies for Education*, OECD Publishing.
- OECD (2012), *Let's Read Them a Story! The Parent Factor in Education*, PISA, OECD Publishing.

Statistical publications
- OECD (2014), *Highlights from Education at a Glance*, OECD Publishing.

Methodological publications
- OECD (2004), *OECD Handbook for Internationally Comparative Education Statistics: Concepts, Standards, Definitions and Classifications*, OECD Publishing.
- OECD/Eurostat/UNESCO Institute for Statistics (2015), *ISCED 2011 Operational Manual: Guidelines for Classifying National Education Programmes and Related Qualifications*, OECD Publishing.

Online databases
- *OECD Education Statistics*.

Websites
- OECD Centre for Educational Research and Innovation (CERI), *www.oecd.org/edu/ceri*.
- OECD Education at a Glance (supplementary material), *www.oecd.org/education/education-at-a-glance-19991487.htm*.

Overview

An indication of long-term trends in educational attainment can be obtained by comparing the current attainment levels of younger and older adults. Tertiary attainment levels have increased considerably over the past 30 years. On average across OECD countries, 41% of 25-34 year-olds have a tertiary attainment, compared with 25% of 55-64 year-olds. Canada, Korea and Russia lead in the proportion of young adults (25-34 year-olds) with a tertiary attainment, with 55% or more having reached this level of education. In Ireland, Korea and Poland, there is a difference of 25 percentage points or more between the proportion of young adults and older adults who have attained this level of education.

In 2014, over 30% of the population aged between 25 and 64 has attained tertiary level education in more than half of the OECD countries. On average across OECD countries, 24% of adults now have only primary or lower secondary levels of education, 43% have upper secondary education and 34% have a tertiary qualification.

Educational attainment

As a percentage of total population in that age group

	Population aged 25-34						Population aged 25-64					
	Below upper secondary		Upper secondary or post-secondary non-tertiary		Tertiary		Below upper secondary		Upper secondary or post-secondary non-tertiary		Tertiary	
	2000	2014	2000	2014	2000	2014	2000	2014	2000	2014	2000	2014
Australia	31.7	13.3	36.9	38.6	31.4	48.1	41.2	22.9	31.3	35.2	27.5	41.9
Austria	..	10.0	..	51.6	..	38.4	..	16.1	..	54.0	..	29.9
Belgium	24.7	17.7	39.3	38.0	36.0	44.2	41.5	26.4	31.4	36.7	27.1	36.9
Canada	11.7	7.4	39.9	34.9	48.4	57.7	19.3	10.0	40.6	36.4	40.1	53.6
Chile	..	20.0	..	52.7	..	27.3	..	38.6	..	40.3	..	21.1
Czech Republic	7.6	5.4	81.2	64.7	11.2	29.9	14.1	6.8	75.0	71.7	11.0	21.5
Denmark	13.1	17.8	57.6	40.0	29.3	42.1	20.2	20.4	54.0	43.8	25.8	35.8
Estonia	9.0	11.0	59.7	48.6	31.3	40.4	15.3	8.9	55.8	53.6	28.9	37.5
Finland	13.7	9.8	47.6	49.9	38.7	40.3	26.8	13.5	40.5	44.7	32.6	41.8
France	23.6	14.7	45.0	41.2	31.4	44.1	37.8	25.2	40.7	42.7	21.6	32.1
Germany	15.1	12.7	62.6	58.9	22.3	28.4	18.3	13.1	58.2	59.8	23.5	27.1
Greece	31.3	18.3	44.8	43.0	23.9	38.7	50.7	31.7	31.6	40.2	17.7	28.1
Hungary	18.7	13.0	66.6	54.9	14.7	32.1	30.8	16.9	55.2	59.7	14.0	23.4
Iceland	..	26.2	..	33.2	..	40.6	..	26.7	..	36.2	..	37.1
Ireland	27.0	9.9	43.2	39.3	29.8	50.8	42.7	21.2	35.7	37.8	21.6	41.0
Israel	..	9.2	..	44.8	..	46.0	..	14.6	..	36.8	..	48.5
Italy	43.6	26.2	46.0	49.7	10.4	24.2	57.9	40.7	32.7	42.4	9.4	16.9
Japan	..	..	..	..	..	..	..	..	..	..	..	..
Korea	6.7	1.7	56.4	30.6	36.9	67.7	31.7	15.0	44.4	40.4	23.9	44.6
Luxembourg	31.8	13.1	45.3	33.9	22.9	52.9	39.1	18.0	42.6	36.0	18.3	45.9
Mexico	62.9	54.4	19.6	21.0	17.5	24.6	70.9	66.3	14.5	15.1	14.6	18.5
Netherlands	25.7	14.8	47.7	40.9	26.6	44.3	35.1	24.1	41.5	41.5	23.4	34.4
New Zealand	31.3	18.9	..	40.7	..	40.4	36.8	25.9	..	38.4	..	35.6
Norway	6.6	18.6	58.5	32.4	34.9	49.0	14.8	18.1	56.8	40.2	28.4	41.8
Poland	10.6	5.8	75.2	51.6	14.2	42.6	20.1	9.5	68.5	63.5	11.4	27.0
Portugal	68.2	35.3	18.9	33.2	12.9	31.4	80.6	56.7	10.5	21.6	8.8	21.7
Slovak Republic	6.3	7.5	82.5	62.6	11.2	29.8	16.2	9.2	73.4	70.5	10.4	20.4
Slovenia	14.6	6.1	66.1	55.8	19.3	38.1	25.2	14.3	59.1	57.1	15.7	28.6
Spain	44.6	34.4	21.3	24.1	34.1	41.5	61.7	43.4	15.7	21.9	22.6	34.7
Sweden	12.7	18.2	53.6	35.9	33.6	46.0	22.4	18.4	47.4	42.9	30.1	38.7
Switzerland	10.2	9.0	64.2	45.0	25.6	46.0	16.1	12.0	59.7	47.8	24.2	40.2
Turkey	72.3	50.5	18.9	24.7	8.9	24.8	76.7	64.4	14.9	18.9	8.3	16.7
United Kingdom	33.2	13.8	37.9	37.1	28.9	49.2	37.4	20.8	36.9	36.9	25.7	42.2
United States	11.8	10.0	50.1	44.3	38.1	45.7	12.6	10.4	50.9	45.3	36.5	44.2
EU 28	..	..	..	..	..	..	..	..	..	..	..	..
OECD	24.8	16.8	49.5	42.4	25.9	40.8	35.0	23.6	43.6	42.7	21.5	33.6
Brazil	..	39.2	..	45.5	..	15.3	..	53.6	..	32.7	..	13.7
China	93.9	..	6.1	..	..	..	95.4	..	4.6	..	..	..
India	..	..	..	..	..	..	..	..	..	..	..	..
Indonesia	..	60.0	..	29.7	..	10.3	..	69.0	..	22.5	..	8.5
Russian Federation	..	5.2	..	36.6	..	58.2	..	5.3	..	40.4	..	54.3
South Africa	..	22.6	..	72.1	..	5.2	..	35.1	..	58.3	..	6.6

StatLink *http://dx.doi.org/10.1787/888933336678*

Population that has attained tertiary education

Percentage, 2014

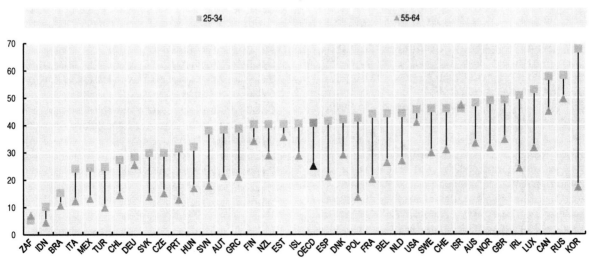

StatLink *http://dx.doi.org/10.1787/888933335606*

TEACHERS' SALARIES

Teachers' salaries represent the largest single cost in formal education and have a direct impact on the attractiveness of the teaching profession. They influence decisions to enrol in teacher education, become a teacher after graduation, return to the teaching profession after a career interruption, and/or remain a teacher (as, in general, the higher the salaries, the fewer the people who choose to leave the profession).

Definition

Salary structures usually define the salaries paid to teachers at different points in their careers. Deferred compensation, which rewards employees for staying in organisations or professions and for meeting established performance criteria, is also used in teachers' salary structures. OECD data on teachers' salaries are limited to information on statutory salaries at four points of the salary scale: starting salaries, salaries after 10 years of service, salaries after 15 years of experience, and salaries at the top of the scale. Salaries are for those teachers who have the typical qualification (i.e. that have the qualification held by the largest proportion of teachers across the teaching force). Qualifications beyond the minimum required to enter the teaching profession can lead to wage increases in some countries.

Comparability

Teachers' statutory salaries are one component of teachers' total compensation. Other benefits, such as regional allowances for teaching in remote areas, family allowances, reduced rates on public transport and tax allowances on the purchase of cultural materials, may also form part of teachers' total remuneration. There are also large differences in taxation and social-benefits systems in OECD countries. All this should be borne in mind when comparing salaries across countries.

In most OECD countries, teachers' salaries increase with the level of education they teach.

Overview

Teachers' salaries vary widely across countries. The salaries of lower secondary school teachers with 15 years of experience and typical qualification range from less than USD 15 000 in Estonia, Hungary, to more than USD 60 000 in Canada, Germany, the Netherlands and the United States and exceed USD 100 000 in Luxembourg.

Between 2000 and 2013, teachers' salaries rose, in real terms, in all countries with available data, except Denmark (upper secondary), France and Italy. However, in most countries, salaries increased less since 2005 than between 2000 and 2005.

Salaries at the top of the scale for teachers with typical qualifications are, on average, 64%, 66%, 65% and 66% higher, respectively, than starting salaries in pre-primary, primary, lower secondary and upper secondary education. The difference tends to be greatest when it takes many years to progress through the scale. In countries where it takes 30 years or more to reach the top of the salary scale, salaries at that level can be more than 90% higher, on average, than starting salaries..

On average across OECD countries with available data, teachers' salaries decreased, for the first time since 2000, by around 5% at all levels of education between 2009 and 2013. The economic downturn may also have an influence on the supply of teachers. In general, when the general economy is weak, and there is high unemployment among graduates and low graduate earnings, teaching might seem to be a more attractive job choice than other occupations.

Sources
• OECD (2015), *Education at a Glance*, OECD Publishing.
Further information
Analytical publications
• OECD (2013), *PISA 2012 Results: What Makes Schools Successful? Resources, Policies and Practices (Volume IV)*, PISA, OECD Publishing.
• OECD (2012), *Preparing teachers and developing school leaders for the 21st century: Lessons from Around the World*, OECD Publishing.
• Schleicher, A. (2011), *Building a High-Quality Teaching Profession: Lessons from around the World*, OECD Publishing.
Online databases
• *OECD Education Statistics*.
Websites
• OECD Education at a Glance (supplementary material), *www.oecd.org/education/education-at-a-glance-19991487.htm*.
• TALIS (OECD Teaching and Learning International Survey), *www.oecd.org/talis*.

Teachers' statutory salaries at different points in their careers
Primary education

| | 2005 = 100 | | Equivalent USD using PPPs | | | |
| | Change in salary after 15 years experience | | Starting salary | Salary after 10 years experience | Salary after 15 years experience | Salary at top of scale |
	2000	2013	2013	2013	2013	2013
Australia	..	111.1	39 177	56 335	56 335	56 521
Austria	91.0	101.2	32 610	38 376	43 015	64 014
Belgium	..	..	..	..	..	..
Canada	..	..	39 608	63 557	66 702	66 702
Chile	..	..	17 733	23 736	26 610	37 110
Czech Republic	..	..	17 033	17 529	18 273	20 795
Denmark	93.8	101.9	45 860	50 958	52 672	52 672
Estonia	85.3	131.4	13 004	13 233	13 233	17 015
Finland	87.4	107.2	32 356	37 453	39 701	42 083
France	104.8	93.8	27 254	31 229	33 500	49 398
Germany	..	107.9	51 389	60 449	63 221	67 413
Greece	..	74.1	17 760	22 460	25 826	34 901
Hungary	63.1	67.7	10 647	12 177	13 061	17 362
Iceland	..	88.5	26 046	29 165	31 145	31 145
Ireland	83.2	109.1	34 899	50 248	56 057	63 165
Israel	99.5	126.4	19 806	25 732	29 869	51 855
Italy	94.5	93.9	27 509	30 262	33 230	40 437
Japan	..	93.9	27 627	41 036	48 546	60 878
Korea	..	96.9	29 357	44 193	51 594	82 002
Luxembourg	..	139.9	68 873	91 203	102 956	123 406
Mexico	87.3	109.0	15 944	20 779	26 533	34 048
Netherlands	..	..	36 456	45 228	54 001	54 001
New Zealand	..	..	29 124	43 292	43 292	43 292
Norway	..	114.9	41 177	44 538	44 538	48 662
Poland	..	121.8	15 220	20 402	24 921	25 980
Portugal	..	84.8	30 806	33 740	36 663	57 201
Slovak Republic	..	..	11 116	13 351	15 650	16 869
Slovenia	86.2	100.0	25 134	31 077	38 261	45 764
Spain	..	95.2	36 422	39 468	42 187	51 265
Sweden	..	109.2	32 991	36 817	38 175	43 595
Switzerland	..	..	..	..	..	..
Turkey	99.4	114.2	25 295	26 107	27 139	29 342
United Kingdom	..	..	..	..	..	..
United States	82.0	98.4	41 606	53 799	59 339	66 938
EU 28	..	..	..	..	..	..
OECD	89.4	102.8	29 807	37 795	41 245	48 706
Brazil	..	..	..	..	..	..
China	..	..	..	..	..	..
India	..	..	..	..	..	..
Indonesia	..	..	..	..	..	..
Russian Federation	..	..	..	..	..	..
South Africa	..	..	..	..	..	..

StatLink ▄▆▇ http://dx.doi.org/10.1787/888933336663

Age distribution of teachers in secondary education
2013

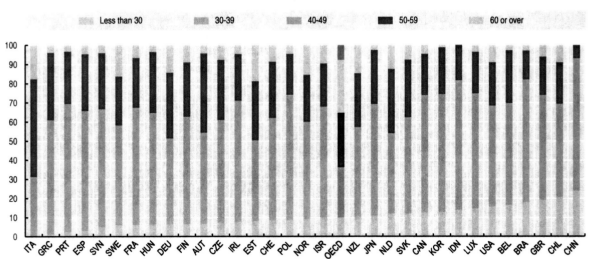

StatLink ▄▆▇ http://dx.doi.org/10.1787/888933335596

EDUCATIONAL EXPENDITURE

Expenditure on education is an investment that can foster economic growth, enhance productivity, contribute to personal and social development and reduce social inequality. The proportion of total financial resources devoted to education is one of the key choices made by governments, enterprises, students and their families. The demand for high-quality education, which can translate into higher costs per student, must be balanced against other demands on public expenditure and the overall tax burden. Policy makers must also balance the importance of improving the quality of educational services with the desirability of expanding access to educational opportunities.

Definition

Expenditure on institutions is not limited to expenditure on instruction services but includes public and private expenditure on ancillary services for students and their families, where these services are provided through educational institutions.

In principle, public expenditure includes both direct expenditure on educational institutions and educational related public subsidies to households administered by educational institutions. Private expenditure is recorded net of these public subsidies attributable to educational institutions; it also excludes expenditure made outside educational institutions (such as textbooks purchased by families, private tutoring for students and student living costs).

Comparability

Expenditure data were obtained by a special survey conducted in 2012 which applied consistent methods and definitions. Expenditure data are based on the definitions and coverage for the UNESCO-OECD-Eurostat data collection programme on education; they have been adjusted to 2012 prices using the GDP price deflator. The use of a common survey and definitions ensures good comparability of results across countries.

The level of expenditure on educational institutions is affected by the size of a country's school age population, enrolment rates, level of teachers' salaries, and the organisation and delivery of instruction. At the primary and lower secondary levels of education (corresponding broadly to the 5-14 year-old population), enrolment rates are close to 100% in OECD countries, and changes in the number of students are closely related to demographic changes. This is not as much the case in upper secondary and tertiary education, because part of the concerned population has left the education system.

Sources
• OECD (2015), *Education at a Glance*, OECD Publishing.

Further information

Analytical publications
• OECD (2016), *Trends Shaping Education*, OECD Publishing.
• OECD (2015), *Reviews of National Policies for Education*, OECD Publishing.

Methodological publications
• OECD/Eurostat/UNESCO Institute for Statistics (2015), *ISCED 2011 Operational Manual: Guidelines for Classifying National Education Programmes and Related Qualifications*, OECD Publishing.
• UNESCO Institute for Statistics (UIS), OECD and Eurostat (2013), *UOE Data Collection on Education Systems*, UIS, Montreal.

Online databases
• *OECD Education Statistics*.

Websites
• OECD Education at a Glance (supplementary material), *www.oecd.org/education/education-at-a-glance-19991487.htm*.

Overview

In 2012, primary, secondary and post-secondary non-tertiary education accounted for more than two thirds of expenditure on educational institutions, or 3.7% of the GDP, on average across OECD countries. New Zealand spent more than 5% of its GDP on these levels of education, while the Czech Republic, Hungary, Indonesia, Latvia, Russia and Turkey spent 3% or less.

In 2012, the OECD average level of annual expenditure per student for primary, secondary and post-secondary non-tertiary education was USD 8 982. Between 2000 and 2012, a period of relatively stable student enrolment at these levels, spending per student increased in every country, rising by 35% on average.

Expenditure on primary, secondary, post-secondary non tertiary institutions

	Annual expenditure per student (USD converted using PPPs for GDP)				2005 = 100						As a percentage of total expenditure	
	Primary	Secondary			Primary, secondary, post-secondary non tertiary institutions						Primary, secondary, post-secondary non tertiary institutions	
		Lower secondary	Upper secondary	All secondary	Change in expenditure		Change in number of students		Change in expenditure per student		Public sources	Private sources
	2012	2012	2012	2012	2000	2012	2000	2012	2000	2012	2012	2012
Australia	7 705	10 574	9 581	10 165	82.6	130.2	92.9	106.2	88.9	122.6	82.4	17.6
Austria	9 563	13 632	14 013	13 806	..	..	..	..	..	..	96.0	4.0
Belgium	9 581	11 670	12 210	12 025	..	114.7	90.9	96.5	..	118.9	96.3	3.7
Canada	9 680	..	11 695	..	83.7	114.7	99.1	96.4	84.4	118.9	91.0	9.0
Chile	4 476	4 312	3 706	3 909	95.8	139.5	98.6	89.6	97.2	155.7	78.0	22.0
Czech Republic	4 728	7 902	7 119	7 469	76.8	113.7	107.4	84.8	71.5	134.2	91.0	9.0
Denmark	10 953	11 460	9 959	10 632	86.1	80.7	95.1	..	90.5	..	97.2	2.8
Estonia	5 668	6 524	7 013	6 791	..	105.0	121.2	80.7	..	130.1	99.1	0.9
Finland	8 316	12 909	8 599	9 985	82.6	112.2	95.4	98.1	86.6	114.4	99.3	0.7
France	7 013	9 588	13 070	11 046	99.3	104.2	101.8	100.7	97.5	103.4	91.0	9.0
Germany	7 749	9 521	12 599	10 650	..	..	..	..	..	..	86.5	13.5
Greece	..	..	..	..	77.2	..	100.5	..	..	..	..	..
Hungary	4 370	4 459	4 386	4 419	68.4	75.2	104.3	90.5	65.5	83.1	94.2	5.8
Iceland	10 003	10 706	7 541	8 724	72.9	98.5	94.4	100.2	77.2	98.4	96.0	4.0
Ireland	8 681	11 087	11 564	11 298	69.0	138.5	97.0	109.4	71.2	126.6	95.7	4.3
Israel	6 931	..	..	5 689	99.2	154.0	94.1	111.8	105.5	137.7	88.9	11.1
Italy	7 924	8 905	8 684	8 774	96.4	89.6	98.6	99.3	97.8	90.2	95.5	4.5
Japan	8 595	9 976	10 360	10 170	98.5	106.3	109.2	94.2	90.3	112.8	92.9	7.1
Korea	7 395	7 008	9 651	8 355	68.9	125.2	102.1	86.3	67.5	145.1	83.9	16.1
Luxembourg	20 020	20 247	20 962	20 617	..	96.4	..	..	..	..	97.8	2.2
Mexico	2 632	2 367	4 160	3 007	80.4	118.7	94.6	107.2	85.0	110.7	82.8	17.2
Netherlands	8 185	12 227	12 368	12 296	82.3	113.1	96.7	101.4	85.1	111.6	86.7	13.3
New Zealand	7 069	8 644	10 262	9 409	..	..	..	..	..	..	82.5	17.5
Norway	12 728	13 373	15 248	14 450	86.8	112.5	94.5	103.8	91.8	108.3	..	..
Poland	6 721	6 682	6 419	6 540	89.8	124.6	109.7	77.0	81.9	161.9	92.0	8.0
Portugal	6 105	8 524	8 888	8 691	99.6	122.6	111.0	97.4	89.7	125.8	85.2	14.8
Slovak Republic	5 415	5 283	5 027	5 152	73.6	124.7	108.1	78.6	68.1	158.7	88.1	11.9
Slovenia	9 015	9 802	6 898	8 022	..	97.6	..	89.3	..	109.2	91.0	9.0
Spain	7 111	9 137	9 145	9 141	92.3	110.4	106.9	107.4	86.4	102.8	88.7	11.3
Sweden	10 312	10 966	11 329	11 177	88.3	102.7	98.4	91.0	89.7	112.9	100.0	0.0
Switzerland	13 889	16 370	17 024	16 731	86.6	110.5	100.1	96.6	86.5	114.3	88.5	11.5
Turkey	2 577	2 448	3 524	2 904	71.0	164.8	92.5	106.6	76.7	154.7	85.4	14.6
United Kingdom	10 017	10 271	9 963	10 085	..	112.1	112.6	103.7	..	108.1	84.0	16.0
United States	11 030	11 856	13 059	12 442	86.2	104.2	97.7	99.5	88.2	104.8	92.0	8.0
EU 28	..	..	..	..	..	..	..	..	..	..	..	..
OECD	8 247	9 627	9 876	9 518	84.4	113.9	100.9	96.6	84.5	120.6	90.6	9.4
Brazil	3 095	2 981	3 078	3 020	65.8	181.7	98.2	86.5	67.0	210.0	..	..
Indonesia	1 180	915	1 067	981	..	..	..	..	..	..	90.6	9.4
Russian Federation	..	..	..	5 345	65.7	150.7	..	87.8	..	171.7	96.7	3.3
South Africa	2 431	..	..	2 440	..	..	..	..	..	..	..	..

StatLink http://dx.doi.org/10.1787/888933336128

Total public expenditure on primary to tertiary education, change between 2008 and 2012

As a percentage of total public expenditure, 2008 = 100, 2012 constant prices

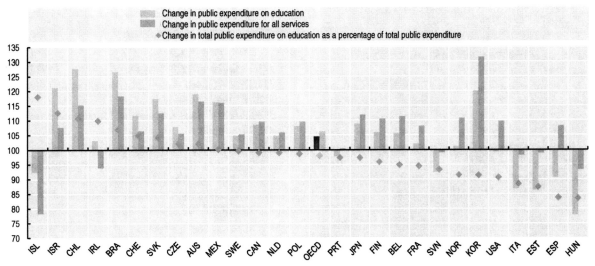

StatLink http://dx.doi.org/10.1787/888933334944

EXPENDITURE IN TERTIARY EDUCATION

Educational institutions in OECD countries are mainly publicly funded, although there are substantial and growing levels of private funding at the tertiary level. At this level, the contribution to the costs of education by individuals and other private entities is more and more considered an effective way to ensure funding is available to students regardless of their economic backgrounds.

Definition

Covered are public and private expenditure on schools, universities and other private institutions delivering or supporting educational services. Other private entities include private businesses and non-profit organisations, e.g. religious organisations, charitable organisations and business and labour associations. Expenditure by private companies on the work-based element of school- and work-based training of apprentices and students is also taken into account.

Private expenditure is recorded net of public subsidies to educational institutions; it also includes expenditures made outside educational institutions.

Comparability

The data on expenditure were obtained by a survey conducted in 2011 which applied consistent methods and definitions. Expenditure data are based on the definitions and coverage for the UNESCO-OECD-Eurostat data collection programme on education; they have been adjusted to 2012 prices using the GDP price deflator. The use of a common survey and definitions ensures good comparability of results across countries.

Educational expenditure in national currency for 2012 is converted into equivalent USD by dividing the national currency figure by the purchasing power parity (PPP) index for GDP. PPPs are used because market exchange rates are affected by many factors that are unrelated to the purchasing power of currencies in different countries.

Overview

In 2012, the average level of expenditure per tertiary student, across OECD countries, was USD 15 028. Spending per student at tertiary level ranged from USD 8 000 or less in Chile, Indonesia, Latvia, South Africa and Turkey to more than USD 20 000 in Canada, Norway, Sweden, Switzerland, the United Kingdom, and the United States and even more than USD 30 000 in Luxembourg.

Expenditure on tertiary education amounts to more than 1.5% of GDP in more than half of all countries, and exceeds 2.0% in Canada (2.5%), Chile (2.5%), Korea (2.3%) and the United States (2.8%). Five countries devote less than 1% of GDP to tertiary education, namely Brazil (0.9%), Italy (0.9%), Indonesia (0.8%), Luxembourg (0.4%) and South Africa (0.7%).

High private returns to tertiary education suggest that a greater contribution to the costs of education by individuals and other private entities may be justified, as long as there are ways to ensure that funding is available to students regardless of their economic backgrounds.

The proportion of expenditure on tertiary institutions covered by individuals, businesses and other private sources, including subsidised private payments, ranges from 5% or less in Finland and Norway (tuition fees charged by tertiary institutions are low or negligible in these countries), to more than 40% in Australia, Canada, Chile, Hungary, Israel, Japan Korea, New Zealand, the United Kingdom and the United States, and to over 70% in Korea. Of these countries, in Korea and the United Kingdom, most students are enrolled in private institutions (around 80% in private universities in Korea; 100% in government-dependent private institutions in the United Kingdom).

Sources
- OECD (2015), *Education at a Glance*, OECD Publishing.

Further information

Analytical publications
- OECD (2016), *Trends Shaping Education*, OECD Publishing.
- OECD (2015), *Reviews of National Policies for Education*, OECD Publishing.
- OECD (2014), *Higher Education Management and Policy*, OECD Publishing.

Methodological publications
- OECD/Eurostat/UNESCO Institute for Statistics (2015), *ISCED 2011 Operational Manual: Guidelines for Classifying National Education Programmes and Related Qualifications*, OECD Publishing.

Online databases
- OECD Education Statistics.

Websites
- OECD Education at a Glance (supplementary material), *www.oecd.org/education/education-at-a-glance-19991487.htm*.

Expenditure on tertiary institutions

| | Annual expenditure per student by educational institutions for all services (USD converted using PPPs for GDP) | | | All tertiary excluding R&D activities | 2005 = 100 | | | | | | As a percentage of total expenditure | |
| | Tertiary (including R&D activities), 2012 | | All tertiary | | Change in expenditure | | Change in number of students | | Change in expenditure per student | | Public sources | Private sources |
	Short-cycle tertiary	Bachelor's, master's, doctoral or equivalent level		2012	2000	2012	2000	2012	2000	2012	2012	2012
Australia	8 267	18 795	16 859	10 455	83.5	132.6	..	132.8	..	99.8	44.9	55.1
Austria	15 071	15 641	15 549	11 616	..	..	..	..	..	..	95.3	4.7
Belgium	8 212	15 785	15 503	10 156	..	123.6	94.4	119.4	..	103.5	89.9	10.1
Canada	15 348	25 525	22 006	15 788	83.6	113.0	..	..	..	..	54.9	45.1
Chile	4 186	9 409	7 960	7 600	84.4	186.8	73.1	177.6	115.5	105.2	34.6	65.4
Czech Republic	16 645	10 304	10 319	6 807	65.3	172.2	72.3	129.6	90.2	132.9	79.3	20.7
Denmark	..	..	..	..	86.5	..	97.8	..	88.5	..	..	..
Estonia		8 206	8 206	4 690	..	158.0	85.5	96.8	..	163.3	78.2	21.8
Finland	..	17 863	17 863	10 728	87.6	117.5	95.0	99.9	92.2	117.6	96.2	3.8
France	12 346	16 279	15 281	10 361	93.0	118.7	95.3	104.1	97.6	114.0	79.8	20.2
Germany	8 265	17 159	17 157	10 025	..	..	..	..	..	..	85.9	14.1
Greece	..	..	..	..	42.0	..	67.5	..	62.1	..	..	..
Hungary	2 897	9 658	8 876	7 405	80.5	79.0	63.9	93.1	126.0	84.9	54.4	45.6
Iceland	9 665	9 373	9 377	..	69.9	107.2	67.6	119.7	103.4	89.6	90.6	9.4
Ireland	..	..	14 922	11 418	102.4	125.3	85.2	113.6	120.2	110.3	81.8	18.2
Israel	6 366	13 777	12 338	7 710	82.7	117.1	80.2	114.4	103.1	102.4	52.4	47.6
Italy	..	10 071	10 071	6 369	93.0	107.3	89.7	94.4	103.8	113.7	66.0	34.0
Japan	10 532	18 557	16 872	..	93.7	114.2	98.9	96.0	94.8	119.0	34.3	65.7
Korea	5 540	11 173	9 866	8 026	78.6	142.1	93.4	103.1	84.2	137.9	29.3	70.7
Luxembourg	3 749	34 739	32 876	21 358	..	..	..	..	..	..	94.8	5.2
Mexico	..	..	8 115	6 647	73.5	135.3	82.8	133.3	88.8	101.5	69.7	30.3
Netherlands	11 580	19 305	19 276	12 505	84.6	124.9	85.3	122.5	99.2	101.9	70.5	29.5
New Zealand	10 289	14 543	13 740	10 841	..	..	..	..	..	..	52.4	47.6
Norway	..	20 016	20 016	12 010	83.2	108.2	87.8	103.5	94.8	104.5	96.1	3.9
Poland	8 229	9 811	9 799	7 692	57.7	112.9	59.7	88.4	96.7	127.7	77.6	22.4
Portugal	..	9 196	9 196	4 917	71.4	102.9	90.4	108.3	79.0	94.9	54.3	45.7
Slovak Republic	..	9 022	9 022	6 191	66.9	151.7	71.3	117.0	93.8	129.6	73.8	26.2
Slovenia	6 874	11 615	11 002	8 888	..	103.0	..	94.8	..	108.7	86.1	13.9
Spain	9 394	13 040	12 356	8 983	87.0	116.9	107.5	117.5	80.9	99.5	73.1	26.9
Sweden	5 897	24 025	22 534	10 589	86.7	121.0	82.3	101.9	105.3	118.7	89.3	10.7
Switzerland	..	..	25 264	11 632	76.4	111.2	75.6	128.0	101.1	86.9	..	..
Turkey	..	..	7 779	5 557	76.8	192.8	71.9	158.6	106.9	121.5	80.4	19.6
United Kingdom	..	..	24 338	18 593	..	..	..	105.1	..	..	56.9	43.1
United States	..	..	26 562	23 706	78.1	124.5	88.6	129.7	88.2	96.0	37.8	62.2
EU 28	..	..	..	..	..	..	..	..	..	..	..	..
OECD	8 968	15 111	15 028	10 309	79.6	126.7	83.6	114.9	96.5	111.0	69.7	30.3
Brazil	..	..	10 455	9 595	78.9	148.8	70.4	160.5	112.1	92.7	..	..
Indonesia	..	..	2 089	..	..	..	..	..	..	..	70.7	29.3
Russian Federation	5 183	9 115	8 363	7 641	44.3	141.9	..	142.3	..	99.7	63.5	36.5
South Africa	..	..	10 885	..	..	..	..	..	..	..	..	..

StatLink http://dx.doi.org/10.1787/888933336062

Share of public expenditure on tertiary institutions
Percentage

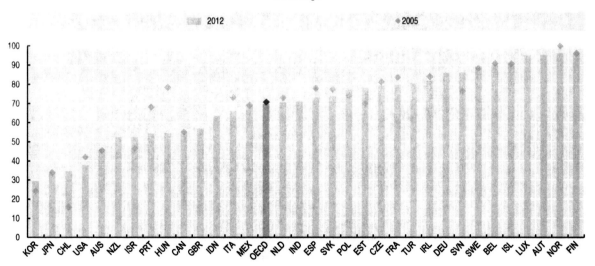

StatLink http://dx.doi.org/10.1787/888933334885

GOVERNMENT

GOVERNMENT EXPENDITURES, REVENUES AND DEFICITS

Net lending reflects the fiscal position of government after accounting for capital expenditures. Positive net lending means that government is providing financial resources to other sectors and negative net lending means that government requires financial resources from other economic sectors.

While general government net lending is an important concept in the *System of National Accounts* (SNA) accounting framework and provides the basis for sound international comparisons, net lending is not necessarily the key fiscal measure targeted by governments. Some countries for example manage their budgets using broader notions that incorporate the positions of public corporations and others focus on more narrow concepts such as central government.

Definition

Total general government expenditures include the following items: intermediate consumption; compensation of employees, subsidies, social benefits and social transfers in kind (via market producers); other current transfers; property income; capital transfers (payable); the adjustment for the net equity of households in pension funds reserves; gross capital formation; and net acquisition of non-financial non-produced assets. It also includes taxes on income and wealth and other taxes on production that governments may be required to pay.

Revenues include taxes (on corporations and households, and those on income, wealth, production and imports), social security contributions, property income and other income.

Comparability

The biggest issue affecting comparability across countries concerns the scope of the government sector. In many countries, hospitals, for example, are classified outside of the government sector and are instead recorded as public corporations on the grounds that they charge market prices for their services. EU countries have adopted a 50% rule, i.e. sales should cover at least 50% of the operating costs to qualify the relevant units as market producers outside government.

Another potential area where comparability may be affected relates to the determination of public ownership. The SNA requires that "control" be the determining factor for recording a non-market producer inside or outside government, and describes a number of criteria that can be used to assess this requirement. Recognising that this is non-trivial it includes a practical recommendation that a 50% rule relating to ownership should be adopted.

Generally however, the comparability of figures for countries is very high. For most general government expenditures there is little scope for ambiguity in treatment and the quality of underlying data is very good, so the level of comparability is good. Data for all countries are on a consolidated basis, except Canada (which consolidates only current transfers) and New Zealand.

Overview

Since the onset of the financial crisis, most OECD countries have recorded fiscal deficits. In 2010, deficits larger than 10% of GDP were recorded for Ireland, the United States, Greece and Portugal. The large deficit in Ireland of 32.3% partly reflected one-off payments to support the financial system. In contrast, four countries recorded surpluses, most notably in Norway (at 11%). In 2014, fiscal balances improved in most OECD countries for which data are available. Two countries had deficits greater than 7.0%: Japan (minus 8.5%) and Portugal (minus 7.2%)

There is a big variation in the shares of government expenditure and revenue as a percentage of GDP across OECD countries. Looking at revenues in 2014, seven countries reported revenues as a percentage of GDP of less than 35.0%: the lowest were reported for Mexico (24.5%) and the United States (33.1%). On the other hand, six countries reported revenues as a percentage of GDP greater than 50.0%: the highest were recorded for Denmark (58.4%), Finland (54.9%), and Norway (54.7%).

Sources

• OECD (2015), *National Accounts of OECD countries*, OECD Publishing.

Further information

Analytical publications

• OECD (2015), *OECD Economic Outlook*, OECD Publishing.
• OECD (2015), *OECD Economic Surveys*, OECD Publishing.

Methodological publications

• OECD (2008), *OECD Glossary of Statistical Terms*, OECD Publishing.

Online databases

• OECD National Accounts Statistics.
• OECD Economic Outlook: Statistics and Projections.

Websites

• Financial statistics, *www.oecd.org/std/fin-stats*.
• Sources & Methods of the OECD Economic Outlook, *www.oecd.org/eco/sources-and-methods*.

General government revenues and expenditures

As a percentage of GDP

	Net lending				Revenues				Expenditures			
	2000	2005	2010	2014 or latest available year	2000	2005	2010	2014 or latest available year	2000	2005	2010	2014 or latest available year
Australia	-1.1	1.6	-4.6	-2.6	35.1	36.3	32.2	34.0	..	..	..	..
Austria	-2.0	-2.5	-4.4	-2.7	48.3	48.5	48.3	50.0	50.3	51.0	52.7	50.9
Belgium	-0.1	-2.6	-4.0	-3.1	49.0	48.9	49.3	52.0	48.6	50.8	52.4	54.8
Canada	2.9	1.7	-4.9	-1.6	43.4	40.1	38.3	37.7	..	..	..	..
Chile	..	..	0.0	-0.4	..	..	..	..	..	..	..	..
Czech Republic	-3.5	-3.1	-4.4	-1.9	36.9	38.7	38.6	40.6	40.4	41.8	43.0	42.1
Denmark	1.9	5.0	-2.7	1.5	54.6	56.2	54.3	58.4	52.7	51.2	57.1	56.9
Estonia	-0.1	1.1	0.2	0.7	36.3	35.1	40.7	38.7	36.4	33.9	40.4	38.3
Finland	6.9	2.6	-2.6	-3.3	54.9	51.9	52.1	54.9	48.0	49.3	54.8	57.6
France	-1.3	-3.2	-6.8	-3.9	49.8	49.7	49.6	53.6	51.1	52.9	56.4	57.0
Germany	0.9	-3.4	-4.2	0.3	45.6	42.8	43.0	44.6	44.6	46.0	47.1	44.1
Greece	..	..	-11.2	-3.6	..	..	41.3	46.4	..	..	..	..
Hungary	-3.0	-7.8	-4.5	-2.5	44.2	41.7	45.0	47.4	47.2	49.6	49.6	49.4
Iceland	1.2	4.5	-9.8	-0.1	42.6	45.9	39.6	45.6	..	..	..	44.1
Ireland	4.9	1.3	-32.3	-3.9	35.8	34.7	33.3	34.4	30.9	33.3	65.6	39.5
Israel	-3.4	-4.2	-4.1	-3.5	44.7	41.8	37.6	37.7	48.2	45.9	41.6	41.2
Italy	-1.3	-4.2	-4.2	-3.0	44.2	43.0	45.6	48.2	45.5	47.1	49.9	50.9
Japan	-7.5	-4.8	-8.3	-8.5	31.3	31.6	32.4	33.9	..	36.4	40.6	42.4
Korea	4.4	1.6	1.0	1.2	29.1	31.0	32.0	33.2	24.7	29.5	31.0	31.8
Luxembourg	5.7	0.2	-0.5	1.4	42.0	42.7	43.3	43.8	36.9	43.0	44.2	43.1
Mexico	..	1.6	-0.6	0.1	..	21.1	23.0	24.5	..	..	..	..
Netherlands	1.9	-0.3	-5.0	-2.4	43.6	42.1	43.2	43.9	41.8	42.3	48.2	46.2
New Zealand	1.7	4.6	-6.7	-0.4	39.3	42.1	40.7	39.7	..	..	..	..
Norway	15.1	14.8	11.0	9.1	57.1	56.9	56.0	54.7	..	42.1	45.0	44.0
Poland	-3.0	-4.0	-7.5	-3.3	39.0	40.5	38.1	38.8	..	..	..	..
Portugal	-3.2	-6.2	-11.2	-7.2	39.4	40.5	40.6	44.5	42.6	46.7	51.8	50.4
Slovak Republic	-12.0	-2.9	-7.5	-2.8	40.0	36.7	34.5	38.9	51.8	39.4	41.9	40.9
Slovenia	-3.6	-1.3	-5.6	-5.0	42.5	43.6	43.6	44.8	46.1	44.9	49.2	60.1
Spain	-1.0	1.2	-9.4	-5.9	38.1	39.5	36.2	38.6	39.1	38.3	45.6	45.1
Sweden	3.2	1.8	0.0	-1.7	56.8	54.5	51.1	50.1	53.6	52.7	52.0	53.4
Switzerland	-0.4	-1.2	0.3	-0.2	33.7	32.8	33.3	33.5	..	34.0	32.9	33.5
Turkey	..	..	-2.9	-0.8	..	..	37.3	36.6	..	..	40.2	37.4
United Kingdom	1.2	-3.5	-9.7	-5.7	39.0	39.2	39.1	38.2	37.8	42.7	48.7	45.0
United States	0.8	-4.1	-12.0	-4.9	34.5	32.3	30.9	33.1	33.7	36.4	42.6	39.0
EU 28	..	..	..	..	..	..	..	..	..	..	..	..
OECD	..	..	..	..	..	..	..	..	..	..	..	..
Brazil	..	..	-2.8	-2.2	..	..	..	..	..	..	..	..
China	-7.0	-0.2	1.5	1.2	..	..	..	..	..	..	..	..
India	..	..	..	..	..	..	..	..	..	..	..	..
Indonesia	..	..	..	..	..	..	..	..	..	..	..	..
Russian Federation	..	6.0	-1.2	0.3	..	40.2	38.5	40.2	..	34.2	39.3	38.7
South Africa	..	..	-3.1	-4.1	..	..	..	..	..	..	..	..

StatLink ⟶ http://dx.doi.org/10.1787/888933336228

General government net lending

As a percentage of GDP

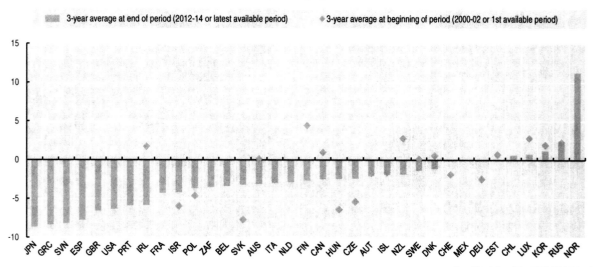

StatLink ⟶ http://dx.doi.org/10.1787/888933335038

GOVERNMENT DEBT

The accumulation of government debt is a key determinant of the sustainability of government finance. Apart from net acquisitions of financial assets, changes in government debt over time reflect the accumulation of government deficits/surpluses.

The government debt-to-GDP ratio, calculated as the amount of total gross government debt of a country as a percentage of its Gross Domestic Product (GDP), is one of the indicators of the health of an economy.

Definition

Generally, debt is defined as all liabilities that require payment or payments of interest or principal by the debtor to the creditor at a date or dates in the future.

Consequently, all debt instruments are liabilities, but some liabilities such as equity and investment fund shares and financial derivatives are not debt. Debt is thus obtained as the sum of the following liability categories: monetary gold and Special Drawing Rights (SDRs), currency and deposits; debt securities; loans; insurance, pension, and standardised guarantees; and other accounts payable. Importantly, debt securities are valued at market prices.

Comparability

The comparability of data on general government debt can be affected by the delineation of the government sector. The degree of consolidation within the government sector may also have an impact on the international comparability of data. Consolidated data are provided by all OECD countries, except: Chile, Japan, and Mexico.

The status and treatment of government liabilities in respect of their employee pension plans in the national accounts is diverse, making international comparability of government debt difficult. In particular, the 2008 SNA recognises the importance of the liabilities of employers' pension schemes, regardless of whether they are funded or unfunded. However, for pensions provided by government to their employees, countries have some flexibility in the recording of the unfunded liabilities. A few OECD countries, such as Australia, Canada, Iceland, Sweden and the United States, record unfunded liabilities of government employee pension plans in general government debt data. To enhance the comparability across OECD countries, an adjusted debt-to-GDP ratio is calculated for all countries by excluding from the gross debt these unfunded pension liabilities. For the aforementioned five countries, a debt-to-GDP ratio including unfunded pension liabilities, measures the impact of this recording on the ratio. For Australia, the difference between the two ratios accounts for 22.5% of GDP in 2014.

All countries compile data according to the 2008 SNA "System of National Accounts, 2008" with the exception of Chile, Japan, and Turkey, where data are compiled according to the 1993 SNA.

Overview

In 2014, 19 OECD countries recorded adjusted debt-to-GDP ratios above 60% compared with 12 countries in 2007. In 2014, countries that recorded the highest debt-to-GDP ratios were Greece (180%), Italy (156%), and Portugal (150%). Japan recorded the highest debt ratio at 239% in 2013, the latest year available. In 2014, the lowest debt-to-GDP ratios were found in Estonia (14%) and Chile (23%).

Ireland recorded the highest increase in its debt-to-GDP ratio between 2007 and 2014 (98 percentage points), reaching a level of 125% in 2014. Other countries with a considerable increase of more than 50 percentage points in the period 2007-14 were Spain (76 percentage points), Portugal (72 percentage points) and Slovenia (68 percentage points). By contrast, Norway's government debt, as a percentage of GDP, declined by 23 percentage points between 2007 and 2014.

The rapid rise in debt-to-GDP ratios from 2007 reflects reduced tax revenues, increases in government budget deficits and the cost of government interventions to support the financial system.

Sources
- OECD (2015), "Financial Balance Sheets", *OECD National Accounts Statistics* (Database).

Further information

Analytical publications
- Bloch, D. and F. Fall (2015), "Government Debt Indicators: Understanding the Data", *OECD Economics Department Working Papers*, No. 1228, OECD Publishing.
- OECD (2015), *OECD Economic Outlook*, OECD Publishing.

Statistical publications
- OECD (2015), *National Accounts at a Glance*, OECD Publishing.
- OECD (2014), *National Accounts of OECD Countries, Financial Balance Sheets*, OECD Publishing.

Methodological publications
- OECD, et al. (2009), *System of National Accounts*, United Nations, New York.

Websites
- Financial statistics, *www.oecd.org/std/fin-stats*.

Adjusted general government debt (excluding unfunded pension liabilities)
As a percentage of GDP

	2002	2003	2004	2005	2006	2007	2008	2009	2010	2011	2012	2013	2014
Australia	23.9	20.9	21.4	21.0	19.7	19.5	20.7	25.4	28.5	33.1	36.6	37.0	40.7
Austria	73.4	72.0	71.3	75.8	72.4	68.7	74.0	86.3	90.3	91.3	97.5	93.6	102.2
Belgium	118.0	114.4	110.1	107.6	99.7	93.5	100.8	109.2	107.4	109.8	119.9	117.7	129.3	
Canada	84.8	80.3	76.5	75.8	74.9	70.4	74.7	87.4	89.5	93.1	95.9	92.3	94.6
Chile	..	..	..	17.4	14.1	12.2	12.4	13.4	15.6	18.3	18.8	19.4	23.1
Czech Republic	30.1	32.6	32.2	31.9	31.6	30.3	34.2	41.0	45.8	48.1	57.8	57.9	57.0
Denmark	58.1	56.1	52.4	45.1	40.5	34.6	42.0	49.5	53.8	60.6	61.5		58.0	60.6
Estonia	7.6	8.4	8.6	8.2	8.0	7.2	8.4	12.6	11.9	9.4	12.9	13.4	13.6
Finland	48.2	49.2	49.4	46.5	43.1	39.1	38.3	49.2	55.1	57.5	63.4	64.4	71.0
France	74.6	78.5	80.0	81.7	76.9	75.6	81.5	93.2	96.8	100.7	110.4	110.1	119.2
Germany	61.3	64.8	67.7	70.3	68.4	64.3	68.1	75.6	84.1	83.5	86.4	81.6	82.2
Greece	111.0	105.7	107.2	111.3	115.8	113.1	117.4	134.7	128.4	110.7	167.0	181.7	179.8
Hungary	60.0	60.7	64.1	67.1	70.7	71.5	75.0	84.1	86.0	95.0	97.9	95.9	99.3
Iceland	..	39.9	34.8	26.5	32.1	30.2	70.9	85.6	90.9	97.5	95.5	87.8	..
Ireland	34.1	32.9	31.5	31.4	27.6	27.4	47.5	67.8	84.6	109.2	129.7	133.0	125.4
Israel	94.9	100.2	98.0	95.7	85.4	81.3	81.0	84.0	80.3	78.6	79.0	77.0	..
Italy	116.9	114.2	114.6	117.4	115.0	110.6	112.9	125.9	124.8	117.8	136.0	143.2	156.2
Japan	161.8	172.3	178.8	180.2	180.0	180.0	184.2	207.3	210.6	226.5	234.8	239.3	..
Korea	..	..	..	..	..	..	..	..	..	..	..	..	..
Luxembourg	12.3	13.2	14.1	12.4	11.9	11.6	19.2	18.9	26.2	27.0	30.6	30.0	33.7
Mexico	..	42.5	38.0	35.5	34.9	37.9	41.9	44.3	40.8	46.4	49.6	48.7	..
Netherlands	56.9	58.0	58.0	57.1	51.0	48.2	61.0	63.7	67.6	71.6	77.4	76.4	81.0
New Zealand	..	..	..	..	..	..	..	..	..	..	..	..	..
Norway	38.7	48.0	49.9	46.9	57.8	55.6	54.2	48.1	48.4	33.8	34.5	34.8	32.4
Poland	..	54.8	53.7	54.4	54.5	50.9	53.9	57.1	60.7	61.1	60.7	62.6	65.9
Portugal	66.8	70.6	76.7	80.0	79.4	78.1	82.8	96.1	104.1	107.8	136.9	140.7	149.9
Slovak Republic	49.4	47.5	45.1	38.1	36.0	34.5	33.5	42.0	46.9	49.4	57.7	60.7	60.1
Slovenia	34.0	33.5	34.3	33.4	33.3	29.1	28.3	42.5	46.8	50.4	60.6	79.5	97.3
Spain	59.3	54.4	52.5	50.0	45.7	41.7	47.1	61.7	66.5	77.5	92.0	103.8	117.7
Sweden	57.7	56.6	56.0	56.9	51.0	45.4	44.0	47.2	44.8	45.1	45.3	47.3	53.8
Switzerland	58.9	57.4	58.1	56.1	50.1	49.9	46.1	44.9	43.5	43.3	44.5	..	..
Turkey	..	..	..	..	..	..	..	54.3	52.5	47.8	46.4	39.7	..
United Kingdom	46.0	45.6	48.9	50.8	50.0	51.0	61.7	75.5	88.0	101.5	106.6	102.6	113.6
United States	55.2	58.2	65.1	64.3	63.0	63.1	71.7	84.8	93.4	97.6	101.0	103.2	103.4
EU 28	..	..	..	..	..	..	..	..	..	..	..	..	..
OECD	..	..	..	..	..	..	..	..	..	..	..	..	..
Brazil	..	..	..	..	..	..	..	..	..	..	..	..	..
China	..	..	..	..	..	..	..	..	..	..	..	..	..
India	..	..	..	..	..	..	..	..	..	..	..	..	..
Indonesia	..	..	..	..	..	..	..	..	..	..	..	..	..
Russian Federation	..	..	..	..	..	..	..	..	..	..	..	..	..
South Africa	..	..	..	..	..	..	..	..	..	..	..	..	..

StatLink ⟲ http://dx.doi.org/10.1787/888933336216

General government debt-to-GDP (including unfunded pension liabilities)
As a percentage of GDP

	2002	2003	2004	2005	2006	2007	2008	2009	2010	2011	2012	2013	2014
Australia	40.7	38.3	37.5	36.7	36.3	34.1	35.1	43.3	46.9	50.8	62.8	58.5	63.2
Canada	101.3	96.3	91.7	90.5	89.1	84.3	88.5	102.1	103.8	106.8	109.4	105.7	107.6
Iceland	..	66.1	59.6	49.7	54.9	49.8	95.7	109.4	114.6	122.1	120.2	112.2	..
Sweden	64.2	63.0	62.5	63.6	57.6	51.9	50.7	54.5	51.9	52.8	53.4	55.9	62.5
United States	70.5	71.4	79.2	78.5	76.2	76.5	92.3	105.7	116.0	121.6	124.7	123.8	123.2

StatLink ⟲ http://dx.doi.org/10.1787/888933336815

EXPENDITURES ACROSS LEVELS OF GOVERNMENT

The responsibility for the provision of public goods and services and redistribution of income is divided between different levels of government. In some countries, local and regional governments play a larger role in delivering services, such as providing public housing or running schools. Data on the distribution of government spending by both level and function can provide an indication of the extent to which key government activities are decentralised to sub-national governments.

Definition

Data on government expenditures are derived from the *OECD Annual National Accounts*, which are based on the *System of National Accounts* (SNA), a set of internationally agreed concepts, definitions, classifications and rules for national accounting. The general government sector consists of central, state and local governments and the social security funds controlled by these units. Data on the distribution of general government expenditures across levels of government exclude transfers between levels of government and thus provide a rough proxy of the overall responsibility for providing goods and services borne by each level of government. For the central level of government, data on expenditures are shown here according to the *Classification of the Functions of Government*. Data on central government expenditures by function include transfers between the different levels of government.

Comparability

Data for Australia, Korea, Japan and Turkey on the distribution of general government expenditures across levels of government include transfers between levels of government. The state government category is only applicable to the nine OECD countries that are federal states: Australia, Austria, Belgium, Canada, Germany, Mexico, Spain (considered a quasi-federal country), Switzerland and the United States. Local government is included in state government for Australia and the United States.

Social security funds are included in central government in Ireland, New Zealand, Norway, the United Kingdom and the United States. Australia does not operate government social insurance schemes. The OECD average does not include Chile and Turkey for general government expenditures across levels of government and does not include Canada, Chile, Mexico, New Zealand and Turkey for central government expenditures by function. Data for Australia refer to 2012 rather than 2013 for government expenditures across levels of government and data for Iceland refer to 2012 rather than 2013 for central government expenditures by function.

Overview

Across the OECD, in 2013, 42.8% of general government expenditures were undertaken by central government. Sub-central governments (state and local) covered 37.8% and social security funds accounted for the remaining 19.4%. However, the level of fiscal decentralisation varies considerably across countries. In Ireland, for example, 90.4% of total expenditure is carried out by central government, representing an increase of 8.4 percentage points from 2007, by contrast, state and local governments in Belgium, Canada, Germany, Spain, Switzerland and Mexico (federal or quasi-federal states) account for a larger share of public expenditures than the central government.

In general, central governments spend a relatively larger proportion of their budgets on social protection (e.g. pensions and unemployment benefits), general public services (e.g. executive and legislative organs, public debt transactions) and defence than state and local governments. In half of OECD countries, expenditures on social protection represent the largest share of central government budgets. In Belgium and Spain, central governments allocate over 60% of their budgets to general public services.

Sources
- OECD (2015), *Government at a Glance*, OECD Publishing.

Further information

Analytical publications
- OECD (2013), *Value for Money in Government*, OECD Publishing.

Statistical publications
- OECD (2015), *National Accounts of OECD Countries*, OECD Publishing.
- OECD (2014), *National Accounts at a Glance*, OECD Publishing.
- OECD (2014), *Quarterly National Accounts*, OECD Publishing.

Online databases
- *"General Government Accounts: Government expenditure by function"*, OECD National Accounts Statistics.
- *"National Accounts at a Glance"*, OECD National Accounts Statistics.
- *Government at a Glance*.

Websites
- Government at a Glance (supplementary material), *www.oecd.org/gov/govataglance.htm*.

Structure of central government expenditures by function

Percentage, 2013 or latest available year

	General public services	Defence	Public order and safety	Economic affairs	Environmental protection	Housing and community amenities	Health	Recreation, culture and religion	Education	Social protection
Australia	..	..	..	..	..	..	..	..	..	..
Austria	35.7	1.8	3.4	10.8	0.8	0.1	4.0	1.0	9.9	32.5
Belgium	67.2	3.0	3.7	7.4	1.2	0.0	2.8	0.2	4.8	9.7
Canada	..	..	..	..	..	..	..	..	..	..
Chile	..	..	..	..	..	..	..	..	..	..
Czech Republic	12.4	2.5	5.4	14.1	0.8	0.9	5.0	1.2	14.0	43.7
Denmark	29.4	3.1	2.2	6.0	0.4	0.4	11.3	2.4	9.7	35.0
Estonia	17.4	6.4	6.5	12.1	1.5	0.0	7.4	4.0	9.0	35.8
Finland	22.7	5.2	3.9	11.6	0.7	0.7	11.4	2.5	12.6	28.7
France	31.2	7.6	5.6	12.8	0.5	1.7	1.1	1.4	16.8	21.3
Germany	30.1	8.3	1.2	9.4	1.1	0.5	1.6	0.5	1.4	45.9
Greece	40.4	4.3	3.7	29.4	0.5	0.1	5.0	0.7	8.4	7.4
Hungary	31.6	1.3	5.4	16.2	0.9	0.6	16.3	3.7	11.2	12.9
Iceland	24.1	0.1	4.0	11.2	1.0	2.2	22.1	3.3	9.3	22.7
Ireland	18.0	1.0	3.7	6.5	0.6	0.4	18.3	1.3	11.3	38.8
Israel	17.6	16.7	4.3	7.1	0.3	0.5	13.4	2.6	16.6	20.8
Italy	30.5	4.0	5.8	12.0	0.6	1.0	11.4	1.4	11.2	22.2
Japan	35.1	4.8	1.5	12.7	1.2	3.3	9.3	0.1	5.5	26.4
Korea	25.5	12.5	4.8	19.2	1.1	1.3	3.6	1.4	19.5	11.2
Luxembourg	19.5	1.2	3.1	11.1	1.6	1.9	2.0	2.0	15.8	42.0
Mexico	..	..	..	..	..	..	..	..	..	..
Netherlands	28.4	4.5	6.8	9.4	0.7	0.3	6.0	1.3	18.4	24.4
New Zealand	..	..	..	..	..	..	..	..	..	..
Norway	22.9	3.8	2.4	9.4	0.8	0.1	15.5	1.7	3.9	39.4
Poland	22.1	7.0	8.9	9.0	0.8	0.9	5.1	1.0	16.7	28.5
Portugal	38.9	2.9	5.1	6.1	0.1	0.3	16.5	1.0	15.0	14.1
Slovak Republic	21.7	4.9	12.4	11.7	1.7	0.9	8.6	3.1	15.6	19.4
Slovenia	14.1	2.3	4.9	32.0	0.7	0.6	9.2	2.7	12.5	21.1
Spain	72.7	4.3	4.9	8.3	0.2	0.0	1.2	1.0	0.7	6.7
Sweden	32.1	4.8	3.8	9.8	0.5	0.5	4.1	1.1	5.8	37.8
Switzerland	25.7	7.4	1.6	20.7	1.7	0.0	0.5	0.8	9.9	31.9
Turkey	..	..	..	..	..	..	..	..	..	..
United Kingdom	14.2	5.5	4.1	6.3	0.9	4.0	18.1	1.2	10.6	35.2
United States	13.5	16.3	1.5	5.6	0.0	1.8	25.8	0.1	2.7	32.8
EU 28	..	..	..	..	..	..	..	..	..	..
OECD	23.9	9.8	3.1	8.9	0.5	1.7	15.3	0.7	7.2	28.9
Brazil	..	..	..	..	..	..	..	..	..	..
China	..	..	..	..	..	..	..	..	..	..
India	..	..	..	..	..	..	..	..	..	..
Indonesia	..	..	..	..	..	..	..	..	..	..
Russian Federation	..	..	..	..	..	..	..	..	..	..
South Africa	..	..	..	..	..	..	..	..	..	..

StatLink ⟶ http://dx.doi.org/10.1787/888933336171

Distribution of general government expenditures across levels of government

Percentage, 2007-13

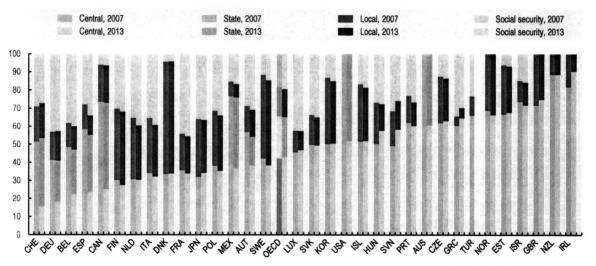

StatLink ⟶ http://dx.doi.org/10.1787/888933334999

GENERAL GOVERNMENT EXPENDITURES AND REVENUES PER CAPITA

Governments spend money to provide goods and services and redistribute income. To finance these activities governments raise money in the form of revenues (e.g. taxation) and/or borrowing. The amount of revenues and expenditures per capita provide an indication of the importance of the public sector in the economy across countries. Variations across countries however can also reflect different approaches to the delivery of public services (e.g. such as the use of tax breaks rather than direct expenditures).

Definition

Data are derived from the *OECD Annual National Accounts*, which are based on the *System of National Accounts (SNA)*, a set of internationally agreed concepts, definitions, classifications and rules for national accounting. The general government sector consists of central, state and local governments and the social security funds controlled by these units. The underlying population estimates are based on the SNA notion of residency. They include persons who are resident in a country for one year or more, regardless of their citizenship, and also include foreign diplomatic personnel, and defence personnel; together with their families and students studying and patients seeking treatment abroad, even if they stay abroad for more than one year. The "one year" rule means that usual residents who live abroad for less than one year are included in the population, while foreign visitors (for example, vacationers) who are in the country for less than one year are excluded.

Comparability

Differences in the amounts of government revenues and expenditures per capita in some countries can be related to the fact that individuals may feature as employees of one country (contributing to the GDP of that country via production), but residents of another (with their wages and salaries reflected in the Gross National Income of their resident country). The OECD average does not include Chile and Turkey.

Overview

On average in the OECD area, governments collected on average USD 14 852 PPP per capita in revenues in 2013, while spending represented USD 16 491 PPP per capita in the same year.

Luxembourg and Norway collected the largest government revenues per capita in the OECD, above USD 30 000 PPP per capita reflecting the large number of cross-border workers and high corporate taxes in Luxembourg and oil revenues in Norway. These two countries also spent the most per citizen (above USD 26 000 PPP).

The governments of Mexico and Turkey collected the smallest revenues per capita; below USD 7 000 PPP. Likewise, government expenditures in these countries were also much lower than average (below USD 7 000 PPP per capita). In general, central European countries also collect comparatively less revenues per capita, and also spend less than most OECD countries.

On average across OECD countries revenues per capita increased, in real terms, at an annual rate of 2.4% between 2009 and 2013 whereas a slight decrease was recorded for expenditures per capita (0.2%) over the same period.

Sources
• OECD (2015), *Government at a Glance*, OECD Publishing.
Further information
Analytical publications
• OECD (2015), *OECD Economic Outlook*, OECD Publishing.
• OECD (2015), *Value for Money in Government*, OECD Publishing.
Statistical publications
• OECD (2015), *National Accounts at a Glance*, OECD Publishing.
• OECD (2015), *National Accounts of OECD Countries*, OECD Publishing.
Online databases
• "General Government Accounts, SNA 2008 (or SNA 1993): Main aggregates", OECD National Accounts Statistics.
• Government at a Glance.
Websites
• Government at a Glance (supplementary material), www.oecd.org/gov/govataglance.htm.

General government revenues and expenditures per capita

US dollars, current prices and PPPs

	General government revenues per capita				General government expenditures per capita			
	2009	2011	2013	2014	2009	2011	2013	2014
Australia	13 402	14 279	15 216	..	15 730	16 197	16 379	..
Austria	19 824	21 247	22 352	22 733	21 985	22 375	22 931	23 830
Belgium	18 028	20 323	21 578	21 894	20 092	22 010	22 800	23 285
Canada	15 153	15 785	16 338	16 715	16 904	17 343	17 503	17 441
Chile	..	..	..	..	..	..	..	..
Czech Republic	10 248	11 364	11 832	..	11 731	12 138	12 168	..
Denmark	21 392	23 727	24 534	26 108	22 506	24 624	24 998	25 551
Estonia	8 850	9 221	9 938	10 589	9 288	8 941	9 993	10 422
Finland	19 610	21 470	22 022	22 308	20 561	21 879	23 033	23 576
France	17 279	18 982	19 913	20 340	19 774	20 886	21 448	21 851
Germany	16 465	18 393	19 171	19 695	17 590	18 756	19 107	19 400
Greece	11 791	11 683	12 257	12 011	16 443	14 408	15 422	12 942
Hungary	9 610	10 010	11 044	11 822	10 568	11 245	11 618	12 459
Iceland	15 394	15 845	17 636	..	19 129	17 954	18 466	..
Ireland	13 957	15 050	15 913	17 066	19 746	20 775	18 563	19 079
Israel	9 986	11 381	12 094	..	11 525	12 377	13 424	..
Italy	15 546	16 195	16 720	16 965	17 331	17 433	17 747	18 036
Japan	10 531	11 341	12 273	..	13 349	14 364	15 338	..
Korea	9 531	10 439	10 951	..	9 905	10 133	10 509	..
Luxembourg	35 569	38 995	40 295	..	36 000	38 639	39 518	..
Mexico	3 294	3 867	4 144	..	3 380	3 880	4 128	..
Netherlands	18 973	19 801	20 554	20 894	21 398	21 809	21 605	21 975
New Zealand	11 971	12 861	13 892	..	12 835	13 982	14 036	..
Norway	31 715	35 925	36 341	36 740	25 904	27 488	28 905	30 660
Poland	7 254	8 614	9 052	9 585	8 655	9 695	10 004	10 378
Portugal	10 597	11 478	12 446	12 665	13 167	13 461	13 774	13 935
Slovak Republic	8 274	9 136	10 186	10 732	10 100	10 167	10 871	11 524
Slovenia	11 636	12 415	13 033	13 539	13 322	14 193	17 232	15 010
Spain	11 420	11 773	12 418	12 834	15 014	14 851	14 668	14 805
Sweden	20 779	22 449	23 182	23 406	21 064	22 484	23 795	24 270
Switzerland	16 785	18 360	19 132	..	16 409	17 948	19 086	..
Turkey	5 306	6 470	..	..	6 249	6 612	..	..
United Kingdom	14 116	14 330	15 214	15 345	18 044	17 120	17 410	17 598
United States	14 188	15 354	17 564	..	20 135	20 632	20 513	..
EU 28	..	..	..	..	..	..	..	..
OECD	12 729	13 747	14 852	..	15 683	16 214	16 491	..
Brazil	4 521	5 291	5 685	5 471	4 946	5 663	6 173	6 474
China	..	..	..	..	..	..	..	..
India	756	921	1 079	1 134	1 155	1 313	1 473	1 553
Indonesia	1 222	1 537	1 736	1 768	1 352	1 591	1 938	1 997
Russian Federation	7 282	9 192	..	..	8 058	8 339	..	..
South Africa	..	..	..	..	..	..	..	..

StatLink ⟨⟩ http://dx.doi.org/10.1787/888933336180

General government revenues and expenditures per capita

US dollars, current prices and PPPs, 2013 and 2014

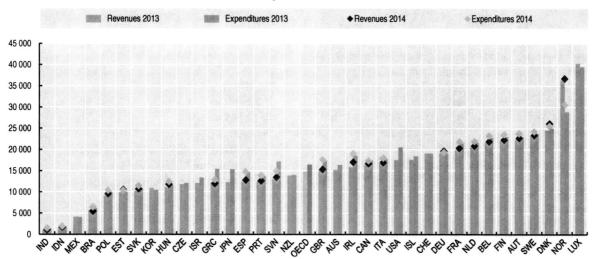

StatLink ⟨⟩ http://dx.doi.org/10.1787/888933335009

GENERAL GOVERNMENT PRODUCTION COSTS

Decisions on the amount and type of goods and services governments produce, as well as on how to produce them, vary across countries. While some governments choose to outsource a large portion of their production of goods and services to non-governmental or private entities, others decide to produce the goods and services themselves.

Definition

Governments use a mix of their own employees, capital and outside contractors (non-profit institutions or private sector entities) to produce goods and services. The latter is often referred to as "outsourcing".

This concept and methodology of production costs builds on the existing classification of public expenditures in the System of National Accounts (SNA), a set of internationally agreed concepts, definitions, classifications and rules for national accounting. Specifically, government production costs include: compensation costs of general government employees; goods and services used and financed by general government (including, in SNA terms, intermediate consumption and social transfer in kind via market producers paid for by government); and, other production costs (which include SNA terms, consumption of fixed capital, i.e. depreciation of capital, and other taxes on production less other subsidies on production). The data include government employment and expenditures for output produced by the government for its own use.

Comparability

Data include some cross-country differences, for example, some countries do not record separately for social transfers in kind via market producers in their national accounts. Thus, the costs produced by non-government entities paid for by government may be understated in those countries. The OECD average for production costs does not include Chile and Turkey.

Overview

In 2013, the production costs of government services and goods represented on average 21.3% of GDP in the OECD, ranging from 32.3% in Finland to 12.3% in Mexico.

Between 2007 and 2013, the share of government production costs in GDP increased on average by 1.1 percentage points across OECD countries. This increase was primarily driven by increases in the cost of goods and services produced by private and non-profit agencies (0.7 percentage points). Few countries experienced a reduction in production costs over the same period. In Israel and Greece the decline took place mainly through a lower share of costs of goods and services used and financed by government, whereas in Hungary, Poland and Portugal it took place through a lower share of compensation of government employees.

In terms of the structure of production costs, on average, production by governments' own employees is still somewhat higher than outsourcing: compensation of employees accounts for 45.2% of the cost of producing government goods and services, compared to 41.9% paid to non-governmental actors for intermediate goods and services or to deliver services directly to households. Other production costs represent the remaining 12.9% of total government production costs.

In 2013 government outsourcing represented, on average, 8.9% of GDP in the OECD. However, its importance varies greatly ranging from 3.0% of GDP in Mexico to 17.1% of GDP in the Netherlands. Among OECD countries, Belgium, Japan, Germany and the Netherlands dedicated the largest shares (over 60%) for their resources to outsourcing goods and services through direct third party provision. In contrast, Denmark, Israel and Switzerland spent the majority of outsourcing in intermediate consumption.

Sources
- OECD (2015), *Government at a Glance*, OECD Publishing.

Further information

Analytical publications
- OECD (2015), *Value for Money in Government*, OECD Publishing.
- OECD (2008), *The State of the Public Service*, OECD Publishing.

Statistical publications
- OECD (2015), *National Accounts at a Glance*, OECD Publishing.
- OECD (2015), *National Accounts of OECD Countries*, OECD Publishing.

Online databases
- *"General Government Accounts, SNA 2008 (or SNA 1993): Main aggregates"*, OECD National Accounts Statistics.
- *Government at a Glance*.

Websites
- Government at a Glance (supplementary material), *www.oecd.org/gov/govataglance.htm*.

Production costs for general government

As a percentage of GDP

	Compensation of employees			Costs of goods and services used and financed by general government			Other production costs			Total		
	2007	2013	2014	2007	2013	2014	2007	2013	2014	2007	2013	2014
Australia	9.2	9.6	..	8.9	9.1	..	2.0	2.1	..	20.2	20.8	..
Austria	10.4	10.6	10.6	9.3	10.3	10.3	2.8	3.1	3.1	22.5	24.0	24.0
Belgium	11.4	12.5	12.5	10.3	11.9	12.0	2.1	2.3	2.4	23.7	26.7	26.9
Canada	11.4	12.1	11.8	8.5	9.5	9.3	2.8	3.4	3.3	22.7	24.9	24.5
Chile	..	8.4	..	..	..	..	..	..	..	..	..	..
Czech Republic	7.0	7.3	7.1	10.4	10.9	10.8	4.4	4.6	4.4	21.9	22.8	22.3
Denmark	15.3	16.8	16.9	9.6	11.0	11.0	2.9	2.9	2.8	27.8	30.6	30.7
Estonia	9.4	10.7	11.1	7.1	8.4	8.5	1.9	3.0	3.1	18.4	22.0	22.6
Finland	12.6	14.4	14.3	10.9	14.3	14.6	3.0	3.5	3.5	26.5	32.3	32.4
France	12.4	12.9	13.0	10.0	11.1	11.1	3.4	3.8	3.8	25.7	27.9	27.9
Germany	7.3	7.7	7.7	11.0	12.8	12.9	2.1	2.3	2.2	20.4	22.8	22.8
Greece	10.9	12.0	12.0	9.2	7.1	6.7	2.5	3.5	3.5	22.6	22.6	22.2
Hungary	11.5	10.2	10.6	9.2	9.7	9.9	3.4	3.6	3.5	24.1	23.5	24.0
Iceland	14.1	14.2	..	10.3	11.2	..	1.7	2.0	..	26.1	27.4	..
Ireland	10.1	10.7	10.0	6.8	7.3	7.4	1.8	1.8	1.6	18.7	19.8	19.0
Israel	10.5	10.5	..	12.4	11.9	..	2.2	2.0	..	25.0	24.4	..
Italy	10.2	10.3	10.1	7.5	8.3	8.3	3.0	3.3	3.3	20.7	21.9	21.7
Japan	6.2	6.0	..	10.2	12.8	..	2.8	3.0	..	19.2	21.7	..
Korea	6.9	6.8	6.8	7.3	8.1	8.1	2.4	2.9	3.0	16.6	17.8	17.9
Luxembourg	7.4	8.3	8.4	7.6	8.8	8.9	1.8	2.2	2.2	16.8	19.3	19.5
Mexico	8.0	9.2	..	2.5	3.0	..	0.1	0.1	..	10.6	12.3	..
Netherlands	8.6	9.3	9.2	15.2	17.1	16.8	3.1	3.5	3.4	26.9	29.9	29.4
New Zealand	9.2	9.4	..	10.5	11.0	..	2.3	2.2	..	21.9	22.6	..
Norway	12.1	13.6	13.9	7.4	8.0	8.3	2.5	3.0	3.1	22.0	24.7	25.3
Poland	10.4	10.3	10.2	7.8	7.8	8.1	2.4	2.3	2.4	20.7	20.4	20.6
Portugal	13.1	12.4	11.8	7.5	7.7	7.8	2.3	2.7	2.6	22.9	22.8	22.3
Slovak Republic	7.2	8.5	8.7	9.2	10.2	10.6	3.3	3.6	3.6	19.8	22.2	22.9
Slovenia	10.4	12.5	11.6	7.4	8.9	8.7	2.4	3.0	2.9	20.2	24.4	23.2
Spain	9.9	10.9	10.8	7.4	8.0	7.8	2.1	2.7	2.7	19.5	21.6	21.3
Sweden	12.3	12.6	12.7	10.4	12.0	12.0	5.7	6.0	6.0	28.4	30.6	30.6
Switzerland	6.9	7.5	..	5.0	5.4	..	2.6	2.9	..	14.5	15.8	..
Turkey	7.0	..	..	8.7	..	..	..	..	..	..	..	..
United Kingdom	10.6	9.7	9.5	10.8	11.5	11.3	1.3	1.5	1.5	22.8	22.8	22.4
United States	10.1	10.0	..	6.8	6.8	..	2.6	2.9	..	19.4	19.6	..
EU 28	..	..	..	..	..	..	..	..	..	..	..	..
OECD	9.5	9.6	..	8.3	8.9	..	2.5	2.8	..	20.2	21.3	..
Brazil	..	..	..	..	..	..	..	..	..	..	..	..
China	7.8	..	..	..	..	..	..	..	..	..	..	..
India	..	..	..	..	..	..	..	..	..	..	..	..
Indonesia	..	..	..	..	..	..	..	..	..	..	..	..
Russian Federation	8.7	..	..	8.8	..	..	0.3	..	..	17.8	..	..
South Africa	11.7	14.3	..	10.0	13.5	..	2.0	2.0	..	23.7	29.8	..

StatLink http://dx.doi.org/10.1787/888933336198

Structure of general government production costs

Percentage, 2013

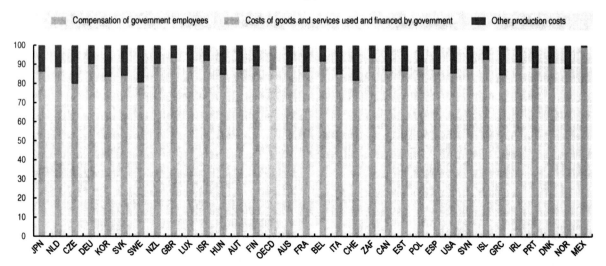

StatLink http://dx.doi.org/10.1787/888933335016

SOCIAL EXPENDITURE

Social expenditures are a measure of the extent to which countries assume responsibility for supporting the standard of living of disadvantaged or vulnerable groups.

Definition

Social expenditure comprises cash benefits, direct in-kind provision of goods and services, and tax breaks with social purposes. Benefits may be targeted at low-income households, the elderly, disabled, sick, unemployed, or young persons. To be considered "social", programmes have to involve either redistribution of resources across households or compulsory participation. Social benefits are classified as public when general government (that is central, state, and local governments, including social security funds) controls the relevant financial flows. All social benefits not provided by general government are considered private. Private transfers between households are not considered as "social" and not included. Net total social expenditure includes both public and private expenditure. It also accounts for the effect of the tax system by direct and indirect taxation and by tax breaks for social purposes.

Comparability

For cross-country comparisons, the most commonly used indicator of social support is gross (before tax) public social expenditure relative to GDP. Measurement problems do exist, particularly with regard to spending by lower tiers of government, which may be underestimated in some countries. Public social spending totals reflect detailed social expenditure programme data till 2011-12, national aggregated for 2012-13 and estimates for 2014.

Data on private social spending are often of lesser quality than for public spending.

No data on net expenditure are currently available for Switzerland. Net data for New Zealand and Poland have been estimated on the basis of information available for 2009.

For non-OECD countries, data are not strictly comparable with OECD countries.

Overview

Gross public social expenditure increased from about 16% in 1980 to 18% in 1990 and to 22% of GDP in 2014 across OECD countries. Since 2009 and after the global financial crisis it has stayed around this level. Spending was highest, at over 30% of GDP, in France and Finland, and lowest, at 10% of GDP or below, in Chile, Korea and Mexico. Keeping measurement-related differences in mind, non-OECD countries have lower levels of social protection than OECD countries, particularly Indonesia and India. The three biggest categories of social transfers are pensions (on average 8% of GDP), health (6%) and income transfers to the working-age population (5%). Public spending on other social services exceeds 5% of GDP only in the Nordic countries, where the public role in providing services to the elderly, the disabled and families is the most extensive.

In 2011, gross private social spending was highest (at just over 10% of GDP) in the United States and lowest (at less than 1% of GDP) in the Czech Republic, Estonia, Hungary, Mexico, New Zealand, Poland, Spain and Turkey.

Moving from gross public to net total social expenditure not only leads to greater similarity in spending levels across countries it also changes the ranking among countries. Austria, Greece, Finland, Slovenia, Luxembourg, New Zealand and Poland drop 5 to 10 places in the rankings while Australia, Canada, Japan, the Netherlands and the United Kingdom move up the rankings by 5 to 10 places. As private social spending is so much larger in the United States compared with other countries its inclusion moves the United States from 23rd to 2nd place when comparing net total social spending across countries.

Sources
• OECD (2015), *Social Expenditure Statistics* (Database).

Further information

Analytical publications
• Adema, W., P. Fron and M. Ladaique (2011), "Is the European Welfare State Really More Expensive? Indicators on Social Spending, 1980-2012; and a Manual to the OECD Social Expenditure Database (SOCX)", *OECD Social, Employment and Migration Working Papers*, No. 124.
• OECD (2015), *Integrating Social Services for Vulnerable Groups*, OECD Publishing.
• OECD (2011), *Doing Better for Families*, OECD Publishing.

Statistical publications
• OECD (2014), *Society at a Glance: Asia/Pacific*, OECD Publishing.
• OECD (2014), *Society at a Glance: OECD Social Indicators*, OECD Publishing.

Websites
• Mental health and work, *www.oecd.org/employment/emp/mental-health-and-work.htm*.
• OECD Family Database, *www.oecd.org/social/family/database.htm*.
• Social and welfare issues, *www.oecd.org/social*.
• Social Benefit Recipients Database (SOCR) (supplementary material), *www.oecd.org/social/soc/recipients.htm*.
• Social Expenditure Database (SOCX) (supplementary material), *www.oecd.org/social/expenditure.htm*.

Public, private and total net social expenditure

As a percentage of GDP

	Public expenditure								Private expenditure				Total net expenditure
	1990	2000	2009	2010	2011	2012	2013	2014	1990	2000	2010	2011	2011
Australia	13.1	17.2	17.4	17.2	17.8	18.3	19.0	19.0	0.9	4.4	3.1	3.3	19.8
Austria	23.4	26.1	28.6	28.6	27.7	27.9	28.3	28.4	2.2	1.9	2.0	2.0	24.3
Belgium	24.9	24.5	29.1	28.8	29.4	30.3	30.9	30.7	1.6	1.7	2.0	2.1	27.4
Canada	17.6	15.8	18.5	17.9	17.4	17.4	17.2	17.0	3.2	4.9	4.7	4.6	20.7
Chile	9.8	12.7	11.2	10.5	10.1	10.2	10.0	..	0.5	1.2	4.0	4.1	13.1
Czech Republic	14.6	18.8	20.3	19.9	20.1	20.2	20.5	20.6	..	0.3	0.7	0.8	19.3
Denmark	25.0	26.0	29.7	29.9	30.1	30.2	30.2	30.1	2.1	2.4	4.8	5.1	26.1
Estonia	..	13.8	19.8	18.8	16.8	16.2	16.1	16.3	..	..	0.0	0.0	14.2
Finland	23.8	23.3	28.3	28.7	28.3	29.4	30.6	31.0	1.1	1.2	1.2	1.2	23.4
France	24.9	28.4	31.5	31.7	31.4	31.5	32.0	31.9	1.9	2.6	3.6	3.6	31.3
Germany	21.4	26.2	27.6	26.8	25.5	25.4	25.6	25.8	3.0	3.1	3.2	3.2	25.3
Greece	16.5	19.2	24.4	24.2	25.7	26.1	24.3	24.0	2.1	2.1	1.9	1.9	23.7
Hungary	..	20.5	24.7	23.5	22.6	22.3	22.1	22.1	..	0.0	0.3	0.2	20.6
Iceland	13.5	15.0	18.5	17.9	18.1	17.5	17.1	16.5	3.0	4.2	5.8	5.9	20.4
Ireland	17.2	13.1	23.4	23.3	22.3	22.0	21.9	21.0	1.4	1.3	1.9	1.9	21.9
Israel	..	16.8	15.8	15.7	15.6	15.5	15.5	..	..	2.3	2.4	2.4	15.7
Italy	21.4	23.3	27.8	27.8	27.5	28.1	28.7	28.6	2.1	1.8	2.2	2.2	25.4
Japan	11.1	16.3	22.0	22.1	23.1	..	..	..	0.2	3.6	3.5	3.7	25.6
Korea	2.8	4.8	9.4	9.0	9.0	9.6	10.2	10.4	0.4	2.7	2.4	2.7	11.6
Luxembourg	19.1	19.6	24.3	23.0	22.5	23.4	23.4	23.5	..	0.1	1.7	1.7	19.1
Mexico	3.2	5.0	7.7	7.8	7.7	7.9	..	..	0.1	0.1	0.2	0.2	7.7
Netherlands	25.6	19.8	23.1	23.7	23.5	24.1	24.6	24.7	6.1	7.3	7.4	7.4	25.8
New Zealand	21.2	18.9	21.0	21.0	20.7	21.0	20.8	..	0.2	0.5	0.5	0.5	18.8
Norway	21.9	20.8	22.8	22.4	21.8	21.7	22.0	22.0	1.9	2.0	2.1	2.2	19.3
Poland	14.9	20.3	20.7	20.7	20.1	20.1	20.7	20.6	..	..	0.0	0.0	16.8
Portugal	12.4	18.6	25.3	25.2	24.8	24.8	25.8	25.2	0.9	1.5	1.8	1.9	24.0
Slovak Republic	..	17.8	18.5	18.4	18.1	18.3	18.7	18.4	..	0.8	1.0	0.9	17.6
Slovenia	..	22.8	23.0	23.9	24.0	24.0	23.8	23.7	..	0.0	1.1	1.2	21.6
Spain	19.7	20.0	26.1	26.7	26.8	27.1	27.3	26.8	0.2	0.3	0.5	0.5	24.8
Sweden	28.5	28.2	29.4	27.9	27.2	27.7	28.2	28.1	1.2	2.6	3.2	3.2	24.6
Switzerland	12.8	17.2	19.7	19.5	19.3	19.7	19.9	19.4	4.4	6.6	7.0	7.0	..
Turkey	5.5	..	13.2	12.6	12.2	12.3	12.5	..	..	..	..	..	11.1
United Kingdom	16.3	18.4	23.9	22.8	22.7	23.0	22.5	21.7	5.0	7.6	6.2	6.2	26.1
United States	13.1	14.2	18.5	19.3	19.0	18.7	18.6	19.2	7.3	8.8	10.8	10.9	28.8
EU 28	..	..	..	..	..	..	..	..	..	..	..	..	..
OECD	17.5	18.6	21.9	21.7	21.4	21.6	21.7	21.6	..	2.9	3.2	3.2	21.7
Brazil	..	..	..	16.7	..	..	..	..	..	..	..	..	..
China	..	..	7.0	..	..	9.0	..	..	..	..	..	..	..
India	..	..	2.7	..	..	..	..	..	..	..	..	..	..
Indonesia	..	..	2.0	..	..	..	..	..	..	..	..	..	..
Russian Federation	..	..	..	..	12.8	..	..	..	..	..	..	..	..
South Africa	..	..	..	..	..	8.7	..	..	..	..	..	..	..

StatLink ━━ http://dx.doi.org/10.1787/888933336616

Public, private and total net social expenditure

As a percentage of GDP, 2011

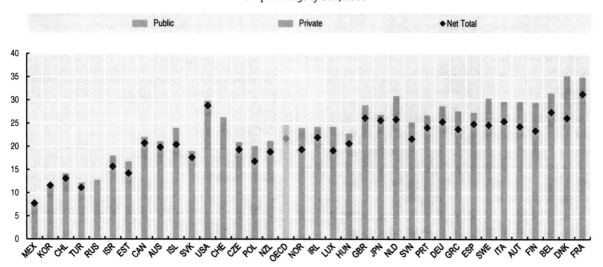

StatLink ━━ http://dx.doi.org/10.1787/888933335530

PENSION EXPENDITURE

Pension systems vary across countries and no single model fits all. Generally, there is a mix of public and private provision. Public pensions are statutory, most often financed on a pay-as-you-go (PAYG) basis – where current contributions pay for current benefits – and managed by public institutions. Private pensions are in some cases mandatory but more usually voluntary, funded, employment-based (occupational) pension plans or individual retirement savings plans (personal pensions).

Definition

Old-age pension benefits are treated as public when relevant financial flows are controlled by general government (i.e. central and local governments or social security funds). Pension benefits provided by governments to their own employees and paid directly out of the government's current budget are also considered to be public. Public pensions are generally financed on a PAYG basis, but also include some funded arrangements. All pension benefits not provided by general government are within the private domain.

Private expenditures on pensions include payments made to private pension plan members (or dependants) after retirement. All types of plans are included (occupational and personal, mandatory and voluntary, funded and book

reserved), covering persons working in both the public and private sectors.

Comparability

Public pension expenditures come from the *OECD Social Expenditure* (SOCX) database while pension expenditures for private pension arrangements come from the *OECD Global Pension Statistics* (GPS) database. The GPS database provides information on funded pension arrangements, which includes both private and public pension plans that are funded.

Although the GPS database covers all types of private pension arrangements for most countries, private pension expenditure data for Austria, Canada, Germany, Greece, Hungary, Luxembourg, the Netherlands, Switzerland, the United Kingdom and the United States only relate to autonomous pension funds. A break in series for Mexico reflects the inclusion of occupational pension plans registered by CONSAR since 2005. The large increase in private pension expenditures between 2008 and 2009 for Iceland reflects the increase in the number of people retiring due to the unemployment peak after the bank crisis and the passing of a special temporary Act allowing people to withdraw limited amounts of money from personal pension plans.

Overview

Public spending on old-age benefits averaged 7.9% of GDP in 2011, compared with private pension benefits of an average of 1.6% of GDP in the same year (in the countries for which data are available that year). Public spending on old-age pensions is highest – greater than 10% of GDP – in Austria, Belgium, Finland, France, Germany, Greece, Italy, Japan, Poland, Portugal, Slovenia and Spain. By contrast, Australia, Chile, Iceland, Korea and Mexico spend 4% of GDP or less on public old-age pensions.

Private expenditure on old-age benefits is the highest in Australia, Denmark, Iceland, the Netherlands, Switzerland and the United States, where it exceeds 4% of GDP in 2013. However, private benefit spending remains negligible in around a third of OECD countries.

The share of private pensions in total expenditures on old-age benefits exceeds 50% only in Australia and Iceland in 2011. The average share of private pensions in the total in 2011 is 19%.

Over time, public pension expenditures have grown a little faster than national income: from an average of 6.8% of GDP in 2000 to 7.9% in 2011.

Expenditure on private pensions has also grown over the last years, from an average of 1.4% of GDP in 2008 to 1.6% in 2013.

Sources
- OECD (2015), *OECD Pensions Statistics* (Database).
- OECD (2015), *OECD Social Expenditure Statistics* (Database).

Further information

Analytical publications
- OECD (2014), *OECD Pensions Outlook*, OECD Publishing.
- OECD (2009), *OECD Private Pensions Outlook 2008*, OECD Publishing.

Statistical publications
- OECD (2015), *OECD Pensions at a Glance*, OECD Publishing.
- OECD (2013), *Pensions at a Glance: Asia/Pacific*, OECD Publishing.

Methodological publications
- OECD (2005), *Private Pensions: OECD Classification and Glossary*, OECD Publishing.

Websites
- Pension Markets in Focus, *www.oecd.org/pensions/private-pensions/pensionmarketsinfocus.htm*.
- Social Expenditure Database (SOCX) (supplementary material), *www.oecd.org/social/expenditure.htm*.

Public and private expenditure on pensions
As a percentage of GDP

	Public expenditure						Private expenditure					
	2000	2005	2008	2009	2010	2011	2008	2009	2010	2011	2012	2013
Australia	3.8	3.3	3.6	3.5	3.4	3.5	5.5	4.6	4.5	4.5	4.8	5.1
Austria	12.2	12.4	12.4	13.4	13.5	13.2	0.2	0.2	0.2	..	..	0.3
Belgium	8.9	9.0	9.4	10.0	10.0	10.2	2.5	3.1	2.8	3.6	1.2	1.2
Canada	4.2	4.0	4.1	4.4	4.3	4.3	2.2	2.5	2.8	2.8	2.9	3.0
Chile	7.3	3.7	3.3	3.6	3.4	3.2	2.0	1.7	1.9	2.2	2.3	2.3
Czech Republic	7.2	7.0	7.4	8.3	8.5	8.9	0.3	0.4	0.4	0.5	0.6	0.3
Denmark	5.3	5.4	5.2	5.8	5.9	6.2	4.0	4.1	4.4	4.8	5.0	5.9
Estonia	6.0	5.3	6.2	7.9	7.8	6.9	..	0.0	0.0	0.0	0.0	0.1
Finland	7.6	8.4	8.4	10.0	10.3	10.3	0.5	0.6	0.6	0.6	0.7	0.6
France	11.8	12.4	12.6	13.5	13.6	13.8	..	0.3	0.4	0.3	0.3	0.4
Germany	11.2	11.5	10.6	11.3	11.0	10.6	0.1	0.3	0.2	0.2	0.2	0.2
Greece	10.8	11.8	12.4	13.1	13.6	14.5	0.0	0.0	0.0	0.0	0.0	0.0
Hungary	7.6	8.5	9.7	10.8	9.8	10.0	0.2	0.2	0.2	0.2	0.2	0.1
Iceland	2.2	2.0	1.8	1.7	1.7	2.1	3.6	6.0	5.2	6.0	5.4	5.2
Ireland	3.1	3.4	4.1	5.0	5.2	5.3	..	..	..	..	..	..
Israel	4.7	4.9	4.6	4.8	4.7	4.8	1.6	1.6	1.6	1.6	1.6	1.7
Italy	13.7	14.0	14.6	15.6	15.8	15.8	0.3	0.2	0.2	0.2	0.3	0.3
Japan	7.3	8.5	9.2	10.1	10.0	10.2	..	..	..	..	..	..
Korea	1.4	1.5	2.0	2.1	2.2	2.2	0.7	1.0	1.3	1.3	1.7	2.3
Luxembourg	7.5	7.2	7.0	8.0	7.6	7.7	0.0	0.1	0.1	0.1	0.1	0.1
Mexico	0.8	1.2	1.4	1.7	1.8	1.8	0.2	0.3	0.3	0.3	0.3	0.4
Netherlands	5.0	5.0	4.8	5.3	5.4	5.5	3.3	3.6	3.7	3.9	4.0	4.1
New Zealand	4.9	4.2	4.4	4.6	4.7	4.9	1.4	1.9	1.4	1.3	1.4	1.7
Norway	4.8	4.8	4.6	5.2	5.3	5.4	0.9	1.1	1.0	1.0	1.0	1.0
Poland	10.5	11.4	10.9	11.4	11.3	10.8	0.0	0.0	0.0	0.0	0.0	0.0
Portugal	7.9	10.3	11.3	12.3	12.5	13.0	1.3	1.0	0.7	0.8	0.4	0.4
Slovak Republic	6.3	6.2	5.7	7.0	7.0	7.0	..	..	0.2	0.2	0.2	0.2
Slovenia	10.5	9.9	9.5	10.8	11.2	11.4	0.0	0.0	0.0	0.5	0.9	0.5
Spain	8.6	8.1	8.6	9.5	10.1	10.5	0.6	0.6	0.6	0.7	0.7	0.6
Sweden	7.2	7.6	7.4	8.2	7.7	7.4	1.2	1.2	1.3	1.3	1.5	1.6
Switzerland	6.5	6.6	6.1	6.6	6.5	6.6	4.8	5.0	4.6	4.6	4.7	4.8
Turkey	4.9	5.9	6.7	7.8	7.7	7.5	0.1	0.1	0.1	0.0	..	..
United Kingdom	5.3	5.5	5.6	5.9	5.6	5.6	2.7	3.0	3.1	3.0	3.1	3.1
United States	5.6	5.7	5.9	6.5	6.6	6.7	4.1	4.1	4.4	4.4	4.8	5.2
EU 28	..	..	..	..	..	..	..	..	..	..	..	..
OECD	6.8	7.0	7.1	7.8	7.8	7.9	1.4	1.5	1.5	1.6	1.6	1.6
Brazil	..	..	..	..	..	..	0.9	0.9	0.9	1.2	..	0.6
China	..	..	..	..	..	..	..	..	..	..	..	..
India	..	..	..	..	..	..	..	..	..	..	..	..
Indonesia	..	..	..	..	..	..	..	..	..	0.1	..	..
Russian Federation	..	..	..	..	..	..	..	..	..	0.1	..	0.1
South Africa	..	..	..	..	..	..	6.2	5.7	5.3	3.9	3.9	4.3

StatLink http://dx.doi.org/10.1787/888933336488

Public and private expenditure on pensions
As a percentage of GDP, 2011

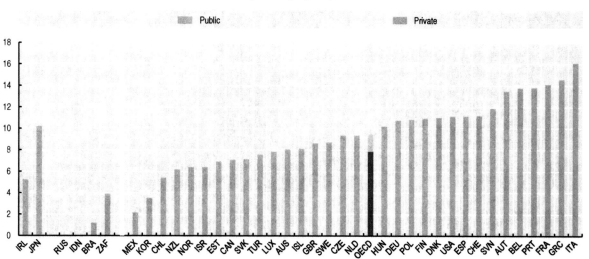

StatLink http://dx.doi.org/10.1787/888933335347

OFFICIAL DEVELOPMENT ASSISTANCE

Promoting economic and social development in partner countries has been a principal objective of the OECD since its foundation. The share of national income devoted to official development assistance (ODA) is a key indicator of a country's commitment to international development. A long-standing United Nations target is that developed countries should devote 0.7% of their gross national income (GNI) to ODA.

Definition

ODA is defined as government aid designed to promote the economic development and welfare of developing countries. Loans and credits for military purposes are excluded. Aid may be provided bilaterally, from donor to recipient, or channelled through a multilateral development agency such as the United Nations or the World Bank. Aid includes grants, "soft" loans and the provision of technical assistance. Soft loans are those where the grant element is at least 25% of the total.

The OECD maintains a list of developing countries and territories; only aid to these countries counts as ODA. The list is periodically updated and currently contains over 150 countries or territories with per capita incomes below USD 12 745 in 2013. Data on ODA flows are provided by the 29 OECD members of the Development Assistance Committee (DAC).

Comparability

Statistics on ODA are compiled according to directives drawn up by the DAC. Each country's statistics are subject to regular peer reviews by other DAC members.

As part of its overall engagement strategy, the DAC encourages donors that are not members of the Committee, to report their aid flows to the OECD/DAC Secretariat. This reporting is voluntary and currently about 20 non-DAC bilateral donors as well as about 35 multilateral agencies (regional development banks, UN agencies, international financial institutions, etc.) provide their data on their outflows to developing countries to the DAC.

Overview

From 1960 to 1990, official development assistance (ODA) flows from the 29 OECD countries of the Development Assistance Committee (DAC) to developing countries rose steadily. By contrast, total ODA as a percentage of DAC countries' combined gross national income (GNI) fell between 1960 and 1970, and then oscillated between 0.27% and 0.36% for a little over twenty years. Between 1993 and 1997, ODA flows fell by 16% in real terms due to fiscal consolidation in donor countries after the recession of the early 1990s.

Aid then started to rise in real terms in 1998, but was still at its historic low as a share of GNI (0.22%) in 2001. Since then, a series of high-profile international conferences have boosted ODA flows. In 2002, the *International Conference on Financing for Development*, held in Monterrey, Mexico, set firm targets for each donor and marked the upturn of ODA after a decade of decline. In 2005, donors made further commitments to increase their aid at the Gleneagles G8 and UN Millennium + 5 summits. In 2005 and 2006, aid peaked due to exceptional debt relief operations for Iraq and Nigeria.

In the past 15 years, net ODA has been rising steadily and has increased by nearly 70% in real terms since 2000. In 2014, net ODA flows from DAC member countries totalled USD 137.2 billion, marking an increase of 1.2% in real terms over 2013 and surpassing the all-time high in 2013. As a share of GNI, ODA was 0.30%.

Sources
- OECD (2015), *OECD International Development Statistics* (Database).

Further information

Analytical publications
- Keeley, B. (2009), *International Migration: The Human Face of Globalisation*, OECD Insights, OECD Publishing.
- OECD (2015), *Development Co-operation Report*, OECD Publishing.
- OECD (2015), *OECD Development Co-operation Peer Reviews*, OECD Publishing.
- OECD (2015), *The Development Dimension*, OECD Publishing.
- OECD (2014), *Perspectives on Global Development*, OECD Publishing.
- OECD (2012), *Aid Effectiveness 2011, Progress in Implementing the Paris Declaration, Better Aid*, OECD Publishing.

Statistical publications
- OECD (2015), *Geographical Distribution of Financial Flows to Developing Countries*, OECD Publishing.
- OECD and World Trade Organization (2015), *Aid for Trade at a Glance*, OECD Publishing.

Online databases
- OECD International Development Statistics.

Websites
- Development finance statistics, *www.oecd.org/dac/stats*.

Net official development assistance

	As a percentage of gross national income						Millions of US dollars					
	2009	2010	2011	2012	2013	2014	2009	2010	2011	2012	2013	2014
Australia	0.29	0.32	0.34	0.36	0.33	0.31	2 762	3 826	4 983	5 403	4 846	4 382
Austria	0.30	0.32	0.27	0.28	0.27	0.28	1 142	1 208	1 111	1 106	1 171	1 235
Belgium	0.55	0.64	0.54	0.48	0.45	0.46	2 610	3 004	2 807	2 315	2 300	2 448
Canada	0.30	0.34	0.32	0.32	0.28	0.24	4 000	5 214	5 459	5 650	4 947	4 240
Czech Republic	0.12	0.13	0.13	0.12	0.11	0.11	215	228	250	220	211	212
Denmark	0.88	0.91	0.85	0.83	0.85	0.86	2 810	2 871	2 931	2 693	2 927	3 003
Finland	0.54	0.55	0.53	0.53	0.54	0.60	1 290	1 333	1 406	1 320	1 435	1 635
France	0.47	0.50	0.46	0.45	0.41	0.37	12 602	12 915	12 997	12 028	11 339	10 620
Germany	0.36	0.39	0.39	0.37	0.38	0.42	12 079	12 985	14 093	12 939	14 228	16 566
Greece	0.19	0.17	0.15	0.13	0.10	0.11	607	508	425	327	239	247
Iceland	0.35	0.29	0.21	0.22	0.25	0.22	34	29	26	26	35	37
Ireland	0.55	0.52	0.51	0.47	0.46	0.38	1 006	895	914	808	846	816
Italy	0.16	0.15	0.20	0.14	0.17	0.19	3 297	2 996	4 326	2 737	3 430	4 009
Japan	0.18	0.20	0.18	0.17	0.23	0.19	9 467	11 058	11 086	10 605	11 582	9 266
Korea	0.10	0.12	0.12	0.14	0.13	0.13	816	1 174	1 325	1 597	1 755	1 857
Luxembourg	1.04	1.05	0.97	1.00	1.00	1.06	415	403	409	399	429	423
Netherlands	0.82	0.82	0.75	0.71	0.67	0.64	6 426	6 357	6 344	5 523	5 435	5 573
New Zealand	0.28	0.26	0.28	0.28	0.26	0.27	309	342	424	449	457	506
Norway	1.06	1.05	0.96	0.93	1.07	1.00	4 081	4 372	4 756	4 753	5 581	5 086
Poland	0.09	0.08	0.08	0.09	0.10	0.09	375	378	417	421	487	452
Portugal	0.23	0.29	0.31	0.28	0.23	0.19	513	649	708	581	488	430
Slovak Republic	0.09	0.09	0.09	0.09	0.09	0.09	75	74	86	80	86	83
Slovenia	0.15	0.13	0.13	0.13	0.13	0.13	71	59	63	58	62	62
Spain	0.46	0.43	0.29	0.16	0.17	0.13	6 584	5 949	4 173	2 037	2 348	1 877
Sweden	1.12	0.97	1.02	0.97	1.01	1.09	4 548	4 533	5 603	5 240	5 827	6 233
Switzerland	0.44	0.39	0.46	0.47	0.46	0.51	2 310	2 300	3 051	3 052	3 200	3 522
United Kingdom	0.51	0.57	0.56	0.56	0.71	0.70	11 283	13 053	13 832	13 891	17 871	19 306
United States	0.21	0.20	0.20	0.19	0.18	0.19	28 831	29 656	30 966	30 652	31 267	33 096
DAC Countries total	0.31	0.31	0.31	0.28	0.30	0.30	120 558	128 369	134 971	126 911	134 832	137 222

StatLink ᴍᴙ http://dx.doi.org/10.1787/888933336440

Distribution of net ODA from all sources by income group and by region

Million US dollars

	2004	2005	2006	2007	2008	2009	2010	2011	2012	2013	2014
By income group											
Least developed countries	25 560	25 911	28 847	33 953	39 068	40 222	44 268	45 204	42 722	47 968	43 726
Other low-income countries	1 262	1 471	1 521	2 126	2 473	2 986	2 849	3 670	4 143	4 635	3 933
Lower middle-income countries	17 100	27 111	31 985	23 155	24 958	30 512	29 607	29 753	30 072	37 035	37 549
Upper middle-income countries	14 946	32 461	20 333	20 613	23 562	15 814	13 615	18 514	16 566	15 221	17 687
More advanced developing countries	540	377	641	715	858	883	754	16	27	37	..
By region											
Europe	3 627	4 062	5 082	4 334	5 379	5 794	5 892	8 945	8 076	7 437	8 613
North of Sahara	3 176	2 667	2 854	3 370	4 226	3 176	2 660	4 068	4 740	8 784	7 354
South of Sahara	26 222	32 415	40 869	34 720	39 627	42 465	43 483	45 467	44 418	46 014	44 321
North and Central America	3 437	3 271	3 497	3 484	4 322	4 352	6 809	5 890	4 706	4 616	4 439
South America	2 938	2 855	3 322	2 940	3 754	3 773	2 780	4 252	4 259	3 924	4 212
Far East Asia	6 006	8 391	6 529	7 286	7 019	8 249	7 489	5 316	6 133	5 858	6 173
South and Central Asia	9 340	11 655	11 430	14 090	15 982	18 465	18 708	20 238	17 627	20 628	19 754
Middle East	7 620	25 512	14 203	14 518	19 914	10 379	9 486	11 363	8 736	16 904	25 081
Oceania	939	1 161	1 199	1 309	1 533	1 560	1 868	2 240	2 179	2 149	1 863

StatLink ᴍᴙ http://dx.doi.org/10.1787/888933336823

Net official development assistance
2014

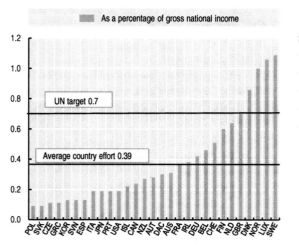

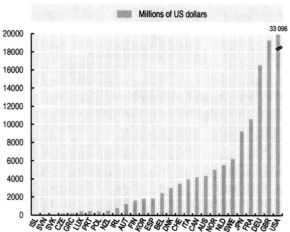

StatLink ᴍᴙ http://dx.doi.org/10.1787/888933335308

TAXES ON THE AVERAGE WORKER

Taxes on the average worker measure the ratio between the amount of taxes paid by the worker and the employer on the country average wage and the corresponding total labour cost for the employer. This tax wedge measures the extent to which the tax system on labour income may discourage employment.

Definition

The taxes included are personal income taxes, employees' social security contributions and employers' social security contributions. For the few countries that have them, it also includes payroll taxes. The amount of these taxes paid in relation to the employment of one average worker is expressed as a percentage of their labour cost (gross wage plus employers' social security contributions and payroll tax).

An average worker is defined as somebody who earns the average income of full-time workers of the country concerned in Sectors B-N of the *International Standard Industrial Classification* (ISIC Rev.4). The average worker is considered single without children, meaning that he or she does not receive any tax relief in respect of a spouse, unmarried partner or child.

Comparability

The types of taxes included are fully comparable across countries. They are based on common definitions agreed by all OECD countries.

While the income levels of workers in Sectors B-N differ across countries, they can be regarded as corresponding to comparable types of work in each country.

The information on the average worker's income level is supplied by the Ministries of Finance in all OECD countries and is based on national statistical surveys. The amount of taxes paid by the single worker is calculated by applying the tax laws in each country. These tax wedge measures are therefore derived from a modelling exercise rather than from the direct observation of taxes actually paid by workers and their employers.

Overview

In 2014, taxes on an average single worker without children represented 36% of their total labour costs across OECD countries on average. This tax wedge ranged between 7% in Chile to around 56% in Belgium.

The average tax wedge has decreased by 0.7 percentage points since 2000. However, there are important differences between countries. Of the 34 OECD countries, 11 countries have experienced an overall increase in the taxes on an average worker since 2000. The countries with the largest increases were Iceland, Japan, Korea and Mexico. Of the 25 countries that have experienced an overall decline, the largest decreases were in Denmark, Hungary, Israel and Sweden.

Sources
• OECD (2015), *Taxing Wages*, OECD Publishing.

Further information

Analytical publications
• OECD (2011), "Taxation and Employment", *OECD Tax Policy Studies*, No. 21, OECD Publishing.
• OECD (2007), *Benefits and Wages*, OECD Publishing.
• OECD (2006), "Encouraging Savings Through Tax-preferred Accounts", *OECD Tax Policy Studies*, No. 15, OECD Publishing.
• Torres, C., K. Mellbye and B. Brys (2012), "Trends in Personal Income Tax and Employee Social Security Contribution Schedules", *OECD Taxation Working Papers*, No. 12.

Statistical publications
• OECD (2015), *Revenue Statistics*, OECD Publishing.
• OECD and Economic Commission for Latin America and the Caribbean (2015), *Latin American Economic Outlook*, OECD Publishing.

Online databases
• OECD Tax Statistics.

Websites
• Tax and Benefit Systems: OECD indicators, *www.oecd.org/els/social/workincentives*.
• Tax policy analysis, *www.oecd.org/tax/tax-policy*.
• Taxing wages (supplementary material), *www.oecd.org/tax/tax-policy/taxing-wages*.

GOVERNMENT • TAXES

TAXES ON THE AVERAGE WORKER

Taxes on the average worker
As a percentage of labour cost

	2003	2004	2005	2006	2007	2008	2009	2010	2011	2012	2013	2014
Australia	28.2	28.2	28.5	28.3	27.7	26.9	26.7	26.8	26.7	27.2	27.4	27.7
Austria	47.4	48.3	48.1	48.5	48.8	49.0	47.9	48.2	48.5	48.8	49.2	49.4
Belgium	55.7	55.4	55.5	55.5	55.6	55.9	55.7	55.9	56.1	56.0	55.7	55.6
Canada	31.7	31.9	31.9	31.8	31.3	31.3	30.5	30.4	30.7	30.8	31.0	31.5
Chile	7.0	7.0	7.0	7.0	7.0	7.0	7.0	7.0	7.0	7.0	7.0	7.0
Czech Republic	43.2	43.5	43.7	42.5	42.9	43.4	42.0	42.1	42.6	42.5	42.5	42.6
Denmark	42.4	41.0	40.9	41.0	41.1	40.9	39.5	38.3	38.4	38.5	38.2	38.1
Estonia	42.3	41.5	39.9	39.0	39.0	38.4	39.2	40.1	40.3	40.4	39.9	40.0
Finland	44.8	44.2	44.4	44.0	43.9	43.8	42.5	42.3	42.3	42.5	43.1	43.9
France	50.1	50.3	50.5	49.7	49.7	49.8	49.8	49.9	50.0	50.1	48.9	48.4
Germany	53.2	52.2	52.1	52.3	51.8	51.3	50.8	49.1	49.7	49.6	49.2	49.3
Greece	39.9	41.4	41.2	42.3	42.1	41.5	41.3	40.1	43.2	42.9	41.6	40.4
Hungary	50.8	51.7	51.1	51.9	54.5	54.1	53.1	46.6	49.5	49.5	49.0	49.0
Iceland	31.5	31.9	32.1	31.8	30.5	30.9	30.5	33.4	34.1	33.8	34.1	33.5
Ireland	24.4	24.1	23.5	23.0	22.2	22.3	24.7	25.8	25.8	25.9	27.1	28.2
Israel	27.7	26.4	25.5	24.3	24.9	22.9	21.3	20.7	20.8	20.4	20.4	20.5
Italy	46.0	46.3	45.9	46.1	46.4	46.6	46.8	47.2	47.6	47.7	47.9	48.2
Japan	27.4	27.3	27.7	28.8	29.3	29.5	29.2	30.2	30.8	31.3	31.6	31.9
Korea	16.4	17.0	17.3	18.2	19.7	20.0	19.5	20.1	20.5	21.0	21.3	21.5
Luxembourg	33.5	33.9	34.7	35.3	36.3	34.7	33.9	34.3	36.3	36.0	37.2	37.6
Mexico	16.7	15.2	14.7	15.0	15.9	15.1	15.3	15.5	18.7	19.0	19.2	19.5
Netherlands	37.2	38.8	38.9	38.4	38.7	39.2	38.0	38.1	38.0	38.8	37.0	37.7
New Zealand	19.5	19.7	20.0	20.4	21.1	20.5	18.1	17.0	15.9	16.4	16.9	17.2
Norway	38.1	38.1	37.2	37.4	37.5	37.6	37.3	37.3	37.6	37.4	37.3	37.0
Poland	38.2	38.4	38.7	39.0	38.2	34.7	34.1	34.2	34.3	35.5	35.6	35.6
Portugal	37.4	37.4	36.8	37.5	37.3	36.9	36.5	37.1	38.0	37.6	41.4	41.2
Slovak Republic	42.5	42.2	38.0	38.3	38.4	38.8	37.7	37.9	38.8	39.6	41.1	41.2
Slovenia	46.2	46.3	45.6	45.3	43.3	42.9	42.2	42.5	42.6	42.5	42.4	42.5
Spain	38.6	38.8	39.0	39.1	39.0	38.0	38.3	39.7	40.0	40.6	40.7	40.7
Sweden	48.2	48.4	48.1	47.8	45.3	44.8	43.2	42.8	42.8	42.9	43.0	42.5
Switzerland	22.4	22.2	22.2	22.1	22.4	21.9	22.0	22.1	22.3	22.1	22.1	22.2
Turkey	42.2	42.8	42.8	42.7	42.7	39.9	37.4	37.4	37.4	37.4	37.6	38.2
United Kingdom	33.8	33.9	33.9	34.0	34.1	32.8	32.4	32.6	32.5	32.1	31.4	31.1
United States	29.9	29.8	29.8	29.9	30.3	29.8	30.1	30.5	29.7	29.8	31.4	31.5
EU 28	..	..	..	..	..	..	..	..	..	..	..	..
OECD	36.3	36.3	36.1	36.1	36.1	35.7	35.1	35.1	35.6	35.7	35.9	36.0
Brazil	..	..	..	..	..	..	..	..	..	..	..	..
China	..	..	..	..	..	..	..	..	..	..	..	..
India	..	..	..	..	..	..	..	..	..	..	..	..
Indonesia	..	..	..	..	..	..	..	..	..	..	..	..
Russian Federation	..	..	..	..	..	..	..	..	..	..	..	..
South Africa	..	..	..	..	..	..	..	..	..	..	..	..

StatLink http://dx.doi.org/10.1787/888933336653

Taxes on the average worker
As a percentage of labour cost

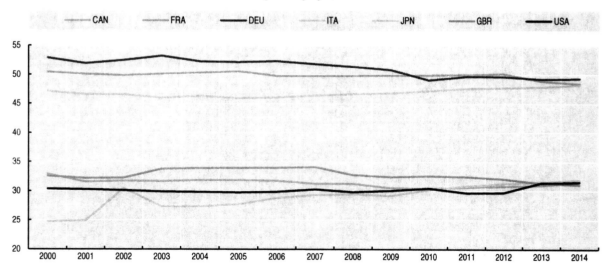

StatLink http://dx.doi.org/10.1787/888933335585

OECD FACTBOOK 2015-2016 © OECD 2016

197

TOTAL TAX REVENUE

Total tax revenue as a percentage of GDP indicates the share of a country's output that is collected by the government through taxes. It can be regarded as one measure of the degree to which the government controls the economy's resources.

Definition

Taxes are defined as compulsory, unrequited payments to general government. They are unrequited in the sense that benefits provided by government to taxpayers are not normally in proportion to their payments. Data on total tax revenue refer to the revenues collected from taxes on income and profits, social security contributions, taxes levied on goods and services, payroll taxes, taxes on the ownership and transfer of property, and other taxes.

Taxes on incomes and profits cover taxes levied on the net income or profits (gross income minus allowable tax reliefs) of individuals and enterprises. They also cover taxes levied on the capital gains of individuals and enterprises, and gains from gambling.

Taxes on goods and services cover all taxes levied on the production, extraction, sale, transfer, leasing or delivery of goods, and the rendering of services, or on the use of goods or permission to use goods or to perform activities. They consist mainly of value added and sales taxes. Note that the sum of taxes on goods and services and taxes on income and profits is less than the figure for total tax revenues.

Comparability

The tax revenue data are collected in a way that makes them as internationally comparable as possible. Country representatives have agreed on the definitions of each type of tax and how they should be measured in all OECD countries, and they are then responsible for submitting data to the OECD that conform to these rules.

Overview

The tax burden continued to rise in OECD countries in 2014, increasing by 0.2 percentage points to an average 34.4% of GDP. The increase is calculated by applying the unweighted average percentage change for 2014 in the 30 countries providing data for that year to the overall average tax to GDP ratio in 2013. The rate of increase was lower than in 2013 and 2012 when the average tax burdens were 34.2% and 33.8%. Of those 30 countries, the total tax revenues as a percentage of GDP rose in 16 and fell in 14 compared with 2013.

The 2014 tax burden is the highest ever recorded OECD average tax to GDP ratio since the OECD began compiling this measure in 1965. Historically, the tax burden reached its previous peak of 34.2% of GDP in the year 2000. It then fell back slightly between 2001 and 2004 but rose again between 2005 and 2007 to an average of 34.1%. During the financial crisis, the OECD tax burden declined sharply to 32.7% in 2009 (a fall of 1.4 percentage points) before rising over the next 5 years to 34.4% in 2014 (an increase of 1.7 percentage points).

Sources
- OECD (2015), *Revenue Statistics*, OECD Publishing.

Further information

Analytical publications
- OECD (2014), *Consumption Tax Trends*, OECD Publishing.
- OECD (2013), *Global Forum on Transparency and Exchange of Information for Tax Purposes*, OECD Publishing.
- OECD (2011), *OECD Tax Policy Studies*, OECD Publishing.

Statistical publications
- OECD (2015), *Taxing Wages*, OECD Publishing.

Methodological publications
- OECD and Council of Europe (France) (2011), *The Multilateral Convention on Mutual Administrative Assistance in Tax Matters*, OECD Publishing.
- OECD (2010), *Model Tax Convention on Income and on Capital: Condensed Version*, OECD Publishing.

Online databases
- OECD Tax Statistics.

Websites
- Global Forum on Transparency and Exchange of Information for Tax Purposes, *www.oecd.org/tax/transparency*.

Total tax revenue

As a percentage of GDP

	2002	2003	2004	2005	2006	2007	2008	2009	2010	2011	2012	2013	2014
Australia	29.8	29.9	30.3	29.9	29.5	29.7	27.0	25.8	25.6	26.3	27.3	27.5	..
Austria	42.5	42.3	41.8	40.9	40.4	40.5	41.4	41.0	40.8	41.0	41.7	42.5	43.0
Belgium	43.6	43.1	43.2	43.1	42.8	42.6	43.0	42.1	42.4	43.0	44.0	44.7	44.7
Canada	32.8	32.7	32.5	32.3	32.6	32.3	31.5	31.4	30.4	30.2	30.7	30.5	30.8
Chile	19.0	18.7	19.1	20.7	22.0	22.8	21.4	17.2	19.5	21.2	21.5	20.0	19.8
Czech Republic	33.5	34.4	34.7	34.5	34.1	34.3	33.5	32.4	32.5	33.4	33.8	34.3	33.5
Denmark	45.4	45.6	46.4	48.0	46.4	46.4	44.9	45.2	45.3	45.4	46.4	47.6	50.9
Estonia	31.1	30.8	31.1	29.9	30.4	31.1	31.3	34.9	33.2	31.9	32.1	31.8	32.9
Finland	43.3	42.4	41.8	42.1	42.2	41.5	41.2	40.9	40.8	42.0	42.7	43.7	43.9
France	42.1	42.0	42.2	42.8	43.1	42.4	42.2	41.3	41.6	42.9	44.1	45.0	45.2
Germany	34.4	34.6	33.9	33.9	34.5	34.9	35.4	36.1	35.0	35.7	36.4	36.5	36.1
Greece	32.5	31.0	30.0	31.2	30.3	31.2	31.0	30.8	32.0	33.5	34.5	34.4	35.9
Hungary	37.4	37.4	37.2	36.8	36.7	39.6	39.5	39.0	37.3	36.5	38.6	38.4	38.5
Iceland	34.3	35.6	36.6	39.4	40.4	38.7	35.1	32.0	33.3	34.4	35.2	35.9	38.7
Ireland	27.4	28.3	29.1	29.2	31.0	30.4	28.6	27.6	27.5	27.4	27.9	29.0	29.9
Israel	34.2	33.5	33.5	33.8	34.4	34.3	31.9	29.7	30.4	30.8	29.7	30.6	31.1
Italy	39.7	40.1	39.3	39.1	40.6	41.7	41.6	42.1	41.8	41.9	43.9	43.9	43.6
Japan	25.8	25.3	26.1	27.3	28.1	28.5	28.5	27.0	27.6	28.6	29.4	30.3	..
Korea	22.0	22.7	22.0	22.5	23.6	24.8	24.6	23.8	23.4	24.2	24.8	24.3	24.6
Luxembourg	38.0	38.1	37.0	38.3	36.3	36.6	37.2	39.0	38.1	37.9	38.8	38.4	37.8
Mexico	16.2	17.1	16.8	17.7	17.9	17.6	20.7	17.2	18.5	19.5	19.5	19.7	19.5
Netherlands	35.2	34.6	34.8	36.1	36.4	36.1	36.5	35.4	36.2	35.9	36.1	36.7	..
New Zealand	33.2	33.1	34.1	36.0	35.4	34.0	33.3	30.5	30.6	30.9	32.4	31.4	32.4
Norway	42.3	41.6	42.3	42.6	42.8	42.1	41.5	41.2	41.9	42.0	41.5	40.5	39.1
Poland	33.2	32.6	32.2	33.3	33.9	34.8	34.5	31.5	31.4	32.0	32.3	31.9	..
Portugal	31.4	31.5	30.3	30.9	31.5	32.0	31.9	30.0	30.6	32.5	32.0	34.5	34.4
Slovak Republic	32.7	32.4	31.4	31.2	29.3	29.2	29.1	28.9	28.1	28.7	28.5	30.4	31.0
Slovenia	37.2	37.3	37.4	38.0	37.6	37.1	36.4	36.2	36.9	36.5	36.8	36.8	36.6
Spain	33.4	33.3	34.3	35.3	36.1	36.5	32.3	29.8	29.9	31.3	32.1	32.7	33.2
Sweden	45.2	45.5	45.6	46.6	46.0	45.0	44.0	44.1	43.2	42.5	42.6	42.8	42.7
Switzerland	27.5	26.8	26.5	26.5	26.4	26.1	26.7	27.1	26.5	27.0	26.9	26.9	26.6
Turkey	24.6	25.9	24.1	24.3	24.5	24.1	24.2	24.6	26.2	27.8	27.6	29.3	28.7
United Kingdom	33.3	32.9	33.4	33.8	34.4	34.1	34.0	32.3	32.8	33.6	33.0	32.9	32.6
United States	24.9	24.4	24.6	25.9	26.6	26.7	25.2	23.0	23.2	23.6	24.1	25.4	26.0
EU 28	..	..	..	..	..	..	..	..	..	..	..	..	..
OECD	33.5	33.5	33.4	33.9	34.1	34.1	33.6	32.7	32.8	33.3	33.8	34.2	34.4
Brazil	31.7	31.2	32.1	33.1	33.1	33.4	33.8	33.1	33.2	35.0	35.6	35.7	..
China	..	..	..	..	..	..	..	..	..	..	..	..	..
India	..	..	..	..	..	..	..	..	..	..	..	..	..
Indonesia	..	..	..	..	..	..	..	..	..	..	..	..	..
Russian Federation	..	..	..	..	..	..	..	..	..	..	..	..	..
South Africa	..	..	..	..	..	..	..	..	..	..	..	..	..

StatLink ▄▄▄ http://dx.doi.org/10.1787/888933336702

Total tax revenue

As a percentage of GDP

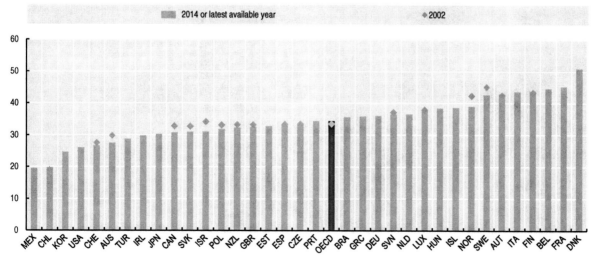

StatLink ▄▄▄ http://dx.doi.org/10.1787/888933335636

HEALTH

LIFE EXPECTANCY

Life expectancy at birth continues to increase steadily in OECD countries, going up on average by 3 to 4 months each year, with no sign of slowing down. These gains in longevity can be attributed to a number of factors including improved lifestyle and better education, and progress in health care.

Higher national income (as measured by GDP per capita) is generally associated with higher life expectancy at birth, although the relationship is less pronounced at higher levels of national income.

Life expectancy in OECD countries varies not only by gender, but also by socio-economic status as measured, for instance, by education level. A higher education level not only provides the means to improve the socio-economic conditions in which people live and work, but may also promote the adoption of healthier lifestyles and facilitate access to appropriate health care.

Overview

In 2013, life expectancy on average across OECD countries reached 80.5 years, an increase of more than ten years since 1970. Japan, Spain and Switzerland lead a large group of 25 OECD countries in which life expectancy at birth now exceeds 80 years.

Although the life expectancy in emerging economies such as India, Indonesia, Brazil and China remains well below the OECD average, these economies have achieved considerable gains in longevity over the past decades, with the level converging rapidly towards the OECD average. There has been much less progress in countries such as South Africa (due mainly to the epidemic of HIV/AIDS), and Russia (due mainly to the impact of the economic transition in the 1990s and a rise in risk increasing behaviours among men, notably rising alcohol consumption).

The gender gap in life expectancy stood at 5.3 years on average across OECD countries in 2013, with life expectancy reaching 77.8 years among men and 83.1 years among women. While the gender gap in life expectancy increased substantially in many OECD countries during the 1970s and early 1980s to reach a peak of almost seven years in the mid-1980s, it has narrowed during the past 25 years, reflecting higher gains in life expectancy among men than among women.

On average among 16 OECD countries for which recent data are available, people with the highest level of education can expect to live six years longer than people with the lowest level of education at age 30 (53 years versus 47 years). These differences in life expectancy by education level are particularly pronounced for men, with an average gap of almost eight years. The differences are especially large in Central and Eastern European countries (Slovak Republic, Estonia, Czech Republic, Poland and Hungary), where the life expectancy gap between higher and lower educated men is more than ten years. This is largely explained by the greater prevalence of risk factors among lower educated men, such as tobacco and alcohol use. Differences in other countries such as Sweden, Italy, the Netherlands and Norway are less pronounced.

Definition

Life expectancy at birth measures how long, on average, people would live based on a given set of age-specific death rates. However, the actual age-specific death rates of any particular birth cohort cannot be known in advance. If age-specific death rates are falling (as has been the case over the past decades), actual life spans will be higher than life expectancy calculated with current death rates.

Comparability

The methodology used to calculate life expectancy can vary slightly between countries. This can change a country's estimates by a fraction of a year. Life expectancy at birth for the total population is calculated by the OECD Secretariat for all OECD countries, using the unweighted average of life expectancy of men and women.

Sources
- OECD (2015), *OECD Health Statistics* (Database).

Further information

Analytical publications
- OECD (2015), *How's Life? Measuring Well-being*, OECD Publishing.
- OECD (2010), *Health Care Systems: Efficiency and Policy Settings*, OECD Publishing.

Statistical publications
- OECD (2015), *Health at a Glance*, OECD Publishing.
- OECD (2014), *Health at a Glance: Asia/Pacific*, OECD Publishing.
- OECD (2014), *Health at a Glance: Europe*, OECD Publishing.

Websites
- Health at a Glance (supplementary material), *www.oecd.org/health/healthataglance*.
- OECD Health Statistics (supplementary material), *www.oecd.org/els/health-systems/health-statistics.htm*.

Life expectancy at birth
Number of years

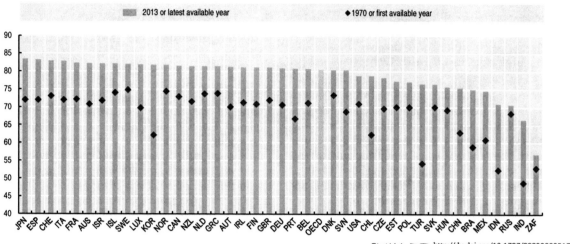

StatLink *http://dx.doi.org/10.1787/888933335172*

Variation in life expectancy by sex
Number of years, 2013 or latest available year

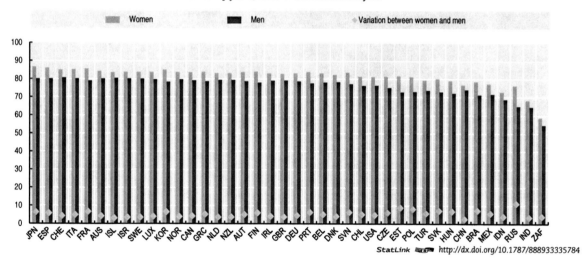

StatLink *http://dx.doi.org/10.1787/888933335784*

Gap in life expectancy at age 30 by sex and educational level
Gap in years, 2012 or latest year

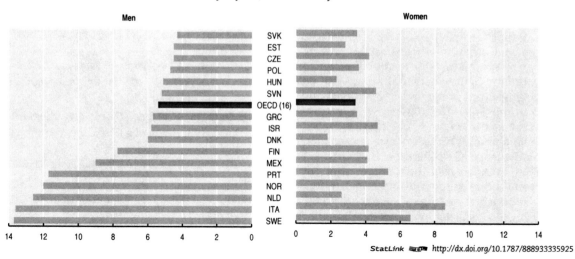

StatLink *http://dx.doi.org/10.1787/888933335925*

INFANT MORTALITY

Infant mortality, the rate at which babies and children of less than one year of age die, reflects the effect of economic and social conditions on the health of mothers and newborns, the social environment, individual lifestyles as well as the characteristics and effectiveness of health systems.

Many studies use infant mortality as a health outcome to examine the effect of a variety of medical and non-medical determinants of health. Although most analyses show that higher health spending tends to be associated with lower infant mortality, the fact that some countries with a high level of health expenditure do not exhibit low levels of infant mortality suggests that more health spending is not necessarily required to obtain better results.

Overview

In most OECD countries, infant mortality is low and there is little difference in rates. In 2013, the average in OECD countries was less than four deaths per 1 000 live births, with rates being the lowest in Iceland, Slovenia, Finland, Estonia and Japan. A small group of OECD countries still have comparatively high infant mortality (Mexico, Turkey and Chile), although in these three countries infant mortality has reduced considerably over the past few decades.

In some of the emerging economies (India, South Africa and Indonesia), infant mortality remains above 20 deaths per 1 000 live births. In India, one-in-twenty-five children die before their first birthday, although the rates have fallen sharply over the past few decades. Infant mortality rates have also reduced greatly in Indonesia.

In the United States, the reduction in infant mortality has been slower than in most other OECD countries. In 2000, the US rate was below the OECD average, but it is now higher.

In OECD countries, around two-thirds of the deaths that occur during the first year of life are neonatal deaths (i.e., during the first four weeks). Birth defects, prematurity and other conditions arising during pregnancy are the main factors contributing to neonatal mortality in developed countries. With an increasing number of women deferring childbearing and a rise in multiple births linked with fertility treatments, the number of pre-term births has tended to increase. In a number of higher-income countries, this has contributed to a levelling-off of the downward trend in infant mortality over the past few years. For deaths beyond a month (post-neonatal mortality), there tends to be a greater range of causes – the most common being SIDS (sudden infant death syndrome), birth defects, infections and accidents.

Definition

The infant mortality rate is the number of deaths of children under one year of age, expressed per 1 000 live births.

Comparability

Some of the international variation in infant mortality rates is related to variations in registering practices for very premature infants. While some countries register all live births including very small babies with low odds of survival, several countries apply a minimum threshold of a gestation period of 22 weeks (or a birth weight threshold of 500 grams) for babies to be registered as live births. To remove this data comparability limitation, the data are based on a minimum threshold of 22 weeks of gestation period (or 500 grams birth weight) for a majority of OECD countries that have provided these data. However, the data for some countries (e.g. Canada and Australia) continue to be based on all registered live births, resulting in some over-estimation.

Sources
- OECD (2015), *OECD Health Statistics* (Database).

Further information

Analytical publications
- OECD (2015), *How's Life? Measuring Well-being*, OECD Publishing.
- OECD (2011), *Doing Better for Families*, OECD Publishing.
- OECD (2009), *Doing Better for Children*, OECD Publishing.

Statistical publications
- OECD (2015), *Health at a Glance*, OECD Publishing.
- OECD (2014), *Health at a Glance: Asia/Pacific*, OECD Publishing.
- OECD (2014), *Health at a Glance: Europe*, OECD Publishing.

Websites
- Health at a Glance (supplementary material), *www.oecd.org/health/healthataglance*.
- OECD Health Statistics (supplementary material), *www.oecd.org/els/health-systems/health-statistics.htm*.

Infant mortality rates

Deaths per 1 000 live births, 2013 or latest available year

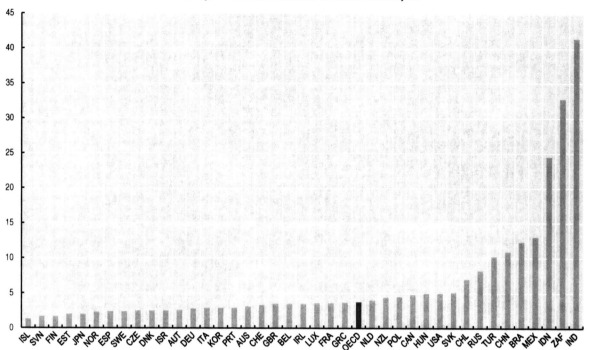

StatLink ⬛ http://dx.doi.org/10.1787/888933335136

Trend in infant mortality in selected OECD countries

Deaths per 1 000 live births, 2000-13 or latest available period

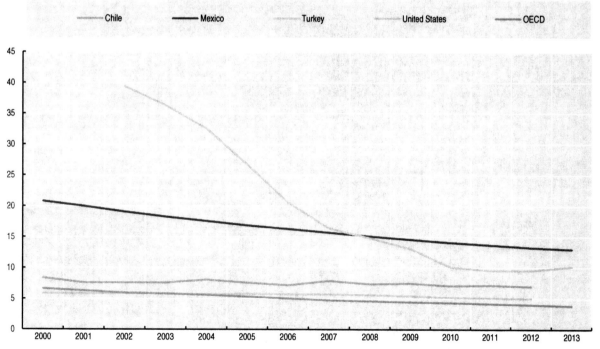

StatLink ⬛ http://dx.doi.org/10.1787/888933335775

SUICIDES

Suicide is a significant cause of death in many OECD countries, accounting for over 150 000 deaths in 2013. A complex set of reasons may explain why some people choose to attempt or commit suicide. A high proportion of people who have attempted or committed suicide are suffering from psychiatric disorders such as severe depression, bipolar disorder and schizophrenia. The social context in which an individual lives is also important. Low income, alcohol and drug abuse, unemployment and social isolation are all associated with higher rates of suicide.

Early detection of psycho-social problems in high-risk groups by families and health professionals is an important part of suicide prevention campaigns, together with the provision of effective support and treatment. Many countries are developing national strategies for prevention, focusing on at-risk groups.

Overview

Suicide rates in 2013 were lowest in Turkey, Greece, Mexico, Italy and Israel, at seven or fewer deaths per 100 000 population, although the number of suicides in certain countries may be under-reported because of the stigma associated with the act or data unreliability associated with reporting criteria. Suicide rates are also low in South Africa and Brazil. Korea had the highest suicide rate with nearly 30 deaths per 100 000 population, followed by Russia, Hungary, Japan and Slovenia with nearly 20 deaths per 100 000 population.

Mortality rates from suicide are three-to-four times greater for men than for women across OECD countries. In Poland and the Slovak Republic, men are seven times more likely to commit suicide than women. The gender gap is narrower for attempted suicides, reflecting the fact that women tend to use less fatal methods than men. Suicide is also related to age, with young people aged under 25 and elderly people especially at risk. While suicide rates among the latter have generally declined over the past two decades, less progress has been observed among younger people.

Since 1990, suicide rates have decreased by around 30% across OECD countries, with the rates being halved in countries such as Hungary, Denmark, Luxembourg and Finland. In Estonia, after an initial rise in the early 1990s, the rates have also fallen sharply. On the other hand, death rates from suicides have increased in Korea, Chile, Mexico, Russia, Greece, Poland, Japan and the Netherlands. In Japan, there was a sharp rise in the mid-to-late 1990s, coinciding with the Asian financial crisis, but rates have started to come down in recent years. In Korea, suicide rates rose steadily over the past two decades peaking around 2010, before starting to come down. Suicide is the number one cause of death among teenagers in Korea.

Definition

The World Health Organization defines suicide as an act deliberately initiated and performed by a person in the full knowledge or expectation of its fatal outcome.

Mortality rates have been directly age-standardised to the 2010 OECD population to remove variations arising from differences in age structures across countries and over time. The source is the WHO Mortality Database. Deaths from suicide are classified to ICD-10 codes X60-X84.

Comparability

Comparability of data between countries is affected by a number of reporting criteria, including how a person's intention of killing themselves is ascertained, who is responsible for completing the death certificate, whether a forensic investigation is carried out, and the provisions for confidentiality of the cause of death. The number of suicides in certain countries may be under-estimated because of the stigma that is associated with the act, or because of data issues associated with reporting criteria. Caution is required therefore in interpreting variations across countries.

Sources
- OECD (2015), *OECD Health Statistics* (Database).

Further information

Analytical publications
- OECD (2015), *Mental Health and Work*, OECD Publishing.
- OECD (2015), *OECD Health Working Papers*, OECD Publishing.
- OECD (2014), *Making Mental Health Count*, OECD Publishing.

Statistical publications
- OECD (2015), *Health at a Glance*, OECD Publishing.
- OECD (2014), *Health at a Glance: Asia/Pacific*, OECD Publishing.
- OECD (2014), *Health at a Glance: Europe*, OECD Publishing.

Websites
- Mental Health, *www.oecd.org/health/mental-health.htm*.
- OECD Health Statistics (supplementary material), *www.oecd.org/els/health-systems/health-statistics.htm*.

Suicide rates

Age-standardised rates per 100 000 population, 2013 or latest available year

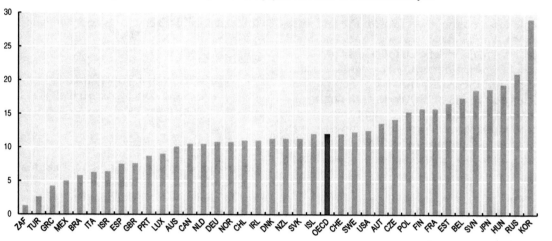

StatLink ⟨⟩ http://dx.doi.org/10.1787/888933335565

Trends in suicide rates

Age-standardised rates per 100 000 population

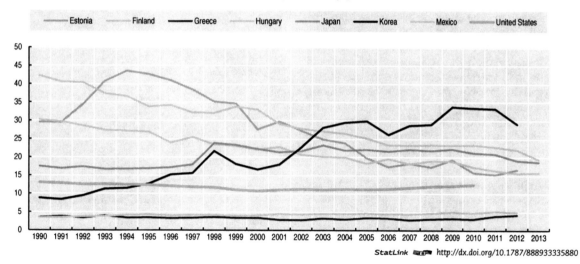

StatLink ⟨⟩ http://dx.doi.org/10.1787/888933335880

Change in suicide rates

Percentage, 1990-2013 or latest available period

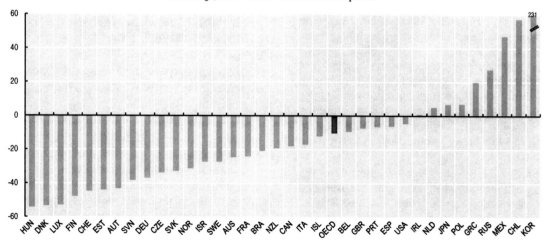

StatLink ⟨⟩ http://dx.doi.org/10.1787/888933336003

SMOKING

Tobacco kills nearly 6 million people each year, of whom more than 5 million are from direct tobacco use and more than 600 000 are non-smokers exposed to second-hand smoke. Tobacco is a major risk factor for at least two of the leading causes of premature mortality – cardiovascular diseases and cancer, increasing the risk of heart attack, stroke, lung cancer, cancers of the larynx and mouth, and pancreatic cancer, among others. In addition, it is a dominant contributing factor for respiratory diseases such as chronic obstructive pulmonary disease. Smoking in pregnancy can lead to low birth weight and illness among infants. Smoking remains the largest avoidable risk factor for health in OECD countries and worldwide.

Definition

The proportion of daily smokers is defined as the percentage of the population aged 15 years and over who report smoking every day.

Comparability

International comparability is limited due to the lack of standardisation in the measurement of smoking habits in health interview surveys across OECD countries. Variations remain in the age groups surveyed, the wording of questions, response categories and survey methodologies (e.g. in a number of countries, respondents are asked if they smoke regularly, rather than daily; and if they smoke cigarettes rather than all types of tobacco). In addition, self-reports of behaviours may suffer from social desirability bias that may potentially limit cross-country comparisons.

Overview

The proportion of daily smokers in the adult population varies greatly, even between neighbouring countries. Nineteen of 34 OECD countries had less than 20% of the adult population smoking daily in 2013. Rates were lowest in Sweden, Iceland, Mexico and Australia (less than 13%). Rates were also less than 13% in Brazil and India, although the proportion of smokers among men is high in India at 23%. On the other hand, smoking rates remain high in Greece in both men and women, and in Indonesia where more than one in two men smoke daily. Smoking prevalence is higher among men than among women in all OECD countries except in Sweden and Iceland. The gender gap in smoking rates is particularly large in Korea, Japan and Turkey, as well as in Russia, India, Indonesia, South Africa and China.

Since 2000, smoking rates across most OECD countries have continued to decline, although other forms of smokeless tobacco use, such as snuff in Sweden, are not taken into account. On average, smoking rates have decreased by about one fourth since 2000, from 26% to 20% in 2013. Large reductions occurred in Norway, Iceland, Denmark, Sweden and Ireland, as well as in India.

Much of the decline in tobacco use can be attributed to policies aimed at reducing tobacco consumption through public awareness campaigns, advertising bans, increased taxation, and restriction of smoking in public spaces and restaurants, in response to rising rates of tobacco-related diseases. As governments continue to reinforce their anti-tobacco policies, new strategies such as plain packaging for tobacco products aimed to restrict branding have been implemented (e.g. in Australia) and are being adopted by an increasing number of countries.

There is strong evidence of socio-economic differences in smoking and mortality. People in less affluent social groups have a greater prevalence and intensity of smoking and a higher all-cause mortality rate and lower rates of cancer survival.

Sources
• OECD (2015), *OECD Health Statistics* (Database).

Further information

Analytical publications
• OECD (2015), *Cardiovascular Disease and Diabetes: Policies for Better Health and Quality of Care*, OECD Publishing.
• OECD (2013), *Cancer Care: Assuring Quality to Improve Survival*, OECD Publishing.

Statistical publications
• OECD (2015), *Health at a Glance*, OECD Publishing.
• OECD (2014), *Health at a Glance: Asia/Pacific*, OECD Publishing.
• OECD (2014), *Health at a Glance: Europe*, OECD Publishing.

Websites
• Health at a Glance (supplementary material), *www.oecd.org/health/healthataglance*.
• Health Care Quality Indicators - Cardiovascular Disease and Diabetes, *www.oecd.org/els/health-systems/hcqi-cardiovascular-disease-and-diabetes.htm*.
• OECD Health Statistics (supplementary material), *www.oecd.org/els/health-systems/health-statistics.htm*.

Adult population smoking daily
As a percentage of adult population, 2013 or latest available year

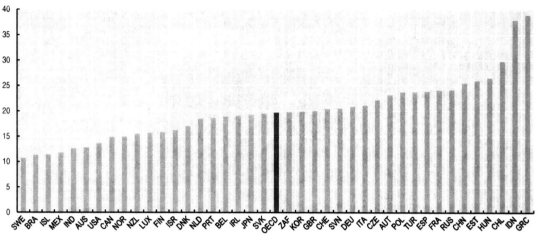

StatLink http://dx.doi.org/10.1787/888933335510

Change in smoking rates
Percentage change over the period 2000-13 or latest available period

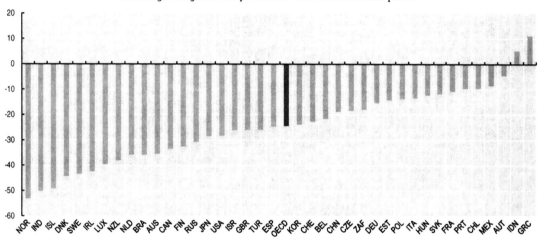

StatLink http://dx.doi.org/10.1787/888933335872

Adult population smoking daily by gender
Percentage of adult population, 2013 or latest available year

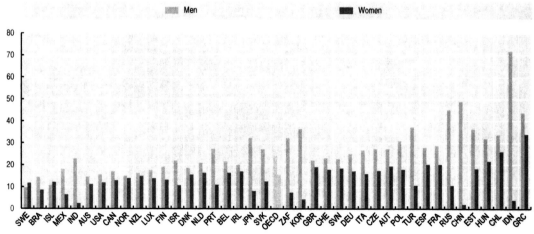

StatLink http://dx.doi.org/10.1787/888933335998

ALCOHOL CONSUMPTION

The health burden related to harmful alcohol consumption, both in terms of morbidity and mortality, is considerable. Alcohol use is associated with numerous harmful health and social consequences, including an increased risk of a range of cancers, stroke, and liver cirrhosis, among others. Foetal exposure to alcohol increases the risk of birth defects and intellectual impairment. Alcohol also contributes to death and disability through accidents and injuries, assault, violence, homicide and suicide.

Definition

Alcohol consumption is defined as annual sales of pure alcohol in litres per person aged 15 years and over. Survey-based estimates of the amount of alcohol drunk by the 20% heaviest drinkers rely on the data analysis of the latest available national health surveys for 13 OECD countries.

Comparability

The methodology to convert alcoholic drinks to pure alcohol may differ across countries. Official statistics do not include unrecorded alcohol consumption, such as home production.

Overview

Alcohol consumption stands at 8.9 litres per adult per year, on average, across OECD countries, based on the most recent data available. Austria, Estonia and the Czech Republic, reported the highest consumption of alcohol with 11.5 litres or more per adult per year in 2013. The lowest alcohol consumption was recorded in Turkey and Israel, as well as in Indonesia and India, where religious and cultural traditions restrict the use of alcohol in some population groups.

Although average alcohol consumption has gradually fallen in many OECD countries since 2000, it has risen in Poland, Chile, Sweden, Mexico, Norway, the United States, Finland, Canada, Iceland and New Zealand, as well as in China, India, Indonesia, Russia and South Africa.

However, national aggregate data does not permit to identify individual drinking patterns and the populations at risk. OECD analysis based on individual-level data show that hazardous drinking and heavy episodic drinking are on the rise among young people and women especially. Men of low socioeconomic status are more likely to drink heavily than those of a higher socioeconomic status, while the opposite is observed in women. Alcohol consumption is highly concentrated, as the large majority of alcohol is consumed by the 20% of the population who drink the most, with some variation across countries. The 20% heaviest drinkers in Hungary consume about 90% of all alcohol, while in France the share is about 50%.

Sources
• OECD (2015), OECD Health Statistics (Database).

Further information

Analytical publications
• Devaux, M. and F. Sassi (2015), "Alcohol consumption and harmful drinking: Trends and social disparities across OECD countries", OECD Health Working Papers, No. 79, OECD Publishing, Paris.
• OECD (2015), Tackling Harmful Alcohol Use, OECD Publishing.
• WHO (2011), Global Status Report on Alcohol and Health, World Health Organization, Geneva.

Statistical publications
• OECD (2015), Health at a Glance, OECD Publishing.
• OECD (2014), Health at a Glance: Asia/Pacific, OECD Publishing.
• OECD (2014), Health at a Glance: Europe, OECD Publishing.

Websites
• Health at a Glance (supplementary material), www.oecd.org/health/healthataglance.
• OECD Health Statistics (supplementary material), www.oecd.org/els/health-systems/health-statistics.htm.
• The Economics of Prevention, www.oecd.org/health/prevention.

Alcohol consumption among population aged 15 and over

Litres per capita, 2013 or latest available year

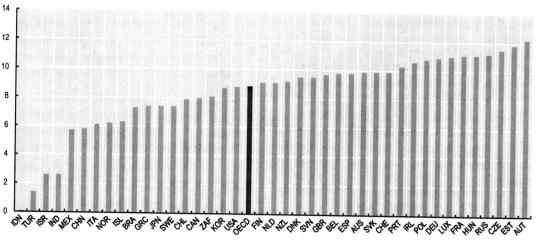

StatLink ⬛⬛⬛ http://dx.doi.org/10.1787/888933334837

Change in alcohol consumption among population aged 15 and over

Percentage change in litres per capita over the period 2000-2013 or latest available period

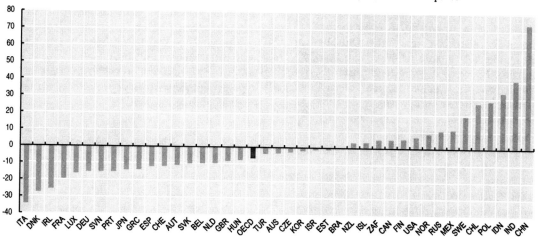

StatLink ⬛⬛⬛ http://dx.doi.org/10.1787/888933335756

Share of total alcohol consumed by the 20% of the population who drink the most

Share, 2012 or latest year available

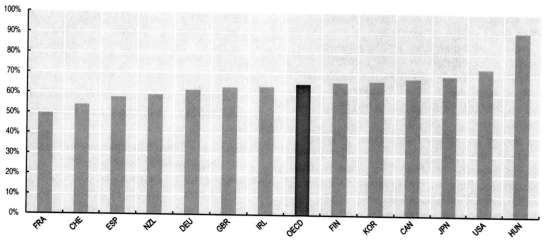

StatLink ⬛⬛⬛ http://dx.doi.org/10.1787/888933335903

OVERWEIGHT AND OBESITY

Obesity is a known risk factor for numerous health problems, including hypertension, high cholesterol, diabetes, cardiovascular diseases, respiratory problems (asthma), musculoskeletal diseases (arthritis) and some forms of cancer. The rise in overweight and obesity is a major public health concern, threatening progress in tackling cardiovascular diseases.

A number of behavioural and environmental factors have contributed to the long-term rise in overweight and obesity rates in OECD countries, including the widespread availability of energy dense foods and more time spent being physically inactive. These factors have created obesogenic environments, putting people, and especially those socially vulnerable, more at risk of obesity.

Overview

Based on the latest available surveys, more than half (53.8%) of the adult population in OECD countries report that they are overweight or obese. In countries where height and weight were measured (as opposed to self-reported), this proportion is even greater, at 57.5%. The prevalence of overweight and obesity among adults exceeds 50% in no less than 22 of 34 OECD countries. In contrast, overweight and obesity rates are much lower in Japan and Korea and in some European countries (France and Switzerland), although even in these countries rates have been increasing.

The prevalence of obesity, which presents even greater health risks than overweight, varies about six fold across OECD countries, from a low of less than 5% in Japan and Korea, to over 32% in Mexico and the United States. Across OECD countries, 19% of the adult population is obese. Obesity rates in men and women are similar in most countries. However, in Chile, Mexico and Turkey, as well as Russia and South Africa, a greater proportion of women are obese, while the reverse is true in Slovenia.

The prevalence of obesity has increased over the past decade in all OECD countries. In 2013, at least one in five adults was obese in twelve OECD countries, compared to one in eight a decade ago. Since 2000, obesity rates have increased by a third or more in 14 countries. The rapid rise occurred regardless of where levels stood a decade ago. Obesity increased by around 45% in both Denmark and Australia, even though the current rate in Denmark is less than half that of Australia.

The rise in obesity has affected all population groups, regardless of sex, age, race, income or education level, but to varying degrees. Evidence from Canada, the United Kingdom, France, Italy, Mexico, Spain, Switzerland and the United States shows that obesity tends to be more common in lower educated groups, especially in women.

Definition

Overweight and obesity are defined as excessive weight presenting health risks because of the high proportion of body fat. The most frequently used measure is based on the body mass index (BMI), which is a single number that evaluates an individual's weight in relation to height (weight/height2, with weight in kilograms and height in metres). Based on the WHO classification, adults with a BMI from 25 to 30 are defined as overweight, and those with a BMI of 30 or over as obese.

Comparability

The BMI classification may not be suitable for all ethnic groups, who may have equivalent levels of risk at lower or higher BMI. The thresholds for adults are also not suitable to measure overweight and obesity among children.

For half of the countries, overweight and obesity rates are self-reported through estimates of height and weight from population-based health interview surveys. However, the other half of OECD countries derives their estimates from health examinations. These differences limit data comparability. Estimates from health examinations are generally higher, and more reliable than estimates from health interviews. The OECD average is based on both types of estimates (self-reported and measured) and, thus, may be underestimated.

Sources
- OECD (2015), *OECD Health Statistics* (Database).

Further information

Analytical publications
- Devaux, M. et al. (2011), "Exploring the Relationship between Education and Obesity", *OECD Journal: Economic Studies*, Issue No. 1, OECD Publishing.
- OECD (2010), *Obesity and the Economics of Prevention: Fit not Fat*, OECD Publishing.

Statistical publications
- OECD (2015), *Health at a Glance*, OECD Publishing.
- OECD (2014), *Health at a Glance: Europe*, OECD Publishing.

Websites
- Health at a Glance (supplementary material), *www.oecd.org/health/healthataglance*.
- Obesity Update, *www.oecd.org/health/obesity-update.htm*.
- OECD Health Statistics (supplementary material), *www.oecd.org/els/health-systems/health-statistics.htm*.
- The Economics of Prevention, *www.oecd.org/health/prevention*.

Obesity rates among the adult population

Percentage of population aged 15 and over, 2013 or latest available year

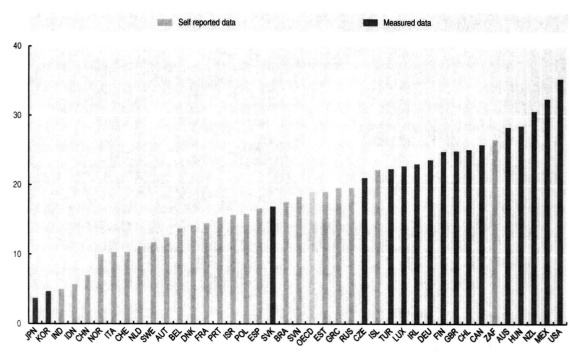

StatLink ▦▤▦ http://dx.doi.org/10.1787/888933335299

Increasing obesity rates among the adult population

Percentage of population aged 15 and over, 2000-13 or latest available period

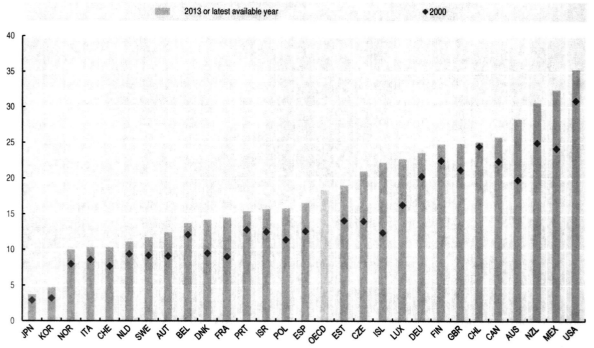

StatLink ▦▤▦ http://dx.doi.org/10.1787/888933335819

DOCTORS

Doctors play a central role in health systems. There are concerns in many OECD countries about current or future shortages of doctors, in particular of general practitioners and doctors practising in rural regions or deprived urban areas.

Projecting the future supply and demand of doctors is difficult because of high levels of uncertainties regarding their retirement patterns, migration patterns on the supply side, and changing health needs of ageing populations and health spending growth on the demand side.

Definition

Practising physicians are defined as the number of doctors providing care for patients. Generalists include doctors assuming responsibility for the provision of continuing care to individuals and families, as well as other generalist/non-specialist practitioners. Specialists include paediatricians, obstetricians/gynaecologists, psychiatrists, medical specialists and surgical specialists. Medical doctors not further defined include interns/residents if they are not reported in the field in which they are training, and doctors not elsewhere classified. The numbers are based on head counts.

Comparability

In several countries (Canada, France, Greece, Iceland, the Netherlands, the Slovak Republic and Turkey), the data include not only physicians providing direct care to patients, but also those working in the health sector as managers, educators, researchers, etc. This can add another 5-10% of doctors. Data for Chile and Portugal refer to all physicians licensed to practice (resulting in a large overestimation of the number of practising doctors in Portugal, of around 30%). Data for Spain include dentists up to 2010, while data for Belgium include stomatologists. Data for India are likely over-estimated as they are based on medical registers that are not regularly updated to account for migration, death, retirement, and people registered in multiple states.

Not all countries are able to report all their physicians in the two broad categories of specialists and generalists because of missing information.

Overview

Between 2000 and 2014, the number of physicians has grown in most OECD countries, both in absolute number and on a per capita basis. The growth rate was particularly rapid in countries which started with lower levels in 2000 (Turkey, Korea and Mexico), but also in countries which already had a large number such as Greece and Austria. In Greece, the number of doctors per capita increased strongly between 2000 and 2008, but has stabilised since then. The number of doctors has also increased strongly in Australia and the United Kingdom, driven mainly by a strong rise in the number of graduates from domestic medical education programmes. On the other hand, the number of physicians per capita remained fairly stable since 2000 in Estonia, France, Israel and the Slovak Republic.

In nearly all countries, the balance between generalist and specialist doctors has changed over the past few decades, with the number of specialists increasing much more rapidly. As a result, there were more than two specialists for every generalist in 2013, on average across OECD countries. In many countries, specialists earn more and have seen their earnings grow faster than generalists. This creates a financial incentive for doctors to specialise, although other factors such as working conditions and professional prestige also influence choices.

Nearly all OECD countries exercise some control over medical school intakes, often by limiting the number of training places, for example in the form of a *numerus clausus*. Ireland and Denmark had the highest number of medical graduates per 100 000 population in 2014. Graduation rates were the lowest in Israel, Japan and Turkey. In most OECD countries, the number of new medical graduates has gone up since 2000.

Sources
- OECD (2015), *OECD Health Statistics* (Database).

Further information

Analytical publications
- Ono, T., G. Lafortune and M. Schoenstein (2013), "Health Workforce Planning in OECD Countries: A Review of 26 Projection Models from 18 Countries" *OECD Health Working Papers*, No. 62, OECD Publishing.
- OECD (2008), "The Looming Crisis in the Health Workforce: How can OECD Countries Respond?", *OECD Health Policy Studies*, OECD Publishing.

Statistical publications
- OECD (2015), *Health at a Glance*, OECD Publishing.
- OECD (2014), *Health at a Glance: Asia/Pacific*, OECD Publishing.
- OECD (2014), *Health at a Glance: Europe*, OECD Publishing.

Websites
- OECD Health Statistics (supplementary material), *www.oecd.org/els/health-systems/health-statistics.htm*.

Practising physicians
Per 1 000 inhabitants

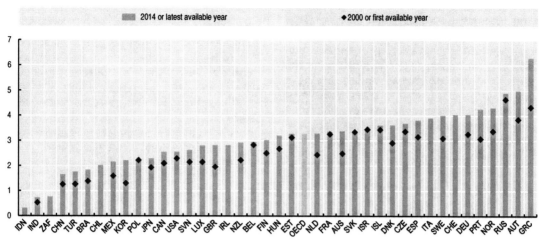

StatLink ᵐᵉᵗ http://dx.doi.org/10.1787/888933334872

Categories of physicians
As a percentage of total physicians, 2013 or latest available year

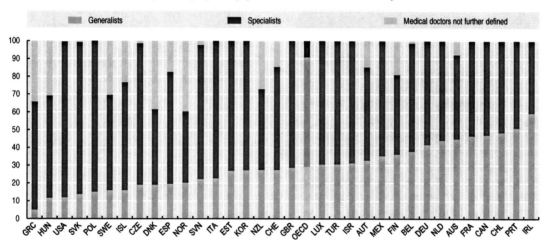

StatLink ᵐᵉᵗ http://dx.doi.org/10.1787/888933335765

Medical graduates
Per 100 000 inhabitants

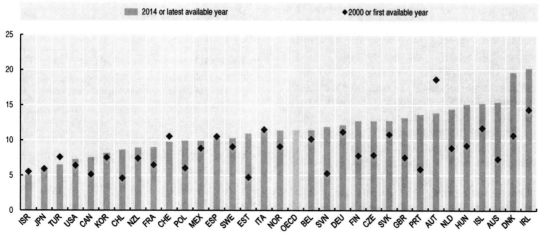

StatLink ᵐᵉᵗ http://dx.doi.org/10.1787/888933335914

NURSES

Nurses are usually the most numerous health profession, outnumbering physicians on average across OECD countries by almost three to one. However, there are concerns in many countries about shortages of nurses, and these concerns may well intensify in the future as the demand for nurses continues to increase and the ageing of the "baby-boom" generation precipitates a wave of retirements among nurses. These concerns have prompted actions in many countries to increase the training of new nurses combined with efforts to increase the retention of nurses in the profession.

Overview

On average across OECD countries, there were around 9 nurses per 1 000 population in 2014. The number of nurses per capita was highest in Switzerland, Norway, Denmark, Iceland and Finland, with more than 14 nurses per 1 000 population. The number of nurses per capita in OECD countries was lowest in Turkey, Mexico and Greece. The number of nurses per capita was also low compared with the OECD average in the emerging economies, such as Indonesia, India, South Africa, and Brazil where there were fewer than 1.5 nurses per 1 000 population in 2013, although numbers have been growing quite rapidly in Brazil in recent years.

The number of nurses per capita increased in almost all OECD countries over the past decade. This was the case in countries that already had a high density of nurses in 2000 such as Switzerland, Norway and Denmark, but also in Korea, Portugal and France which used to have a relatively low density of nurses. The number of nurses per capita declined between 2000 and 2014 only in Israel and the Slovak Republic.

In 2013, there were about three nurses per doctor on average across OECD countries, with about half of the countries reporting between two to four nurses per doctor. The nurse-to-doctor ratio was highest in Finland, Japan, Ireland and Denmark (with at least 4.5 nurses per doctor). It was lowest in Greece (with only about half a nurse per doctor) and in Turkey and Mexico (with only about one nurse per doctor).

There were 47 newly graduated nurses per 100 000 population on average across OECD countries in 2014. The number was highest in Korea, Denmark and Switzerland, and lowest in Mexico, Luxembourg, the Czech Republic, Spain, Turkey, Israel and Italy, with less than half the OECD average. Nurse graduation rates have traditionally been low in Mexico, Turkey, Israel and Spain, four countries which report a relatively low number of nurses per capita. In Luxembourg, nurse graduation rates are also low, but many nurses are foreign-trained.

Definition

The number of nurses includes all those employed in public and private settings providing services to patients ("practising"), including the self-employed. In those countries where there are different levels of nurses, the data include both "professional nurses" who have a higher level of education and perform higher level tasks and "associate professional nurses" who have a lower level of education but are nonetheless recognised and registered as nurses. Midwives and nursing aids who are not recognised as nurses are normally excluded.

Comparability

In several countries (France, Greece, Iceland, Ireland, Italy, the Netherlands, Portugal, the Slovak Republic, Turkey and the United States), the data include not only nurses providing direct care to patients, but also those working in the health sector as managers, educators, researchers, etc. Data for Chile refer to all nurses who are licensed to practice (less than one-third are professional nurses with a university degree). About half of OECD countries include midwives because they are considered as specialist nurses.

Austria reports only nurses employed in hospitals, resulting in an under-estimation.

Sources
• OECD (2015), OECD Health Statistics (Database).

Further information

Analytical publications
• Buchan, J. and S. Black (2011), "The Impact of Pay Increases on Nurses' Labour Market: A Review of Evidence from Four OECD Countries", OECD Health Working Papers, No. 57.
• Delamaire, M. and G. Lafortune (2010), "Nurses in Advanced Roles: A Description and Evaluation of Experiences in 12 Developed Countries", OECD Health Working Papers, No. 54.

Statistical publications
• OECD (2015), Health at a Glance, OECD Publishing.
• OECD (2014), Health at a Glance: Asia/Pacific, OECD Publishing.
• OECD (2014), Health at a Glance: Europe, OECD Publishing.

Websites
• OECD Health Statistics (supplementary material), www.oecd.org/els/health-systems/health-statistics.htm.

Practising nurses
Per 1 000 inhabitants

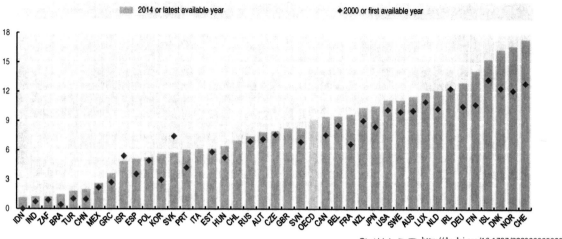

StatLink ⟲ http://dx.doi.org/10.1787/888933335283

Ratio of nurses to physicians
2013 or latest available year

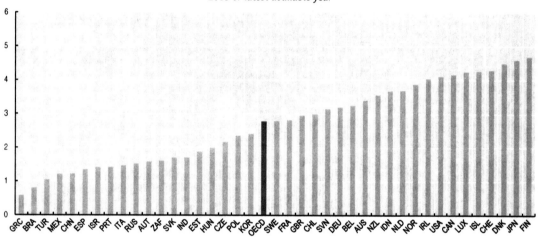

StatLink ⟲ http://dx.doi.org/10.1787/888933335801

Nursing graduates
Per 100 000 inhabitants

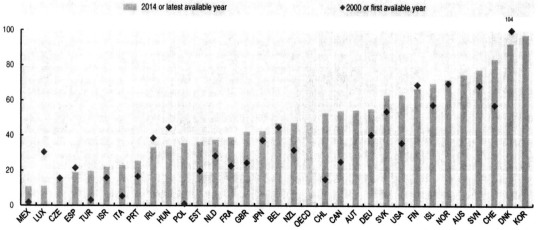

StatLink ⟲ http://dx.doi.org/10.1787/888933335941

HEALTH EXPENDITURE

In most OECD countries, spending on health is a large and growing share of both public and private expenditure. Health spending as a share of GDP had been rising over recent decades but has stagnated or fallen in many countries in the last couple of years as a consequence of the global economic downturn. The financial resources devoted to health care vary widely across countries, reflecting the relative priority assigned to health as well as the diverse financing and organisational structures of the health system in each country.

For a more comprehensive assessment of health spending, the health spending to GDP ratio should be considered together with *per capita* health spending. Countries having a relatively high health spending to GDP ratio might have relatively low health expenditure *per capita*, while the converse also holds.

Definition

Expenditure on health measures the final consumption of health goods and services (i.e. current health expenditure). This includes spending by both public and private sources (including households) on medical services and goods, public health and prevention programmes and administration, but excludes spending on capital formation (investments). Medical services can be provided in inpatient and outpatient settings or in some cases in day care facilities or at the home of the patient.

Comparability

OECD countries are at varying stages of reporting health expenditure data according to the definitions proposed in the 2011 manual A *System of Health Accounts* (SHA). While the comparability of health expenditure data has improved recently, some limitations do remain, in particular on the measurement of long-term care expenditure and administrative services.

The data generally refer to current health expenditure and therefore exclude capital formation (investments). However, data for Brazil, China, India, Indonesia, Russia and South Africa include investments. Public and private expenditure for the United Kingdom include investments, whereas total expenditure does not. The Netherlands report compulsory co-payments by patients to health insurers under social security rather than under households' out-of-pocket payments, resulting in an overestimation of the public spending share and an underestimation of the private spending share. In Luxembourg, health expenditure is for the insured population rather than the resident population.

For Australia, Ireland and Luxembourg 2013 data refer to 2012.

Overview

Trends in the health spending-to-GDP ratio are the result of the combined effect of changes in GDP and health expenditure. The 2000s were characterised by a period of health spending growth above that of the overall economy so that health expenditure as a share of GDP rose sharply in many OECD countries. As a result, the average share of GDP allocated to health climbed from 7.2% in 2000 to 8.3% in 2008. The health spending-to-GDP ratio jumped sharply in 2009 to reach 9.0% on average as overall economic conditions rapidly deteriorated but health spending continued to grow or was maintained in many countries. In the context of reducing public deficits, the subsequent reductions in (public) spending on health have resulted in the share of GDP first falling and since stabilising as health expenditure growth has become aligned to economic growth in many OECD countries. In 2013, health spending accounted for 8.9% of GDP on average across OECD countries.

There remain large variations in how much OECD countries spend on health as a share of GDP. In 2013, the share of GDP allocated to health was the largest by far in the United States (16.4%), followed by the Netherlands and Switzerland (both 11.1%). Turkey, Estonia and Mexico spent 6% or less of their GDP on health.

Sources
- OECD (2015), *OECD Health Statistics* (Database).
- For non-OECD member countries: World Health Organization (WHO), *Global Health Observatory Data Repository* (Database).

Further information

Analytical publications
- OECD (2010), *Value for Money in Health Spending*, OECD Health Policy Studies, OECD Publishing.

Statistical publications
- OECD (2015), *Government at a Glance*, OECD Publishing.
- OECD (2015), *Health at a Glance*, OECD Publishing.

Methodological publications
- OECD, Eurostat and World Health Organization (2011), *A System of Health Accounts*, OECD Publishing.

Websites
- OECD Health Statistics (supplementary material), *www.oecd.org/els/health-systems/health-statistics.htm*.

Public and private expenditure on health
As a percentage of GDP

	Public expenditure				Private expenditure				Total			
	2000	2005	2010	2013 or latest available year	2000	2005	2010	2013 or latest available year	2000	2005	2010	2013 or latest available year
Australia	5.2	5.5	5.8	5.9	2.4	2.5	2.7	2.8	7.6	8.0	8.5	8.8
Austria	7.0	7.2	7.7	7.7	2.3	2.4	2.4	2.4	9.2	9.6	10.1	10.1
Belgium	5.9	6.9	7.7	8.0	2.0	2.1	2.2	2.3	8.0	9.0	9.9	10.2
Canada	5.8	6.4	7.4	7.2	2.5	2.7	3.2	3.0	8.3	9.1	10.6	10.2
Chile	3.3	2.4	3.0	3.4	3.1	4.1	3.7	3.9	6.4	6.6	6.7	7.3
Czech Republic	5.1	5.6	5.8	6.0	0.6	0.8	1.2	1.1	5.7	6.4	6.9	7.1
Denmark	6.7	7.6	8.8	8.8	1.4	1.5	1.6	1.6	8.1	9.1	10.4	10.4
Estonia	4.0	3.8	4.9	4.6	1.2	1.1	1.3	1.3	5.2	5.0	6.1	6.0
Finland	4.8	5.7	6.1	6.5	1.9	2.0	2.1	2.2	6.7	7.7	8.2	8.6
France	7.5	8.0	8.4	8.6	2.0	2.2	2.4	2.3	9.5	10.2	10.8	10.9
Germany	7.7	7.8	8.3	8.4	2.1	2.5	2.7	2.6	9.8	10.3	11.0	11.0
Greece	4.4	5.6	6.2	6.0	2.8	3.4	3.0	3.1	7.2	9.0	9.2	9.2
Hungary	4.7	5.6	5.0	4.8	2.1	2.5	2.7	2.6	6.8	8.1	7.7	7.4
Iceland	7.3	7.4	7.1	7.1	1.7	1.7	1.7	1.7	9.0	9.2	8.8	8.7
Ireland	4.2	5.2	5.9	5.5	1.4	1.7	2.6	2.6	5.6	6.9	8.5	8.1
Israel	4.3	4.3	4.4	4.4	2.4	2.7	2.5	2.9	6.8	7.2	7.0	7.5
Italy	5.5	6.5	7.0	6.8	2.1	1.9	1.9	2.0	7.6	8.4	8.9	8.8
Japan	5.9	6.6	7.8	8.5	1.4	1.5	1.7	1.7	7.4	8.1	9.5	10.2
Korea	2.0	2.8	3.7	3.8	2.0	2.3	2.7	3.0	4.0	5.0	6.5	6.9
Luxembourg	4.8	6.0	6.1	5.5	1.1	1.2	1.1	1.2	5.9	7.2	7.2	6.6
Mexico	2.2	2.5	2.9	3.2	2.7	3.4	3.3	3.0	4.9	5.9	6.2	6.2
Netherlands	4.7	6.7	9.1	9.7	2.4	2.8	1.4	1.4	7.0	9.5	10.4	11.1
New Zealand	5.8	6.6	7.9	7.6	1.6	1.7	1.9	1.9	7.5	8.2	9.7	9.5
Norway	6.3	6.9	7.5	7.6	1.4	1.4	1.4	1.3	7.7	8.3	8.9	8.9
Poland	3.6	4.0	4.6	4.5	1.6	1.8	1.8	1.9	5.3	5.8	6.5	6.4
Portugal	5.9	6.8	6.9	6.1	2.4	2.7	2.9	3.1	8.3	9.4	9.8	9.1
Slovak Republic	4.7	5.0	5.6	5.6	0.6	1.6	2.2	2.0	5.3	6.6	7.8	7.6
Slovenia	6.0	5.9	6.3	6.2	2.1	2.1	2.3	2.5	8.1	8.0	8.6	8.7
Spain	4.9	5.5	6.7	6.3	2.0	2.2	2.3	2.5	6.8	7.7	9.0	8.8
Sweden	6.3	6.8	6.9	9.2	1.1	1.5	1.5	1.7	7.4	8.3	8.5	11.0
Switzerland	5.2	6.1	6.7	7.3	4.2	4.2	3.7	3.7	9.3	10.3	10.5	11.1
Turkey	2.9	3.5	4.2	4.0	1.8	1.7	1.2	1.1	4.7	5.1	5.3	5.1
United Kingdom	5.3	6.4	7.6	7.3	1.4	1.5	1.5	1.5	6.3	7.4	8.6	8.5
United States	5.5	6.6	7.9	7.9	7.0	8.0	8.5	8.5	12.5	14.6	16.4	16.4
EU 28	..	..	..	..	..	..	..	..	..	..	..	..
OECD	5.2	5.8	6.4	6.5	2.1	2.3	2.4	2.4	7.2	8.1	8.8	8.9
Brazil	2.8	3.4	4.1	4.4	4.2	4.8	4.6	4.7	7.0	8.3	8.7	9.1
China	1.8	1.8	2.7	3.1	2.9	2.9	2.3	2.5	4.6	4.7	5.0	5.6
India	1.2	1.0	1.2	1.3	3.2	3.3	2.7	2.7	4.3	4.3	3.8	4.0
Indonesia	0.6	0.7	1.0	1.1	1.1	1.8	1.7	1.8	1.8	2.5	2.7	2.9
Russian Federation	3.3	3.2	3.7	3.1	2.2	2.0	3.2	3.4	5.4	5.2	6.9	6.5
South Africa	3.4	3.4	4.0	4.3	4.9	5.4	4.6	4.6	8.3	8.8	8.7	8.9

StatLink ᴹᵞᴸ http://dx.doi.org/10.1787/888933336500

Public and private expenditure on health
As a percentage of GDP, 2013

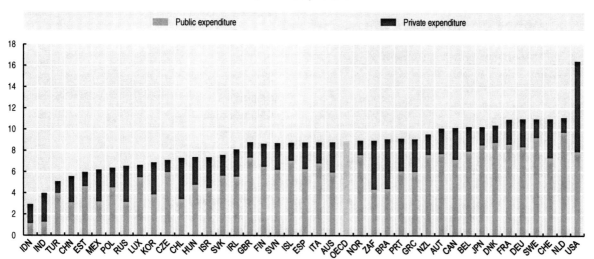

StatLink ᴹᵞᴸ http://dx.doi.org/10.1787/888933335371

Analytical index

ORGANISATION FOR ECONOMIC CO-OPERATION AND DEVELOPMENT

The OECD is a unique forum where governments work together to address the economic, social and environmental challenges of globalisation. The OECD is also at the forefront of efforts to understand and to help governments respond to new developments and concerns, such as corporate governance, the information economy and the challenges of an ageing population. The Organisation provides a setting where governments can compare policy experiences, seek answers to common problems, identify good practice and work to co-ordinate domestic and international policies.

The OECD member countries are: Australia, Austria, Belgium, Canada, Chile, the Czech Republic, Denmark, Estonia, Finland, France, Germany, Greece, Hungary, Iceland, Ireland, Israel, Italy, Japan, Korea, Luxembourg, Mexico, the Netherlands, New Zealand, Norway, Poland, Portugal, the Slovak Republic, Slovenia, Spain, Sweden, Switzerland, Turkey, the United Kingdom and the United States. The European Union takes part in the work of the OECD.

OECD Publishing disseminates widely the results of the Organisation's statistics gathering and research on economic, social and environmental issues, as well as the conventions, guidelines and standards agreed by its members.

OECD PUBLISHING, 2, rue André-Pascal, 75775 PARIS CEDEX 16
(30 2015 04 1 P) ISBN 978-92-64-23256-3 – 2016